IT'S STRICTLY PERSONAL

A NOSTALGIC MOVIE MEMOIR OF 1975-1982 OR: WHY SHARKS, BOXERS, GALAXIES, ALIENS AND BRITISH SPIES MATTERED TO GEN X'ERS LIKE ME!

Eric Friedmann

NEWMAN SPRINGS PUBLISHING
320 Broad Street
Red Bank, NJ 07701

First originally published by Newman Springs Publishing 2018

This is entirely a work of nonfiction taken from the deepest roots of my personal childhood and teenage memories. However, in cases of specific information and facts, particularly television premiere broadcast dates, I'm grateful for the use of public Internet sources as Merriam-Webster, Wikipedia, and YouTube, as well as my own personal vintage collection of *HBO guides* and *TV Guide* magazines from the 1970s and 1980s.

My thoughts, feelings, opinions, and personal interpretations of the selected motion pictures in this book are my own. Any similarity to thoughts, feelings, opinions, and personal interpretations of others, living or deceased, regarding the same motion pictures, whether published or not, is purely coincidental.

ISBN 978-1-64096-263-7 (Paperback)
ISBN 978-1-64096-264-4 (Digital)

Printed in the United States of America

For my son, Sam,
whose own love of film
inspires and encourages me.

CHAPTER CONTENTS

1982

Please Allow Me to Introduce Myself

I love movies!

Movies are history. History is movies. Movies are life. Life is movies. Like history and life, respectively, movies are subject to our own individual interpretations, thoughts, feelings, and memories. Movies constitute an emotional form of *time travel* that allows us to drift backward and take stock of the different periods of our personal lives. How we choose to remember specific movies and the period of history they represented at the time of their theatrical release may differ greatly between different people. My own personal memories of the first time I saw such classics as *Jaws* and *Star Wars* may be entirely different from how you remember such cinematic events (you may have even *hated* them, though that would be hard to imagine). Some may experience a movie in the theater for the first time, thinking it's a good one, and then simply write it off until they go to the movies again. Others, like myself, may long to see it again to absorb the experience even fuller into their lives and interpret (or *re*interpret) the meaning it holds for them.

As we get older, I believe we fondly reflect on the past. It's almost unavoidable. How many times have you looked back at movies, television, and music from when you were a kid or a teenager and said something corny and cliché like, "Ah, those were the days!" Trouble is, even what we may define as *"the day"* differs depending on who does the reflecting. Those born following the end of World War II, the "baby boomers," recall *"the day"* as, perhaps, the decade of the 1950s, when television and rock and roll were new, and low-budget science fiction and horror film double features (often categorized as

9

"B" movies) were all the rage at local movie theaters and drive-ins. For a Generation X man as myself, I'm sure my reflections of personal movie history and what constitutes *"the day"* differs from others. Those born during the Gen X era recall a time that saw the rise of the personal computer, arcade video games, and MTV.

Before I dive too much deeper into the true intentions of this book you're about to read, I feel it's important to clearly define one or two terms and ask ourselves a question or two that will greatly aid in making my points clear. First, let's define what a Gen Xer, someone born during the Generation X period, is. In simple terms, as defined on *Merriam-Webster*, it's *"the generation of Americans born in the 1960s and 1970s"* (though other sources are willing to stretch that time period as late as 1981). That being the case, since I was born in 1967, I would say I absolutely qualify as a Gen Xer. Let's also ask a question: you've heard of the term *comfort food*, correct? Again, by *Merriam-Webster's* definition, it's *"food prepared in a traditional style having a usually nostalgic or sentimental appeal."* Chicken soup, fried chicken, meat loaf, and macaroni and cheese tend to fall into this category (my wife and son can surely attest to the mac and cheese example).

By that logic, consider the idea of *comfort movies*. This isn't exactly an original term I've created (I wish it were). Its definition may vary, depending on the source. By the public's definition, it's *"a film one watches that one has seen a minimum of one hundred times and it never gets old. Typically a comedy, it is usually watched on a lazy day at home. If you only see this film on TV, you'll probably watch it without changing the channel."* That's quite an opinion. Whomever came up with that one provides every possible scenario short of describing the weather and what's cooking in the kitchen (probably comfort food). Additional definitions include *"a movie that a person likes to watch and fall asleep to and feel comfortable doing so because they've seen the movie countless times and they know it forward and backward"* and *"like comfort food, a comfort movie is a movie that one watches to feel less like shit and a movie that evokes many positive and lovely feelings in that one person."* I suppose all these definitions possess certain validity, but in the end, I believe that opinions are like excuses … everybody's got one.

If I were to come up with my own original meaning for what truly defines a *comfort movie*, I'd mix things up a little. Yes, our favorite films that we've seen so many times to the point of irritating dialogue memorization *do* make us feel better about ourselves when we're feeling low. Yes, they're a simple way to kill a couple of hours that we choose to commit to movie-watching without devoting a whole lot of time *thinking* about what we're watching. I have, on many occasions, watched a movie from my own comfort list that I know will raise my spirits when I need cheering up. But I prefer to go beyond the superficial meaning of what a comfort movie can achieve. For me, the true comfort movie transports me back to a period of time in my life and childhood when things were simpler and the movies, in my opinion, were better. This again, is strictly relevant to one's own experience, feelings, and interpretations of what was *"simpler"* and *"better"* to them. My father (and others of his generation) would claim the 1950s were the defining era for such emotions of simplicity. Just sit in the same room with him while he's listening to his favorite songs of the Doo-Wop era and you'll see how the comfort of that music puts him back in *"that special place"* that's uniquely his.

Our own memories and interpretations of movies are strictly a personal issue, and there's no right or wrong answer in how we allow these movies to affect our lives. The traditional motive of escapism behind the movies has always been a valid issue in my life. You see, my parents, while being very loving people, were also constantly fighting with each other and creating an environment that housed a tone of chaos and instability. As a kid, I sometimes wondered if they were just simply insane (for that matter, was *I* insane too?). To be able to lose myself for a couple of hours in the darkened movie theater meant pretending my troubled world at home didn't exist. The movies existed to comfort me and guide me through tough times, as well as good times too. The release of some movies were even oddly timed to coincide with specific events in my family's history, but I'll get deeper into that later.

This leads us to an important question behind my writing here: given the entire history of cinema that spans more than one hundred years and given the fact that I've been alive on this earth for fifty years, why do I chose to focus my attention and memories on only an eight-year period between 1975 and 1982? The reasons are two-fold: The first being it was these eight years that I consider to be the crust of my childhood and teen upbringing, age eight to sixteen. The second being it was during these eight years when the movies had the strongest meaning and impact for me. The movies were changing. They were the bigger and faster products of new and exciting young filmmakers, and they took us into deeper experiences of fantasy and fun. As a child with his eyes wide open, who longed for the escape of his turbulent home environment, it was a thrill to be there and watch it happen.

While it seems that everyone out there with an opinion and a computer keyboard has what they believe to be their "best list of movies" or their specific quantity of movies *"you must see before you die,"* and I suppose I'm no different, it was these eight years that comprise what I've determined to be my list of comfort movies and my personal reasons behind them. However, let me stress that I'm not here to provide just another opinionated list of movies I feel are better than others in the hopes that you'll take my words to heart and go out to immediately watch them (the web is full of that stuff). There are numerous credible and entertaining sources for cinematic history and fact out there, depending on what exactly it is you're looking for in a good read. Although I don't hold a formal education in cinema studies or any professional position in the motion picture business, I have, over many years, read my more-than-fair-share of critical and analytical books on cinema and the many gifted directors that shaped its history including Stanley Kubrick, Steven Spielberg, Martin Scorsese, Alfred Hitchcock, David Lynch, Woody Allen, Orson Welles, Frank Capra, and Federico Fellini.

If you're looking for the history of American moviemaking during the era of World War II, then I urge you to read *Five Came Back: A Story of Hollywood and the Second World War* by Mark Harris. If the decade of the 1970s is more your focus, then you won't do better than *Easy Riders, Raging Bulls: How the Sex-Drugs-and-Rock "N" Roll Generation Saved Hollywood* by Peter Biskind. On the other hand, if your interests are strictly limited to the great blockbusters of our generation, then you won't go wrong with *Blockbuster: How Hollywood Learned to Stop Worrying and Love the Summer* by Tom Shone. If you'd like to read about specific movies that shaped and changed the popular culture throughout history, then *The Movies That Changed Us* by Nick Clooney is for you. Finally, if you're simply looking for some good 'ol fashioned lists of recommended movies and the good reasons to put them on your list of what to watch, then there's all three volumes of *The Great Movies* by the late Chicago film critic Roger Ebert.

The intent of this book is a personal *memoir* of movies and not so much a critical look (well, maybe *some* criticism) at them or those who were behind the making of them and how it all went down. That's been done many times already and I do my best not to copy what others have done already. I'm *not* a professional film journalist, nor do I pretend to be, because there are enough of them out there in the business who can put a far superior seal on the true meaning of cinema than I can. Consider me more like the everyday, ordinary, average, informal movie guy who's here to tell you a story through the eyes of my personal life and the meaningful memories that movies played in the structure of my growing from boyhood into manhood.

I watch a movie every night during the same two or three hours the average person watches TV. As a kid, I lived and breathed movies because I longed for the fantasy and escape of other worlds and other experiences that didn't exist in my own everyday life. If it was out there on the screen and advertised in the Arts & Leisure section of the Sunday New York Times, then I wanted to go see it, regardless of what sort of movie it was or what it was about (this section of the Sunday newspaper was my movie *bible* of what was playing and what was coming soon). Ironically though, my access to the movies seemed few and far between. Not to suggest that I rarely went to the movies, it just often required a struggle to get my parents to drag their lazy butts out of the house and take me and my younger brother Kevin to the neighborhood movie theater. This, after all, was no longer a time before the advent of the television set when families were traditionally going to the movies every weekend. This was decades later when people like my mother and father had to have sufficient motivation to go to the movies, which very often involved some nagging and whining from their two boys. Typically, if they could avoid it, they generally considered going to the movies a waste of their time and money that was better spent on more practical matters.

Believe it or not, I remember the first movie I ever saw on screen. It was 1974, I was seven years old, and it was a film called *The Lords of Flatbush* with Sylvester Stallone and Henry Winkler, released before their infamous characters of Rocky Balboa and Arthur Fonzarelli made them household names. To be honest though, I didn't actually *see* the movie. Technically, it was simply my father putting me in the back seat of his four-door, tan-colored Pontiac and taking me with him to the Century's Route 110 Drive-In Theatre in Melville, Long Island, as he watched a triple bill of movies while I was in the back seat drinking my *Yoo-Hoo*. I was only a child and had no clue what I was looking at up there on the screen beyond the front windshield (I think the bill also included a rerelease of Robert Altman's *M*A*S*H*. I recognized the title because the TV show was already on CBS). Still, for the first time in my life, I *was* sitting there watching the screen and everything it displayed in front of my little eyes. It was confusing and incomprehensible to my young mind, but there it was, nonetheless—a little boy's introduction to the magic of the movies. Sometime later, my father and I returned to that same drive-in so he could see Mel Brooks's *Young Frankenstein*. Again, not quite understanding what I was watching, the black and white images of the dark castle on a stormy night and the giant monster who danced to "Puttin' on the Ritz" were immediately taking ahold of me. After that night, we never returned to that drive-in again, and it was (sadly) demolished in 1983 to make way for a Marriott Hotel, which still stands there today.

Those of us born in the 1960s and 1970s, the Gen Xers as we're often called, recall a time before the Blu-Ray and DVD player, the laser disc player, the VCR and the Sony Betamax. It was a time when, if you wanted to see your favorite movie again after its first theatrical run, you basically had two choices: a) hope the studio would rerelease the movie in theaters for a limited engagement or; b) wait for the movie to air on a pay-TV cable channel or on free television. For kids like me whose parents weren't willing to pay extra money to subscribe to a premium pay movie channel like HBO or Showtime, it meant waiting patiently for two to three years for the movie to premiere on any of the three major TV networks, ABC, NBC, and CBS. Despite the long wait and the aggravation of sitting through a movie with commercials, these were still days of great movie-watching. Perhaps it was the idea that if you don't have easy access to something on a regular basis, then it's so important to you when you *do* manage to get what you want. In other words, when you don't go to the movies too often and television becomes your primary source of movie experiences, then you treasure everything you can get from it.

*****

Beginning with the year 1975 and moving forward through the year 1982, I shall discuss, critique, and analyze selected movies as they pertained to my own personal life, feelings, and memories as a kid who experienced them between the ages of eight and sixteen. I won't go into great depths of what the movie is about and what I think of it, but rather about how the movie and its cultural impact (if any) affected my life at the time that I saw it as a child or teenager and then again in my adulthood. What I also feel is important to share with you is that a movie's impact on my life didn't necessarily mean I was there to witness it firsthand on screen when it was released in theaters. What exactly does that mean? Am I cheating? No, of course not. I don't actually believe that a movie *has* to be seen firsthand on screen in the theater for its cultural impact and its marketing tactics to reach a child's (or adult's) life and give it the effective impact.

If you were there in 1975 and 1977 when *Jaws* and *Star Wars* were global phenomenons, you remember and perhaps even agree that even if you couldn't see them for yourself, it was impossible not to feel the effects of their success. If you were unable to see *Jaws* immediately, perhaps you were still nervous about stepping into the ocean when you went to the beach due to all the hype. If you were unable to see *Star Wars* for a while because tickets were repeatedly sold out that entire summer, perhaps you still headed to your local record store and purchased the double-soundtrack album by John Williams and hummed the iconic opening theme. Perhaps you even collected some of the "early bird" original series of action figures made by Kenner Products during the 1977 holiday season. Such indirect impacts from the movies *can* happen and they *do* happen. I say that with conviction because they happened to me repeatedly, and that's part of what I'll share with you in this book.

Let's, of course, not forget about television and its important role in all of this. Today, as we knock ourselves out trying to live in the twenty-first century world of endless movie choices that include Blu-Ray and DVD purchases, the DVR machine, downloading, and streaming, it may take great effort to recall the dependence one once had on the TV set for enjoying movies at home back in the '70s and '80s. Movie collectability in the form of video tapes (both Beta and VHS), laser discs, and the Capacitance Electronic Disc (CED) *did* exist back then, but they were generally considered too expensive in the beginning by most consumers to be mainstream. TV was still free, and even if it wasn't *completely* free beyond the first thirteen channels, the average monthly cost of a pay-movie channel was about ten dollars, which was a lot cheaper than the hundreds of dollars a video machine and individual movies cost the average consumer. So it's important to note that the existence of network television and motion picture broadcasts throughout my selected years play a critical role in my personal movie memories and experiences.

Bear in mind though that it's impossible for me to discuss *all* the great movies that fall into this eight-year period. While we of sophisticated cinematic taste cannot ignore important films like *Dog Day Afternoon, Taxi Driver, Network, Midnight Express, The Deer Hunter, Apocalypse Now,* and *Raging Bull,* let's remember that I was just a *kid* back then with no possibility of my parents allowing me anywhere near these films (my exposure and appreciation of these titles came later in my college years when I had free access to video tape rentals).

What I shall do is introduce each selected film of each year in their chronological order of theatrical release date in the United States and examine each of them by their cultural and historical impact, as well as how my life related to it, either in a small or big way, good or bad. My writing of each year shall also include popular, noteworthy, and important films of the era that were rereleased in theaters and also made their television broadcast premiere during that same eight-year period. For some of the films I loved and remember very well, I'll have a whole lot to say. For others that I didn't so much, I may have a lot less. Some of these films were major blockbusters that met with critical and audience acclaim and are still very popular with moviegoers today. Others were considered major flops by critics and audiences that I, nonetheless, have a personal fondness for, the reasons which I'll tell you about. I'll begin by describing how I felt about a film when I first saw it as a kid and its impact on me at the time of its original release (*Then*), followed by how I look at that same film today as an adult (*Now*).

So now, if you'll permit me some of your valuable reading time, allow me to take you along with me back to the wonderful and weird years of 1975 to 1982; when the new theatrical motion picture releases of the time, their rerelease limited engagements and their eventual pay-tv and free television broadcasts managed to turn the life of a small child from eight to sixteen into a die-hard movie fanatic with his own stories to tell, his feelings to share, and his memories to reflect upon. It's my hope that perhaps as you're reading this book, I'll have done my job effectively, and you too will remember a time that *"takes you back"* and maybe even *"puts you in that special place"* of movie comfort ... because after all, as far as I'm concerned, it's *strictly personal.*

THE YEAR WAS 1975 ...

- The war in Vietnam ends as Saigon falls to communist forces, resulting in the massive evacuations of South Vietnamese and Americans. South Vietnam unconditionally surrenders as the capital is taken.
- The unemployment rate peaks at 9.0 percent, ending the Post-World War II employment boom.
- Facing bankruptcy, New York City's mayor, Abraham Beame, is unsuccessful in obtaining President Gerald Ford's support for a federal bailout. The incident prompts the *New York Daily News* to run its infamous headline, "Ford to City: Drop Dead," which referred to a speech in which Ford flatly declared that he would veto any bill calling for a federal bail-out of New York City.
- Teamsters Union president Jimmy Hoffa is reported missing in Detroit, Michigan.
- Muhammad Ali defeats Joe Frazier in the "Thrilla in Manila" heavyweight championship boxing match.
- *Saturday Night Live* airs for the first time on NBC.

... AND THERE WERE MOVIES

From the legendary moment that the mighty fin of the Carcharodon carcharias or the Great White shark broke through the depths of the deep oceans of the fictitious locale known as Amity Island in New England, 1975 was the year that would forever change the definition, the cultural impact, and Hollywood's financial potential of the traditional blockbuster. Not to suggest that Steven Spielberg's *Jaws*, from the best-selling novel by Peter Benchley, was the first blockbuster to grace the big screen. The first one can be traced to as far back as 1915 with D. W. Griffith's silent film *Birth of a Nation*. This highly controversial film and its hard portrayal of blacks, whites, and the rise of the Ku Klux Klan was, in fact, a commercial success. Victor Fleming's 1939 film *Gone with the Wind* was phenomenally popular, becoming the highest grossing film up to that point and still remains one of the most successful films in box office history. William Wyler's 1959 film *Ben-Hur* became the second highest grossing film just after *Gone with the Wind*. Big name films that followed over the decades, including *The Sound of Music, The Godfather, The Exorcist,* and *The Towering Inferno* were huge success with audiences at the box office.

It was *Jaws*, however, that finally broke new ground with the blockbuster's potential for success during the summer season from May through August and inevitably set the bar for generations to come. As much as I wish I could start our journey together with the biggest movie of 1975 and subsequently, one of the greatest films of all time, sadly, I cannot. I was a mere child of seven years old at the start of 1975 (I turned eight on May 7th) and at such a tender, young age, whenever your parents are willing to take you to the movies, they're going to search the newspaper ads for more family and child-friendly content. That being the case, the pickings were slim. Remember, this was a time before Disney/Pixar Studios and Dreamworks Animation provided an array of family film choices that usually incorporates the use of computer-generated imagery (CGI). In the 1970s, the best available cinema for children were Disney Studios cartoon and live action G-rated rereleases, and perhaps a few films that depicted friendly, furry animals of the wilderness and even a few cute doggies. Quite stale, by today's family comparisons. But hey, it was what it was, and kids like me were stuck with it.

Escape to Witch Mountain
Directed by John Hough
(March 21, 1975, U.S. Release Date)

Then

This film by Disney Studios was exactly what a seven-year-old child (who didn't know from anything better) needed for solid movie entertainment. The stars were kids, they had magic powers, they fought bad guys, they escaped to safety in a flying RV, and eventually left for home in a spaceship designed to likely precede anything Steven Spielberg might dream up years later. There was a particular moment in the movie when Tony used his magic powers to defend himself against a bully he had to live with in the orphanage he'd been placed in. I loved this scene as a kid because, admittedly, there had been times I was bullied at school by other kids, and to watch one take a bit of a licking on screen felt like true joy for me.

It was pure Disney magic at its best for the 1970s, and I treasured the experience when my father took me and Kevin to see it at a local movie theater in the same suburban town of Melville, where I experienced the drive-in movie theater. It was also a decade when movies for children were few and far between, and I think Disney Studios knew that and did their best to fill the void for kids and their parents. Just a year or two later, there was a summer-long film festival of double-features which Disney called the *Disney Summer Hit Parade* that offered a classic animated film paired with a live action film, both G-rated. This sort of double bill, which ran throughout

21

the summer, was like a gift from movie heaven for my father, who was very often the one responsible for taking his two boys to the movies when he was willing to cave in to the request. It left little to think about in terms of risk content, and there was no doubt that the movies were perfectly fun and safe for all children to enjoy, and it all began for me with *Escape to Witch Mountain*.

Now

We now live in a time in which speed and action matter a great deal on the movie screen. Even in a traditional family film, if you're going to hold a moviegoer's attention, both young and old, things have to move at a reasonable pace. Today, I likely wouldn't bother exposing my twelve-year-old son to *Escape to Witch Mountain*; not even years ago when he was much younger. He would have likely stared at me with a look of boredom on his face and asked, "Daddy, are you kidding me with this?"

For myself, despite whatever magic the film may have possessed when I was a child, it's riddled, nonetheless, with childish antics and musical stunts that I no longer have the patience to sit through. You see, as a rule, I generally don't have the tolerance for musicals and the idea of sitting through dancing puppets and dolls as they're controlled by children with magic powers simply doesn't sit well with me anymore.

There are those that say the inner child within us never dies, and I suppose that may be a valid point when it comes to certain motion pictures. But there are also undeniably some movies where that child within us will *not* live forever, and that appears to be the case with me and *Escape to Witch Mountain*. Perhaps, instead, I should give the film's 2009 remake *Race to Witch Mountain*, with Dwayne Johnson, a look.

The Return of the Pink Panther
Directed by Blake Edwards
(May 21, 1975, U.S. Release Date)

Then

Fans of the popular Pink Panther franchise may not recall this, but *The Return of the Pink Panther* was (and still is, I believe) G-rated, making it perfectly safe for my father to take his sons to see. By this time, I was eight years old, but that hardly meant I'd matured in any way in my understanding of everything I watched on screen. Cartoons, furry animals, and children with magic powers were, after all, easy to understand and appreciate. A bumbling French detective and a stolen diamond that takes the moviegoer to exotic lands overseas were not.

Still, the key words here for a child are bumbling detective. I didn't need to understand the plot details surrounding the diamond heist or those who were ultimately behind it. I only needed to watch and enjoy the antics of this silly man called Peter Sellers bumping into walls, slipping on floors, crashing through windows, fighting with his Asian servant, dodging bullets, and surviving bomb explosions in the same manner that any Looney Tunes cartoon character may have survived the same explosion. I was laughing my little, young butt off and not fully understanding why.

Even the sheer madness of Chief Dreyfuss, played by Herbert Lom, and his insane, desperate attempts to kill Inspector Clouseau had me laughing in stitches. It's also very likely that I was naïve enough to think that Peter Sellers was actually a Frenchman. Sometimes an accent is so thick and so outrageous, you may actually think that it's genuine. At least, that's what a child thinks when he's eight year-old and doesn't know any better. He's just grateful that his daddy took him to the movies to have some fun.

Now

There are, according to my research, eleven *Pink Panther* films since the first one, simply called *The Pink Panther*, graced the big screen back in 1963 (one of them, the third one, released in 1968 called *Inspector Clouseau*, stars Alan Arkin in the title role instead of Peter Sellers), including three that were released after Sellers died and two remakes with Steve Martin in the title role.

That's a whole lot of comedy that I can only call, in my opinion, redundant. In my vast collection of DVD and Blu-Ray titles, *The Return of the Pink Panther* is the only film in the entire franchise that I've deemed worthy of my time and ownership. This is not only because I still find myself laughing with much enthusiasm at the antics of the late, great Mr. Sellers in his comedic stunts and pitfalls that I think greatly outsoar the other films, but also because I think this film carries with it a more intricate plotline in terms of the details behind the theft of the Pink Panther diamond itself; the same plot element that confused me as a child. Although the final resolution of who actually stole the diamond is completely anti-climactic and even boring, I still find myself sitting in suspense as I watch the thief carefully make his way into the chamber where the diamond rests and skillfully removes it without setting off any of the security alarms. For a film that isn't meant to be a heist film, essentially, it still manages to achieve a certain degree of tension in its depiction of crime.

I must confess, however, the film's G-rating by today's standards and practices of what is considered visually and politically correct in our society, may be highly questionable. While there's certainly no significant violence that I can complain about, there are moments of gunfire and explosions. There are also moments in Seller's dialogue that would likely be considered racist today, as he often refers to his loyal sidekick Cato as his *"little yellow friend."* Back in the 1970s, an era when a character like Archie Bunker of CBS's *All in the Family* was spewing out an array of offensive and racist references every week on network television, such a reference to an Asian man uttered on the big screen may have easily been overlooked, tolerated, or even gone completely unnoticed.

Today, how seriously we wish to take that sort of dialogue in a harmless *Pink Panther* film is strictly dependent on how easily we may take offense to such matters. It is, perhaps, a small and questionable price to pay for the comedic talents of the late Peter Sellers in this particularly entertaining film. While it may never live up to the madness and genius of his talent in Stanley Kubrick's classic films *Lolita* and *Dr. Strangelove or: How I Learned to Stop Worrying and Love the Bomb*, it still remains a high level of entertaining silliness that I continue to treasure to this day, when I choose to crave some silly entertainment from my childhood.

Jaws

Directed by Steven Spielberg
(June 20, 1975, U.S. Release Date)

Then

For a period of more than two years, in between *The Exorcist* and *Star Wars, Jaws* was the highest grossing motion picture of all time. It was the movie that instilled the fear of going swimming in the ocean and asking ourselves what lurked beneath us in the water (a fear many still possess today) in the same fashion that Alfred Hitchcock's *Psycho* instilled in some, the fear of taking a shower. It's a nostalgic reason many tourists love to visit Martha's Vineyard in Massachusetts (I've still yet to visit, myself).

This is it! The big one of 1975 when the oceans came alive (hey, that rhymes). The colossal film by legendary director Steven Spielberg that ushered in the new era and definition of motion picture blockbusters, aggressive marketing campaigns, and wider theatrical distribution that continues to live on today. You'll recall earlier when I said that a movie's impact on my life didn't necessarily mean that I was there to witness it firsthand in the movie theater at the time of its initial release. Here's the first example where I hope to validate that point. I was almost completely unaware of *Jaws* during the three-month period that constituted the summer of '75, save the occasional glance at the movie section in my father's copy of the local newspaper.

It was in September that things opened up for me. I returned to elementary school to enter the third grade, and something had

26

changed since last spring. Kids around me were in a frenzy as they walked around the school humming a strange and steady tune that sounded like, *"Dun-dun-dun-dun-dun-dun-dun-dun-dun-dun!"* Some of them were walking up to me and enthusiastically asking the big question, "Did you see *Jaws* over the summer?" It was with great shame that only an eight-year-old kid can feel that I quietly replied, "No." Something unusual was definitely happening to me. There was a major movie phenomenon going on in the world, and it seemed as if I was the only kid in the entire third grade who had no idea what the hell was going on. What to do? Naturally, I went before my father and asked if he'd take me to see *Jaws*. His answer was an unconditional, uncompromising "NO!" Apparently while other kids were being taken to the scariest movie of the year by their moms and dads, I was deemed too young to be able to handle such terror on screen. That didn't stop me from begging, of course, and beg I did, for months to come because it seemed the movie refused to leave the theaters.

To make matters worse, the movie's marketing and merchandising, including a kid's game featuring a plastic shark with snapping jaws by Ideal, started to hit the television airwaves. There were magazine covers that included *Time*, *People*, and even *Mad*. There were comic parodies that included skits on *Saturday Night Live* (John Belushi playing a great Matt Hooper) and *The Carol Burnett Show* (Harvey Corman playing a great Quint). We were living in a *Jaws* world where moviegoers were repeatedly returning to the movie theater for more (selfish bastards!), and I was prevented from seeing it even once by a pair of overprotective parents (if you're detecting a little anger on my part, you're right). Yes, I was young, I was naïve, and I was obsessed with *Jaws*, without ever setting foot near the movie.

Now I'll describe the power and influence a major movie's rerelease has over a child living in a world that's still years away from personal movie collectibility. One year after its first run, *Jaws* was back in theaters for the summer of 1976. Do you think that one year and being one year older made a difference with my strict parents? Of course not! Beg and plead I did and denied I still was. Its rerelease by Universal Pictures was nothing more than a severe slap in my face; a brass ring being waved around in my little face in the form of newspapers ads and TV promo commercials. Oh, how I cried, "No fair, no fair!" Jump ahead another three years to the summer of 1979 (the movie's first sequel had already come and gone) when *Jaws* was once again rereleased on the big screen for a special limited two-week engagement. The trailer and the reissue poster were teasing me with *"If you forgot what terror was like, it's back."* No, I hadn't forgotten what terror was like because I'd been denied the experience of remembering it in the first place … twice. But I gave it another try, and the result was still the same. Despite the fact the 1978 sequel was considered lighter in the terror department, my parents still held their conviction that the original movie was just *"too intense for younger children,"* including me at the age of twelve.

Let's now move forward to the power of network television and how things finally changed for me after four long years. It was a cold day in November 1979, and I was standing on line with my mother at the supermarket, thumbing through that week's issue of *TV Guide* while we waited for our turn with the cashier. Slowly I turned the pages, waiting to see if anything caught my attention to watch that week. Try to imagine a kid's face lighten up and brighten up when he sees a full-page ad announcing the world premiere of *Jaws* right before his eyes. This was one of those wonderful and ecstatic moments in a kid's life (well, *this* kid's life anyway) when the *ABC Sunday Night Movie* was about to finally rescue me from what seemed like an ongoing conspiracy toward me over the past four years. But the night to come was not to be without a certain degree of negotiation and compromise. A Sunday night was, of course, a school night and that meant my homework had to be completely finished, and I very likely was going to have to take a nap for a couple of hours in order to compensate for the extra time I'd be staying awake to watch the entire two-and-a-half-hour duration it would take to air the movie along with the inevitable commercials.

I cannot fully account as to why only a matter of several months since the movie's two-week engagement made such a huge difference with my parents in allowing me to finally see *Jaws*, but I can only presume that standards of TV edits and censors were enough to cut me the slack I needed to finally get what I wanted. So on Sunday,

November 4, 1979, at eight thirty in the evening on ABC Channel 7 in New York, the voice of the one and only Ernie Anderson filled the airwaves and he seemed to be saying these words, with John Williams's iconic score in the background, to a very grateful twelve-year-old boy … *"Tonight, an* ABC Sunday Night Movie *special. Tonight, the most exciting movie ever made comes to television. The movie that made motion picture history. Tonight, get ready for* Jaws. *Roy Scheider, Robert Shaw, Richard Dreyfuss in the biggest adventure ever. First time on television. And now … get ready … for* Jaws."

Ernie had no idea, but I *was* ready, because I'd waited four long, damn years to be ready! This was a feeling that I and perhaps only a small number of other kids could possibly comprehend and appreciate because as I've previously described, most of the other parents in my world had been lenient and allowed their kids to see the movie on the big screen when it was new, or at the very least, allowed them to watch it uncut and uninterrupted when it had been on HBO over the past summer.

So it began … the first fatality of this great movie, and I could immediately appreciate the fear behind the great phenomenon. My first thought was that my parents had been completely wrong regarding the traumatic impact of this movie because there was no blood to be seen when the girl was killed, only a lot of violent thrashing about. Still, it wasn't too difficult to see the fear that lied beneath the water in *not* seeing what was there. By the time the next victim, the ten-year-old boy, was struck by the great white shark, the impact was more obvious and just a little more red in color despite TV's obvious edits. What followed for the next hour or so was the fun and the drama of some of the best actors of the past two decades, particularly its three main stars, Scheider, Dreyfess, and Shaw.

During the July Fourth beach gathering, I recall feeling severely cheated when I learned the initial shark fin sighting was nothing more than a practical joke played by two kids. But the movie was smart in immediately discarding that hoax and substituting it with the real thing only seconds later. The killing of the pond victim in the rowboat was frightening, and even though I couldn't tell exactly how ABC had edited it, it was easy to see that the scene had been cut to a degree to reduce the bloody violence (I'd discover later, of course, that the man's severed leg is seen in the uncut version).

By the time the movie reached the point of being out at sea with our three heroes, I was practically on the edge of my bed because it was clear that I would to see the mighty shark a lot more now. Like many others before me must have reacted, I nearly jumped when the shark first appeared after Roy's classic line of *"Come on down here and chum some of this shit!"* Of course, the word *shit* was edited for television, naturally. Throughout the sea battle that followed, I was dumbfounded by the great strength and survival of the shark because, by all physical accounts, it looked like Quint and his men were truly kicking the shark's butt. It would never be enough though. The shark kept coming back for more right up until the moment where he infamously leaped onto the deck of the boat and finally claimed the life of Quint in his jaws (pun definitely intended). This was a violent moment despite the required edits of TV. I'd learn later they specifically deleted the scene where blood comes spewing out of Quint's mouth just before he dies.

It was almost time for *Jaws* to end, but not before the last remaining hero would give it all he had. As the shark came closer to his final victim and John Williams's music got more intense, I could only presume that in the end, Chief Brody would win the day. It wasn't so much after his great line of *"Smile, you son of a bitch!"* (again, the word *bitch* edited out for television) that got me excited, or even the great explosion that followed, but his loud and joyous laughter following *that*, that literally had me standing up and shouting, "Yeah!" No joke—I stood up and shouted, prompting my father to walk into my room and ask me *why* I'd just shouted. He'd seen the movie back in '75, so he *had* to have known why.

Now

Jaws remains not only one of my favorite films of all time, but one of the top ten I would absolutely have to have with me were I ever stranded on a desert island (come on, you've all taken that little quiz before, haven't you?). It is, in my opinion, with all due respect to the magic of *Star Wars, Indiana Jones, E.T., Die Hard,* and *Batman, still* the greatest summer blockbuster movie of all time. It is a film I watch every July Fourth weekend (in addition to other times during the year) in the same fashion that many watch *It's A Wonderful Life* every Christmas Eve. Oddly, I rarely watch it during the so-called off-season because I have, like many others I suppose, adapted the film as *the* quintessential summer movie. Why not? Everything about it, from the beaches to the sun to the surf, spells the very essence and spirit of summer. It's a film that affectionately defined my summer seasons in the Hamptons of Long Island, where my family once had a home.

Beyond its obvious excitement, I consider *Jaws* to be a truly human motion picture, each of the main characters representing a rather definitive form of social class persona. Roy Scheider as Chief Martin Brody, in his own way, represents the traditional white middle-class citizen existing to preserve a respectable and traditional level of law and order in a small town filled with white middle-class citizens. Richard Dreyfuss as Matt Hooper, perhaps meant to portray a leftover symbolic physical example of the 1960's hippie culture, is, nonetheless, a modern man of the era's technology and gadgetry without necessarily possessing the much-needed experience he needs to hunt sharks and destroy them. The charismatic Robert Shaw as Quint, on the other hand, represents the *true* law and order of Amity Island. The seaman's personality of working class toughness seems irrational, if not frightening and out of control, yet remains the only likelihood of any safety and survival for the people of this island. The combination of these three ... well, dare I call them *stereotypes* ... gives us a mixed variation of human beings who must ultimately come together to approach and defeat a great and powerful menace of the open sea. In the end, ironically, it's the common, everyday man of Martin Brody who destroys the monster with a single bullet to the air tank inside his jaws.

Although I've seen and owned the film in its most pristine and uncompromising forms on VHS, DVD, and high definition Blu-Ray disc throughout my youth and adulthood, every time I watch it, somewhere in the back of my mind is the voice of the late Ernie

Anderson and the *ABC Sunday Night Movie* initiating a twelve-year-old boy into a small degree of movie manhood. For that, I remain eternally grateful.

The Adventures of the
Wilderness Family
Directed by Stewart Raffill
(December 19, 1975, U.S. Release Date)

Then

Returning now to 1975, remember that I'm still eight years old and good ol' fashioned, wholesome family movies that are safe to take your kids to are still scarce. This is also the time to tell you that my parents had recently divorced after eleven years of marriage (more on that later), leaving my father with his weekly (as opposed to the traditional and legal bi-weekly) visits with his boys. Thus, the family film, in whatever shape or form it came in, was a form of rescue for my dad in having to figure out how to occupy some of his time with me and Kevin.

The Adventures of the Wilderness Family was *not* a movie I asked to see. My father actually fell in love with the prospect of this innocent nature film whose most threatening element for his two small boys would likely just be a large, black bear. Remember, this was a G-rated movie, so bears didn't actually kill or maim people (see William Girdler's 1976 horror movie *Grizzly*, a blatant and shameless *Jaws* rip-off known as *"Jaws with paws,"* if you enjoy a little man-eating blood and guts with your big bears). In fact, when the big, black bear threatened the Robinson family and their home, it was another (friendly) bear who came to their rescue.

I'll admit, however, as a small child, the movie contained enough excitement to keep me interested. But then again, I was simply happy to be going to the movies for any reason, so I may have just as well held the same interest and excitement for something like *Benji*, a very popular (and very cute) doggie movie of the '70s as well. One thing that such a wilderness movie managed to achieve for me was a sense of beauty in the art of film photography. The wonders of the Colorado mountains (despite being filmed in Canada) were grand and majestic. At this age, I didn't know of such men as Director John Ford who made his trademark in the cinematic capture of the American landscape. For now, it was America the beautiful, and that seemed perfectly fine for a kid spending a rainy Saturday afternoon in a darkened movie theater.

Now

Sometimes I ask myself if anyone outside of my own particular age group and generation who grew up with these sort of family films in the '70s remember that they even existed once (I suppose professional film critics and film scholars remember, but then again, it's their job to remember). I had the opportunity to watch this film again many years ago on Cinemax during a time in my adulthood when I was not yet a father. While the beauty of the American landscape could still hold my attention, this is a film that is undoubtedly dated for its time and its place in family viewing. It's a very slow-moving film that can likely only hold a place for those who still have a nostalgic passion for it and the past memories it holds (my father, perhaps). It's a nice enough experience if you watch it with a child at just the right age—an age where large grizzly bears won't scare them and an age where they just might not be bored to tears.

Were it to be remade by Hollywood today, it would likely score at least a PG rating, with more threatening elements of tension and suspense from Mother Nature as well as, perhaps, a stronger and more modern political statement regarding our forests, our environment, and the harshness of our polluted American cities. The Robinson family would probably not be so damn perfect and wholesome either. Perhaps the marriage would be troubled. Perhaps the kids would have juvenile records.

Perhaps *I* should start writing the potential remake (maybe).

Bugs Bunny: Superstar
Directed by Larry Jackson
(December 19, 1975, U.S. Release Date)

Then

My father, now a divorced man living in Manhattan with two boys to entertain every weekend, needed to know nothing of this movie other than what the movie poster had to say about it. The banner held by Daffy Duck and Porky Pig read, *"You Won't Believe How Much You Missed As A Kid!"* I suppose that was meant for a full-grown adult like my father at the time. For myself, I was still a kid and I couldn't possibly fathom what I may have missed in the world of Bugs Bunny already.

Everyday, upon coming from school, in between snack and homework, there were Bugs Bunny cartoons being shown for half an hour on one of the independent channels. In addition, every Saturday morning, there was an hour of Bugs Bunny and friends on CBS called *The Bugs Bunny/Road Runner Show*, and I never missed any of it. Aside from *The Flintstones*, it's safe to say that Bugs Bunny was my life, and in that regard, life was truly hilarious! The prospect of a full-length motion picture of Bugs Bunny cartoons was *"mother's milk"* to me. However, it turned out to be more than simple cartoon entertainment. This was the first time I witnessed the behind-the-scenes look at cartoon and filmmaking. Never before was I aware of the painstaking artistry that went behind each drawing, each painted animation cell, and each frame filmed for the big screen. I didn't even fully comprehended that there was once a time when all of these great cartoons I enjoyed on TV every day had once been shown on the big screen before the main feature. Unfortunately, even by '75, the time-honored tradition of showing a cartoon before the movie had practically been phased out.

Now

It's only as an adult that you can truly learn a thing or two about a movie you haven't seen since you were a small child. To date, *Bugs Bunny: Superstar*, the full-length motion picture as it was made back in 1975, has never been individually released on American Region 1 DVD or Blu-Ray disc. This is why I still maintain a working VCR in my life because I was recently able to purchase a new and factory-sealed VHS copy of this out-of-print movie at a reasonable price on eBay. What little there is of it available on DVD is part of the *Looney Tunes Golden Collection, Volume 4,* and I understand the quality of the content is considerably unrestored. Having recently watched it again for the first time in decades, I can not only say it still holds up today in bringing back some of the greatest cartoon memories of my life, but also further educates me in the film's background and production stories.

The animator behind this movie, the late Bob Clampett (who resembled the late Roy Orbison back then), was the primary crust behind everything that went into this feature. It was actually not produced by Warner Brothers, but rather Hare-Raising Films, which Clampett held the role as primary developer of their cartoons. Clampett took credit for several of the iconic Warner character, claiming *he* was the actual creator of Bugs Bunny, having used Clark Gable's carrot-munching scene from Frank Capra's 1934 film *It Happened One Night* as his inspiration. As a result, the entire documentary infuriated the artists at Warner Brothers.

No doubt, these are entertaining and valuable pieces of behind-the-scenes cinematic information and history of cartoon creating pre-CGI for an adult who is passionate about film. As a kid back in '75, however, it was simple enough to spend a Saturday afternoon at the movies to see how real men in the real world up there on the big screen created a wonderful array of priceless cartoons that have entertained and inspired generations of children and the adults they inevitably turn out to be.

*****

This is the last film of 1975 I shall discuss in any great detail.

I shall, for this year and the other years to follow, cap it off by discussing not only some additional experiences with movies of the time, whether I saw them on the big screen or not, but also the influence of the movies that were shown on TV. Some shall include broadcast debut of movies that were released prior to 1975 since they first caught my attention.

It was in late November of that year that my life underwent a dramatic change when I finally learned that my parents were not *getting* divorced, but actually already *were* divorced. Apparently, it was finalized back in September, and Kevin and I learned about it for the first time from my father following the Thanksgiving holiday weekend. As you might *not* expect from a typical eight-year-old child, my initial reaction was not a negative one. Realizing that my parents were constantly fighting and there was an ongoing environment of tension and hostility in the household (the primary escape that going to the movies brought me), the only feeling I experienced was relief. I was just a child, and all I could focus on, upon hearing the news, was that the fighting would end. Upon further reflection, I also realized that I'd spend my weekends with my father at his Manhattan apartment, and that likely meant more fun, more leisure, and more movies. There was a small catch, however. He had a new girlfriend named Mindy. Just prior to Christmas, we arrived at his new apartment in Gramercy Park on Saturday morning to meet her for the first time. I was nervous, but going against the grain of how most children would traditionally react, I took to her almost immediately. She was pretty, fun-loving, and high-spirited, which is exactly what a child needed when his own mother was experiencing her own personal feelings of bitterness following the divorce and, unfortunately, found its way into the home environment during the week with her.

As that day dragged closer to dusk and we were planning an evening of take-out food together, I stumbled upon something I'd never seen before. It was a guide, but not the traditional *TV Guide* I'd seen before. This was a mini booklet with a cover depicting the bright colors of red, orange, and yellow. On the left side of the guide were the words *On Air* with December 1975 printed underneath it. On the right side of the guide were three letters I'd never seen before—*HBO*, with the words *Home Box Office* printed underneath it. Underneath that was what really caught my attention, and that was the movie title of a major blockbuster hit that was in theaters just one year before, *The Towering Inferno.*

Inside the guide were numerous pictures and schedule listing of not just this movie, but many others. *Wait a second—just what was this I was looking at?* My father told me he was paying for an extra channel every month that showed movies without commercials, though he didn't specifically identify his new service by the name HBO, but rather simply stated that he was paying for cable TV. HBO, cable TV, extra channel, I didn't care what the proper name for it was. This was something new that I never knew existed before—the latest hit movies on television without commercials. My visitation weekends with my father and Mindy had just jumped up a considerable amount of points. For the first time, I was going to watch *The Towering Inferno* on television, uncut and uninterrupted. I'd heard of the movie a year ago simply by staring at the promo ads in the newspaper, which depicted the tall skyscraper engulfed in fire, so I didn't need to guess what it was about. So, that evening, by the time 8 p.m. rolled around and the consumption of take-out fried chicken had been completed, we all sat in front of one of the most modern color televisions available at the time, ready to watch the movie.

Two and a half hours later, I was not only enlightened, but also just a little freaked out by what I'd just watched. Enlightened because this was the first disaster film I saw during an era when this partic-ular genre gained widespread popularity with moviegoers ever since

George Seaton's film *Airport* in 1970. It seemed I was just starting to understand what all the fuss was about because *The Towering Inferno* proved to be sheer excitement and intense drama for my movie tastes, limited as they still were. Freaked out because watching a raging inferno in the world's tallest building taking the lives of so many people is a frightening thing and because my father was a living in a rather tall apartment building. Still, he must've felt that watching a raging fire was a far less traumatic experience than watching a monster shark eat people because he had no reservations about letting me and Kevin watch the movie (I wonder how my mother would've felt about it had she been there).

There was a Christmas tree flashing in the corner of the living room. That night, I couldn't remember if he'd unplugged the tree before retiring, but I do remember the idea of an electrical element like that running all night in an apartment building after having just watched *The Towering Inferno* didn't sit right with me. I have the vaguest memory of waking up in the middle of the night and checking the living room. It would seem that childish paranoia and the power of the disaster motion picture took its toll on an eight-year-old boy (thanks so much for doing that to me, Irwin Allen!).

The year 1975 also introduced me to a new (new to *me*, anyway) and tremendously popular character in the world of English spies, James Bond. By that year, the most current Bond movie on screen was *The Man with the Golden Gun* with the late Roger Moore, but I knew nothing of that yet. My introduction that year was when *Diamonds Are Forever* premiered on the *ABC Friday Night Movie* and *You Only Live Twice* premiered on the *ABC Sunday Night Movie*. I saw only bits and pieces of each movie, and it's unlikely that I fully understood exactly what I was watching. However, I was, for the first time, watching the intrigue, action, and excitement that was James Bond played by Sean Connery. It was a small yet effective introduction to the exotic life of the world's greatest motion picture spy because my love and fascination for Bond movies hasn't left me since, both on screen and TV.

And that, my friends, was the year 1975 for me.

THE YEAR WAS 1976 ...

- Patty Hearst is found guilty for her participation in the robbery of a bank in San Francisco.
- The Apple computer company is formed by founders Steve Jobs and Steve Wozniak.
- The United States holds a coast-to-coast Bicentennial to celebrate the 200th anniversary of its declaration of independence.
- In New York City, postal worker David Berkowitz also known as "the Son of Sam" strikes for the first time in a series of attacks that terrorize the city for the next year.
- The Cincinnati Reds sweep the New York Yankees in four games to win the World Series championship.
- In the US Presidential Election, Jimmy Carter defeats Gerald Ford to become the thirty-ninth president of the United States.

... AND THERE WERE MOVIES!

In the spring of 1976, my parents were (thankfully) divorced, my father had a downtown Manhattan apartment, a girlfriend named Mindy, and I seemed to easily adjust to a new childhood lifestyle of a weekday home on Long Island and a weekend home in New York City.

That summer, my father gave me the option of choosing not to attend day camp if I didn't want to. I immediately jumped at the chance not to go. While most kids my age enjoyed the daily grind and activities of camp, I was typically frustrated with the task of getting up early during the summer to meet the bus, as well as the entire structured system of the whole program, which felt no different than going to school. At the age of nine, I longed for the freedom of summer to do *what* I wanted *when* I wanted with as few rules as possible. With the prospect of day camp behind me forever, I'd spend the bulk of my free time with my father and Mindy in Manhattan and enjoy the benefits of the Long Island beach club they'd taken membership with. This also meant extra time for movies when the weather wasn't cooperating.

However, the spring and summer movies of '76 weren't exactly kind to a kid. Beyond the Disney Studio double feature rereleases I previously described, as well as a new live action movie about a horse that played football called *Gus* (I've never seen it), titles like *All The President's Men, The Omen,* and *The Outlaw Josey Wales* were hardly appropriate for me. I suppose my father could've taken me to see something as safe and (somewhat) innocent as Mel Brooks's *Silent Movie,* but I'm guessing it simply slipped his attention. Knowing my attention span as a child, I likely would've been bored to tears by a movie without dialogue anyway.

In the end, all that was left for me during the summer of '76 was a so-called family comedy about California little league baseball players.

The Bad News Bears

Directed by Michael Ritchie
(April 7, 1976, U.S. Release Date)

Then

My grandmother Sally (on my father's side) and I were very close. One of the greatest pleasures of my childhood was spending weekends with her at her home on Ocean Avenue in Brooklyn. During the summer of '76, Kevin and I would often divide our weekend time between my father and Mindy and my grandmother. It was she who took us to see *The Bad News Bears* under the presumption it would be just what it appeared to represent on the movie poster—a perfectly safe and wholesome family film about baseball. That turned out to be a *false* presumption.

The California Bears were a bunch of misfit kids somewhere in the neighborhood of my own age that I could relate to (or at least *try* and relate to). They were underdogs who were constantly laughed at and picked on by other boys in the league because they couldn't play baseball to save their lives. While I didn't fully understand the idea of drunken behavior (yet), watching Walter Matthau stumble around through his daily grind of coaching and cleaning swimming pools, wondering when and where he'd get his next beer, was amusing enough in itself. As a kid, the visual laughs of grown-ups acting silly and irresponsible was funny to watch, even if I didn't fully understand why.

I felt disappointed and grossly let down when the Bears, after all of their hardwork and resilience, lost the championship game in the end. Still, it was the character of Tanner Boyle who saved my negative feelings in the end when he shouted, *"Hey Yankees … you can take your apology and your trophy and shove 'em straight up your ass!"* Oh, I knew very well that wasn't a particularly nice thing for a little kid to say, but oh, man, it felt so good to hear after such an unfair loss. My grandmother, poor woman, was surely stunned by what she'd taken her little grandsons to see. Why she didn't force us to leave the theater as soon as she heard the first unpleasant remark of racist profanity from one of those little, foul-mouthed hooligans is beyond me. Who could blame her for taking us though? The movie was PG-rated, and it appeared safe enough for kids.

The Bad News Bears had its television premiere on the *ABC Friday Night Movie* on September 28, 1978. I likely missed it because I recall traveling to Florida with my family over that weekend before returning Sunday night. This was a time before the existence of affordable recording devices for TV and movies. If you weren't there in front of your set when it aired, you were out of luck. Though I can only imagine the movie must've been heavily edited to delete all its offensive words of racism and bigotry. Had it not been, my parents would have surely made me turn the TV off if they caught me watching it.

Now

It takes a few decades and some recent revisiting with an old movie like *The Bad News Bears* to reminded myself just what sort of content was considered safe and uncontroversial enough for a PG-rating back in the '70s. It remains a childhood favorite and has stayed with me not only as a fun film, but a rather exciting sports film as well. Not at the level of a climactic championship fight or Olympic event, mind you, but at the level that continues to remind us of the spirited tradition of the great game of baseball in the lives of children and their parents who support them. By comparison of today's standards of child and adolescent antics, the adventures of the Bears is surely a lame experience, if not a boring one. But those of my generation who watched *The Little Rascals* on TV after school and recall a time when the antics of wild kids were still at a safe and respectable level can cherish a time when the Bears were a comforting part of our lives and our growth (this is what it was like to be a kid in the '70s).

The Bears were, and still are, a group of shocking little punk kids to ever hit the ballfield. Tanner Boyle, played by Chris Barnes, may go down in history as the most short-tempered, racist, foul-mouthed, little creep in what is supposed to be an entertaining family film about Little League baseball. Though I have to give him credit for having the guts not to allow himself or his friends (even the ones he doesn't care for, like Timmy Lupus) to be bullied by the older and meaner kids. The words "family film" must also be reconsidered carefully here not only for back then, but by today's standards of acceptable entertainment for children and pre teens in an age where being politically correct about every little thing is deemed so important. My son is now three years older than I was when I went to see the movie in '76, and I'm *still* not ready to show him *The Bad News Bears*.

I'm not someone who's particularly offended by vulgarity or racism in fiction even when such dialogue is spoken by child actors. In the end, they're just movies, and if we're going to get offended and all bent-out-of-shape by every little thing we see and hear on screen, then we may as well just stick with Bugs Bunny and *The Flintstones*. Questionable dialogue is clearly used for comic effect that's meant to be appreciated by grown-ups rather than their children. The film is profane, rude, and cynical, but it's made with irresistible humor that's honest, unforced, and held together by credible performances by Walter Matthau, Tatum O'Neil, and the rounded-out cast of hopeless Bears who try to make the great American pastime of baseball and the spirit of athletic competition as much fun as possible.

Rocky

Directed by John G. Avildsen
(November 21, 1976, U.S. Release Date)

———※《◎》※———

Then

In May 1977, my parents decided to give their failed marriage another try after just over a year and a half. They didn't legally remarry. Instead, my father simply ended his relationship with Mindy, moved out of his Manhattan apartment, and went back into our Long Island home to pick up where he and my mother had previously left off. Within a month of that little event, they'd sold our house and we moved into a high-end apartment complex called North Shore Towers. This was (and still is) a luxurious complex of three highrise buildings in Floral Park (also on Long Island) complete with a golf course, tennis courts, indoor and outdoor swimming pool, and an array of indoor, lower level amenities including shops, restaurants, health club, and a *private movie theater*. Yes, you read that right—an actual 460-seat movie theater strictly for the residents (though in recent years, it has opened to the public). Try to imagine just how big a deal this is for a kid like me obsessed with movies. For the first time in my life, the joy of going to the movies would be as quick and easy as an elevator ride. The movies they featured were often second run, anywhere from four to six months after their initial theatrical release. The waiting period hardly mattered to me though. Every week, there was something new, and with it came an additional movie poster to announce the next attraction a week or two later.

That June, having lived there for less than a month, my father announced one night that he was taking me and Kevin downstairs to see *Rocky*. I was excited to finally break in the private theater, but I was, admittedly, unfamiliar with the movie aside from newspaper ads which featured only the title in white letters against a black background. I knew nothing of the story, who Sylvester Stallone was (my memory of him in *The Lords of Flatbush* non-existent) or that it had recently won the Oscar for Best Picture of 1976. My father had seen it (twice), and if he was willing to take us to see it, it must be safe enough for kids to watch.

Exciting is hardly the appropriate word to describe watching *Rocky* for the first time at the age of ten. This wasn't a movie filled with thrills, chills, spills, or even laughter. For the first time in my (limited) moviegoing experience, I was watching straight drama between grown-ups who each appeared to be trying to find themselves in the grimy city of Philadelphia. Rocky Balboa was an interesting character who believed in the good and positive side of life's challenges. He saw past Adrian's shyness and awkwardness and won her over after only their first date on ice skates. He saw past Paulie's nastiness and accepted him as a loyal friend. He was also a man with a heart who wanted to succeed as a boxer and was willing to take on his training by Mickey, who could be as equally nasty as Paulie.

Rocky was my first grown-up sports movie. Even before the championship fight sequence, I got caught up in Rocky's training sequences. The big one, the one with *"Gonna Fly Now"* came as somewhat of a surprise to me. I'd heard that song for months now on the radio, but it wasn't until that night I learned it was from this movie. Things were coming together for me now in the movie and the song (this is a ten-year-old's brain at work, so these things matter). I could now place the man with the music and see just how inspirational the proper song and soundtrack could make one feel when watching a story of determination, strength, and spirit.

The big fight was an experience I've still never forgotten. It was the excitement the movie was lacking up until now. It was bloody and brutal, and it made me want to stand up and cheer. My father, bless his heart, screamed with joy at the screen whenever Rocky laid

47

some good punches onto his opponent, Apollo Creed. Throughout the fourteenth round, I was sitting on the edge of my seat to see what would happen because the drama behind Bill Conti's music was so strong. By the fifteenth round, I felt I couldn't handle any more of this. Was Rocky going to win or lose? By all physical accounts of the fight, Rocky appeared to be the winner. I was sure of it. Then the roof caved in on me.

For the first time, I learned the movies were not always kind, fair, or justified. I can still recall the gape in my mouth when I realized Rocky had lost the big fight. I even had to confirm with my father if he had, in fact, lost because I didn't understand what the words *split decision* meant. By the time it was over and we were on our way to the elevator to take us back upstairs to our apartment, I was left to contend with the injustice of Rocky's fate. I felt disillusioned, and quite frankly, ripped off! I thought this just couldn't be the end of it all. Rocky had to triumph somehow because he deserved it (he *would* triumph eventually ... and repeatedly).

Rocky made its network television debut on CBS on February 4, 1979. This was one of the few times I got to watch an entire movie on TV from start to finish that I'd previously seen on screen. This airing gave me and my family another chance to relive, catch up, and perhaps even understand Rocky's character better before we found ourselves standing in line at the local movie theater for the next chapter in the story, *Rocky II*, which was already in production. We all knew it was just a matter of months before we'd be cheering for the legendary underdog all over again.

Now

As I write these words, it's been more than forty years since *Rocky's* original release date. Since then, we've seen sequels, some good and some bad, and the recent spin-off *Creed*. We've seen opponents in the form of a Mohawk-wearing badass and a gigantic Russian brute who barely spoke. Throughout all of it, the ten-year-old boy inside me has never lost touch with the powerful importance of Rocky's original down-and-out underdog story and what it meant to me and to the world. *Rocky*, to this day, remains a defining and dramatic tale of one's personal stake in the world of professional sports. The emotions I experience when I watch this film today haven't changed since I was a kid. I feel for Rocky and I cheer for Rocky as anyone who would cheer for the poor slob who gets the girl and turns himself into a prince. I still get caught up in all the bloody brutality of the big fight. But even more important, I still get pissed off at the end when Rocky loses the fight. Decades later, I still feel the emotional impact of his unfair loss.

I often ask myself what Sylvester Stallone was thinking when he wrote Rocky's loss in the original screenplay. Back then, I suppose he knew the character would go on to win the title three years later, but I also wonder just how much he anticipated the full-blown, if not *overblown*, franchise it would turn out to be over the course of the next several decades. How would Stallone feel if I were to stand in front of him and tell him that *Rocky IV* and *Rocky V* are, in my opinion, two of the worst films I've ever had the displeasure of watching? He'd probably tell me that's my opinion and I'm entitled to it, and then ask me what I thought of *Rocky Balboa*. I'd be completely honestly with him and tell him I didn't think it was all that bad, but essentially, I considered it no more or less than a remake of the original *Rocky*.

Today, I believe that Martin Scorsese's *Taxi Driver* deserved the Oscar for Best Picture of 1976 instead of *Rocky* because in the end, it's simply the better, the more powerful, and the more thought-provoking film. However, I understand and appreciate how a simple film of human strength and determination by a newcomer like Stallone, a man who at the time was compared to men like Paul Newman, Al Pacino, and Marlon Brando, could outweigh a tale of the deranged and violent mind of Robert DeNiro driving through the filthy streets of New York City in the '70s. I suppose it's simple triumph over tragedy.

King Kong

Directed by John Guillermin
(December 17, 1976, U.S. Release Date)

Then

It began with an advance teaser full-page black and white movie poster image in the Arts & Leisure section of the *Sunday New York Times* in December 1975; an image of the mighty King Kong straddled atop the Twin Towers of the World Trade Center in New York City (the towers falsely featured as an all-glass facade as opposed to the tube-frame steel construction they really were), holding a blonde woman in one hand and a giant fighter jet in the other. At the top of the poster, the caption read, "There still is only one King Kong." The bottom of the poster featured the real kicker that read, "One year from today Paramount Pictures and Dino De Laurentiis will bring to you the most exciting original motion picture event of all time."

I'll ask you now to try and get inside the head of an eight-year-old child because something inside me snapped when I saw this full-page image for the first time. By this time, I'd been to the movies only a few times and with the exception of a festival of Bugs Bunny cartoons, everything I'd seen on screen was new and unfamiliar. The game had just changed. As a child of my generation, monster movies and famous monsters themselves were something of an obsessive form of entertainment, and *King Kong* was simply the reigning champion of all monsters. Still, I needed to calm down because according to the poster, I'd have to wait an entire year before any of this would happen.

Let's now jump ahead several months to the summer of 1976. The entertainment section of the daily newspapers and weekly magazines my father subscribed to were constantly reporting the on-location filming of *King Kong* in New York City and the massive crowds of extras that were part it. My growing anticipation suffered even more with the knowledge of knowing all of this was taking place somewhere outside of my father's apartment building. It was in the air; the new Dino De Laurentiis remake of *King Kong* was coming soon, and I was gearing up for it. I should also point out that although I was already very familiar with the legendary character of Kong, I *still* hadn't seen the original 1933 film from beginning to end (only bits and pieces on TV).

The movie was finally released in theaters on Friday, December 17, 1976, but I had to wait an entire twenty-four hours before Kevin and I saw it at the Loews Astor Plaza theater in Times Square; a theater, I might add, with a huge screen. We waited in line to buy tickets, but thankfully, weren't shut out. I remember as we waited, I strayed away for a moment and opened the door to the theater, the previous show still in progress. I caught only a glimpse of Jeff Bridges and Jessica Lange seated at a bar table talking and immediately ordered myself to get back in line with my family. I'd waited this long, and there was no point in ruining things with an advance visual tease.

As we seated ourselves and the theater eventually darkened, I reminded myself of the significance of this day. This was the first PG-rated film I would be seeing on the big screen. This movie would officially take me from young boyhood to slightly older boyhood by exposing me to some adult themes, including a little bad language and maybe even a little blood. After some adult drama and some breathtaking on-location photography on a Hawaiian island, I was finally witnessing the great, legendary monster in all his colorful and powerful glory. For the first time, I witnessed a motion picture that could easily classify itself as a blockbuster event. The movies were no longer so sweet and innocent for me anymore. No more animation, no more cute, cuddly animals, and no more sappy, happy endings that were perfectly safe for children. Things had just gotten bigger, badder, meaner, and more spectacular with a new world of thrills, danger, and fear.

While I sat there, taking all of it in with the greatest of pleasure, there were some sequences that grabbed me and stayed with me long after I left the theater. The first was Dwan's sacrifice by the native tribe and the eventual arrival of Kong. This entire sequence was tremendously epic in scope, choreography, cinematography, and its musical score. It was dark, menacing, and terrifying to watch poor Dwan await the arrival of the great beast, apparently so high on the native's narcotics that she was barely aware of her surroundings and what was happening to her. Then the trees began to rustle, the camera got in real close to the ape's eyes and mouth, the music of John Barry got louder and louder, and we knew the great monster was coming closer and closer. Then the mighty ape stopped, looked down at who was before him, and roared to a volume that could have surely brought down the house. This was the roar that I and every other fan in the movie theater that day had waited an entire year to hear.

The second sequence was Kong's breaking through the great wall. This scene too was shown on a great, epic scale. Rather than simply try to push the big doors open as he had in the original '33 version, Kong unleashed all his anger and his roaring fury as he smashed the wall and doors, bit by bit, piece by piece until finally breaking through, his arms raised in a gesture that represented a loud, great victory. Unlike the original movie, Kong didn't destroy the native village, but was immediately trapped in a pit filled with chloroform. I suppose I found that omission of destruction disappointing at the time, but I'd learn much later how sometimes it's best not to copy an original movie's content too much.

The third and final sequence was Kong's final stand atop the Twin Towers in New York City, both the climb and the battle against the military helicopters. I've always been fascinated with the Twin Towers and the way they dramatically pierced the skyline of the city ever since I first saw them in the distance when riding in the car to Manhattan from Long Island. I knew nothing of their history or architectural significance as a child, but I appreciated the aesthetic awe and wonderment of such tall buildings. When I first learned that Kong would climb the Twin Towers in the remake, it made sense to choose these newer, iconic buildings. He'd already climbed the Empire State Building, so why repeat it? I remember the audience gasping in awe when Kong leaped from one tower to the other during his final battle. At the climactic moment when Kong suffered the bloody massacre of the helicopter's bullets, it was clear that he wasn't just going to die, but that everyone in the theater would likely grieve over it too. Kong's death was sad, particularly when he used his last breath to gaze upon the woman he loved. I think Kevin (age five at the time) even cried.

When the movie ended two hours and fifteen minutes later, we strolled out of the theater to find a taxi to take us home, and I felt like a changed kid. At that time, I couldn't fathom movies getting any better than the grand screen spectacle I'd just witnessed. I begged my father to take us to see it again when it was rereleased in the spring of 1977, and he did (bless the guy!). The new *King Kong* was now my favorite movie of all time, and it would remain that way until the summer of 1977, when a certain little science fiction space movie would say a great, big hello to the world.

For the time being, I was gripped with *King Kong* fever that included my desire to own any of the marketing merchandise I could get my hands on, including a metal lunch box, a plastic drinking cup from the local 7-11, and a movie-related board game by Ideal. I was even determined to see another monster movie released in the United States a short time later, called *Godzilla vs. Megalon*, because the movie poster depicted both monsters standing on each of the Twin Towers as fighter jets and helicopters swarmed above them, promising what looked like a spectacular battle. I didn't see this movie on screen, but when I finally watched it a couple of years later on TV, I learned to my horrible disappointment that no such scene and no such battle existed in this otherwise awful movie. This was, perhaps, my first lesson in the deceptions of life. A beautifully graphic and colorful movie poster will not only deceive but will outright *lie* to you when it wants to cash in on another movie's popularity and success (I still think it's a great looking poster though).

It seemed like a lot longer at the time, but I only had to wait just under two years before *King Kong* had its television premiere on the *NBC Big Event* in September 1978 over the course of two nights with additional footage added that hadn't been seen in the original theatrical release. Wait a minute! What was this? *New scenes* added to an already great movie? More *Kong* to enjoy over *two* nights instead of one? I'd never heard of such a thing before (though I later learned the 1974 disaster movie *Earthquake* was also aired in the same manner on NBC in September '76). I discovered, however, even at the age of eleven, that more footage isn't necessarily better footage. All that really took place, with the exception of one added scene of Kong rampaging down a New York City street and throwing a car into the side of a building as it explodes on impact, were simply extensions of scenes already in the original version. Sequences like the battle between Kong and the giant python, the smashing of the native village wall, and the climb up the Twin Towers just took a little longer to run their course. As a kid, I was hardly that discriminating. It was simply an opportunity for me to enjoy one of my favorite blockbuster movies for a longer period of time.

Now

I've grown up, but I've never let go of the kid in me who loved *King Kong*. However, I've learned over the course of time watching the original '33 black and white classic, that bigger is not necessarily better. Anyone with a sincere appreciation for quality cinema would surely agree that the original surpasses any of its remakes for many reasons that include actor performances and its overall movie-making technology during an era when special effects artist like Willis O'Brien were helping to shape things for the future. *Kong '76* is not the better movie, and it's hardly perfect. It's greatest flaw by today's standards is, by far, the cheap-looking ape suit worn by special effects artist Rick Baker. But we must consider the fact that stop-motion animation had been played to death in the original Kong, and CGI effects were still decades away. I believe that cheap ape suit or not, the makers behind Dino De Laurentiis did the best they could with the technologies of the time, and the suit can be easily compensated for with excellent acting by Jeff and Jessica, fine photography, and a haunting musical score by John Barry. To define *Kong '76's* technological achievement ... well, let's just say that where *Kong '33* made great achievements in stop-motion animation and Peter Jackson's 2005 remake made great achievements in CGI effects to compete with Steven Spielberg's *Jurassic Park*, *Kong '76* makes its impressive achievement in the use of modern hydraulics for the design and movement of the great ape's arms and hands, particularly when he picks up and holds Jessica Lange.

There's one element that I believe makes *Kong '76* better than its predecessor. Despite the fact that Fay Wray made quite a name for herself as the original "Scream Queen" of the movies, I enjoy Lange a whole lot more because she actually takes the time to get to know the big ape. She talks to him, shouts at him, and even hits him in the face when she's enraged. The remake puts in the effort to acknowledge the inevitable bond of trust and affection that develops between beauty and beast, right up until the moment when Kong is fighting atop the Twin Towers and she tries to protect him against the attacking helicopters. It's also, perhaps, the one film that truly glorifies the Twin Towers more than any other in history. You can tell just by looking at the great movie poster designed by John Berkley. It's also managed to take on a different shape and meaning for me since the tragic events of September 11, 2001 and the destruction of the Twin Towers by cowardly acts of terrorism. The two soaring structures serve as more than just the great ape's climbing destination but actual *characters* for the thrilling and bloody climax of Kong's demise.

Back then, the Twin Towers had recently opened in 1973 and gained international fame when French high wire acrobatic performer Philippe Petit performed repeated walks between the towers on a steel tightrope on the morning of August 7, 1974. Following the release of *King Kong*, mountain-climber George Willig was discovered climbing the south tower of the World Trade Center on the morning of May 26, 1977. He was arrested at the top and fined one dollar and ten cents; one cent for each of the skyscraper's 110 stories, by then New York City Mayor Abraham Beame. Since the events of the 9-11 attacks, which I personally witnessed standing on the streets of Manhattan, I cannot watch the '76 version of *King Kong* without taking a moment to reflect on what those two buildings meant to the world and to a certain nine-year-old boy who was forever transformed when he witnessed for the first time on the big screen, the greatest and mightiest monster of all time. I'm grateful for that memory.

*****

This is the last film of 1976 I shall discuss in any great detail.

I shall cap off by discussing the influence of films released prior to 1975 shown on TV because they were noteworthy films that first caught my attention during this eight-year period.

Let's begin with *Gone with the Wind*, the famous 1939 Civil War film I first heard of as a kid. I'd seen it parodied on some Bugs Bunny cartoons and also in a skit on *The Carol Burnett Show*. I'd also heard people mockingly coin the phrase, "Frankly, my dear, I don't give a damn!" On November 6, 1976, Hollywood's best remembered film was making its TV premiere on the *NBC Big Event* over a period of two nights, and I was going to finally see this big movie for the first time. The network promised "the television premiere of the most eagerly awaited motion picture of them all!" and it was to start on a Saturday night with a three-hour big event. This, like *The Towering Inferno*, was another night with my father and Mindy as we enjoyed some take-out dinner before the big show began.

This was the first old (and classic) movie I ever saw in *color*. I can't say I understood everything I watched, but I was old enough to appreciate the concept and horrors of the Civil War, while fascinated by its colorful cinematography, including the famous scene of Scarlett O'Hara, Rhett Butler, and Melanie Hamilton escaping burning Atlanta and the raging inferno behind them. I loved the fire's orange glow and how it ignited the scene's sense of danger and intensity. Of course, as a kid, I wasn't thinking those exact words. I very likely thought something simple like, "That's cool!" While I didn't know it at the time, the movie's airing was the highest-rated television program ever presented on a single network (that's cool too). Unfortunately, the thrill of the evening and the three-hour big event was not meant to continue to its conclusion. The next night was Sunday, and I had to go to school the next day, which meant I'd miss out on part 2 because my mother ordered me to go to bed at my usual weeknight time. I was left incomplete and unfinished in my cinematic knowledge of *Gone with the Wind* until many years later when I finally owned a VCR and movie rentals were an easy trip to the neighborhood video store. Very unfair, but I'm still grateful for the opportunity that NBC and movies on TV gave me as a kid … even for just one night.

As previously mentioned for '75, TV and ABC were responsible for my introduction to the movies of James Bond. The year 1976 continued this trend with the premiere of *Live and Let Die* on the *ABC Sunday Night Movie* in October 1976. I loved that movie and still do today, though my childhood memories are pretty vivid in that I think I was a little freaked out when I first experienced the notion of large serpents, man-eating alligators, a large man with a hook in place of his hand, and deadly voodoo magic.

Prior to that was the premiere of *On Her Majesty's Secret Service* on the *ABC Monday Night Movie* in February 1976 (again, there's a great difference between what I experienced then and what I know to be true today). Back then, I watched bits and pieces of what appeared to be a great James Bond action movie with some great skiing and bobsledding sequences that lasted over the course of two nights on TV. Today, I've learned the truth behind this ABC broadcast was nothing short of an unacceptable abomination. Apparently, the network, in an effort to stay ahead of CBS and NBC during "sweeps" month, decided to air the movie over a period of two nights one week apart at ninety minutes each night. It featured severe reedits at the beginning, custom optical effects at new points of its transition, and an inexplicable (and infamous) narration added to explain newly-added flashbacks. This was clearly *not* the accurate representation of the film United Artist and director Peter Hunt released in 1969, but rather a desperate attempt by a television network to hold onto its viewing audience. All of this, while remaining an interesting piece of TV broadcast history, is practically irrelevant today because I have never and still don't consider this to be one of the better Bond movies in the franchise.

Finally, we'll end the year with a television event that forever changed the way I looked at (and continue to look at) the annual American holiday of Thanksgiving. On New York's Channel 9, WOR-TV in the Tri-State region of the United States, there began a festival of classic monster movies that was repeated annually until 1985. On this historic occasion, the network aired *Mighty Joe Young, King Kong vs. Godzilla,* and *Son of Kong.* At the age of eight, I was hardly a serious critic of monster movies, even the badly-dubbed Japanese ones. These movies were all the rage of childhood entertainment, and to be able to watch them on TV during my holiday off from school was considered pure gold. The broadcast ratings were seemingly good enough for the network to include the Friday after Thanksgiving in the monster movie line-up by adding a few extra Japanese Godzilla movies. However, the original '33 version of *King Kong* wasn't part of the line-up in '76. That would take another year, and it would be the first time I'd finally seen the legendary classic from beginning to end.

And that, my friends, was the year 1976 for me.

THE YEAR WAS 1977 ...

- The TV mini-series *Roots* begins its hugely successful run on ABC.
- The July blackout of New York City results in looting and other criminal chaos.
- David Berkowitz, *"the Son of Sam"* serial killer is finally arrested in Yonkers, New York City, after more than a year of brutal murders.
- Elvis Presley, considered the king of rock and roll, dies at the age of forty-two at his home in Graceland.
- Anti-gay speaker Anita Bryant is famously hit in the face with pies by gay rights activists, thus resulting in her political fallout.
- The New York Yankees achieve championship victory when Reggie Jackson hits three homeruns in the final game of the World Series against the Los Angeles Dodgers.

... AND THERE WERE MOVIES!

In June 1977, my parents were back together and we moved to North Shore Towers. While it was a (seemingly) positive experience to have both of them under the same roof again, I must confess that I felt some sadness in knowing I'd never see Mindy again. In addition to these changes, for the first time since I was three years-old, my family rented a home for the summer of '77 in the town of Westhampton Beach on Long Island (a town complete with two neighborhood movie theaters, I might add).

Even before my parents' unprecedented domestic reunion, and before the move to an apartment complex with a private movie theater, and before the inevitable release of George Lucas's huge gift to the world of science fiction, movies were about to get a little more serious for a kid who was on the verge of hitting the big double digits of ten years old. It began, as it often did, with the browsing of the Sunday paper and the sight of a large 747 jumbo airliner crashing into the sea and lying at its bottom. It continued later with a frightening image of the Goodyear Blimp crashing into the stands of a football stadium during the Super Bowl (though I wouldn't see that John Frankenheimer movie until many years later).

Disasters in the movies wouldn't end with previous films like *The Poseidon Adventure, Earthquake,* and *The Towering Inferno.* They were about to hit home in a small way for a child who, at that time, had still never flown in an airplane before.

Airport '77

Directed by Jerry Jameson
(March 11, 1977, U.S. Release Date)

Then

By 1977, I'd heard of both previous *Airport* movies, but saw neither
of them. Like other movies before, my first image of the new one,
Airport '77, was a full-page ad in the *Sunday New York Times*. It was a
split image of the large 747 airliner making contact with the water as
it crashes into the Bermuda Triangle at the upper part and the plane
sitting at the bottom of the water moments later at the lower part. I
remember staring at this image for several minutes because there was
something very chilling about the prospect of what was happening
to this airplane. Somehow, in my young mind, I'd determined that
such an airline disaster seemed *possible*. Unlike the newspaper image
of the large blimp crashing into a large stadium in *Black Sunday*, I
could somehow picture the reality of this underwater situation happening in real life.

The Bermuda Triangle and the myths surrounding it, in which
ships and airplanes mysteriously disappeared, were not unheard of
within the small circle of fourth grade ten-year-old children. Now
it looked as if Hollywood had taken the *Airport* franchise to the
next level and decided to play upon the fear of such myths. While
I stood there staring at the paper with a chill in my body, I was also
filled with excitement at the prospect of seeing such a movie. It was
PG-rated, so I figured I had a good chance with my father. I wasted

no time and immediately asked him if we could see it. He took the paper from me, stared at the ad for a moment, and said, "I guess so." Well, *that* was easy!

When you're a kid watching a disaster movie, *any* disaster movie, all you really want to see is the disaster. This meant that any of the complicated plotting surrounding the priceless works of art aboard the aircraft and the means by which the hijackers took over the plane was material that probably went right over my head, or perhaps I just didn't care that much. Once the 747 took off, however, that's when I knew I needed to prepare myself and countdown the minutes until everyone on board was in trouble. From the moment the passengers passed out from the gas and the plane was overtaken, I was ready for anything. I can actually recall my father telling me to sit still in my seat. When the plane finally crashed into the water and the music got louder and more dramatic, you could've easily carried me out on a stretcher from the tension and the excitement I felt. Once the plane sank and settled to the bottom of the water, I calmed down a bit. Now it was simply a matter of time before the survivors were rescued. The rest of the movie was a thrilling underwater adventure. It was my first moviegoing experience in which I found myself sucked into the adventures and dangers of being underwater (I hadn't seen the James Bond movie *Thunderball* yet, and *The Deep* was still months away from release).

When the movie ended, there was only one thing on my mind other than the fact that I'd really enjoyed *Airport '77*, and that was the fact that I'd still never flown in a plane before. I wondered how long it would be before that actually happened and how a kid like me, who'd grown up in the era of disaster movies in which airplanes got into real trouble, would handle his first flight. Well, that flight took place about a year and a half later in September 1978, returning from Florida to New York. I'm happy to say I didn't allow Hollywood's grim version of air travel to get the better of me. I simply sat close to my father and waited for the trip to be over (today, of course, I have far more sophisticated and realistic reasons to hate the process of air travel).

Like *King Kong* before it, *Airport '77* premiered on the *NBC Big Event* in September 1978 (the same week as the *Kong* premiere) over a period of two nights with approximately seventy-five minutes of trims and unused footage. I could see there was a definite pattern taking place in television airings of popular movies by generously extending them in an effort to hold people's attention longer. Whether or not it worked was dependent, I suppose, on what the viewer thought of the extra footage. In the case of *Airport '77*, the extra time was mostly devoted to flashbacks, giving us an insight to each of the main character's lives before they took the ill-fated flight that landed them at the bottom of the water. Like *Kong* on TV before it, I recognized that more footage didn't necessarily make a better movie, just an unnecessarily longer one. Well, as the old saying goes, sometimes less is more, even with a disaster movie.

Now

I've caught up on all the *Airport* films in the franchise. The original *Airport*, based on Arthur Haley's novel, is far from perfect but offers solid performances by some of Hollywood's best actors of the time. The film consists of more personal drama behind its characters than true disaster, which is easily predictable, even up to the point where we know that everything will turn out okay in the end. Still, it paved the way for an entire decade of the disaster genre, even before men like Irwin Allen took it to the extreme.

I saw *Airport 1975* when it premiered on *NBC Saturday Night at the Movies* on April 22, 1978. As a kid with no cinematic taste yet, I loved every minute of it because my suspension of disbelief was at its maximum. I loved the mid-air collision, I loved the idea of the stewardess flying the plane on her own, and I loved how her pilot boyfriend could be transported and inserted from the air into the plane to bring it down to safety. This was complete suspension of disbelief. Today, despite being a fan of most of Charlton Heston's work, you couldn't pay me enough money to watch this turkey with its hokey story and spectacularly bad acting. The only good feelings I've taken away from it are the parodies, as seen in a skit on *The Carol Burnett Show* and the 1980 comedy *Airplane!*

You may be surprised to find that a less-than-popular movie like *Airport '77* still continues to hold up very well with me over the decades. The intricate plotting of the art heist and the hijacking not only make a whole lot of sense to me now, but actually work a great deal better as cause and motive inevitably leading up to the great disaster than the other three *Airport* films. The performances, particularly by Jack Lemmon, Brenda Vaccaro, George Kennedy, and even the great James Stewart as the millionaire art collector are solid enough to hold it all together. The film is also greatly aided with realistic portrayals of the Navy's rescure operations and procedures, which are claimed to be real at the film's end. I've owned a copy of the film since becoming available on VHS, but I had the opportunity to watch the extra long version on TV when I was in college. While my opinions of the unnecessary extra footage remain the same when I was a kid, one element of the longer version does, in fact, catch my attention today. If you've ever been a fan of ABC's *Lost*, then you're familiar with the ongoing part of the plotline in which the show uses flashbacks to show the lives of the crash survivors before they took the ill-fated flight that landed them on the mysterious island. I can't help but wonder if the show's creator, J.J. Abrams, and his writers were not inspired by the similar flashback footage used to make *Airport '77* longer on television. Perhaps they just ripped it off directly.

Annie Hall

Directed by Woody Allen
(April 20, 1977, U.S. Release Date)

Then

Question: If you were the parent of a ten-year-old boy in 1977, would you have taken him to see Woody Allen's *Annie Hall*? His two previous films, *Sleeper* and *Love and Death*—yes, I can see that. They were goofy, wacky, easy for a kid to laugh at, and in the same spirit as any of the *Pink Panther* movies, even if they didn't understand the whole story. *Annie Hall*, on the other hand, would require some degree of understanding in the world of adult wit and romantic situations, and really, what ten-year-old kid would have any of *that*? Even more, what six-year-old younger brother would have any of that? Still, the movie was safely PG-rated, contained no apparent profanity or violence, and my parents were dying to see it, so they decided to drag their two boys along with them.

From the moment the movie began, I immediately experienced something very different. The star of the movie, this Woody Allen guy, was standing there on the screen in front of a bare background and talking to us. He was talking to *me*. This was unheard of for me. Who *does* this in a movie? Within moments of my confusion and bewilderment, however, a smile developed on my face. My god, this was brilliant! A movie whose story and actor *interacts* with the audience. From the moment that Allen's opening remarks were concluded, I knew then and there I was going to enjoy *Annie Hall* very much, even if I didn't fully understand what was going on.

The more I thought about it though, the more it occurred to me that the subject of love, relationships, and their inevitable break-ups were not that hard to comprehend, even for a ten-year-old boy. In between, however, there were unconventional moments throughout the movie that truly surprised me because I simply didn't know that such creative liberties existed in the movies. These included the scene where Alvy and Annie are having a drink and talking on her apartment building rooftop, all the while their inner thoughts displayed on the screen to be read like subtitles, as well as the sudden transition to cartoon animation depicting Alvy's troubled relationship with Annie through the eyes of the Wicked Queen from *Snow White and the Seven Dwarfs*.

As I found myself laughing throughout the movie, I recall my mother leaning over and whispering in my ear.

"Eric, do you understand what you're laughing at?"
"I think so."

Was that *really* the truth? I'd like to think it was, rather than just my trying to appear as if I could keep up with an adult-themed movie. Whether it was true or not, there was no denying I'd not only been introduced to the neurotic (yeah, like I knew what the word *neurotic* meant back then) world of Woody Allen, but also to a new and altogether different style of moviemaking and dialogue. I suppose when you're a kid, you'll embrace any opportunity to discover something different and unprecedented in life, even when you're simply sitting in your seat in a darkened movie theater. I can thank my parents for that.

Now

Despite a long and dramatic career that has spanned many decades, *Annie Hall* remains, to this day, my favorite Woody Allen film above all others. Some of the reasons are due to the same unconventional filmmaking styles that I was fortunate enough to recognize even as a kid. Perhaps even more than some of his other films of a more serious tone as *Interiors, Manhattan, Hannah and Her Sisters,* or *Crimes and Misdemeanors, Annie Hall* exposes a world of grown-up New Yorkers in the 1970s and just how neurotic, psychotic, and truly messed up their lives can be, but also with just the right added blend of comedy and silliness to bring it to a realistic level that those of us in real life can truly relate to.

Beyond basic comedy, however, is the deep, philosophical, and psychoanalytical theme behind Woody Allen's character of Alvy Singer, who's not too unlike Marcello Mastroianni's self-determined character in Federico Fellini's *8 ½*. Alvy confesses to us about his concerns over aging and death though while still suggesting he's not morose about such matters. The fantasy elements regarding how we may deal with life's irritating situations are intriguing. How many times have we often thought about how great it would be to really embarrass or humiliate some obnoxious person on a movie line who simply won't shut his mouth (in today's world, however, such a fantasy would probably exist on a commuter train with someone who insists on talking loudly and publicly on their smart phone)? As Allen so eloquently puts it, *"Boy, if life were only like this."* He knows that as human beings, we can be weak, if not terribly flawed creatures. We simply need to acknowledge it and, perhaps, even have a little fun with it, as he chooses to. The fact is, one cannot claim to have fully experienced the world of so-called grown-up drama unless we've experienced the good, the bad, and the ugly side of it all, and believe me, there's plenty of it to go around in life. As Woody himself states at the end of the film, we continue to put ourselves through all of it because some of us simply *"need the eggs."*

Since *Deconstructing Harry* in 1997, I've lost touch with (or perhaps interest) Woody Allen's film career and the messages behind his work. Perhaps it's the years, the mileage, or simply the man's age, but I'm just not laughing much anymore, nor am I getting anything new or significant from his definition of who and what people are today. Perhaps this is why I embrace a film like *Annie Hall*. Also, no matter how much time passes or what comes to define human interactions during each era of life, we're all still just muddling around through the streets of our existence like Alvy and Annie; waiting to see what will happen next and who it will happen with, all the while wondering why we're doing it in the first place. Perhaps times do change, but people inevitably don't.

Star Wars

Directed by George Lucas
(May 25, 1977, U.S. Release Date)

Then

"When and where did you first see *Star Wars*?"

I've asked that very question to others on social media, and the answers I've received are often quite detailed. Many remember the very day they first saw the movie in 1977, the exact movie theater they saw it in, how long they waited in line to get inside, whether or not the show was sold out, and how long they waited before seeing it again ... and again ... and again. For those of us who grew up in the late '70s, *Star Wars* was a cinematic rite of passage to a world that never existed before. If *Jaws* got the summer blockbuster up on its feet, then *Star Wars* cemented it into the foundation of our lives. Aside from James Bond, no other film franchise in history has had as much of a generational effect and transition as *Star Wars*. Those of us who were there at the very beginning devoted six years of our lives to the original trilogy. We saw the movies, we read the books, we listened to the soundtracks, and we begged our parents to buy as all those action figures and other assorted toys.

Those who grew up in the 1990s had the limitations of video cassette tapes and TV sets to experience the trilogy; that is, until 1997 when all three movies were rereleased as *special editions* for a limited run in theaters. Those who grew up later at the start of the twenty-first century had the prequel trilogy to keep them happy (or *not*, depending on how they felt about them). Finally, those who are growing up now in this decade are the children of the new Disney-owned *Star Wars* franchise that includes a variety of CGI TV shows, the latest episodes following the original saga (*The Force Awakens* and *The Last Jedi*), and stand-alone movies (*Rogue One* and *Solo*). For someone like my twelve-year-old son, it's almost impossible for him to conceive the idea that a long time ago, far, far away, there was just a stand-alone movie that took the world by storm. It had no episode number and no subtitle of *A New Hope*. It was a movie simply called *Star Wars* that opened on May 25, 1977, without fanfare, without marketing hype, or word-of-mouth. It's hard to imagine now, but it was a movie that could've easily bombed.

Up until then, sci-fi movies for my generation were grim pieces of dystopian societies like the *Planet of the Apes* saga, *THX-1138*, *Soylent Green*, and *Logan's Run*. Even Stanley Kubrick's *2001: A Space Odyssey* was a real thinking piece that didn't necessarily paint a positive picture for man's future and his relationships with computer machinery and artificial intelligence. *Star Wars* was a much more fun time at the movies, but it would've been difficult to know that just by looking at the movie poster and newspaper ads. Those who saw it in its opening weeks were likely taking a large leap of faith based on positive critical reviews and, perhaps, even their fondness for George Lucas's previous film, *American Graffiti*. By June of that summer, the word was out—you just *had* to see *Star Wars*! That being the case, I'll describe the conditions in which I almost saw *Star Wars* for the first time (yes, I said *almost*).

My family and I were still living in our Long Island home when the movie opened. Across the street lived my best friend in the neighborhood whom I shall call *David H.* It was a Saturday afternoon, and we were playing together at his house. His father asked if we'd like to go to a movie. The answer was obvious, but David H. and I needed to agree on what to see. He suggested something new that was playing at the local movie theater called *Star Wars*. I rejected the idea for the simple reason that I'd never heard of it before. I asked if there were any monster movies playing anywhere (perhaps I wanted his answer to be *Godzilla vs Megalon*). He told me that there *were* monsters in *Star Wars*, but I held my conviction and continued to reject the idea (ten-year-old boys are not necessarily *smart* ten-year-old boys). I felt determined that whatever we saw should be something familiar to the both of us. We finally came to an agreement and went to see (I can hardly bring myself to say this) *For the Love of Benji*. Yes, I actually opted out of seeing the newest and greatest space fantasy blockbuster of all time so I could watch a silly sequel about a little, brown dog wandering an island in Greece. What David H. must've thought of me, I can't even imagine.

It eventually gets better. Jump ahead two months to August. My father announces that he's finally taking me and Kevin (and my grandmother) to see *Star Wars*. I was happy, of course, but I wasn't exactly jumping out of my skin because I still wasn't fully aware of what I was about to see because my access to public word-of-mouth and marketing hype wasn't too great. We drove nearly an hour to a neighborhood theater in East Hampton, Long Island, got our tickets and seats easily and without waiting or hassle. When the lights went out and the movie's opening crawl began, I remember feeling disappointed because I didn't like starting off a movie that required me to read what the story was about. That disappointment lasted only through the extent of the crawl because as soon as the camera panned downward and the great Star Destroyer shot its way across the screen above the planet Tatooine, my eyes widened, my mouth opened, and I was caught in its grip.

The age of ten felt like the perfect age to experience *Star Wars*. It was a glorious age when a little boy started to break away from childish entertainment and discover the true meaning of heroes and adventure on screen. The ancient mythology of the hero and the villain were incomprehensible to me, but as someone filled with curiosity, wonderment, and awe, men like Luke Skywalker and Han Solo defined what a young boy wished *he* could be in the fantasies of his own mind.

The action surrounding the rescue of Princess Leia aboard the Death Star practically put a laser blaster in my own hand to fight alongside these rebels fighting for intergalactic freedom. The fear of watching our heroes survive the trash compactor had me biting my fingernails. The lightsaber duel between Ben Kenobi and Darth Vader put a sword in my own hands. The spectacular space battle of the Death Star transported my imagination into the cockpit of my own X-Wing fighter to challenge Vader and his stormtroopers in their Tie-Fighters. A child's imagination is already a powerful thing, but Lucas had clearly figured out how to tap into its heart and make it soar. In fact, it was during the climactic space battle that I noticed my grandmother had actually fallen asleep in her seat. To this day, there's an ongoing family joke in which we recall, "Remember when Grandma fell asleep during *Star Wars*?" How could anyone, even an old lady, fall asleep during such a loud movie?

By the end of the movie, I felt so fulfilled and yet so unsatisfied because it was a feeling that I didn't want to end. I asked my father if we could stay in our seats and watch it again (you could still easily do that back then). He said no, and I'm sure I did my best not to hold a grudge against him. What really became intolerable was the fact that I spent much of the remainder of '77 and well into '78 repeatedly asking my parents if I could see it again, and their answer was always no. Not since *Jaws*, had I felt the pinch of being denied access to a popular movie. This was worse, actually, because I'd already seen *Star Wars*, and I knew just how great an experience it was. Every weekend, the movie section of the Sunday paper was there on the table, and every weekend, I had to stare at the images of what was now my favorite movie of all time (sorry, *Kong*) and contend with the fact that I wasn't getting any closer to a second go-around. Unlike today where a blockbuster movie plays for only a few weeks at the local multiplex before making its way to DVD, Blu-Ray, and stream upload, *Star Wars* played continuously in movie theaters for nearly a year and eventually surpassed *Jaws* as the highest grossing film of all time.

For the time being, the closest I got to seeing the movie again was watching *The Making of Star Wars* on ABC on September 16, 1977, just four months after its release, or repeatedly listening to *The Story of Star Wars*, a record album of one hour's worth of action and dialogue from the movie (to be teased like this was just *not* cool!). Thankfully, however, even the most persistent of nagging kids can inevitably get their way. On July 20, 1978, *Star Wars* officially ended its first theatrical run in the United States, but due to its overwhelming popularity, it was given a wide rerelease *the very next day* on July 21st and remained in theaters until the following November (I guess there are some movies you just don't take away from people). There was a great new poster too; a "circus" style oil painting of the beloved characters by Drew Struzan and Charles White III, officially known as the *"Style D"* poster. To this day, this remains one of my favorite movie posters of the original film.

I saw the movie for a second time at a small neighborhood movie theater in the town of Great Neck, Long Island (where my family and I would eventually move to in 1979). While the feeling is inexplicable when you experience something like this for the very first time, it felt more exciting the second time because I not only knew what would happen and when, but I was now a part of something that already set its place in motion picture history. Once wasn't enough. Twice wouldn't be enough, and it didn't have to be this time. My parents agreed to let us stay in our seats and watch it again. In today's age of easy movie collectibility, I'm sure that hardly sounds exciting. But at a time when you could only see a movie again if you went back to the theater and pay for another ticket, watching a movie two times in a row was a big deal for a kid like me.

Still, I was greedy. Even *three* times in one year wasn't enough for me. The movie eventually came to our building's private movie theater, and you can only imagine what my immediate reaction was. Unfortunately, my parents weren't too agreeable to a *fourth* time in a galaxy far, far away. This would take some real doing on my part. In one of my earliest efforts in the art of negotiation, I promised them if they let me see it again, I'd forgo my weekly allowance until the price of the ticket was paid off. They agreed, and believe me, I got the better end of the bargain because a children's movie ticket wasn't expensive back then. This time, they wouldn't have to suffer through it either, because I'd meet a friend at the theater. Yes, I'd definitely scored with this one! To not have seen *Star Wars* again while it was so conveniently playing within the confines of my own building would've been unforgivable.

That *still* wasn't enough. It was rereleased again on August 15, 1979, and this time the movie poster was determined to tempt me back into the theater. It said, *"It's back!"* and *"The Force will be with you for three weeks only."* It also promised, *"EXTRA: See coming attractions for THE EMPIRE STRIKES BACK, the continuing saga of STAR WARS."* Seriously? Was George and 20th Century Fox deliberately going out of their way to mess with me? How was I supposed to ignore these temptations? Didn't they realize there was no way my parents would allow me to see this movie a *fifth* time? It was not to be. It would not be again when it was rereleased on April 10, 1981, for two weeks only, and this time came with a new addition to the opening crawl: *Episode IV—A New Hope.* However, by the time it was rereleased again on August 13, 1982, I was fifteen years old and had gained a little more independence in how, when, and with whom I ventured to the movies. If I chose to see *Star Wars* again and I had the allowance money to spend, the decision was all mine. I chose *yes,* of course, and this time I got to see the new trailer for the next chapter in the saga, *Revenge of the Jedi* (later changed to *Return*). Movie independence is a highly underestimated position in a young boy's life, believe me.

By the time all was said and done, between 1977 and 1982, I'd seen *Star Wars* on the big screen *five* times. By comparison to many die-hard fans, that's insulting low, I'm sure. Those people clearly had money to burn and more agreeable parents than I did. I didn't see the movie again until it premiered on HBO and other pay-cable channels in February 1983. I watched it at friends house's because my parents didn't finally agree to subscribe to HBO until *one month later*, when it was no longer aired (just my terrible luck!). Years later, when I was older and more in control of my own finances, I purchased a brand new VHS copy of the movie from CBS-Fox video at my local neighborhood video store, seven years from the time I first saw the movie back in the summer of '77. I still own that tape, and it sits somewhere among my archived childhood items. By the time it finally made its CBS premiere on February 26, 1984, watching it over a three-hour period seemed futile in an age of movie collectibility. Still, the TV version offered a bonus feature of some interesting commentary on the movie's phenomenon in between the commercials by host Mark Hamill.

All in all, from age ten well into my teens, *Star Wars* was a major *"force"* in my life. I'm truly grateful for that, and I thank its creator from the bottom of my heart for being such an important and influential part of my growing up. *Thank you, George!*

Now

The world of *Star Wars* has changed so much in the more than forty years since the original film first hit movie theaters, that sometimes it's difficult to wrap my head around all of it. What started out as a two-hour motion picture of a fairytale quest inspired by multiple themes and inspirations, including Flash Gordon and Akira Kurosawa's *The Hidden Fortress*, has since become an uncontrollable (excuse the pun) *"empire"* comprised of sequels, prequels, computer-generated TV shows, books, video games, graphic novels, YouTube fan-made videos, smartphone apps … the list is endless.

What *Star Wars* defines for a man my age is another time and another meaning compared to today's generation of fans that fall under the new ownership of the franchise by Disney. Don't get me wrong—I enjoy all eight *Star Wars* films (even the prequels) and believe it or not, I still own some of the old toys I managed to hang onto from when I was a kid (and a few extras purchased on eBay over the years), but the reflections I have of the past are perhaps incomprehensible to those who enjoy it all on a different level today. When I was a kid, *Star Wars* was just simply a great movie.

In the summer of 1996, I went to see *Independence Day* and was surprised to see a trailer for all three films of the original *Star Wars* trilogy set for theatrical rerelease in the spring of 1997 to celebrate the twentieth anniversary of the original film. *Star Wars* would be released on January 31, 1997, as a *special edition* with newly added footage and enhanced digital effects. Despite an initial reaction of curiosity, I wasn't sure how to feel about that. The movie was already perfect as it was, so why change anything? Long story short, I ended up seeing the *special edition* twice for no other reason than it was a rare opportunity to see the film on the big screen all over again. That didn't necessarily mean I was *happy* with what Lucas had done to his movie. As it turned out, *nobody* really was.

I consider myself a movie purist. That means I generally don't approve of a filmmaker going back and changing their work years later. With very few exceptions, I do *not* go for *special editions, director's cuts, final cuts*, or anything of the sort. I'm of the opinion that once a motion picture has had its general release and its impact on the moviegoing public, has established itself, good or bad, you walk away, you leave it alone, and you move on. Sure, I own the *special edition* of the film because it's what's available in high definition Blu-Ray, but I'm fortunate that I still keep a working VCR in my life so I can, once in a while, watch *Star Wars* as it was (as of 1981, anyway) before Lucas got his hot, little hands on it and unacceptably changed things, in particular the infamous issue of who shot who first at the Mos Eisley Cantina (Han Solo *did* shoot first!).

Having vented all that frustration, I'm left only with what *Star Wars* meant to me as a kid and what it still means to me as the adult I am now. It's my favorite film of the entire saga that I watch when I want to remember that I still have an active imagination. It's the film I watch when I need to recall a time when a new step forward in science fiction fantasy had been taken and the world stood up and took notice. It's the film I watch when I want to shake off the stress of the daily grind of adulthood and remember when things in my life were simpler. In short, it's the film I've come to define as my favorite *comfort movie*. It serves to remind us all that we, as fans of great science fiction, are in the ongoing process of committing ourselves to cosmic and character events, revelations, and realizations that play out like a giant inter-galactic soap opera. Mind you, we're not complaining. We love it! Perhaps it's even made some of us happier when life gets us down.

It has for *this* guy!

The Deep

Directed by Peter Yates
(June 17, 1977, U.S. Release Date)

—————————⊷⦿⊶—————————

Then

Looking back on it decades later, I cannot, for the life of me, imagine how I ever got my father to take me to see *The Deep*. One look at the movie poster's tagline, *"Is anything worth the terror of The Deep?"* and you'd think my parents would've shielded me from such a potentially-menacing underwater movie. Still, it was PG-rated and even though it was based on a book by the same man who wrote *Jaws*, it didn't appear to be about anything man-eating. It was, perhaps, simply a matter of my father wanting to see it himself and having to take me with him. I think he'd read the book too because I recall a paperback copy sitting somewhere in the house. I also think he chose it as an alternate to another new disaster-type movie that opened that same weekend, *Rollercoaster*. Having seen the movie poster image of that one as well, I was likely relieved to see *The Deep* instead because the idea of a loop rollercoaster, which I didn't even know existed in real life, unnerved me at an age when a day at Six Flags Great Adventure in New Jersey meant the world to me. I didn't want to spoil that.

Let me take a moment to tell you where I was at this time. It was the summer of '77 and my family had rented a beach house for the entire season. We spent our days surrounded by water of the bay at the back of the house and the Atlantic ocean across the street at the beach. It was a glorious haven to spend my summer months before going back to school again. So, what better way to take in all of that beautiful environment than to go see a movie where the action took place underwater? In other words, when a beach town has a beach or water movie playing at its local theater, you want to go see it to keep up the spirit of your surroundings. I thought that way as a kid, and I still think that way today.

At the age of ten, however, I didn't fully comprehend the concept of sunken World War II ships, drugs, and criminals who wanted to get their hands on them for distribution and profit. I had no understanding of why criminals would use a chicken's foot to paint blood on a woman's body while they held her down helpless on the bed. I don't think I fully realized that I was watching the same actor who'd been in *Jaws* because his appearance was cleaner than Quint's. All I really understood were the adventures and the dangers of underwater scuba diving, and perhaps that was more than enough for me to enjoy watching *The Deep*. There were a couple of sequences involving sharks and a deadly moray eel. I wonder just how I got through the scene when the eel took the head of Louis Gossett Jr. into its mouth? Did my father cover my eyes? Did he also cover my eyes when Jacqueline Bissett infamously appeared in her white, wet T-shirt and bikini bottom? I don't remember anymore. I'd like to think that he was too distracted by her bulging, wet nipples to pay any attention to his little boy sitting next to him (bless him!). When the movie ended after the great, climactic explosion underwater, I felt as if I'd been inaugurated into a world of grown-up adventure and danger that didn't necessarily involve giant apes or battles in outer space. This, I suppose, is how a young boy grew up a little at the movies.

Less than three years later, on February 10, 1980, *The Deep* premiered on the *ABC Sunday Night Movie*, and the apparent tradition of making films longer over a period of two nights with added footage continued. That footage included the wreck of the Goliath with a young Adam Coffin on board during World War II and also a deeper insight into Romer Treece's past, including the murder of his wife by drug dealers. Of course, television editing had to omit much of

Bissett's wet T-shirt shots (damn them!), but at least I was fortunate to have seen that on screen years before. Like *King Kong* and *Airport '77* before it, sitting through (most of) this two-night TV version meant the extension of scenes that previously existed, though I found the new opening World War II sequence interesting and informative to the plot. Perhaps by the age of thirteen, I understood why some footage was left on the cutting room floor and didn't make the final print. Perhaps this was the beginning of my becoming the movie purist that I am today.

Now

The Deep is a highly underrated thriller by director Peter Yates. Those who viewed it negatively back in '77, both critics and audiences, because they were expecting another version of *Jaws*, were only kidding themselves. Although there's terror in the water and a moment or two involving deadly sharks and that dreaded moray eel, author Peter Benchley was clearly trying to break away from what made him famous while still trying to remain in the water, which is what he seemed to enjoy writing about.

Perhaps the story resembled too much of the syndicated TV show *Sea Hunt* with Lloyd Bridges, which ran from 1958 to 1961. If you grew up with that show, then perhaps you have a valid point to fall back on. For my generation who may have only seen the show in reruns, *The Deep* was a solid underwater adventure and still is, in my opinion. Nick Nolte and Jacqueline Bissett are solid actors who feed well off of each other, in and out of the water. But it's surely Robert Shaw who carries this movie to the end. You may claim he's reprising the sort of charismatic role he already portrayed in *Jaws,* but I'd like to think it's a combination of Quint as well as other assorted tough guy characters he'd previously given us, including SPECTRE assassin Donald Grant in the 1963 James Bond film *From Russia With Love* and his most recent role at the time as Major David Kabakov in John Frankenheimer's outstanding terrorist thriller *Black Sunday.*

The Spy Who Loved Me

Directed by Lewis Gilbert
(July 7, 1977, U.S. Release Date)

Then

This was it! I was going to see my first James Bond movie on the big screen, uncut and unedited. I'd have to wait a couple of months until the movie made it to the private theater in its second run, but that hardly mattered to me. This was a major step for a ten-year-old boy who'd already gotten his feet wet in the world of James Bond with bits and pieces of other movies already shown on TV.

From the moment *The Spy Who Loved Me* opened, it seemed I hadn't drifted too far from my last screen experience of *The Deep* because it was an underwater adventure all over again that involved the disappearance of nuclear submarines. All of a sudden though, the movie switched to the snowy ski slopes with Bond being chased by enemy spies who were trying to kill him. Then he was flying! Well, not really flying but performing a daring escape off a cliff by parachute ... and this was all before the opening credits and song by Carly Simon, whom I was actually aware of because I liked one of her older hit songs, *"You're So Vain."*

Because of my limited experience and knowledge of complex plot lines such as nuclear missles, world domination, and the strained relationships and mistrust that still existed between the Soviet Union and much of the rest of the world (England included), the story behind the action went right over my little head. Still, there was incredible spy action and thrills on the screen before me that included chases, exploding helicopters, shootouts, and a cool-looking white car that moved underwater. As for Barbara Bach … well, she was just stunning to look at! Apparently, at age ten, I recognized the visual appeal of beautiful women in the movies (thank you, Jacqueline and thank you, Barbara!).

Let's be honest for a moment; despite even the great action and the beautiful women, what made *Spy* so ultra-cool to me was the character of Jaws. This man (if you could really call him *that*) was an incredible powerhouse of gigantic destruction. This was an enemy that seemingly could not die, and just how was the great James Bond supposed to defeat someone … some*thing* like that? He could lift huge boulders, stop moving vans, and bite through anything with his own steel teeth (those same teeth could get him electrocuted too). What really sent things over the top (in a good way) for me was when Jaws was attacked by a shark (even today, the irony of that is priceless) and *he* ended up biting the shark to death. This was, perhaps, suspension of disbelief even in a James Bond movie, at its ultimate level, but my young mind hardly cared or knew any better. This was incredible fun at the movies, the most I'd had since *Star Wars* (though not better). It seemed the summer blockbuster season of '77 was off to a fantastic start.

Leaving the theater, I recall this little conversation between myself and my father:

"Daddy, does James Bond marry the girl?"
"No."
"How come? I thought he loved her."
"James Bond was married once, but she was killed by his enemy right after the wedding. He won't ever get married again."
"How come?"
"I don't know. Did you enjoy the movie?"
"Oh, yeah! Can we see it again?"
"No."
"Awww!"

The Spy Who Loved Me made its television premiere on the *ABC Sunday Night Movie* on November 9, 1980, and this time, there was no two-night duration and no additional footage that seemed to be the pattern on TV over the last several years. This was the Bond movie as it was, as I remembered it three years earlier. Well, sort of. For this airing, I saw something I'd ever seen before. It was a black title card with a message in white that read *"Although edited for television, some parents may consider this James Bond film unsuitable for younger family members. Viewer discretion is advised."* Seriously? What was the problem? I'd seen the movie myself three years ago, and I didn't recall anything so terrible about it. Was the network concerned about murderous violence by Jaws or perhaps just the display of excessive upper cleavage skin by Barbara Bach? Regardless of their reason, I enjoyed this great Bond movie again, and this time it had some deeper meaning of familiarity to me because I'd also seen *Moonraker* on screen just a year ago and the famous character behind Roger Moore as well as Jaws were like old friends.

Now

While *The Spy Who Loved Me* remains one of my preferred Bond films in the legendary franchise, it has managed to move down a few notches since I was a kid. The action and drama under the direction of Lewis Gilbert, at times, falls short in some sequences. The first example is when Bond and Anya are trying to escape from Jaws in the white van in Egypt and he manages to temporarily stop them by grabbing the back end of it. What could've been a thrilling moment with even a touch of terror is substituted for pure silliness, even in the accompanying soundtrack when they finally escape and the van appears to fall apart as they drive it. Perhaps my sense of humor is off, but it simply doesn't work for me.

Speaking of the soundtrack, I've always believed the music of any Bond film during that period loses something significant when it's not scored by John Barry (that's just *me*). What really disappoints me though, is the climactic destruction of Stromberg's *Atlantis* and the escape of our two heroes done without the dramatic use of any soundtrack music. What should be a sequence of sheer excitement becomes bland in its delivery (do I blame Marvin Hamlisch for that bogus decision?). Still, *Spy* offers the political excitement and tension of nuclear conflict and the twisted vision of a criminal madman seeking global domination in a world he creates by his own hand, in this case, under the sea. In fact, if you take a moment to consider the other two Bond films under Gilbert's direction, *You Only Live Twice* and *Moonraker*, these reoccurring themes are present as well.

Orca: The Killer Whale
Directed by Michael Anderson
(July 22, 1977, U.S. Release Date)

Then

By the summer of 1977, *Jaws* was only two years old and the inferior copycat movies were piling up. This was the "natural horror sub-genre" or movies featuring nature's creatures running amok in the form of mutated and carnivorous beasts, insects, or other animals that were normally considered harmless, turning into cold-blooded killers. Movies like *Grizzly, Tentacles, Day of the Animals, Kingdom of the Spiders, Empire of the Ants,* and *The Island of Dr. Moreau* (actually, I liked that one) showed just how desperate Hollywood was to rip off and cash in on the success of Steven Spielberg's former blockbuster. Many consider *Orca: The Killer Whale* no different from the rest of the lot. I saw it differently though. If *Jaws* was the poison forbidden to me as an innocent eight-year-old boy, then *Orca* was the antidote for that same boy two years later because it was as close as I'd get to seeing the killer shark classic. Unlike the usual Sunday paper, my discovery of *Orca* came from an ad on the back of a Marvel comic book movie adaptation of *Star Wars*, no less. I remember showing the ad to my father, and without even having to ask myself, he asked me if I wanted to see it.

"Isn't this like *Jaws*?" I asked.

"I don't think so," he replied. "I think it's not as scary. Besides, it's on the back of a comic book. How bad could it be?"

(Yes, the man *could* make sense once in a while).

I recall the opening haunting music of Ennio Morricone catching my attention immediately. Moments later, when it appeared that a young diver would be attacked by a great white shark, I thought that my father had been wrong. The attack, however, was not to be because the diver was saved from the shark by a giant killer whale. Unlike the movie poster's implication, this fish ... sorry, *mammal* ... appeared to be a kind creature. This sequence was immediately followed by a formal lesson on the killer whale by a college professor and marine biologist who was also a very pretty woman named Rachel.

Unlike *Jaws*, I learned the cause of the mammal's attack on man was not random, but rather directly provoked by the death of his family by the hands of a shark hunter and his crew. Captain Nolan was not meant to be portrayed as an evil human being, but just a man trying to make a living by doing the wrong thing. The attack on the female and her unborn fetus was particularly sad, brutal, and bloody, perhaps worse than my parents could've conceived. When the scene was over, there was a feeling of sorrow among not only those responsible for the deaths of one of Mother Nature's creatures, but within the theater audience as well. This is where the action began. The orca's acts of revenge on those responsible for hurting him was relentless and thrilling. I was particularly impressed with how the whale could make an entire small seaside village burn in a raging inferno with just a few headbutts into some underwater gas lines. There was almost a feeling of joyous triumph when I watched the orca do what appeared to be a celebratory dive into the water as the town exploded behind him.

As the movie progressed, Nolan appeared remorseful for what he'd done to the whale and his family. But since he couldn't speak to or express to the whale just how sorry he was, he was left with no choice but to face him on the open, icy waters. This entire sequence was hardly what I would've described as a battle at sea, but rather a repeated pattern of the death of a crew person, followed by sorrow and sad music, and then followed by another death, etc., etc., etc. By the time the final showdown approached among the dangerous icebergs of the Canadian waters, Nolan was a broken man. Not only did I feel sorry for the poor guy, but I also didn't want to see him die (my wish wasn't granted). The story clearly had a message that man was meant to pay for his brutal attack against one of nature's kind creatures. Nolan died and Rachel was spared for no other apparent reason than the whale didn't recognize her face as one of the people who tried to harm him. Rachel was (conveniently) rescued by helicopter while standing on an iceberg in the middle of nowhere as the orca headed for home underneath the ice, his future uncertain.

I saw *Orca* a second time a couple of weeks later at the local movie theater in Westhampton Beach on one of those nights when my parents wanted to get their kids out of the house for a couple of hours so they could be alone. Like *The Deep*, it was another one of those times when watching a movie that took place on the water in a seaside town in the Hamptons had significant meaning. The time I waited between its theatrical release and the time it premiered on TV was one of the shortest durations I'm aware of, only a year and a half. It premiered on CBS on November 25, 1978. I remember it was a Saturday night because my family was planning to go out to dinner, as we often did on the weekends. I asked to stay behind so I could watch *Orca*. They obliged me (this was another time when leaving an eleven-year-old boy by himself for a few hours was considered neither neglectful nor dangerous). While it was edited for some bloody content including the death of the female orca and the biting of Bo Derek's leg, the movie, more or less, stayed faithful to its screen version, which was still pretty exciting.

Now

Orca: The Killer Whale, while poorly received back in '77, has gained a cult following ever since. While it can never comare to the original thrills of *Jaws* (or even *Jaws 2*, for that matter), it does possess its own charm and quality in not only its performances by gifted actors like Richard Harris and Charlotte Rampling, but also its message of the consequences in committing brutal attacks on nature's creatures. As a reverend in the film so eloquently puts it,

"You can commit a sin against a blade of grass." I suppose we're meant to take such an important message to heart. It's not a great film by any means, but I'd hardly consider it a dud either. There are some very beautiful moments of cinematography of the Newfoundland country and its waters, but more than that, there's something very beautiful in watching the actions, both good and bad, of the killer whale, a beautiful creature in itself. The whale is meant to be the hero of this film, even if it appears to act unfairly in its quest for vengeance against man.

As an adult, I certainly enjoy watching a woman like Bo Derek before she made herself famous in Blade Edward's *"10."* Even now, when I know it's going to happen, I still wish the poor woman won't lose her precious leg to the great killer whale. It's a film I still enjoy watching during the heart of the summer when I not only recall that childhood moment when I was allowed to get just a little closer to my desire of seeing *Jaws*, but also that feeling you get when you're living in a small town by the sea, even if it's haunted and terrorized by a man-eating fish ... sorry, *mammal.*

Close Encounters of the Third Kind

Directed by Steven Spielberg
(November 16, 1977, U.S. Release Date)

Then

By the end of 1977, I was still unaware of who Steven Spielberg really was. While I knew of *Jaws* over the past two years, a child of eight rarely equates a popular movie with its director. Even when I became aware of this new science fiction movie called *Close Encounters of the Third Kind*, it was because I repeatedly saw copies of the paperback novelization in stores. I was unaware the story was about unidentified flying objects and man's contact with them because the movie poster's visual image of the bright, white light at the end of the long, lonely road hardly relayed that specific message. When I eventually learned what this new movie was about, my immediate reaction was that it couldn't have come out at a better time. *Star Wars* had paved the way for a new movie like *Close Encounters* and a new generation of sci-fi movies to come in the years ahead.

I don't recall needing to ask to see this movie because my mother announced one day that we were taking a bus into Manhattan to the Zeigfeld Theatre on West 54th Street. I remember when we arrived, there was an extensive line waiting to get into this legendary New York City movie theater. Once inside, however, I was treated for the first time to one of the greatest large-scale, single-screen movie palaces in the United States. This entire place was New York's answer to the famous Gruman's Chinese Theater in Hollywood, California, and often used for world premieres and big event press screenings, including *Close Encounters* (unfortunately, the Zeigfeld Theatre permanently closed its doors in January 2016. New York City now has nothing but common multiplexes and a just few art house independent theaters located in Greenwich Village).

The movie began and the tremble of the opening theme kept rising in volume against a black screen, until the music climaxed with a loud shudder and the screen went white to reveal a sandstorm in the Sonora Desert, Mexico. I didn't quite follow the opening scene with the discovery of the old World War II airplanes and also found it frustrating to have to read subtitles in French (my mother didn't have to read them because she speaks and understands the language fluently). But when one of the American men on the team (who understood Spanish) translated the old man's words into *"He says the sun came out last night. He says it sang to him,"* I knew the movie would take off now.

There were incredible sequences of light, color, special effects, and speed, and that was just with the first UFO sighting by Indiana electrician Roy Neary. But I could see there was something spiritual and mystifying taking place here as well. Roy was not only witness to this close encounter (with his half-burned face to go with it), but had clearly been chosen to try and understand something that was going to happen later, and it all seemed to be connected to a mysterious mountain which he couldn't seem to get right in his head. It was also interesting to see he wasn't the only one going through all of this. Others, including Jillian Guiler and her brave little boy Barry, were also touched by an implanted vision. Not only did I grip the arms of my seat when the unseen alien ship overtook Jillian's house and took Barry away, but I also found it difficult to even breathe. When Barry was taken out of his mother's grip and she maniacally chased after the clouds that took him, I remember mother saying, "She's never going to see him again." Was she right?

As the movie continued and Roy was seemingly going mad, it was hard not to laugh at his antics, particularly his playing with his mashed potatoes at the dinner table in front of his family and the insane transformation of the living room into a massive sculpture ground for what he now understood to be the correct shape of the mountain he was destined to envision and eventually find. To his surprise (and ours too), the mountain he sculpted *was* real and it was in the state of Wyoming. I could appreciate the spirituality of the kid inside this grown man because all he wanted were answers to questions of who and what was out there and why they were here. Roy and Jillian's travels, their capture, their escape, and their desperate climb up the Devil's Tower mountain were clearly leading to something spectacular, though I still had no concept of what it would be.

Things settled down for a moment before witnessing an awesome event of mankind. It started a simple line, *"Okay, watch the skies,"* and it all practically exploded after that. The entire sequence of spaceships, bright lights, fabulous color, and John William's seven-note musical theme that became as infamous as the movie itself was a world of undefined magic to the wondrous eyes of a ten-year-old boy. However, despite my experience with *Star Wars* before this, somehow I knew it was wrong to compare the two movies. The final sequence of the alien visitors arriving at Devil's Tower was, in its own right, a classic piece of special effects moviemaking, yet I knew I shouldn't try to compare it with, say, the final battle of the Death Star. Such an attempt was pointless (apples and oranges, my friends).

After the intense excitement of the flying objects, things were quiet again. What would happen now? The background noise began to rumble as something slowly rose behind the great mountain. Then we saw the entire ship. My God, it was beyond huge! It was massive and it was awesome! I couldn't believe that human beings in the real world could actually make a movie like this. Then the door of the mother ship opened. This was it—we were going to see the aliens. They slowly walked out, and they were … human. Wait a minute, they were *human*? For a moment, I sat there feeling grossly let down. This couldn't really be the end result of all I'd just sat through, could it? Thankfully, it wasn't. The people were just being returning to Earth after being taken in the past, Barry included (looks like my mom was wrong).

Moments later, we finally met our friends from another world and they looked like bald-headed children. They couldn't speak, but we on Earth seemed to understand them and they understood us. They were our friends, and we were happy to learn that we were not alone in the universe. When Roy Neary boarded the great mother ship, my first thought was actually *not* the fact that he was leaving Earth and his family forever, but instead, a sense of wonderment of what would become of such an ordinary man who was about to begin a spectacular journey into the unknown. That curiosity was never satisfied because the ship left our planet and the movie ended.

Returning home on the bus, I could swear I still had a big smile on my face. I'd just witnessed true movie magic in a form that not even the great Walt Disney had ever shown me before. I'd been transformed to a world where moviemaking was not only exciting but spiritually enlightening as well (even if I didn't know what *"spiritually enlightening"* meant yet). I even had an awesome movie program my parents bought me after the show to remember it all by. Still, once wouldn't be enough. I went to see this incredible movie again a couple of months later at a second-run movie theater on Long Island with three of my cousins. They hadn't seen it yet, so I had a joyous sense of having the advantage over them. They loved it, of course, except for one of them who was only two years old at the time. I think it freaked her out a bit (she got over it).

We'll jump ahead now about two and a half years later to August 1980 and another full-page movie ad in the *New York Times* informing me of something I was unaware of until that moment. *Close Encounters of the Third Kind* was being rereleased in theaters, but something had changed. The new movie poster depicted Roy Neary being led into the great mother ship by the alien visitors. I remembered this scene well, but there was a lengthy caption written on the poster ...

When over 100 million people saw "Close Encounters of the Third Kind" for the first time, they were dazzled. And they wanted more. NOW THERE IS MORE. Director Steven Spielberg has filmed additional scenes, designed to expand the total experience of the original film. NOW, FOR THE FIRST TIME, FILMGOERS WILL BE ABLE TO SHARE THE ULTIMATE EXPERIENCE OF BEING INSIDE.

Holy crap! Was this for real? There was *more*? Apparently, this version was big enough to call a *special edition*. The mere sound of those two words were practically begging me to get in line at the nearest theater showing it. I suspected though that if I was going to try and see this new version of a movie I already loved, I'd have to act fast because past experiences showed that these theatrical rereleases didn't hang around for too long. Two, three weeks at best, and then it was off to pay-cable movie channels and free television. I asked to see it and, of course, my parents denied my request. It looked like I was screwed and wouldn't see what this *special edition* was all about. But fate unexpectedly intervened. I ended up spending a few days and nights at the house of one of my cousins. After going out to dinner one night with my aunt and uncle, we discovered the movie was playing at the theater within the same shopping complex as the restaurant (the *same* Long Island theater I'd seen the original version the second time; different cousins though).

Here I was—*Close Encounters* for the third time. It started out the same and stayed that way for a while. The first surprise I discovered was that unlike the poster's promise, there was more to experience other than being inside the mother ship. What I didn't expect was the price of *more* in the *special edition* meant a little *less* of the original footage I'd come to be very familiar with. This was *not* cool, in my opinion. The first thing to go was the entire sequence of Roy Neary among his colleagues at the electrical plant where he worked. In its place was a new scene of the discovery of a battleship resting in the desert sand, designed to continue the opening scene of a similar desert discovery. Gone also was the Army briefing sequence immediately following Barry's disappearance in which the common folk were encouraged to disregard the existence of UFOs.

I didn't realize it at the time, but some of the scenes were also rearranged a bit. But what really burned my biscuits was the complete deletion of Roy Neary's madness as he tore his property apart while his frightened family looked on. The scene simply picked itself up with his family exiting the house and getting into the car to make their getaway. We could see Roy was in the process of doing something outdoors, but unless you'd already seen the original version and knew what the deal was, you had no clue as to why his family was leaving him. The continuity of this and the previous new scene of Roy's mental decay in the master bathroom simply were not enough to connect the entire meaning of what was happening to the Neary family. I was only thirteen at the time, but I could clearly see that a strange decision in movie editing had taken place here.

Then it finally came, the new sequence of being *inside* the mother ship that was designed to pull us back into the theater once again. My reaction to this could best be summed up in just one word: *fine*. It was fine. It didn't blow me away. There were more lights, more color, more music, and more images of Roy Neary in his red jumpsuit and even a bizarre, downward rain effect at the end of the sequence before it resumed the scene outside the mother ship. It was fun to watch but didn't necessarily *"expand the total experience of the original film"* for me. None of the new scenes really did. When it was over, I was, of course, happy to have seen it again on screen, but I felt cheated nonetheless. If this was what *special edition* meant, I wasn't too sure I wanted any part of it.

On November 15, 1981, the *ABC Sunday Night Movie* made it up to me. This was the first time I watched the movie again since that night in August 1980. The *special edition* had previously been released on VHS tape and laser disc, but that did me no good at all (we *still* didn't have a movie player of any sort in our household). The *TV Guide* ad for the movie's TV premiere depicted the original movie poster's artwork of the bright light at the end of the long road, so I (naturally) presumed ABC would air the original version from '77. To my surprise (and others', I'm sure), what they did was fuse *all* the elements and all the scenes of *both* film versions into one longer, continuous feature. Everything that was taken away was back in tact, and that made contending with the newer perhaps less thrilling footage easier to deal with. It was a great version, and when it aired again in December 1984, the family *finally* had its first VCR and I recorded the movie, actually taking the time to edit out the commercials. It was beautiful!

I held onto that homemade recording for more than ten years (until I wore it down and wore it out) and finally purchased an official VHS copy of the *special edition* as released by Columbia Pictures. I was always happy to have *Close Encounters* in my life, in one version or another.

Now

Steven Spielberg once said in an interview with Barbara Walters on ABC's prime time news program *20/20,* just before the 1994 Academy Awards, that he'd like to be best remembered for *E.T. The Extra Terrestrial* and *Schindler's List* and it's more than possible that will be the case. For me, however, despite all the outstanding films that has defined his lengthy career, I will forever consider *Close Encounters of the Third Kind* to be my favorite Spielberg film; a film that so effectively defined my childhood.

Over the years, the film has been defined by three versions: the original theatrical version, the *special edition,* and the 1997 *director's edition*, which does some of the same fusing that ABC did on TV, though the sequence inside the mother ship is still omitted from the final cut. Apparently, Spielberg never wanted that particular sequence in the first place, but made a marketing deal with Columbia Pictures in order to get the funding he needed to shoot the other new scenes that made his 1980 cut. At this point, when it comes to ultimately determining and interpreting *Close Encounters* as a whole, I've given up trying to pointlessly compare "Coke" with "Pepsi." All three versions have their merits and their faults. While my childhood memories still prefers the original theatrical version, I tend to switch around my viewings when choosing between the three that are available on a single high definition Blu-Ray disc. Although, over time, I've come to develop a strange notion regarding the *special edition* of the film.

It involves Roy Neary finally stepping inside the great mother ship. What I'll tell you now is a totally wild and unsubstantiated theory regarding what happens to Roy inside the ship, and I have no doubt that just about every other fan of this great film would likely tell me that I'm completely crazy and should go take a flying leap off of Devil's Tower.

Take a moment to consider the final shot inside the mother ship when we're meant to be looking up via Roy's point of vision. Suddenly, like a great falling rain, something comes showering downward, presumably toward and perhaps even on top of Roy. Cut immediately back to the scene outside the ship when all the remaining men are gathered together to watch Carlo Rambaldi's extra-terrestrial creation standing before them as they offer each other communication. If we were to put together exactly just how this moment follows the last one inside the ship, is it not at all possible that the extra-terrestrial we now look upon *is* Roy Neary? Is it not possible that the so-called *"rain shower"* we just witnessed inside the ship actually transformed Roy Neary into perhaps what he was always longing to be throughout the film ... something other than what he really was? He has sacrificed his profession, his family, and his life on Earth to reach his destiny and fulfill his dreams, so why is it completely inconceivable that his new alien friends simply understood this desire and accommodated him to make him one of *them*? Like I said, it's a highly far-fetched theory, and I realize, of course, that I'm reaching for the impossible with this one. Still, it's a thought-provoking premise that I like to ponder over whenever I watch the *special edition* of *Close Encounters*.

I'll conclude my discussion of this film by sharing something very personal with you that clearly expresses the impact and meaning Spielberg's films, particularly *Close Encounters*, has had on my life. In May 2007, when I turned the milestone age of forty, I wrote a letter to Mr. Spielberg which I (of course) never expected to be received by or responded to by the man himself. The intention was for me to express my feelings and experiences in writing at such a pivotal age. I now take great pleasure in sharing this letter with you, as it was originally written more than ten years ago ...

Dear Mr. Spielberg,

On May 7th of this year, I will finally reach my 40th birthday. As you yourself may appreciate, when a man reaches a milestone age such as this, he takes a moment to take some stock of where his life has been, where it is going and those who may have influenced it. While I cannot claim that a single person has influenced my life, I am writing this letter to you in the hopes that you will take a moment to read how the films of your career have made a significant difference in my life. If you'll bear with me for a moment longer, I'd like to share a quick story with you.

On September 11, 2001, like many other New Yorkers, I stood on a sidewalk in Greenwich Village watching the horrors of that day unfold. What followed after were days of images and intense media coverage on every TV channel. Finally, when I felt I could not take it any longer, I searched for something of entertainment value; something to help me forget. I came across Close Encounters of the Third Kind *on one of the cable channels, already in progress. Before I knew it, my memory was back in year 1977 when I was 10 years old, seeing this film for the first time at the Ziegfeld Theatre in New York City, and first discovering what true magic was like on the movie screen.*

And so, Mr. Spielberg, I'd like to take this opportunity to say to you, from the sincerest part of my heart, thank you for being, perhaps, the only evidence of any real magic in this troubling and confusing world. Thank you for a body of work and cinematic achievements that have made a significant difference in my life and the way I try to keep an optimistic view of our world and the world that I will try to one day explain to my son. Perhaps it will begin when I sit down to watch E.T. *with him for the very first time.*

It is my sincere hope that this letter will not only one day find you personally, but that perhaps I will one day have the privilege of meeting you in person, shaking your hand, and thanking you face to face.

Keep the magic alive. It makes a difference.

It's naïve for a grown man like myself to think that Mr. Spielberg may have or may still some day still read this letter (or maybe even this book), but one can dream.

The Goodbye Girl

Directed by Herbert Ross
(November 30, 1977, U.S. Release Date)

Then

The average child is probably not too enthusiastic about romantic comedies. I wasn't either. But I loved to laugh and I loved to go to the movies no matter what was playing, so I was more than willing to tag along when my parents wanted to see *The Goodbye Girl*. Immediately, there was some familiarity to it. The movie took place in Manhattan, and I'd already come to know the big city on screen through *King Kong* and *Annie Hall*. The movie also had little Quinn Cummings from ABC's *Family*. Most of all, it starred Richard Dreyfuss, and I practically felt like an expert on the man, having seen him in *Close Encounters* twice already. The character of Paula McFadden seemed like quite an oddball to me, practically to the point of making my own mother seem totally normal. She had spirit and spunk (as did her daughter Lucy) which also included her feelings of deep sorrow and regret when something bad happened to her. She and Lucy were set to move to California with her actor boyfriend when they suddenly discovered that he'd taken off without them.

Having already survived my parent's divorce and reconciliation, I had a somewhat limited knowledge of grown-ups and their heartaches. Really, I was just waiting for Richard Dreyfuss to show up. When his character of Elliot Garfield finally *did* show up at their apartment in the middle of the night claiming it rightfully belonged to him, it seemed pretty obvious that despite their despising each other in the beginning, he and Paula would eventually fall in love (the movie poster indicated as much). Still, recalling *Annie Hall*, I realized that the true humor behind any romantic comedy is sitting back and watching what happens to two people as they travel the road toward falling in love.

I discovered just how funny Dreyfuss was in a role that had nothing to do with UFOs. Every time he spoke to and bickered with Paula, he was almost never serious, and even when he was, there was still a touch of that wise guy in his voice and his manner. It was the sequence of the failed stage production of William Shakespeare's *Richard III* that really got me laughing. This was, I think, the first time I'd ever seen a movie where a man spoke in a highly effeminate voice. My father was cracking up every time Dreyfuss spoke like that, and I believe someone else's laughter is highly contagious, especially when you're a kid. It was also the first time I'd ever seen an actor play a state of drunkenness too. When Elliot was sitting on the ledge of the apartment reading the horrific reviews the show had gotten after its first performance, I laughed at that too, because I knew what it meant to be drunk (rest assured my parents did *not* get drunk. Some things you just pick up on in life by yourself).

When Elliot's big break came along in the form of a movie role, he needed to leave New York immediately. It looked like Paula and Lucy would be left in the dumps all over again. Their love was saved in the end by none other than a guitar left behind by Elliot for Paula to have restrung. I didn't entirely comprehend the meaning behind the guitar, but it appeared to mean that Elliot would return to the woman he loved and all would be happily ever after. That must've been a nice thing for me because I remember feeling disappointed when the movie was over following that final scene in the rain. I suppose Elliot and Paula had gotten to me, and I wanted to see what would happen to them next. If nothing else, *The Goodbye Girl* was a good lesson to a kid in the structure of the American romantic comedy. It taught me that love is likely destined to hit major snags along the way and it's a moment of curious wonder to see if the two people involved are going to survive them or not.

Now

Little has changed in my positive perception and appreciation for *The Goodbye Girl*. I still don't get too enthusiastic about the average American romantic comedy because I feel the formula never changes from film to film. I mean, come on ... boy and girl meet, boy has a best friend who's obnoxious, girl has a best friend who's either goofy or gay (or both), boy and girl fall in love, boy and girl hit a snag, boy and girl almost always get past it and end up together (blah, blah, blah, blah). Honestly, just give me an old-fashioned, tear-jerking love story instead. They feel a lot more real to me.

There *is* the small share of romantic comedies though that have caught my attention and my appreciation during the course of my adult years, but it's still *The Goodbye Girl* that wins my heart and my ability to laugh at love, relationships, and the overall silly inconsistencies of the people involved. Richard Dreyfuss remains priceless in the role I consider one of the best of his career. He proves just how versatile he is in a role that was miles away from what he'd previously done in two of Steven Spielberg's back-to-back blockbusters. The scenes of *Richard III* are some of the funniest I've seen since Mel Brooks's stage production of *Springtime for Hitler* in his 1968 film *The Producers*. He surely deserved the Oscar he received for Best Actor of 1977.

Saturday Night Fever

Directed by John Badham
(December 16, 1977, U.S. Release Date)

Then

King Kong, Star Wars, and *Close Encounters of the Third Kind* may have had a strong hand in shaping the excitement of my inner imagination as a kid, but it was, by far, the star of John Travolta, the musical sensation of the Bee Gees, and the movie called *Saturday Night Fever* that truly changed my moviegoing experiences. You see, this was the first R-rated movie I ever saw on screen at the tender age of ten.

By December 1977, it was impossible not to be aware and feel the effects of this film. Even if I didn't see the movie for a while, the television hype of the new American dance movie, the stardom it brought Travolta following his run on *Welcome Back, Kotter,* as well as the smash songs of the double-album soundtrack were impossible to ignore. New material by the Bee Gees was all over the radio, in particular *"Stayin' Alive," "How Deep is Your Love,"* and *"Night Fever."* At that age, my musical tastes were focused on the rock and roll of artists like Elton John. But when I heard the Bee Gees for the first time, I knew that not only was I going to be a new fan of the *Brothers Gibb,* but disco music as well. By the time *Fever* solidified its place in the popular culture of the time, kids my age seemed to be into only two musical groups: the Bee Gees and Kiss. That was it. No other group seemed to exist at that time (though I also discovered the music of the Steve Miller Band. Leave it to me to be the minority of the group).

Getting back to my first R-rated movie experience, it was a significant moment for me because it represented a symbolic rite of passage from being a boy and becoming a *man* ... at least in the world of moviegoing anyway. From the moment the movie faded in on the Manhattan skyline, I was already in familiar geographical territory. My grandmother lived in Brooklyn too, so I felt a certain kinship with that borough. After a brief montage of Bay Ridge, the music started. "*Stayin' Alive*" pulsated from the theater speakers as Travolta strutted his stuff down the busy sidewalk. My first thought was, *This is cool!* When the profanity began with "*Fuck the future!*", I knew I'd graduated to manhood that included profanity, racism, gang fights, attempted rape, and frontal nudity. I was neither shocked nor embarrassed by any of this. On the contrary, I couldn't help but feel that this was how adults behaved in the real world. They argued with each other, they cursed at each other, and they sometimes danced naked on a bar stage. Had this movie not been essentially a story of dance filled with great music, my mother would've made us all get up and leave the theater in the middle so as not to subject her two little boys to any further cinematic filth.

All adult content aside, the character of Tony Manero enthralled me. To begin with, he had on his bedroom walls the same poster of *Rocky* and the legendary 1976 swimsuit poster of Farrah Fawcett-Majors as I did. He may have just been a paint store worker during the day, but on Saturday nights, he was the star of the neighborhood because he could tear up the dance floor with his talented moves, and the girls loved him. Well, most of them did. The one girl he wanted to connect with more than anyone both on and off the dance floor, Stephanie, was the one who challenged him the most. She was only a year older than him, but she acted far superior nonetheless. Still, when they danced together, they created magic. At the pivotal moment when Tony did his big solo dance to "*You Should Be Dancing,*" I simply didn't want it to end. When he stepped off the dance floor, I remember asking my mother, "Will he dance again? I want him to dance again." When Tony finally did dance again, with

Stephanie to *"More Than a Woman,"* I was disappointed. I expected that when the big dance contest finally arrived, Tony and Stephanie would tear up the floor with the same energy and speed the Puerto Rican couple showed following them. Instead, it was a slow, rather romantic dance with kissing that left me feeling cheated when it was over. *Is that it?* I thought.

Imagine my surprise when Tony and Stephanie actually *won* the contest with that dud. I wasn't the only one who couldn't believe this though. Tony himself couldn't believe it either, and he was mad as hell! While I couldn't completely understand the workings of an adult mind struggling with maturity, it appeared that Tony was starting to grow up a little. He seemed to understand that he couldn't live with a prize he hadn't genuinely earned, and he lashed out at those around him because of it, his longtime friends and Stephanie included (he even tried to attack her in the back seat of a car).

After an all-night New York City subway ride to *"How Deep Is Your Love"* in which he actually was *not* mugged or killed, Tony made good, and he and Stephanie would be friends from now on. They hugged, the right side of the picture faded out to the end credits, and the Bee Gees were singing again. The movie was over, and I wanted more. To ask my parents to see this racy, violent movie filled with profanity and nudity again was pointless though. I was smart enough to know I'd just gotten away with something very significant, and it was best not to push my luck. I felt blessed to have seen *Saturday Night Fever* during the era when disco music dominated our musical pop culture. I certainly couldn't go to real discos, but I felt fortunate to have taken part in the movie culture version of it, even if only for one time. Someday the movie would be on TV, and I would (hopefully) get to watch it again.

Instead, something else happened. In the spring of 1979, *Saturday Night Fever* was rereleased in theaters and it had changed in a big way. It was now rated PG. Hollywood had not only heard my cries of longing to repeat the movie's experience, but also the cries of many other American kids and teenagers who weren't old enough to see the R-rated version by themselves during its first theatrical run. To read the rerelease movie poster's lengthy tagline, it was clear that

Paramount Pictures was taking no prisoners in tempting everyone back into the theater, and *everyone* appeared to be the keyword in their new poster marketing campaign ...

> *IT IS NOW RATED PG. Because we want everyone to see John Travolta's performance ... because we want everyone to hear the #1 group in the country, the Bee Gees ... because we want everyone to catch "Saturday Night Fever."*

Once again, Hollywood demanded that I get my little butt back in gear for a second run. I went to my parents with this one, and I didn't have to fight very hard for it. They agreed to let me and Kevin see the movie again, but there was a small catch. They would drive us into Manhattan, drop us off at the movie theater, and let us sit through the movie *twice* while they went off to do a lot of shopping. If this was what they called a *catch*, then I'd gladly take it. I should point out (again) that not only was sitting through a movie more than once without paying for another ticket not a big issue back in the '70s, but parents also felt confident enough that their children would be safe left all alone and without adult protection in a strange New York City movie theater. Today, I think both of them would've been arrested on charges of child neglect and endangering the well-being of minors for pulling that one.

As a kid, I had no concept of Hollywood's standards of editing, censoring, voice dubbing, redubbing, and alternate takes. When Tony's previous line of *"Fuck the future!"* became *"To hell with the future!"*, I simply presumed that the scene was re-shot because it sounded natural enough. As the movie progressed, it became obvious that there was some sloppiness involved in de-emphasizing this story down to an acceptable PG level. At other times, specific scenes of a racist or sexually-oriented nature were just removed completely. All in all, *Fever* was stripped down to what it was always likely intended to be in the first place: a movie about the spirit of music and dancing. That spirit remained in the new and cleaner version, and it was just as fun and entertaining as it had been nearly two years ago, despite having lost its obvious power and edge. Perhaps I didn't require so much power and edge. Perhaps all I really needed was some music, some dancing, and a good time at the movies (two times in a row). To date, the only home video release the PG version has seen is on VHS tape, as it was released in the '80s. It hasn't (yet) been released on American Region DVD or Blu-Ray disc. Despite the faults this version contains, I still maintain a VHS copy of the movie and sometimes watch it for no other reason than it brings back the memory of experiencing the movie in the theater for a second (and third) time, as well as to quietly criticize and discriminate between the two film versions.

Nearly three years following its original release, disco music was dead, as the influences of punk and new wave were taking shape in music pop culture with bands like Blondie, The Clash, and The Police. Strangely enough though, 1980 was a somewhat popular year for *Saturday Night Fever* in three stages. At the start of the year, Paramount Pictures paired up the PG-rated version of the movie as a double feature along with its other Travolta blockbuster, *Grease* (I happen to own this double feature movie poster, by the way, and it still looks cool). By February, the movie made its debut on HBO. The channel aired *both* versions of the movie; the PG version during the day and the R version at night (back then, HBO had a programming rule of only showing R-rated movies during the evening after 8 p.m.). Finally, on November 16, 1980, the movie rounded out the year when it premiered on the *ABC Sunday Night Movie*. It was, basically, the same version as the PG release, with little-to-no changes due to television editing restraints. Though the TV version *did* contain several minutes of outtakes that included Tony dancing with Doreen to the song *"Disco Duck,"* Tony unsuccessfully gaining entrance into Stephanie's apartment at his first attempt and his father getting his job back after a long layoff.

When disco "officially" died by the start of the '80s, it was all but declared unpopular and uncool to appreciate the movie and the hit soundtrack. That being the case, even as I started to develop my musical tastes in classic rock, I still indulged in the fun and spirit of *Fever* (both movie and music) rather underground, so to say, when no one else was around. By the time I started college in 1985, I'd listen to the soundtrack late at night when I had the dorm room to myself and no one was around to hear it. You see, these were the years of my young adulthood when I didn't want to be ridiculed for liking the "wrong" music. While everyone else around me was listening to Bon Jovi and Whitesnake, I didn't want to be caught listening to the Bee Gees. Such is strange life, I suppose.

Now

Speaking strictly of the original R-rated version of *Saturday Night Fever*, the film and its childhood impact on my mind, my senses and my memories have never changed. As an adult though, I view it very differently than when I was a kid. Its power and impact, resonating with the public during a time when the nation's culture was weary and exhausted from the effects of the Vietnam War as well as the Watergate scandal under Richard Nixon, cannot be ignored. The people needed a relief after a decade of suffering, and they found it on the dance floors of America's discos every Saturday night. More than anything else, however, I view *Fever* as a film of very deep and valid social implication, and I will attempt to explain exactly why I have come to that rather sophisticated conclusion. Bear in mind, these are the detailed opinions of an analytical movie lover and not a professional psychologist or any other related profession.

First, let's examine the neighborhood of Bay Ridge in Brooklyn that Tony Manero resides in. It is, by all physical accounts, a mixed melting pot of residents that include Italian Americans, African Americans, and Puerto Ricans. The existence of these mixed races isn't always a pleasant environment of peace and social harmony, to say the least. From the moment we first arrive and are introduced to the 2001 Odyssey Disco where Tony and his friends frequent every Saturday night, they're already entertaining themselves by freely using racist and disparaging terms against their Puerto Rican and African American neighbors.

Once inside the disco, amid the pulsating effects of the colorful lights and the loud music, we can see the same mixed melting pot of people who are on the dance floor enjoying their Saturday night of freedom and liberation. Compared to the world of the disco, the outside world practically ceases to exist for many of these dancers. The disco floor is a place for letting go of not only one's daily existence of routine and structure, but to also, perhaps, redefine one's identity, and this is especially true for Tony. By day, he's a mere paint store clerk whose existence in life is no greater than to simply blend in with the rest of the Brooklyn working class while providing extra money to support his family while his father is temporarily out of work. On the dance floor, however, Tony is the superstar of the neighborhood with not only his extraordinary dancing abilities, but also his movie-star-like charms and personality, even resembling Al Pacino to one of the women there. This is the power of the transformation of Saturday night from the mundane to the glamorous for Tony and for all who come seeking the magic of the disco.

Like many social scenes of interaction though, there still exists the so-called cliques of those who'll only interact with each other more regularly and more intensely than others in the same setting. This situation is broken, however, during a pivotal moment in the film's disco sequence when the Bee Gees are singing "*Night Fever*" and slowly, the floor fills with people who have all chosen to do a dance together known as *The Electric Slide*. If you look carefully now at this moment on film, you can easily see that the bonds of racial separation have (at least temporarily) been broken for the artistic and joyous purpose of the dance. Only a short time ago, Tony and his crew were racially slandering other patrons of the disco, and now there appear to be no racial separations because all the people of the disco have come together as one with all their social differences put aside for at least the duration of one song. Even the dance itself is a very finely choreographed set of steps in which all participants must work together as a collective in order for the dance to work (I've never tried to do it myself). On film, it's a beautifully effective scene filled with bright color, music, and the physical appearance of social harmony and understanding. This may easily be attributed to the practical sense of the dance itself requiring the need for all of the people coming together to make it work, but its social significance, in my opinion, seems very clear and very effective.

It's interesting to note also that such strains in human relations don't just occur within the mixed neighborhood races of Bay Ridge, but also within the primary relationships of the film, specifically between Tony and his two female interests, Stephanie Mongano and Annette. While Tony does agree to enter the big dance contest with Annette, it's for no other reason than the fact they'd previously won another dance contest before. It's clear from the beginning that he doesn't respect her as a person and doesn't display any tact by making it clear to her that he wants little to do with her. She claims to love him, but for Tony, she's nothing more or better than a moment of cheap sex in the back seat of a car when he ultimately feels threatened that she'll end up sleeping with one of his friends instead if he doesn't give himself to her first.

Despite both of them gladly using each other sexually when they please, he still disrespects and looks down on her because she's a free-spirited woman who *wants* to have sex uninhibitedly during a decade when sexual politics were practiced so freely and so openly. From the immature perspective of Tony's mind, Annette is someone who must decide whether she's a nice girl or a whore (I'm not using the actual word that he says in the film), with no apparent room for the in-between. By the time he's callously dumped Annette as his dance partner and taken on Stephanie instead, his view of a relationship with a woman has improved only slightly because unlike the common women of the neighborhood, Stephanie has a little more to offer. This is what we're supposed to believe anyway.

Over the years, I've found Stephanie's character more interesting and compelling than Tony's. In her own fashion, she looks down on Tony because he's not educated, still lives with his family, routinely blows all of his earnings every Saturday night at the disco, and is, as she bluntly puts it, *"a jerkoff guy that ain't got his shit together!"* Stephanie acts more mature and places herself on a higher social level than Tony based on nothing more than the most superficial elements of her life that include her job in Manhattan, drinking tea with lemon instead of coffee to blend in with the female executives at her office, shopping at Bonwit Teller, and occasionally being introduced to celebrity clients as part of her job. During a scene at a coffee shop, she appears dumbfounded at the fact that Tony doesn't know who Laurence Olivier is and makes no secret of her superiority over the fact that she does. Still, even when it comes to truly and properly identifying the legendary English actor, she can't seem to come up with a better account of the man's current status other than the fact that he's the one on television who *"does all those Polaroid commercials."*

The fact is that despite Stephanie's ongoing efforts to place herself on a high pedestal above Tony and every other person her age in the neighborhood, she is, like it or not, just like the rest of them with an almost desperate need to hide and compensate for it. She has the right idea of *who* she wants to be but isn't yet as accomplished as she realistically *wants* to be. When finally pushed against the wall during an argument with Tony over an older man she was once involved with, she breaks down and confesses her own human social weakness in not knowing how to effectively do anything at work and requiring the guidance of her older friend in order to make up for it.

Social acceptance and peace in this film appear to only have any validity at the 2001 Odyssey Disco on Saturday nights. Once the work week has arrived again, many of the film's characters revert to their old attitudes of racism and intolerance. At times, these attitudes are displayed with extreme violence. This first occurs when Tony's friend Gus is brutally attacked by a gang of Puerto Rican youths when walking home carrying his groceries for no better reason than being one of the neighborhood Italian kids in the wrong place at the wrong time, and ends up in the hospital. As an act of retaliation later in the film, Tony and his friends strike back by invading the hideout of the Puerto Rican gang they believe to be responsible for Gus's attack and inflict their own personal revenge on them, *"Italian style"* as Tony's friend Joey puts it. Even as this streak of racism and violence appears to be an unstoppable plague in the neighborhood of Bay Ridge, Tony, who is at heart a good and moral kid, can't deny by the film's end that his own beliefs and perspective of life must inevitably change for the better if he's ever going to grow up.

I would not have been the child I was without the impact of *Saturday Night Fever*. I also wouldn't be the adult I am today in terms of how I watch and analyze movies without this film. In a world of cinema and its history, there are some films that are easily forgettable as just another Friday night at the local multiplex. Others are destined to become one of the classic great films, though that category I keep reserved for titles like *Gone with the Wind, Casablanca, Lawrence of Arabia,* and *The Godfather*, to name only a few. *Fever*, while perhaps not a film destined to join the ranks of the titles just mentioned, holds its own place in the history of cinema in how it radically changed our pop culture status at a time when we needed such a change. For that, I'm truly grateful, and so are a lot of other people of that era.

*****

This is the last film of 1977 I shall discuss in any great detail.

Like the two previous years, my television introduction to James Bond movies continued with *The Man with the Golden Gun* premiering on the *ABC Sunday Night Movie* on January 16, 1977. This Bond movie had the unique distinction of airing on TV before the next film, *The Spy Who Loved Me*, was due to hit theaters. Even as a nine-year-old kid, I must confess, I found the notion of the flying car a bit silly, despite having already seen some funny Bond gadgets during the other TV airings I'd seen. The most significant memory I think I have with seeing (most of) this movie for the first time on TV was the actor Hervé Villechaize. At the time of the movie's airing, he meant nothing to me. Nearly a year later, when *Fantasy Island* premiered on ABC and he gained popularity by shouting, *"The plane! The plane!"*, I recall pointing to the little man and exclaiming that he had been in "that James Bond movie on TV last year!" Ah, the things and people a child will remember.

In the fall of '77, *The Poseidon Adventure* had an encore presentation on the *ABC Sunday Night Movie*. This was the first time I saw this great disaster movie after having already seen Irwin Allen's *The Towering Inferno* nearly two years prior on HBO. The underwater thrills and peril of this tale had a particular impact with me, having already enjoyed a small series of underwater adventures on film with *Airport '77, The Deep,* and a related action sequence in *The Spy Who Loved Me.* I also reacted to Pamela Sue Martin because I knew her well on TV as Nancy Drew on ABC's weekly series *The Hardy Boys/ Nancy Drew Mysteries.* Like many other Sunday night movies on TV, I didn't get to see the entire thing because this was still the time before the VCR or any other form of recording device. The next morning, I asked my father how it ended. He told me that six people survived and were rescued in the end. I couldn't believe it. The ocean liner was filled with so many people, and only *six* had survived. I recall some disappointment when my father told me that Gene Hackman's character of Rev. Scott was *not* one of them. The outcome of life and death in the movies can be *so* unfair to a kid.

Although I'd have no part of it at such a young and fragile age, it's worth noting that in November 1977, NBC aired what would come to be known as *The Godfather: The Complete Novel for Television* in which director Francis Ford Coppola, in an effort to raise money to help finance the making of his current project at the time, *Apocalypse Now*, edited the content of both *The Godfather* and *The Godfather— Part II* in chronological order and incorporated additional footage not shown in theaters. Unlike *The Godfather*, which had previously aired on NBC for the first time in 1974, this was the first time any of *The Godfather—Part II* would be shown on television. The film was shown over four consecutive nights. The violence, sex, and language was, of course, toned down for a TV audience, but hardly enough for a ten-year-old boy to witness. I wouldn't see both *Godfather* films until years later in high school when they both aired on HBO, uncut and unedited. Like so many other films I've come to love or even consider masterpieces (like both *Godfather* films), more is not always better. But as previously discussed, longer versions of movies shown on TV over more than one night were quite the rage back in the day. I suppose Coppola knew that and took full advantage of it.

Take a moment to recall my earlier description of the Thanksgiving holiday monster movie festival on Channel 9 WOR-TV back in 1976. One year later, the festival continued but the program on Thursday changed slightly with the network airing of *Mighty Joe Young, King Kong,* and *Son of Kong.* For the first time, I'd finally seen the original 1933 version of *King Kong* in its entirety since seeing the '76 remake and without any restraints of school or bedtime rules. Well, there was one restraint though I didn't know it at the time. Television was cheating me by airing a version in which stricter rules of decency were put into effect by the Motion Picture Production Code since its '33 premiere, with various scenes either trimmed or excised altogether for content considered too racy or violent at the time. I learned much later that these scenes included Kong undressing Ann Darrow and sniffing his fingers, Kong biting and stepping on island natives when he attacks their village, and Kong mistaking a sleeping woman for Ann and dropping her to her death after realizing his mistake. Edited or not, the annual tradition of watching *King Kong* on TV stayed with me until the entire festival was discontinued in 1985. Today, those childhood memories remain as an adult, as I still make it a point to watch my DVD copy of the '33 version of *Kong* every Thanksgiving, whether it's before or long after the big turkey has been consumed. This, by far, is one of the strongest examples I can offer of how movies, movies on television, and our deep childhood memories of them continue to have true meaning in our lives.

Finally, one of the most significant experiences I can tell you about movies on television was the broadcast premiere of *2001: A Space Odyssey* on the *NBC Big Event* on February 13, 1977. Because it was a Sunday night, I didn't get to watch the entire movie, but even if I'd been able to, there's no way I would've been able to fully understand what the hell I was watching. I knew nothing of Stanley Kubrick; the man or his art. I was simply watching a movie about space and astronauts on TV, and it looked really cool, despite being a very quiet movie with almost no dialogue. It's important for me to mention the TV premiere of this classic film because its purpose and impact found me again years later when I was a high school teenager and watched it again. You know what? I hated it! I was an older kid now who'd lived through the generational impact of the fast-paced sci-fi entertainment of the late '70s and early '80s that included two *Star Wars* movies, two *Star Trek* movies, two *Superman* movies, *Battlestar Galactica, Alien, Moonraker,* and Disney's *The Black Hole.* For me to watch such a boring display of space exploration accompanied by classical music instead of an adventurous soundtrack was, to say the least, intolerable. Still, time and cinematic maturity can be kind to almost anything. I gave the movie another look by the time I got to college and … well, long story short, I'm proud and honored to say that *2001: A Space Odyssey* is my favorite motion picture of all time and Stanley Kubrick my favorite film director of all time, and none of it may have ever happened without that first TV airing on NBC planting the original seed.

And that, my friends, was the year 1977 for me.

THE YEAR WAS 1978 ...

- Hollywood film director Roman Polanski flees to France to avoid sentencing after pleading guilty to having unlawful sex with a minor.
- A northeaster blizzard hits the New York metropolitan area, resulting in much damage and human fatalities.
- Serial killer Ted Bundy is captured in Pensacola, Florida.
- The CBS nighttime soap opera *Dallas* is launched and remains on the air until 1991.
- At Camp David, Maryland, Israel's Menachem Begin and Egypt's Anwar Sadat begin the peace process following twelve days of secret negotiations under United States President Jimmy Carter's initiative.
- In Guyana, under the direction of Jim Jones, 909 Americans are discovered dead as a result of a mass murder/suicide.

... AND THERE WERE MOVIES!

In July 1978, my family made an important change that became a part of my life for the next thirty-eight years. During the course of once again renting the same house in Westhampton Beach from the previous summer, they took a drive one day and came across a two-story house about half a mile further down the road that was still under construction and nearing completion. Like the rental, it was also across the street from the beach and the Atlantic ocean. *Unlike* the rental, it was a larger home of four bedrooms, two bathrooms, and plenty of outdoor decking that overlooked the water at the front and rear.

Although my immediate reaction was disappointment when I learned we were interrupting our fun summer rental for something new, it didn't take long for me to realize the value of the family having our own vacation home in the Hamptons. This home saw its highs and lows, its triumphs and tragedies, and almost, quite literally, nearly fell into the ocean during a time of destructive Long Island beach erosion and winter storms during the early 1990s. The house remained in my family for nearly four decades, and I have equated some, if not nearly all of my deepest, fondest memories of love, family, and friends with that precious beach house.

Despite all the years, all the memories, and all the people that have come to define the meaning of that house in my life, it's still the inaugural year of '78 that my mind continues to drift back to when recalling the movies that shaped my childhood and my life. That summer was, in my opinion, very significant in linking not only the blockbusters that were due to be released, but also some previous movies that were still going strong in theaters. While everyone was getting in line to go see new movies like *Grease, Jaws 2, Animal House, Hooper,* and *Heaven Can Wait,* older releases like *Close Encounters, Saturday Night Fever,* and the first official rerelease of *Star Wars* could still be seen if you searched your local newspaper well enough. Put them all together and you had an enormous blockbuster summer season ahead of you. Take notice also that for me, '78 began just as the previous year of '77 had ended—with the magic and star power of John Travolta.

Grease

Directed by Randal Kleiser
(June 16, 1978, U.S. Release Date)

———— ‹‹(◦)›› ————

Then

I was never a real fan of movie musicals. At the time when my father was taking me to see Disney revivals on screen like *Pinocchio* and *Peter Pan*, I impatiently waited for the singing portions of the movie to be over and done with so we could get on with the action. Prior to 1978, even the biggest movie musicals of the '70s like *Cabaret, Fiddler on the Roof,* or even *Willy Wonka and the Chocolate Factory* wouldn't have found their way into my life because I was either unaware of them or I simply had no interest in them.

Grease was different. It was on the Broadway stage since 1972, and even when the movie version was on its way, it was still going strong in ticket sales. Everyone who was a fan of *Saturday Night Fever* and John Travolta knew that *Grease* was coming soon. It was hyped as one of the biggest blockbusters to hit theaters for the summer of '78. I knew it and my parents knew it too, which meant I hardly had to put any effort in getting them to take us to see it once it opened. We drove to Easthampton, and oddly, we must've gone during an off-peak show time, because I don't recall any massive lines or difficulty in choosing good seats.

From the moment the movie opened with the wave of the ocean crashing onto the shoreline, I knew it was definitely summer. I was taken with the beauty of Olivia Newton-John and even more taken with the fact that Travolta was lucky enough to have her as his movie girlfriend. While Danny and Sandy ran along the beach, I recall my father saying, "Looks like *From Here to Eternity*." I had no idea what he meant. When the opening credits began and Frankie Valli was singing the title track of "*Grease*," I suspected that my general prejudices against movie musicals would be suspended for the next two hours because things were starting off real good.

The wild antics of Danny Zuko and his friends Kenickie, Sonny, Doody, and Putzie at Rydell High School were easy to enjoy and laugh at. When Sandy suddenly showed up, it seemed the entire audience was captivated and was wondering what would happen next. How soon would Danny and Sandy find each other? When the big moment finally happened, Danny turned into a real jerk and hurt Sandy's feelings just so he could look like an insensitive big shot in front of his stupid friends. Still, I admired a girl like Frenchy for wanting to stand by Sandy and be her friend. She was clearly the better girl of the Pink Ladies, while Rizzo was the one who wasn't afraid to take risks and do something bad once in a while. Becoming girlfriend to a boy like Kenickie certainly seemed like something risky.

Which brings us to a scene that followed not too long after Kenickie and Rizzo hooked up, when they were kissing like a couple of crazy freaks in the back seat of his car. The two of them stopped for a moment to take a breath, and Kenickie took something out of his wallet which I couldn't easily identify after Rizzo asked him, "*You got something?*" What was that thing? It looked like some sort of large coin to me on the screen and then it apparently broke in Kenickie's hands. Whatever it was, it was old because Kenickie told Rizzo he'd bought it in the seventh grade. Unfortunately, none of the supporting dialogue was helping me identify that thing. When I got older, of course, I realized what Kenickie had in his wallet and broke was a *condom*. At age eleven, however, I knew nothing of prophylactics or the potential consequences of not using them. Well, the whole scene makes sense to me *now* and consequently why Rizzo thought she was pregnant for a time.

To my surprise, I thoroughly enjoyed the musical and dance numbers, especially "*Greased Lightning*." This was a sequence of tough guys in leather jackets doing a dance alongside a red-hot, fast car, which I appreciated as a symbol of manhood. Later, during the scene of the big high school dance, Danny tore up the dance floor with Sandy to Sha-Na-Na's *"Born to Hand Jive"* and even managed to score a high octane victory when he was suddenly dancing with Cha-Cha DiGregorio instead. If I'd previously possessed a healthy male fondness for Travolta in *Fever*, then *Grease* only solidified that feeling. He was clearly a man of men who could sing, dance, and he always got the chicks. Really, what's not to admire about *that* when you're a kid? My mother used to tell me that I wanted to *be* John Travolta when I was a kid. She may have been right.

Aside from the excitement of the music and dancing, *Grease* wasn't without its comedy and action. I laughed myself silly when Sonny, Doody, and Putzie mooned their bare butts for the TV camera during the big dance and also when Sandy slammed the car door and injured Danny's private area at the drive-in movie theater after he tried to put his hand on her breast. The action of the big Thunder Road race was thrilling, though I found the moment when sharp blades came protruding out of the competition's tire very hard to swallow. Looked to me like something out of a James Bond movie rather than a musical. Still, Danny won the big race, and that was something to smile and feel good about. Kid or adult, we always want our heroes to win in the end.

Speaking as a full-blooded heterosexual male who was once a heterosexual boy, we can sometimes recall the moment when we first realized we liked girls ... I mean *really, really* liked girls! For me, that moment originated when I first saw the famous 1976 poster of Farrah in her red swimsuit (I still have that old poster sitting somewhere in my archive collection). That feeling toward the opposite sex only intensified when I saw the transformed image of Olivia with her hair in wild curls and dressed in a skintight black spandex outfit. Try to imagine what a young boy with his mouth dropped down to his lap looks like and you've got a good image of me sitting in my seat. Then she and Danny started singing *"You're The One That I Want."* Wait, I'd heard this song before. It was all over the radio for the last month or two and up until this very moment I had no idea it was from *Grease*. Nice surprise. Lyrics from that song like, "*Tell me about it, stud!*" and "*Feel your way*" were awfully sexy to listen to coming out of Olivia's mouth, even at my age of innocence.

When it was all over and Danny and Sandy magically flew off into the great yonder of the blue skies, the first thing I asked my parents was to buy the movie soundtrack record (yes, I said *record*!). The second thing I asked was if we could see the movie again. Their answer was a firm "maybe." A second time would require some waiting because the theater in East Hampton was the only one showing *Grease* in all of the Hamptons right now and the drive wasn't exactly next door. I hoped it would eventually find its way to the local movie theater in Westhampton Beach.

As Tom Petty sings, "*the waiting is the hardest part.*" The waiting inevitably paid off though. *Grease* came to town, and the family headed to the theater once again to be a part of this blockbuster movie musical sensation of '78. The second time is always better because you know what's going to happen and you know you're going to love it. The unexpected part of the evening came when the movie ended and my father asked the entire family, "Do you want to stay and watch it again?" My mother may have had reservations about the idea, but it looked like she was going to be outvoted by the rest of us because we stayed in our seats and watched the movie for the third time.

Grease played at the town's local theater for well over a month, and as the newspaper movie ads were correctly pushing, "*It gets better every time you see it ... again ... and again ... and again.*" Now you'd think the third time would have been the charm, yes? It wasn't. Some months later when the movie made it downstairs at North Shore Towers for its second run, the family didn't even stop to consider whether or not they'd invest time (and my parent's ticket money) to have another go. We took our seats once again. Just in case you're wondering, we *did* stay in our seats to watched it twice. Clearly, the Friedmanns had become a family of *Grease* addicts with five viewings ... and it *still* wasn't over.

By the summer of 1979, the movie was rereleased and once again, it came to Westhampton Beach. Want to take a wild guess at what happened? We went to see it, but this time only once and this time just me, Kevin, and my father. My mother was emphatically against spending any more money on a movie we'd already seen five times. My father disagreed, and it actually ended up in a fight between the two of them. Against my mother's wishes, I followed my father and enjoyed *Grease* for the *sixth* and final time in the theater. Unfortunately, the price I paid for that sixth viewing was getting into trouble with my mother when I got home. Was it worth it? Probably not, because no kid enjoys that kind of trouble, even if the reward is another trip to the movies. How are you supposed to enjoy a movie knowing the entire time you're sitting there that you're going to get your butt handed to you by your mother when you get home?

By the time it was re-released again in 1980 with the marketing tagline of *"one more time,"* I knew better than to press my already delicate luck by asking to see it again. So, after just six times, I'd hang it up for a while before seeing it again on November 8, 1981, when it premiered on the *ABC Sunday Night Movie*. I was excited to see a movie again that had become such a part of my childhood, much like an old friend. However, I soon discovered that my "old friend" had gone through some very radical and unacceptable changes. ABC, for reasons of both time and content, did a despicable editing job with the movie, to the point of practically butchering it. What was previously a reasonable family film had been stripped down to a very sloppy and poorly-edited farce. Realizing that television standards and practices of what was acceptable and what wasn't was still very different back in 1981 as compared to today, there were nonetheless still edits and cuts made to *Grease* that made no sense to me. Some were very simple ones such as in the song *"Look at Me, I'm Sandra Dee"* and the line that goes *"Would you pull that crap with Annette?"* The word *crap* was inexplicably substituted for the word *one*. Even back in '81, I can't imagine the word *crap* was deemed unacceptable for younger TV ears. That same word was apparently also questionable when Danny was supposed to tell Sonny, *"I'm sure glad you didn't take any of her crap, Sonny. You would have really told her off,"* and instead became, *"Sonny, you really told her off."*

The real abomination was during "*Greased Lightning*," which had song lyrics sloppily removed, leaving what was left of the entire number to sound completely chopped up, like a broken record. Looking back on it now and taking into account the full extent of some of the song's racy lyrics, I realize that you couldn't say (or sing) things like, "*We'll be gettin' lotsa tit!*" and "*The chicks will cream*" and "*She's a real pussy wagon!*" on television. Yes, I get that *now*. But still, these were supposed to be professional TV editors, and I can't help but feel they could've done a much cleaner job in preserving the song. A simple *bleep* or single-word substitution (*scream* instead of *cream*?) would've been a lot better than the mess they aired that night (oh, the heartbreaks a kid has to go through when watching a movie he loves on television!). Still, somebody at ABC must've gotten the message because the next time they aired *Grease* in 1984, they simply deleted the entire song altogether. Was that better or worse? I'll never be sure.

Now

From my perspective, *Grease* has changed so much since first released in the summer of '78, and not necessarily for the better. Don't get me wrong; it remains one of the few movie musicals I still enjoy even today. I cannot imagine a better follow-up to *Saturday Night Fever* during a joyous era of Travolta's career breakthrough following *Welcome Back, Kotter*. Like *American Graffiti* (though not nearly as dramatic), it bridges a gap in the spirited Generation X youth that experienced a decade of decadent disco, punk, and hard rock music, while still managing to fondly reflect on the innocence and naïveté of '50's rock and roll and the mighty Elvis (who'd only been dead a year). It's filled with imagination, fantasy, energy, and vitality, without becoming overly sweet or cheesy.

There's something that's always puzzled me over the last few decades, however, and I wish somebody would offer me a rational explanation for it. Exactly when and how did *Grease* slowly evolve into a *chick* movie? Really, back in the day when the film was new and red hot, it didn't seem that way at all. Girls loved the movie, sure, but boys did too, because we recognized its level of coolness. When we weren't drooling over Olivia and longing to be John, we often found ourselves pretending to be just like the T-Birds singing *"Greased Lighting"* and exchanging wiseguy taunts with each other. Somewhere over the course of time, however, the film became something else that I didn't care for. To see *Grease* revived on Broadway in 1994 with women like Rosie O'Donnel and Brooke Shields playing Rizzo was bad enough. To see the film rereleased in movie theaters back in 2010 as a *"sing-along version"* was just the end of the rope for me. Hollywood and fans were taking a precious motion picture memory away from me and turning it into some pathetic episode of FOX's *Glee* or Disney Channel's *High School Musical.* Most recently, the movie has been transformed into *Grease-Live* on the FOX network in January 2016 (totally unacceptable and unfair, in my opinion!).

For me, the magic, imagination, wit, fun, and validity of *Grease* was and continues to lie in the real cool musical that played continuously in a small neighborhood movie theater in Westhampton Beach during the summer of '78 and made me want to be just like Travolta and have Olivia Newton-John for my girlfriend. Regardless of what's happened to the film since those days, they can't ever take *that* away from me.

Jaws 2

Directed by Jeannot Szwarc
(June 16, 1978, U.S. Release Date)

Then

The movie poster for the new sequel to *Jaws* was reaching out and warning us, *"Just when you thought it was safe to go back in the water ...,"* a warning that's become one of, if not *the* most popular movie poster taglines in motion picture history. For myself, however, it was an opportunity to finally right a great wrong I felt was bestowed upon me three years earlier when my parents wouldn't permit me to see *Jaws*. But how would I sell this one to them? Surely, this all-new sequel would offer much of the same bone-chilling terror the first movie offered, and it was those frightening elements my parents were trying to shield me from. I was three years older now, and an eleven-year-old boy can likely handle the screen's terror better than an eight-year-old of three years prior, right? It was worth a shot, though I couldn't help but predict the answer from my father wouldn't go in my favor. The conversation surprised me when it went something like this:

"Dad, can we go to see *Jaws 2* this weekend?"

"No. *Jaws* is a horror movie."

"But, Dad, this is a different movie. I'm three years older now, and it's playing right in town. Please, Dad!"

(*A brief pause to think about it*) "Okay. I'll check to see what the movie's like first."

My initial feeling at his final response was defeat because when he read up on *Jaws 2* in the newspapers and magazines and listened to the reviews from critics like Rona Barrett and Joel Siegel on TV, he'd surely deny my request. Any movie about shark attacks had to be questionable and deemed too intense for any child to handle. Even the poster itself was working against me by stating that the movie "*May Be Too* Intense *For Younger Children.*"

Opening weekend came and went, and I concluded that my request was going down the tubes. As the next weekend (or the weekend after that, perhaps) approached, my dad shocked me by telling me that he and I would go to see *Jaws 2* in our own beach town that Saturday night. Apparently, through his mildly-extensive research, he learned that this new sequel was considered more tame and less bloody and violent than its predecessor of '75, and that was enough for him to lighten up a bit and let his son see the movie he longed to see. Remembering that I'd not seen the original *Jaws* yet, I was nonetheless familiar enough with the pop culture fame of the first movie to make immediate comparisons from the moment the sequel began.

For starters, the opening music had changed from John Williams pulsating and terrifying chords to soft harp strings (also by Williams). The music was soft and accompanied the visual effects of being underwater quite well. When the camera zoomed in on the underwater sunken wreck of the Orca, I needed to whisper the question to my dad if that was indeed the boat that battled the shark from the first movie. He confirmed that it was. Even before the opening shark attack happened, it was easy to see that it was well on its way. I mean, when you open a shark movie with an underwater sequence involving two divers, there's no other way for the scene to end. This opening was the first example in which my father had described to me how *Jaws 2* was considered a "safer" movie than *Jaws*. The divers were attacked and killed by an unseen great white shark, but the attack was in a sense, a blur. No screaming, no penetrating jaws into the body, and no blood. We knew they were dead, but we had to use our imagination to picture just how badly they died.

The story then reintroduced (or in my case, *introduced*) the audience to the fictional town of Amity Island. It was a beautiful setting with picturesque beaches, calm waters, and a quiet light-house, not too unlike the Hamptons, though I'd learn years later that many scenes were filmed in Florida rather than on-location at Martha's Vineyard. The eventual second attack on the water skier in the ocean was, like the first attack, free of the blood and guts considered "unsafe" for a child to witness. Still, there was a terri-fying premise involved in that the speed of the experienced water skier wasn't sufficient to outrun the speed of the killer shark who was persistently getting closer and closer to its victim. The attack on the boat in which we got to see the face of the shark for the first time and the explosion that followed was a thrilling conclusion to an already intriguing attack.

Much of what happened for a good deal of the movie was a closer, more personal look at Martin Brody as not only a family man, but one who struggled to get the townspeople to believe his word that they had another shark problem on their hands. The missing bodies of the divers and the water skiers weren't conclusive. The half-eaten killer whale found on the beach was easily explained with other rea-sons than a shark attack. Brody's conclusion that he was witnessing a shark approach the ocean swimmers at the town beach, in which he also mistakenly fired his gun, was explained as nothing more than a school of harmless bluefish. The underwater photograph taken while the divers were being attacked at the beginning of the movie seemed like the piece of evidence that would finally prove Brody right. But even that was considered worthless by the important townspeople eager to dismiss it as just mud and seaweed in the water or in the camera lens.

I felt bad for Brody when he was fired from his job for carrying on about the shark so much. I thought to myself, *How will he stop the shark now?* It was when one of the town's teenage boys was killed by the shark in the water (again, not much blood and guts, except in the water when the attack was finished) that the story finally took a direction in which Brody finally got to be the hero. His two sons were out there somewhere on the water with a bunch of other teens on a day's sailing trip, and the great white shark was headed straight for them. There was even an interesting camera shot showing the shark's point of vision toward the sailboats. This was where the trouble really started, from the moment the shark first hit the sailors. After that, nothing seemed to go right for these poor kids. Although only one more of them was actually killed by the shark (again, not very violent), their fate seemed repeatedly doomed. Even when it looked like they were going to be rescued by a water helicopter, the machine was attacked by the shark and the copter sunk, the pilot presumably killed by the shark, though we didn't actually get to see that.

It was clear to me that Brody was to be the sole hero of this movie, as opposed to the team of three hunters I'd heard about in the first movie. When he eventually arrived to the kids, including his own little boy Sean, there seemed little hope of ever getting to safety at the island known as Cable Junction. When all appeared lost, however, Brody came up with an idea involving a huge underwater electrical cable. At this point, I knew very much how the original *Jaws* had ended with its big, glorious explosion. This victory was not to be repeated in the sequel. Instead, the great white shark was electrocuted in a bright, violent fireball that finally sank the great beast into the depths of the ocean. This was an altogether different way to destroy the shark, and I thought it looked really cool. When the movie was over and we headed home, the conversation with my father went something like this:

"So are you going to be afraid to go in the ocean now?"
"No way, Dad! That wasn't very scary, but it was still a great movie! Can we see it again?"
"No."
"Awww!"

Bearing in mind that as a kid, I was always determined to at least *ask* if I could see a movie again if it was rereleased in theaters. There was no exception to this when in February 1980, *Jaws 2* returned in the wake of the successful two-week engagement the original *Jaws* received back in August 1979. The reissue movie poster took advantage of that prior success by featuring *two* sharks under the water and a marketing tagline that said, "*One good bite deserves another. After the sensational return to the screen of Jaws … what could be more terrifying than Jaws 2."* Tempting, indeed. But not tempting enough to wet my dad's appetite for another go-around. I waited an entire year until the movie premiered on the *ABC Sunday Night Movie* on February 15, 1981. It was exactly as I'd remembered it on screen in '78 because, like I said, the movie wasn't particularly violent or bloody to begin with, so there was very little for ABC to edit or delete (thank goodness for that).

Now

Well, I suppose it's necessary for me to ask the most important question first. Is the sequel as good as the original? Of course not. I mean, how could it be? Is it as terrifying? Not at all. Is it as exciting to watch? No to that too. Is it a complete and total disaster? Well, I wouldn't go so far as to say that. What *Jaws 2* is, as I can best explain it, is a good example of Hollywood's approach to mediocre movie-making for its time. In other words, it ain't that great and it ain't that bad either. To it's credit, the first sequel of this overdone franchise (continuing until 1987) offers some exciting and original sequences such as the shark chasing the water skier, the shark getting burned by the flare gun, the shark attacking the harbor patrol marine helicopter and pulling it under the water, the beached killer whale with the enormous shark bite taken out if it, and the shark's final demise by electrocution, which in some ways, outsoars the quick and simple action of the explosion that destroys the first shark, in my opinion. These are all wonderful ideas, which unfortunately tend to fall short in their delivery. It's thrilling to watch the shark fin get closer and closer to the water skier, but it would've been deliciously enticing to watch this girl get hers with a lot more terrifying gore as opposed to the quick underwater camera shots that only provide the obvious implication that she's being torn to pieces. The same can be said for the helicopter pilot whom we don't see after the craft is pulled underwater (even the deleted DVD scene doesn't offer much more than the pilot struggling to stay alive).

How ironic it is that I should be so critical of the lack of violence and gore in *Jaws 2* now, because it was the lack of such that enabled me to see it in the first place back in the summer of '78. While the character of Matt Hooper is noticeably missed, the performances of remaining characters Martin Brody, Ellen Brody, and Larry Vaughan are considerably strong enough to hold the viewer's interest for one more round. For my own personal interests, it remains a strong film in my memory because it'll be forever linked to that first glorious summer my family spent at the beach house that would become a part of my life for decades to come. Today, when I spend the day at the beach, my immediate thought of what to do with the evening to come is to sit down and watch *Jaws 2* and think back to the eleventh year of my childhood when I was finally permitted to experience the exciting thrills that accompanied the great white shark.

For my final thought on this film, consider John Carpenter's breakthrough film *Halloween* (also from '78), the one considered responsible for originating the teenage slasher film. However, were we to really think about it, can we not truly give that honor to *Jaws 2* first? Consider that for its climactic sequences, we have a group of Amity Island fun-loving teenagers who are caught in great peril when they become disabled and adrift in the middle of the ocean and are repeatedly stalked, menaced, and even killed by the great white shark, much in the same tradition that one would have bestowed to a fictional character like Michael Myers, Jason Voorhees, or Freddy Kruger in the 1980s. You see my point? It's much like a teenage slasher film, except with shark teeth rather than butcher knives and machetes.

Or perhaps I'm just really reaching here?

Animal House

Directed by John Landis
(June 28, 1978, U.S. Release Date)

———⟫∘⟪———

Then

"Okay, but don't tell your mother."

Think back to your own childhood and I'll bet that many, if not all of you, heard this line spoken to you by your father (or mother) if he or she was willing to do something to make you happy, but would be highly disapproved by the other half. If you heard a line like that, it meant you won your argument, but the victory came with a degree of caution and maybe even a warning. For me, the victory was finally convincing my father to take me to see *Animal House*, a popular comedy I'd only heard and read about during the summer of '78, but for reasons of obvious vulgarity, would likely never be granted access to. By the end of that year though, the movie made it to our resident movie theater and I may have even seemed a bit older in the eyes of my father. Whatever the reason was, he agreed to take me to see it and the promise I had to agree to was to keep my mouth shut. I couldn't even say anything to Kevin because he'd surely rat me out to my mother.

I'll start out by saying that if *Saturday Night Fever* was an inauguration into the adulthood of R-rated movies, then *Animal House* only confirmed me as a member for life. From the very moment I was introduced to the character of Bluto, as he stood there peeing on the ground outside the Delta House while drinking a beer, I knew something was about to change in my movie viewing. From that moment on, it just got worse and worse in its level of rudeness, crudeness, rowdiness, and disgust—though not to suggest I didn't find reasons to laugh. However, laughter during *Animal House* meant having to understand *what* I was laughing at in the first place. This was a grown-up movie for grown-ups who understood grown-up humor. There was much taking place here that I wasn't old enough to understand or laugh at. I was too young to understand what Greg Marmalard and Mandy Pepperidge were doing in the car and why she was wearing a white glove. I was too young to understand what Otter meant when he described his date for the night as having a pair of *"major league yabos!"* I was too young to understand the phallic, sexual interpretation behind the comparison of cucumber sizes between Otter and Mrs. Wormer in the supermarket, and I was too young to understand the comedy behind Pinto holding a handful of tissue paper when he was alone in the room with a girl. Hell, for all I knew, it may have very well *been* the Germans who attacked Pearl Harbor. What did I know from outrageous and stupid grown-up humor? My father knew, of course, and why he didn't drag me by the hand and out of the movie theater to prevent me from seeing and hearing any more is still beyond my comprehension to this very day.

On the other hand, there was enough slapstick hilarity that I *could* understand to keep me well entertained for nearly two hours. I enjoyed and laughed at moments like a golf ball crashing through a window and landing in a large pot of soup, Douglas Neidermeyer being dragged along the ground by his horse, Bluto stacking his plate with an endless pile of food in the cafeteria and the food fight he starts, the horse suffering a fatal heart attack upon hearing the gun shot, and Bluto smashing the guitar in anger at the Toga party. I even knew why I was laughing when the Playboy bunny went flying though the open window and landed on the boy's bed, to which he shouted out, *"Thank you, God!"* and why Bluto fell to the ground on the ladder after watching the naked blonde girl in front of him on the other side of the window just after he turned to us in the movie theater and raised his eyebrows in mischief (you see, I may have only been eleven, but I *was* already familiar with the visual pleasures of the opposite sex).

When the *second* R-rated movie of my life was over, I felt a little older and a little privileged to have been permitted access to a popular movie that was considered vulgar, gross, and totally inappropriate for a boy my age. I also felt a certain degree of wicked deceitfulness in having done something my mother wouldn't have approved of, but with my father's blessing nonetheless. Like it or not though, it was in the past now and my father couldn't take it back even if he wanted to, and as I'd promised, I didn't tell my mother ... not until I was much older and it was safe to tell her anyway.

I didn't see *Animal House* for the second time until February 15, 1981, when the movie made its television premiere on the *NBC Sunday Night Big Event*. Since I was fortunate enough to see it on screen, I saw just how much editing the network had done, despite advising parental discretion to its viewers. Just about any content that implied disgust or vulgarity had been properly edited for TV viewers. Watching it now seemed no better or worse, no safer or more dangerous, than watching the very short-lived ABC, movie-spawned sitcom, *Delta House*. By the time the movie encored on NBC just over one year later, John Belushi was dead from a drug overdose. The TV announcer proclaimed, *"He was the greatest, and this was his greatest role."* He was likely right.

In my senior year of high school, I was permitted my first gathering of friends to include beer. We watched *Animal House*, and the laughter and exclamation of its most popular quotes by rowdy teenage boys from the basement of our house must've been enough to cause my parents and Kevin their fair share of annoyance. Still, gathered together in front of the TV, watching a vulgar movie and drinking cans of Budweiser was just a part of being teenage boys on the way to manhood. Years later, I wouldn't have gotten through my college years without the joy of watching *Animal House* with friends. It was viewed now at an entirely new level that couldn't possibly compare to the eyes and perspective of an eleven-year-old boy sitting in a movie theater seat next to his father (and not telling his mother).

Now

Today, I cannot viably claim what's considered popular comedy movie viewing by college students. Perhaps it's *The Hangover* franchise or maybe it dates back to the *American Pie* franchise, both of which have no meaning for me. I'd like to think (or imagine, perhaps) that today's kids would take the time to reach further back than that into the archives of raunchy comedy entertainment with not only a classic film like *Animal House*, but also *Caddyshack*, *Porky's*, and *Fast Times at Ridgemont High*. Were they to really sit down and absorb *Animal House*, they'd discover it has as many quotable lines (*"Was it over when the German's bombed Pearl Harbor?"*) as *Casablanca*, *Gone With the Wind*, *Jaws*, and *Star Wars*.

As messy and anarchic as it comes off, *Animal House* assaults our senses nonetheless with an undeniable mix of manic energy. It's comedic effects of the wild times of our college youth couldn't be delivered successfully were it not for the gifted actors involved, including secondary ones as Donald Sutherland and Karen Allen. There are moments in the film where you'd like to think the appropriate response is to be grossed out by tasteless antics such as Bluto pissing on the shoes of Pinto and Flounder, the enormous pile of horse shit in the stable that Flounder must do his push-ups in front of or a blunt line like, *"You can take your thumb out of my ass any time now, Carmine,"* but it's nearly impossible to feel that way when you're laughing so damn hard.

One thing's for sure: 1962 may have been a simpler time of innocence, but you'd never know it because the college campus was still a place of madness and insanity, where the beer flowed every weekend (or every night) and the sole purpose of any red-blooded American male was to get the girl drunk and take her bra and panties off.

Halloween

Directed by John Carpenter
(October 25, 1978, U.S. Release Date)

Then

Like *Jaws* before it, John Carpenter's *Halloween* is a tale of how I came to know and experience a motion picture *after* its initial theatrical release. In October 1978, like so many other times before, I browsed through the Sunday newspaper to see what movies were out there. What I saw on this particular day shocked and horrified me. It was a full-page black and white movie ad of a large, forceful hand clutching a large butcher knife. Above that image was the title *Halloween* and below that image was the tagline that read, "*The Night He Came Home*." My initial reaction to such an image was utter confusion. What did this mean? Up until that very moment, Halloween was a yearly fun tradition of costumes, trick-or-treating, candy, black and white monster movies on TV, and an annual airing of *It's the Great Pumpkin, Charlie Brown*. But now, with this newspaper ad, someone was trying to imply that Halloween was now associated with a large butcher knife stabbing innocent people. I knew that horror movies existed, and up until that time, many of their stories in the '70s had been linked to the idea of possession by the devil, as in *The Exorcist* and *The Omen* (movies I wasn't allowed to see as a kid). This was clearly something new in which the prospect of going out on Halloween night could very well mean getting killed by a maniac with a knife. This was something I did *not* need to see as an impressionable young boy. For the time being, the spirit of Halloween needed to remain fun.

By February 1980, my life was significantly changed again. My parents were split up for the second time and we'd moved some months earlier to the town of Great Neck, Long Island. With the move came the dreaded prospects of a new school and new friends. I was twelve years old then and was attending middle school. I had a new friend whom I shall, for the purpose of this book, call *Greg B.* (remember his name because he'll frequently come up as one who had much to do with how I got to see certain forbidden movies). He and I were as close as I suppose two twelve-year-old boys could be. We hung out together, ate lunch together in the school cafeteria, and sometimes assisted each other with test answers in the classroom if we could get away with it. He and I also had occasional sleepovers together and *always* at his house. The reason they were always at his house was because not only did his family subscribe to HBO, but also because he had his own small color TV set in his room that also carried the channel. As we sat together eating our horrid school lunch, he insisted that we have a sleepover at his house the night of February 9, 1980. When I asked him why that night was so important, he replied, "*Halloween* is on HBO Saturday night!"

By this time in my life, I'd reached a point where I could do some harmless sneaking around to see movies that were considered forbidden by my parents, particularly horror. All I had to do was simply ask if I could have a sleepover at Greg B.'s house, and my request was almost always granted. His parents were also more liberal than my own. They didn't question what we were watching on TV in the privacy of their son's bedroom. Perhaps they didn't know or perhaps they simply didn't care. Either way, it made no difference to me because they existed as a means-to-an-end for me to watch some new, forbidden, movies. So on Saturday, February 9, 1980, after finishing dinner with my friend's parents, we closed his bedroom door and waited for *Halloween* to begin, which would actually not be until around eleven that night. The lateness of the hour would make the prospect of the forbidden horror movie all the more exciting for two young boys looking forward to staying up real late on a

Saturday night. I remember Greg B. handing me the *HBO guide* for that month and reading the description for *Halloween*. Words like *"fast becoming a horror classic," "Don't see this one alone!,"* and *"will have you screaming."* were either strengthening my anticipation for the movie or just plain scaring the crap out of me.

The late-night hour finally arrived and *Halloween* began. The electronic music was chilling and immediately set things up with the scary image of the jack-o'-lantern in the background. The first scene of a house on an ordinary street on Halloween night in 1963 was quiet and simple, and it was perhaps that simplicity that first made me realize that something very bad was probably going to happen very soon. I didn't have to wait too long before I was getting my first taste of innocence lost on Halloween night. Trick-or-treating had just been traded in for the genuine horror of a small child stabbing his sister to death in her own bedroom and without a single drop of blood to be seen. Even while I was watching all of this, somewhere in the back of my mind I couldn't help but wonder just how a small six-year-old child could have the strength to do this to his older sister. Ah, who cared? Horror movies weren't always supposed to make sense, and it didn't stop my friend and I from looking at each other and thinking the same thing; that it was cool to watch an R-rated horror movie without our parents knowing.

The scene of the rain and thunderstorm fifteen years later kept me in silence because I didn't want to miss one word that Dr. Sam Loomis was saying. There was a certain effectiveness in getting to know the character of Michael Myers without actually seeing him (yet) because Loomis was giving us a rather detailed history of who Michael was now and just how dangerous he was considered to be. I wasn't surprised to see him escape the hospital he was being kept at, for if he hadn't, there wouldn't be much of a movie left to watch, would there? Even while I waited to see just what Michael would do next, I eagerly anticipated Dr. Loomis's next move because he always seemed to know what Michael would do next. His reasons were simple enough when he declared over the phone, *"I know him! I'm his doctor!"*

Next came the three pretty babysitters who were also best friends. Ah, this took me back because I'd had my small fair share of high school babysitters when I was younger. I also remember my mother's stern warning of never letting strangers into the house when she was away and Kevin and I were left alone with the babysitter. It became immediately obvious that high school babysitters and an escaped lunatic were *not* going to be a pleasant mix in this movie. While two of the babysitters seemed just silly and girlish, the one named Laurie Strode seemed more like a responsible mother who really cared about the children she was watching. She also loved Halloween and took pleasure in making things fun for the children as the night wore on; making popcorn, carving a jack-o'-lantern, and watching old monster movies on TV.

When the first babysitter, Annie, was killed in the front seat of her car, what I remember most was the music suddenly becoming very loud and violent at the moment her throat was slashed by the masked killer. I was shocked and horrified, but still of an age where I was old enough to recognize when something was just a movie and not real-life. I also enjoyed seeing Laurie's friend Lynda naked for a brief moment (the occasional nudity *mattered* on screen when you're a young boy discovering his active hormones for the opposite sex). When the scene finally arrived when Laurie discovered the dead bodies of her friends (again, no actual blood seen in the movie) in the house across the street, my immediate thought was that I hadn't heard a woman scream like that in the movies since Fay Wray in the 1933 version of *King Kong*. I hadn't yet heard the movie term *"scream queen,"* but I'd just gotten an audible taste of what it meant.

The rest of the movie seemed less bloody horror than relentless terror as Laurie ran and screamed for her life from the slow-moving Michael Myers. Even while she was trying to save her own life, she didn't forget that her first duty as a babysitter was to be courageous and protect the children, which she did by locking them in the closet. She was terrified of Michael, but she knew how to fight back against him, and this is where things really became confusing for me because no matter how many times Laurie struck back, Michael kept getting up and coming back for more. I didn't yet understand the fictional suspensions of disbelief that came with many of the horror movie characters yet to come in the 1980s, but all I kept asking Greg B. was,

"Why won't Michael die?" He had no rational answer. Even at the climactic moment, after Dr. Loomis shot Michael Myers *six* times, the man still supposedly got up, walked away, and disappeared. All we were left with was the prospect that the "boogeyman" did, in fact, exist and had come home for Halloween night.

It was just a short ninety minutes, but I'd just turned a corner in the role that movies played in my life. Watching an uncut, R-rated horror show late at night, even on a small TV set, turned out not to be scary but rather liberating to a young boy always striving to branch out to new and forbidden forms of screen entertainment. Horror and Halloween had changed for me now. It was no longer black and white monster movies by Universal Pictures, nor was it a Halloween TV special of *The Munsters* or *The Addams Family*. The man who made *this* movie had just shown me the true spirit of Halloween lied in its ability to make us think about what could truly scare us, and without hardly a drop of blood to show for it.

Nearly two years passed before I got to watch *Halloween* again, and like some other movies on TV before it, there were changes in content. On Friday, October 30, 1981, the movie made its television debut on NBC. The timing couldn't have been more perfect because the first sequel *Halloween II* had just opened in theaters nationwide that very weekend. I was fourteen years old then and I had the pleasure of my own small TV set to watch in the privacy of my own bedroom. My parents (they were back together *again*) wouldn't bother me tonight because they were preoccupied with watching CBS's *Dallas* in their own bedroom. The dramas and conflicts of the *Ewing* family were much too important to bother worrying about what their oldest son was watching in his room.

When the movie began and NBC issued its warning of *"Parental Discretion Advised. This film contains elements of shock and suspense,"* I thought to myself, *Yeah, right, whatever. Bring it on. I've seen it uncut already.* Clearly, such a horror movie was going to be edited for television wherever the network deemed necessary, but what I didn't realize at the time was how a movie that was originally ninety minutes uncut was going to have to be compensated for to fill in the two-hour television time slot. Like other movies on TV before it, there was new and added footage (twelve minutes filmed by John Carpenter during the production of *Halloween II*, I'd learn later), though this time the movie wouldn't be aired over two nights. The newly-filmed scenes included Dr. Sam Loomis at a hospital board review of Michael Myers and his talking to a then-six-year-old Michael at Smith's Grove, in which he tells him, *"You've fooled them, haven't you, Michael? But not me."* Another added scene featured Dr. Loomis at Smith's Grove examining Michael's abandoned cell after his escape and seeing the word *Sister* scratched into the door (something we'd learn more about in the sequel). Finally, there was a scene in which Lynda came over to Laurie's house to borrow her blouse, just as Annie telephoned asking to borrow the same blouse. Except for the extended courtroom sequence in which Loomis was trying to keep Michael Myers locked up, none of these added scenes really amounted to very much. They took up time, and I suppose that's what was necessary for NBC to air the movie. Unfortunately, I didn't get to see Lynda naked again.

By the time I was in college, I owned *Halloween* uncut on VHS video. When you live in a dormitory and have occasional access to a VCR, you can become quite popular in your own right when you have movies at your disposal. Movie nights in the recreation area of my floor were always fun, particularly at Halloween, when consumption of as many horror movies as possible was always anticipated. My friends and I repeatedly enjoyed watching it during the entire week preceding the annual holiday before we'd inevitably go to fraternity parties in full costume and get drunk (ah, those were the days!).

Now

John Carpenter's original *Halloween* remains one of my top ten favorite horror films of all time. Like Hitchcock's *Psycho* and George A. Romero's *Night of the Living Dead* before it, the film exercises a certain psychological relevance in creating the necessary fear and shock value without overextending itself with needless blood and gore. While it's gone down in the history books of cinema as the one that inaugurated the genre of the slasher film, I have to give it much more significant credit than that. The average slasher film is a mindless experience that almost never respects its own characters beyond the lunatic with the knife or the machete, and in particular, that of its female characters. Prior to *Halloween*, most female victims were considered unsafe and defenseless until they were rescued by their male counterparts. Laurie Strode, as played skillfully by Jamie Lee Curtis, while ultimately needing to be saved by Dr. Sam Loomis and his gun in the end, is nonetheless brave, spirited, intelligent, and uses her instincts to not only protect herself but also the children she's ultimatley responsible for.

I think the late Roger Ebert said it best when he said, *"There is a difference between good and scary movies and movies that systematically demean half the human race. There is a difference between movies that are violent but entertaining and movies that are gruesome and despicable. There is a difference between a horror movie and a freak show."* He also adds, *"As you watch Halloween, your basic sympathies are always enlisted on the side of the woman, not with the killer."*

Carpenter, while never forgetting that it's important to scare the living hell out of us with suspense and fear, clearly respects the women in his film, particularly Laurie Strode. *Halloween*, unlike too many other slasher films, doesn't degrade women. I don't raise this specific issue with the film because I'm looking to score points as a champion for women's rights and respect in the world of motion pictures, but I deem it relevant because, like it or not, most of the victims in horror films are *women*. Carpenter recognizes that his last surviving hero (aside from Dr. Loomis) shall be a woman, and he doesn't seek to disrespect that unavoidable fact.

It's important that I also give the director his proper credit for knowing how to take his time with a horror film and not rush things. Michael Myers doesn't claim his first babysitter victim until approximately fifty-three minutes into the film. It seems that the artist here is purposely building not only the backstory, but also the suspense that'll eventually get the pay-off of the horror show rolling. Even when Michael stabs a young man to death in the kitchen, the camera pauses for a moment to stare at the killer as he slowly cocks his head to focus on (and perhaps even *admire*) the body he's just impaled to the kitchen cabinet door. Again, notice that not a drop of blood is spilled on screen. Even the town of Haddonfield, Illinois, itself is one of the most authentic-looking suburban flavors I've seen on film. There's a very subtle creepiness to the quiet, deserted streets we see late in the day of October 1978, implying that the honored tradition of our homes, our streets, and our families are no longer safe.

Not since Bernard Herman's score for *Psycho* have I ever enjoyed the music of a horror film more. Carpenter, through what I can only describe as electronic genius, creates the ability to start out one way musically and then pile on an entirely new form of music to accompany the appropriate scene. As an example, the music during the scene where Laurie is being chased by Michael is simple and pulsating, much like the infamous theme to *Jaws*, but emanates fear because it's hard hitting nonetheless, implying that evil is on its way and ready to strike.

Like *Jaws* on July Fourth and *It's A Wonderful Life* on Christmas Eve, *Halloween* is a film I *must* watch every Halloween night when it's real late and my family has already retired to bed. It's a film that I still manage to take in and absorb as though it were brand-new every time the credits roll and the music begins, much like the twelve-year-old boy who watched it for the first time uncut on HBO back in February 1980. It is, admittedly, the only *Halloween* film I choose to own. As a practical matter, I suppose owning just the *one* film leaves things hanging in the wind with a certain ambiguity as to how Michael Myers is finally defeated (defeated before being reborn in *Halloween 4*, that is), but it's a personal sacrifice I'm willing to make to avoid the endless examples of how so many credible ideas in cinema, be they horror or other genres, start out pure and unaffected and then shamelessly erode into a series of mindless sequels and remakes. Let's not, of course, forget the Hollywood copycats that were destined to follow. *Halloween* may very well be considered responsible for inevitably spawning too many other infamous, immortal, and refuse-to-die screen killers that include names like Jason and Freddy. Unfortunately, it is what it is (though I wish it weren't).

The Lord of the Rings

Directed by Ralph Bakshi
(November 15, 1978, U.S. Release Date)

Then

During the two years that my family lived at North Shore Towers, the private movie theater offered a *free* screening of a recent family film to its residents once a year on a Saturday afternoon. The first one shown while I was there was *Sinbad and the Eye of the Tiger*. The second was *The Lord of the Rings* sometime in early 1979. This second screening had special significance for me because it was not only one of the few movies at that time I was allowed to go see with friends and without parental supervision, but it was also a major step in how I viewed the art of cartoon animation, because this was no ordinary animated feature. To begin with, it was PG-rated and that was an altogether different ballgame to a young boy whose previous experiences with animated movies had been safely rated G (I didn't know it at the time, but Ralph Bakshi's first animated feature *Fritz the Cat* was X-rated).

From the moment the movie began and the narrator's voice-over told the tale of the nine rings of power, I was already lost. Here lied the second challenge in this feature for my mind and senses. Up until then, my exposure and interpretation of all animation, whether by Walt Disney or the likes of Bugs Bunny, Woody Woodpecker, and *The Flintstones* on TV, was easy enough to understand. *The Lord of the Rings* was something entirely different entirely because it involved a complicated and complex plot of Middle-earth, Hobbits, Dwarfs, Orcs, and Wizards. I didn't even recognize what a hobbit was. I thought they were ordinary boys with hairy feet. The primary story of good versus evil and the power of the One Ring was easy enough to follow I suppose, but the more detailed and specific story points were just simply flying over my little head. I hadn't read the three books by J.R.R. Tolken (I *still* haven't). Ironically, none of this mattered, because I was captivated and enthralled by the action and excitement as told through a form of animation I'd never seen before. There were moments where many characters and even their horses looked like real-life (I'd learn later that this form of animation was a new filmmaking technique known as *rotoscoping*, in which live action footage was actually traced over, frame by frame, to produce an animated look).

The Lord of the Rings was violent, even for a PG-rated feature. There was blood, animated though it may have been, in flows of red and purple during some of the intense battle scenes (my parents would've likely forced me to leave the theater if they'd been there to see what I was watching). This was a new and rather chilling surprise to me as well. Never before had I seen Bugs Bunny, Woody Woodpecker, or Fred Flintstone bleed before—I didn't even know animated characters *could* bleed. As different a reality as this was in the world of animated movies, there was no denying that I and my friends found this screen spectacle to be very, very cool. We didn't always get it, but we loved it nonetheless … and it was a *free* screening too. By the time it ended, good had triumphed, the evil of the orc army was defeated, and the triumph of the Rings was forged in the places of Middle Earth history, or so the narrator was telling us. However, little did I know how much my friends and I had just been cheated by this movie.

Now

For the purpose of writing this book, I recently watched *The Lord of the Rings* for a fresh and honest perspective, though it's not the first time I've watched it since I was eleven. At the start of 2004, once I'd seen all three of Peter Jackson's big screen installments of Tolkien's legendary tales, I needed to watch Bakshi's version to see how it compared to the recent live-action epics. This was the first time I watched the film since that day back in '79, and I was stunned and appalled to realize the animated film covered only the first two books, *The Fellowship of the Ring* and *The Two Towers*, of Tolken's trilogy of books, which left the entire film virtually unfinished. I was clueless to this fact back when I was a kid, and now I finally understood just how much I'd been cheated.

Along with this realization is also some of the filmmaking facts I've learned about Bakshi and his efforts to make his version of *The Lord of the Rings*. The film was originally intended to be distributed as a *Part I* in keeping with the tradition of Tolkien's work (just like Jackson did later). Of course, leave it to the arrogant powers-that-be at United Artists to make the poor decision of releasing the film without any indication that a sequel would follow, fearing that movie audiences would not pay their good ticket money to see merely half a film. It would've been natural for fans to presume that the simple title of *The Lord of the Rings* meant they'd see a film that covered all three books. They were wrong, and they ended up confused. Bakshi himself has stated that he *"would never have made the film if he had known what would happen during the production."* Despite the fact that Bakshi's film is only two-thirds of an original piece of work, it's impossible to deny that his effort possesses some very redeeming qualities. At a time long before CGI, the concept behind the animation involved was very unusual, bold, and daring during a decade when Disney films, whose best efforts of the '70s had been *The Aristocats* and *Robin Hood*, were all but extinct.

The film remains an exciting and impressive visual experience above all else. By this time in our film history, it's likely to be unfairly judged because it has the likes of Jackson's endearing trilogy to compare itself and live up to, and that unfortunately, may be an impossible brick wall to penetrate. To view Bakshi's film now is an exercise in keeping an open and patient mind, as well as recalling a period in time when one man attempted to be the first to bring his own vision of a piece of popular fantasy literature to the screen. Even Jackson himself couldn't deny the influence that Bakshi's film had on his own creations. At first, he denied seeing the film, but then later confessed to first discovering Tolkien's story through Bakshi and considered the film a *"brave and ambitious attempt."*

He was right.

Superman–The Movie

Directed by Richard Donner
(December 15, 1978, U.S. Release Date)

Then

Not since the '76 remake of *King Kong* had I such high anticipations for a new movie. I cannot claim to have had the same anticipations for movies like *Star Wars* and *Close Encounters* because they were unfamiliar territory until becoming popular in their own right. The character of Superman, like Kong, was already legendary. While I wasn't a major fan or reader of *Superman* comic books, I did watch the 1950's TV show with George Reeves everyday after school when it aired in reruns. Superman himself was unmistakable, and now the first major motion picture for the big screen was on its way. When it played at a neighborhood movie theater only ten minutes from where we lived, my parents knew well enough they'd be responsible for taking their sons to see it (asking them was hardly necessary).

The movie started with an image, or perhaps an *homage*, to an old aspect ratio of movie theater curtains parting and the sound of an old projector displaying the words *June 1938* (the year Superman was created by Jerry Siegel and Joe Shuster) and a cover of *Action Comics* depicting art deco rocket ships and an exploding planet. A child's voice told us of a decade during the Great Depression when the responsibility of the *Daily Planet* was to provide the public with truth and clarity. These words then yielded to some very powerful title images accompanied by the opening music of John Williams and inevitably building up into the immortal word that was *SUPERMAN*! Even at the age of eleven, when I was still too young to recognize or understand just how powerful opening credits could be when done effectively, I sat there in amazement, anticipating more … and more.

I was already somewhat familiar with how Superman came to Earth as a baby, but this was the first time I discovered the specific reasons to how and why. Although I'd understand years later with the sequel, the opening trial of the three Kryptonian criminals was confusing, if not unnecessary, to the story that followed. I was anxious to see what would happen to the planet Krypton following Jor-El's ignored warning to evacuate all its citizens. When the baby of Kal-El first appeared, I remember my mother making soft, cooing noises at such an adorable infant. To watch a loving mother and father kiss their baby and say goodbye to him for the last time in their lives was, admittedly, sad. But excitement quickly overtook sadness. The rocket ship blasted off and Kal-El was safe for his new journey to Earth to one day become Superman. I kept thinking the planet Krypton would be destroyed and that would be it. Instead, the scene took its time and showed us the slow and gradual destruction of the planet's interior and its doomed people who attempted to survive in vain. The planet's explosion was dramatic and final.

The journey of Kal-El's ship was intriguing. Rather than just fly through space and eventually land on Earth, the scene again took its time and gave us specific details of the journey. First, the ship passed alongside the three Kryptonian criminals who'd been sentenced to the Phantom Zone which appeared as nothing more than a large sheet of glass. Then we saw close-ups of the baby listening to the recorded voice of his father already beginning to teach him the ways of the people of Earth. There were descriptions of the special powers he'd have (powers we in the audience already likely knew about from comic books and TV) and even a warning never to interfere with human history. Had I known at the time what the art of set-up and pay-off were in a professional screenplay, that specific warning might've had more meaning for me.

When the three-year-old Kal-El finally landed on Earth, met his new adoptive parents, and lifted up the truck that almost crushed

Jonathan Kent, we knew things were about to get started and it was time for the true Superman to be born. As a child, it wasn't always easy for me to appreciate or retain specific moments of powerful dialogue. To this day, however, I won't forget a feeling of sadness and sorrow when, at Jonathan Kent's funeral, young Clark Kent said to his mother, *"All those things I can do ... all those powers ... and I couldn't even save him."* But as I mentioned before, feelings of sadness in a movie such as this are very quickly replaced by the sheer excitement of story and action. Young Clark Kent was about to journey up north where he'd create the Fortress of Solitude and discover just who he was and why he was sent to Earth. In what's best described as an "out of body" experience (though I'd never heard such words when I was a kid), Clark was taken by his father, Jor-El, through time and space to not only fully comprehend his role on Earth as a powerful being from another world, but would also return as an older man by twelve years, his manhood and his colorful costume and cape ready for action.

Never forgetting the familiarity of Superman's story as seen on TV, the arrival of Clark Kent at the Daily Planet in the city of Metropolis (which I could clearly recognize as being filmed in Manhattan), and his introduction to Lois Lane and Jimmy Olson seemed almost routine. Mild suspense and dialogue clearly were leading to something much bigger in which the world would finally recognize the existence of Superman. Such expectations finally paid off during the helicopter disaster sequence at the rooftop of the Daily Planet in which Lois Lane began to fall to her death. Not to worry though—Superman was on the way. What happened next is important to me because for a brief moment, it changed the way I looked at my mother. For as long as I could remember, I'd never seen my mother get excited, joyous, or giddy watching anything fun on the screen that would normally bring out the kid in us (she was just *that* damn serious!). But when Superman showed up in flight to save the falling Lois Lane, grab hold of the falling helicopter and fly them both up to safety, my mother (along with the rest of the audience) clapped her hands and cheered with genuine laughter and excitement. I'd *never* seen her exhibit this sort of fun at the movies before, and I don't think I ever saw her do it again after that. I suppose the powers of Superman extend beyond what we're familiar with, even to someone like my mother.

Superman was here, and now we'd watch him live up to his full potential with a series of daring rescues (including the old, silly cliché of the cat stuck in the tree) and chases. By the time the Daily Planet was committed to exploiting Superman's arrival, Lois Lane was also just as committed to getting as close to Superman as possible. During their interview at her rooftop apartment, it seemed as if they were just killing time with each other when what they really wanted was to get closer. Their flight together through and above the skies of Metropolis was not only visually beautiful, but also touching in the way we could hear Lois's voice-over recite a poem entitled *"Can You Read my Mind?"*.

The story also knew when to be a little silly for the sake of slapstick fun. Meeting Lex Luther, his sidekick Otis and his girlfriend Ms. Teschmacher were meant to make us laugh, and I'm sure we did. But I'll still never forget the reaction I had when I first saw Ms. Teschmacher wearing the sexy black outfit that revealed a large portion of her breasts. Remember, I was twelve then and the fantasies of the opposite sex were just starting to build. That was only natural, of course, but a woman like Valerie Perrine in the late '70s certainly helped to move it along.

During the second and final sequence of Superman's daring exploits and rescues, it was thrilling to watch him show up when he was needed during California's major earthquake orchestrated by Lex Luthor. Never did the strength and power of the man seem more obvious than when he laid down his own body in place of the broken train track and allowed it to safely pass over himself. Even though I never doubted the power of his superhuman abilities, I was still stunned nonetheless to watch this man raise the land's infill to protect and repair the San Andreas Fault Line immediately following the start of the earthquake. Yes, it seemed that there was nothing Superman couldn't save or fix. For a time, however, that may not have been completely true. When all was finally settled down, it appeared that Lois Lane had died during the course of the quake. Wait a second, could this be possible? Was Lois really dead? Like Rocky Balboa losing the big fight, this just didn't seem possible or fair, even for a movie. When Superman arrived at the scene seemingly too late, even he couldn't believe it. He let out a scream of rage and fury that I never thought a righteous man like himself was capable of.

What followed next, I couldn't possibly understand the theoretical physics of at the age of eleven, but it appeared that by flying at an unimaginable speed, Superman could rotate the planet Earth in the opposite direction and physically turn back time. By doing that, the events of the quake and those who suffered from it, including Lois, would be undone and all would be safe despite the fact that Superman had ignored his father's previous warning that he was forbidden to interfere with human history. I suppose sometimes even a man like Superman had to disobey his own daddy in order to do the right thing and save the woman he loved.

Just over two hours later, *Superman—The Movie* could not have ended better. The world was saved, Lois Lane was saved, Lex Luthor and Otis were going to jail, and the human race seemed to have a better understanding of itself and its safety, because as Superman himself put it, *"We're all part of the same team."* Yes, Superman was here to stay; on screen, on lunchboxes, on trading cards, and in our popular culture. It was a moviegoing phenomenon that could've easily rivaled *Star Wars.* It was pure fun, magic, and something I didn't want to end.

In February 1982, *Superman—The Movie* had its television premiere on the *ABC Sunday Night Movie*. Like *King Kong, Airport '77*, and *The Deep* before it, it included additional footage over the course of two nights, bringing its running time (without commercials) to just over three hours. By the end of the first night's airing, the movie stopped short when Lois Lane fell from the helicopter, creating a cliffhanger-type of effect for the end of part one. The next evening, there was a brief recap of what took place the night before and the film continued from where it left off. Some of this new footage included a Kryptonian security officer ordered to hunt down and capture Jor-El for excessive energy use, Superman subjected to machine gun fire, a giant blow torch, and frozen ice while walking through Lex Luthor's underground hideout and a little girl revealed to be Lois Lane aboard a moving train watching a teenage Clark Kent through her binoculars as he's running at a speed faster than the train. Some scenes which included Lex Luther playing the piano just before he lowered Ms. Teschmacher into a den of lions seemed completely pointless and stupid.

By the time I reached my high school teens and finally owned an uncut copy of the movie, it had been restored to its original theatrical version, which was fine by me because by that time, the extra TV footage left very little impression on me. I understood the ineffective waste of time additional footage brought to most motion pictures that were already considered great as they were. Apparently, I was already asking the question of why Hollywood and television couldn't just leave well enough alone. As the old saying goes, why fix it if it ain't broke?

Now

How far we've come since *Superman—The Movie*: three sequels within the original franchise, a 2006 reboot by Bryan Singer, and three *Man of Steel* films (so far). It's easy to claim that the recent Superman films of the twenty-first century are more exciting and offer harder, more fast-paced action than its originators. But the story of Superman, in my opinion, remains a deeply spiritual one of a man from another world trying his best to fit in among people who may or may not fully understand who and what he is. The first *Man of Steel* film of 2013 *does* accomplish this in an admirable and effective manner, but there's a true sensitivity to Christopher Reeve and his performance in the first film that I've never let go of all these years.

The film begins with a strong spirit of family that is most evident in the speech that Marlon Brando as Jor-El makes to his infant son just before taking off on his journey:

> *You will travel far, my little Kal-El. But we will never leave you, even in the face of our deaths. The richness of our lives shall be yours. All that I have,*

all that I've learned, everything I feel—all this and more I bequeath you, my son. You will carry me inside you all the days of your life. You will make my strength your own, and see my life through your eyes, as your life will be seen through mine. The son becomes the father and the father the son. This is all I, all I can send you, Kal-El.

The spirit of family continues in 1950's Smallville in a picture-perfect setting that would've made famed artist Norman Rockwell proud. Knowing full well he's adopted, Clark Kent is nonetheless a content boy as seen through the trusting relationship with his Earth father, Jonathan, and the tender relationship with his mother, Martha, at the time he decides he must leave her to pursue his destiny.

There's also an interesting underlying sexual content to *Superman—The Movie* that I was too young to recognize as a kid. Back then, I didn't understand Lois Lane's almost desperate need to "know" Superman by asking him if he was married as her first interview question, as well as her second question of *"How big are you?"* when what she really meant to ask was *"How tall are you?"* I didn't understand her implications in having him confirm if the rest of his bodily functions were "normal." I didn't understand that she was basically making sure that Superman did, indeed, like women (and liked pleasing them orally too, I suppose) by asking him, *"Do you like pink?"* Well, as movie audiences would've fully expected back then, Superman answered, *"I like pink very much, Lois."* Ah, the hidden sexual and subliminal messages you come to realize as you get older.

Above all, *Superman—The Movie* remains a delightful combination of old-fashioned ideas like heroes, villains, romance, swashbuckling adventure, and groundbreaking special effects that doesn't feel old or dated. It's pure fun and entertainment for a man as myself who's never considered himself an expert (or even an amateur) of the comic book genre. I don't take such stories too seriously and seek to only satisfy my cravings for fun, but with also the right touch of intelligence, charm, and wit. Unlike some of the unfortunate sequels that followed, the film does know when to take itself seriously, in particular with gifted and veteran actors like Marlon Brando and Gene Hackman, while still knowing just when to be cute and fun without being over-the-top campy. It's a film that still takes me back to that glorious moment back in '78 when I learned that my mother, if she truly applied herself, could have just as much fun at the movies as her two boys did when the right moment struck her.

Invasion of the Body Snatchers

Directed by Phillip Kaufman
(December 20, 1978, U.S. Release Date)

Then

The 1978 remake (though I didn't know it was a remake at the time) of *Invasion of the Body Snatchers* was the first movie in a long line of childhood movies in which I'd actually lie to my parents about what I was doing with my friends in order to sneak away and see a movie they'd likely never let me see themselves, many of them often scary movies. This first effort proved very easy, the lie to my parents being that I would spend a couple of hours at a friend's apartment in another part of the complex. The movie was PG-rated, so there would be no trouble getting into the theater. I only needed to scrounge the ticket money out of my weekly allowance. Considering the cost for a child at that resident theater was just a mere one dollar, it wasn't difficult.

Having already experienced the outer space adventures of *Star Wars* and *Close Encounters*, the opening scene of a race of mysterious creatures abandoning their own world to establish themselves in the city of planet Earth's San Francisco was an immediately captivating image. I took special note that the invading entity was more of a plant rather than the stereotypical ugly space creature that had been so typical in the movies before. I can't realistically claim that I fully understood what the alien's assimilation into a pink flower stood for, but I sensed there was real trouble on the way as soon as Brooke Adam's

153

character Elizabeth, picked it, smelled it, and brought it home with her. The people of the city were soon becoming different and changing their personalities in a way that took away all traces of emotion. I could easily comprehend that ordinary people were being copied by these alien invaders, though I didn't follow the concept of public fear and paranoia and what its meaning and even homage to the original black and white movie meant. People were clearly afraid though, and that was enough to create a dark feeling of terror in the movie without the use of unnecessary violence. The secrets behind the great mystery of the alien invaders became clearer when we learned the real danger ordinary people faced was falling asleep, in which their human bodies were copied by alien pods. The scene when Donald Sutherland's character Matthew Bennell was copied in the backyard garden totally freaked me out. No blood or violence, but rather a series of creepy sound effects that accompanied a gross-looking birth of Bennell's alternate version of himself. There was also the image of Bennell sleeping, a sleep that didn't look peaceful but a rather disturbing-looking version of rapid eye movement as he was completely unaware of what was happening to him just a few short feet away.

This was the first time I saw the actor who played Mr. Spock on *Star Trek* in anything else but that iconic character. I was surprised to learn that he was just another one of the copied alien creatures and was determined to do his part in defeating what appeared to be the only good (and human) people left in San Francisco. I remember cringing just a bit when he produced that large hypodermic needle and stuck it into the arms of our two heroes. Now they'd fall asleep, and all hope for the good people of our planet would be lost. But this is actually where the movie became more exciting because now Matthew and Elizabeth were on the run and hiding from the copied human creatures with loud, squeaky, and shrilling voices that filled the night skies of the dark streets, all the while trying not to fall asleep.

After a night of running for their lives, the movie dissolved into a scene of the next morning and Matthew was walking by himself in a rather calm state. It looked to me as if everything had turned out okay with him, and he was merely walking among the copied people of the city in an effort to disguise his true self and perhaps even escape. I fully expected that presumption to be confirmed when his friend Nancy got his attention and told him they didn't get her either. What followed was shocking and horrifying. Matthew slowly opened his mouth and uttered that horrible shriek to reveal that they had indeed not only gotten him in the end, but he was now alerting his comrades to Nancy's presence, which would surely mean the end of her as well. His face was frightening and hideous, an image which I've never forgotten and one that still gives me the slightest case of the "heebeegeebees" even today.

Leaving the theater with my friends, I realized I'd lied to my parents to see this, and I only hoped that no one else in the complex would see me exit the movie and rat me out to them. Nonetheless, I'd achieved forbidden admittance to a scary movie and felt just a little older and a little more privileged for it. I watched the movie again on October 24, 1980, when it premiered on the *ABC Friday Night Movie* and without the supervision of my parents (again, too busy watching *Dallas*). It was, by all accounts of my memory, left more or less in tact, with the obvious edits to language and anything that may have been considered bloody or visually gross, though I can't imagine there was much of that to deal with except for the birth of Matthew Bennell's copy in the backyard garden. That was still pretty creepy, even for an edited-for-television version.

Now

To date, there have been *four* film versions of Jack Finney's original 1955 novel *The Body Snatchers*, including a pointless 2007 version with Daniel Craig and Nicole Kidman. As a general rule, I believe remakes are incapable of outdoing their original film versions. But as an additional general rule, I also believe there are exceptions to that first general rule. Phillip Kaufman's bold version of *Invasion of the Body Snatchers*, in my opinion, not only surpasses its black and white predecessor (though that's still a great film) and the two that followed, but is also one of the best film remakes I've ever seen, particularly in the horror and science fiction genre. It's not only a thrilling sci-fi spectacle, but it also matches the original classic in its horrific tone and effect and manages to exceed it in both conception and execution. It effectively updates itself from the Cold War fear of the '50s with the modern background of the '70s and also a film where the director knows just how to properly borrow the right inspiration from terrifying predecessors like *The Exorcist, Carrie,* and *The Omen,* which knew just how to offer the right amount of fear and creepiness without necessarily going too far overboard with traditional blood, guts, and filth.

The film's PG rating back in the day (today it would've surely earned a PG-13) was a truly scary event not only in story, but in the effect it could have on its viewers who enjoy a good scare or in my case, as a boy who was looking to initiate himself into a good scare. Not that I'm overly proud of having lied to my parents to get to see this movie, but I was never exactly ashamed of it either. After all, I did it again and again in order to see scary movies with my friends, and let's face it—it's not exactly like I was lying in order to steal, cheat, or get involved with the wrong crowd of kids or discover illegal substances. It was just the movies, so I have no regrets about being less-than-an-honest kid.

*****

This is the last film of 1978 I shall discuss in any great detail.

I'll cap things off by discussing the influence of two motion pictures from 1973 which I was fortunate enough to discover during this particular year of my boyhood (unfortunately *The Exorcist* was not one of them. I was still too young). During the summer of '78, when films like *Grease, Jaws 2,* and the rerelease of *Star Wars* were going strong, Universal Pictures rereleased George Lucas's second film *American Graffiti* in theaters. The newspaper ad of the updated movie poster boasted the fact that many of the film's principal actors, who were unknowns back in '73, were now famous and the poster was inviting us to *look again!* It was five years later and Richard Dreyfuss had *Jaws, Close Encounters,* and *The Goodbye Girl* under his belt; Harrison Ford had *Star Wars* under his; and Ron Howard, Cindy

Williams, and Suzanne Somers had ABC's *Happy Days, Laverne & Shirley*, and *Three's Company* under theirs, respectively. The timing and the marketing were perfect for Universal to rake in a little more box office profits from this critically-acclaimed smash hit, coming-of-age comic tale of youth, circa 1962. The rereleased version also promised a few extra minutes of bonus footage and for the first time, shown in full Dolby Stereophonic Sound. I suppose such a promotion really meant something to those who grew up on its Doo-Wop rock and roll soundtrack, as did my father. It was because of my father that I was already familiar with the legacy of *American Graffiti*. He grew up on the music of that era, and he still loved it when I was a kid (he still does today). So when I asked him if he'd take me to see it, he barely hesitated before saying yes.

At first I couldn't believe I was watching a movie made by the same man who'd made *Star Wars*. This was a completely different kind of story, but it made a little more sense to me when my father explained that it was a story based on many of Lucas's experiences when he was the same age as these young people back in the early '60s. It was a simple tale of a group of friends who were spending one last night together after graduating high school before they were destined to go their separate ways to seek their own private futures. I enjoyed watching and laughing at their wild antics, and they did it all without an over-excessive amount of profanity or filth. The most endearing memory I have though, was watching my father lip-sync every word to every Doo-Wop song featured in the film's soundtrack. The man clearly knew his stuff, and I suppose it was watching a movie with someone who could truly take it all to heart that made the experience just a little more special for a boy who was merely experiencing a taste of our pop culture past from a filmmaker who'd already changed his young life with the greatest space fantasy movie ever made. When the movie made its TV premiere on the *NBC Big Event* on February 18, 1979, my father and I sat down to watch it again, and in a very special way, I felt just a little closer to him because of his love for this movie.

Today, my love for *American Graffiti* remains unaltered. It remains a fine testament of who Lucas was before the "empire" of the *Star Wars* universe corrupted his original creativity and is, in my opinion, the best film ever made about youth. It remains a poignant tribute to the things that matter most to us when we're young; the music that defines our life and our generation and our social interactions through the cars we drive. Today's generation of kids whose only definition of their youth is expressed through social media and phone texting may not understand what I'm talking about or what a man like Lucas was trying to say, but it's through *American Graffiti* that we may still understand what it means to be young and carefree and to also be just a little bit afraid of our future as responsible adults.

The second film of '73 was George Roy Hill's *The Sting* when it premiered on the *ABC Sunday Night Movie* on November 5, 1978. I remember it began an hour earlier than the usual broadcast start time of 9 p.m., which meant I could stay up to watch a lot more of, if not all, of the movie on a school night. I immediately recognized the opening music of Scott Joplin's "The Entertainer" because I'd previously heard it in elementary school during a school play. I was also aware of its principal actors, Paul Newman, Robert Redford, and Robert Shaw.

Although I had some knowledge of what a con artist was (though I'd have called such a person a *cheater* at that age), I didn't fully understand the intricate plotting of the cons and scams that took place in the old city of Chicago during the Great Depression of the 1930s. Still, there was a degree of fun and pleasure involved in watching a group of men who were scheming to take away a large amount of money from a hard criminal who was responsible for the murder of their friend. When they managed to pull off their con in the end and I learned that Redford's character was only pretending to be dead after Newman only pretended to shoot him, I felt a huge smile develop on my face, as if I'd been privileged to be let in on the whole thing in the end. This was, perhaps, the first time I learned what the craft of the twist ending and the big pay-off meant in screenwriting. In this case, it meant the good guys won and the bad guys lost, and that's what was most often fun about the movies, even on TV. The film continues to prove just how effective the on-screen chemistry was between the late Paul Newman and Robert Redford.

It was their second (and last) film together after *Butch Cassidy and the Sundance Kid* in 1969, and it's a real shame they never worked together again. It's a simple film that easily influenced others like it of crime, cons, scams, and heists, though none of them, in my opinion, come close to *The Sting's* charm and grace. It can be called a stylish costume piece, but there's just that right touch of deception and nastiness to remind us that it's not just a tale of the innocence of a forgotten era, but rather a twisted reminder that in life, it's not necessarily how you play the game, but how you win it.

And that, my friends, was the year 1978 for me.

THE YEAR WAS 1979 ...

- Full diplomatic relations are established between the United States and the People's Republic of China.
- After nearly fifteen years in exile, the Ayatollah Khomeini returns to Tehran, Iran.
- In Pennsylvania, the most serious nuclear power plant accident in America's history occurs at Three Mile Island.
- Margaret Thatcher becomes Great Britain's first female prime minister.
- The United States Embassy in Tehran, Iran, is seized by a group of Muslim Iranian students, and fifty-two American students and diplomats are held hostage for four hundred forty-four days.
- In Cincinnati, eleven people are killed during a crowded rush for unreserved seats at a concert for The Who.

... AND THERE WERE MOVIES!

For me, the year 1979 pretty much began as the previous year had ended. My family was still living in North Shore Towers, and the new family beach house was sitting tight waiting for us to return for our second season.

Superman—The Movie was still going strong in theaters, and *Star Wars* was taking another theatrical hiatus before it would be rereleased again during the coming summer. The spring of '79 is actually a blur for me because except for sitting through the PG version of *Saturday Night Fever* twice, I recall little of what I went to see at the movies before the summer blockbuster season eventually arrived. I have a vague memory of seeing a sports comedy called *Fast Break* with Gabe Kaplan. I have no memory of it and I haven't seen it since I was a kid, but it makes sense that I'd want to see such a movie because I was a serious fan of *Welcome Back, Kotter*. If Mr. Gabe Kotter was in the movie, I'm sure I expected it to be funny (I don't remember if it was or not).

My moviegoing experiences wouldn't really begin that year until the summer arrived and school was out. I was already anticipating the arrival of the second *Rocky* movie, as well as the new James Bond movie that took place in outer space. Whatever else might fill the gap of time between those two anticipations, I was still to discover. I hardly expected the gap would begin with a musical about the hippie culture of the 1960s.

Hair

Directed by Milos Forman
(March 14, 1979, U.S. Release Date)

Then

My family went to see *Hair* in Westhampton Beach about two months after it was originally released. Having already committed ourselves to sitting through *Grease* six times, it was pretty obvious we'd found a new taste for the modern musical of the '70s. As far as I was aware, my parents had never seen the original Broadway production because the story was nothing they could relate to. These two were married and fully domesticated in 1964 before the entire rock and roll hippie culture ever began, and when it finally did arrive, I'm sure, like many other American conservatives, they believed the entire movement and culture was a harsh insult to what was considered traditional values for the common, decent man and woman. Not to suggest I agree or disagree with such attitudes, but this is what they were like. However, seeing *Hair* was their idea, and I gladly tagged along.

As a twelve-year-old kid, I considered myself reasonably smart enough to figure out most plotlines in the movies I saw. However, for the life of me, as we sat through *Hair*, the fact that the movie took place during the late '60s went completely over my head. Despite the music and the fashion of its cast, I assumed the story took place in the present day. Where my brain was, I don't know. Still, my clue- lessness didn't stop me from becoming engrossed in this musical. A newspaper critic called *Hair* "the Star Wars of musicals," and I was beginning to see why. The movie started out slow with the simple scene of a young man saying goodbye to his father and boarding a bus for New York City. The music started, and before I knew it, the screen exploded into a song and dance frenzy in the middle of Central Park to the song *"Aquarius."*

Musicals being the fun they were for me back then, it mattered little whether or not I understood what was happening when the characters weren't singing and dancing. I didn't comprehend the act of getting stoned or high on mind-altering drugs. I didn't understand that there was a war taking place overseas in a country called Vietnam. I didn't understand the hippie culture or the rebelious nature against modern America that had made them a part of history. I only understood that I was enjoying the fact that the characters of this movie were interesting, colorful, and full of spirit, particularly that of Berger played by this actor I'd never heard of before called Treat Williams (Treat? That was really somebody's *first name?*), and a man who called himself Hud.

The songs had a certain energy and edge to them, unlike the campy fun of those in *Grease*. I remember smiling with a certain wicked joy when I watched Berger brazenly dance across the long dining table at the private party while singing *"I Got Life"* and the title track of *"Hair"* sung in the prison and on the street as Berger strutted his stuff along the sidewalk. As the story progressed closer to climax, even through all the fun of the music, I could see that things were getting more serious. The carefree scenes of Central Park and private parties had switched to a United States Army base. Through trickery, deception, and confusion, Berger ended up in an Army uniform and was mistaken for one of its soldiers. A prank played by a group of misfits had gone very wrong, and Berger was now boarding a plane with other soldiers off to war. Even as he was singing the opening chords of what would become *"Let The Sun Shine In,"* I knew he was going to die, even if we wouldn't actually see it. My feeling was confirmed during the final scene of the movie when his friends stood before his grave as the song continued and closed with a shot of a huge group of people gathered together in Washington DC. Again, I didn't understand that they were protesting our American government's involvement in the Vietnam War. I only recognized the epic conclusion to the song.

Seeing *Hair* as a young boy enabled me to recognize the movie musical as something deeper and darker than the usual material. Remember also that with the exception of *Grease* and any of the '70's live-action Disney rereleases, I'd seen very few musicals on screen to make any comparisons with. I left the theater grateful for being exposed to something a little different, and in a strange way, felt just a little older because of it. I didn't see it again until years later when I was in high school and managed to tape it off HBO. I was surprised to discover that Beverly D'Angleo, the woman who'd played Mrs. Clark W. Griswald in *National Lampoon's Vacation*, was in it the whole time (so was Charlotte Rae and Nell Carter, from NBC's *The Facts of Life* and *Gimme A Break!*, respectively).

Now

As a general rule, I find most movie musicals too cute and too campy for my tastes and patience. I tend to switch the channel if I turn on *Turner Classic Movies* and there's a musical playing. There have, of course, been exceptions. *Grease*, of course, remains a favorite for all of my personal childhood reasons. The 2002 film *Chicago* has some good moments in it, particularly the scene of a large group of sexy jailed women singing and dancing to *"He Had it Coming."* Even the 2005 film version of *Rent* holds my attention with a degree of enthusiasm (this is what happens when you're married to a woman who loves musicals. Sometimes you get dragged to them and it eventually rubs off on you).

For me, to actually claim to have a favorite movie in a genre I don't favor too much is a difficult one. If I take stock of what I appreciate most in a musical; a darker edge and some seriousness while still maintaining a degree of fun to music that's more in the style of rock and roll than the traditional show tune music and lyrics, then my mind and heart still go with the film version of *Hair* and the piece of history it represents. I'm also intrigued with the career progression that Treat Williams has taken since his early (though not his first) motion picture role in this film. I followed him as a boy through his next several roles that included Steven Spielberg's *1941*, Sidney Lumet's *Prince of the City*, and Sergio Leone's *Once Upon a Time in America*. He's an actor I've long admired for his combination of severe intensity and boyish charm, especially when he smiles that devilish smile of his. John Savage later caught my attention when I was old enough to see the late Michael's Cimino's *The Deer Hunter* and even enjoyed his brief cameo role in Spike Lee's *Do The Right Thing*.

Over the years, I've learned just how much the plot and musical soundtrack of the film version of *Hair* differs from the original Broadway production. I've also discovered I don't particularly *care*. I was exposed to the movie theater before the Broadway stage, and like it or not, right or wrong, it's the version my childhood memories and my current adult appreciations cling to. In 2009, I finally saw a revival of *Hair* on Broadway, and while it maintained the same fun I'd expect, I felt disappointed because there was just too much content that differed from the film that had become all too familiar since I was a kid. Were I a greater fan of musicals, then perhaps I would've kept a more open mind about it. But I am, unfortunately, a very stubborn man who allows himself to be held prisoner by his very thick and meaningful childhood feelings and memories of the movies (if I weren't, then you probably wouldn't be reading this book right now).

The China Syndrome

Directed by James Bridges
(March 16, 1979, U.S. Release Date)

Then

By the time I saw *The China Syndrome*, it was more than six months after its initial release and was part of a second-run double feature with Norman Jewison's *And Justice For All*. It was one of those situations when your parents drop you off at the movies by yourself so they can use the time to do their own thing, whatever it may be. Obviously, I didn't object to spending my afternoon at the movies, especially when the second feature was R-rated. Considering, however, that it was December 1979 by the time I saw this movie, I'd already missed the overwhelming controversy surrounding it. I was old enough to understand that nuclear power was considered dangerous and life-threatening by many, but as it turned out, I'd missed out on the subject of life ironically imitating art when the horrific accident at Three Mile Island in Pennsylvania occurred on March 28, 1979, just *twelve days* after *The China Syndrome* opened in theaters (it's just like I said at the beginning of this book: movies are history and history is movies). Realizing now that nothing gives a new movie a little push like public controversy, I'm sure (I hope) that no one at Columbia Pictures at the time would've wished for such a dangerous event to occur just to help encourage movie ticket box office sales.

Watching *The China Syndrome* as a twelve-year-old boy was an exercise in diving into an adult world that didn't involve romance, comedy, or even music and dancing. Although it was virtually impossible for me to fully understand all the intricate details involved in the subject of nuclear power, it was clear that this was a serious subject with dangerous consequences if something ever went wrong. Long before the age we live in now, when things we're not meant to see somehow end up being filmed on camera or a smartphone, I can remember feeling a sense of dangerous fascination when the camera zoomed in on the hand of Michael Douglas as he secretly filmed the crisis that was taking place at the Ventana nuclear power plant, particularly after he'd been previously warned that he wasn't permitted to shoot any activity taking place down at the control room. He'd just disobeyed his orders, and now he had the entire incident on film. Clearly, this was the point of action where the movie was going to really take off from. I remember that feeling of fascination quickly turning to dread during the scene when we learned that the power plant came seriously close to a core meltdown and that all of southern California was very lucky to be alive.

Television news reporter Kimberly Wells was an interesting woman. She was strong, feisty, and genuinely interested in exposing the big story, but she also seemed ready, willing, and able to bow down to those she worked for when she was instructed to back off the big story. As she developed her relationship with the plant supervisor Jack Godell played by Jack Lemmon (I remembered him from *Airport '77*), I couldn't decide if she was doing it because she was just a nice woman or if she was simply using him to get closer to the story. Whatever her reasons, she was an admirable woman whose only true pursuit was the truth. But in this grown-up movie of flawed characters, that also meant lying, cheating, and even murder in order to ultimately hide the truth from the general public. Still, I experienced fascination and dread with *The China Syndrome*, and it wasn't over yet.

By the time Jack Godell, in his own effort to uncover the truth about the power plant's dangers, picked up a gun and took over the control room, my previous feelings and emotions had been replaced outright with genuine fear. Jack was obviously a good man who wanted to do the right thing, but even at my young age, I could clearly recognize when even a good man like Jack was very likely going to die in the end. Even before that inevitably happened, I recall feeling like I wanted to reach out and touch the screen in order to help Jack get his words out more clearly in front of the TV camera. Here he was, with the chance to tell the truth for all those who were watching him, and he was rambling on like a blundering idiot. Now fear was replaced with anger. I wanted to shout out, "Wake up, stupid! Get ahold of yourself and say what you have to say in plain English!" That didn't happen though. In the end, Jack was shot to death by the police just after the television feed was cut off and it looked like the bad guys trying to hide the truth had won.

Having been educated by *The China Syndrome*, what did I learn? I learned the world had real dangers in it that could kill us. I learned that while there are good people out there, even those in the media that choose to risk their jobs and their lives to expose the truth to the people, there are also those who'll stop at nothing to prevent such righteousness. I learned the meaning of the word cover-up and that sometimes dreadful acts as murder (or attempted murder) are carried out by such people. Most of all, I leaned that the movies didn't exist to just show us the fun and the fantastic. Sometimes they existed to show us a piece of the real world as it was with its real dangers and its bad people.

Now

The China Syndrome remains a powerful and effective thriller that raises the very unsettling issues of just how safe or unsafe a nuclear power plant really is. The film is backed up by very well-crafted performances by Jane Fonda, Michael Douglas, and Jack Lemmon. It's a story of fiction, of course, but it's fiction based on very real dangers and real-life incidents that took place at nuclear power plants prior to the film's creation. It works well to frighten us at the possibilities of what can and will go wrong. Even the simplest shot of a graph needle making the wrong move or going in the wrong direction can get our nerves knotted up in a twist. But even these fears wouldn't work as well as they do if they weren't backed up by gifted actors who know how to take our fear to the highest level. The fear is still, nonetheless, a complicated one. Many films offer the fear of real-life dangers that exist in the world. Where I think this succeeds above others is the fact that there's no accompanying soundtrack involved. Think about it: there's no music in the film other than what we might hear in the background at a bar or a party. Like a film shot in real time or even a genuine documentary, we become a part of what's going on in the world and those who seek to either make it better or worse. Because, you see, in the real world, there is no soundtrack score.

While the film's subject matter remains a scary and thought-provoking one, I can't help but wonder how frightened we still need be of nuclear power in the twenty-first century world where the fear and uncertainty of terrorist acts against humanity occupy our minds and hearts more than anything else. With all the protesting we see on TV today against unpopular politicians and cops who shoot unarmed African American citizens, when was the last time a formal protest against nuclear power was organized? When was the last time rock stars like Neil Young and Jackson Browne played a *"No Nukes"* concert? When was the last nuclear power plant accident that caught the world's attention since Chernobyl of the former Soviet Union in 1986?

When was the last time you were *afraid* of nuclear power?

Battlestar Galactica

Directed by Richard A. Colla
(May 18, 1979, U.S. Release Date)

※((◎))※

Then

After *Star Wars* shook up the entire world, ABC's three-hour sci-fi pilot movie of *Battlestar Galactica* may have been the most anticipated television show for the fall '78 season. But I faced a real problem with the premiere of this new show. On that same night of Sunday, September 17, 1978, the second part of the premiere of *King Kong* was concluding on the *NBC Big Event*, and I had a serious choice to make. I'd seen *Kong* already in the theater (twice), so it's not like I'd miss anything I wasn't already familiar with. On the other hand, the first part of the movie featured additional footage not shown in theaters and I'd already gotten caught up in it all over again, so how could I possibly abandon the ride I was on by switching channels and watching something brand new, even sci-fi? In the end, I remained faithful to the giant ape over the new space epic that was already being called a blatant rip-off of George Lucas's masterpiece.

As it turned out, my decision wasn't too unfortunate. While the pilot movie of *Battlestar Galactica* was airing and I was engrossed in a different channel, the three-hour broadcast was interrupted for more than an hour to televise the signing of the Camp David Peace Accords between Anwar Sadat of Egypt and Menachem Begin of Israel, as it was overseen by our own president of the United States, Jimmy Carter. The movie resumed where it left off once the breaking news story was concluded. Had I chosen to watch *Galactica* over *Kong*, I would've only seen a small portion of it before having to go to bed. Now, you'd think that NBC would've interrupted their movie broadcast for the same reason, but despite my great memory being what it is, I honestly cannot recall such a thing happening. My memory tells me that I watched all of part two of *Kong* that night. Is that memory truly and one hundred percent accurate beyond my most reasonable ability? I may never know that without the aid of hypnosis, so I suppose you'll just have to take my word for it.

Following that Sunday night, I watched *Battlestar Galactica* religiously every week until the show was finally cancelled after only one season (I even tried to watch its ABC spin-off *Galactica 1980* some time later, but it didn't hold my interest for too long). But I was watching the original series under a severe handicap because I didn't have the opportunity to see the pilot movie and understand how all of this began. It didn't matter though, because when you're a young boy watching any sort of sci-fi action on screen or TV, plot details almost never matter. You just want to see space battles and laser blasters being fired.

Then, in May 1979, something happened that was, by my experience, completely unprecedented in the world of movies. Universal Pictures released the original three-hour television pilot movie as a reedit and recut theatrical release in theaters. Wait a minute—this thing had already been on TV eight months ago. Why would anyone in their right mind pay good money to see something in the theater that they'd already seen on free TV? I suppose, in my particular case, the key words in that question are "already seen." I *hadn't* seen the pilot, and here was the opportunity to not only make up for that, but to also see it on the big screen.

Battlestar Galactica was released in theaters in a format back in the '70s known as *Sensurround*. Developed in conjunction with Universal, this was an audio-enhancing experience that added extended range to the bass of a movie's sound effects that was more often *felt* than heard, providing a very vivid and realistic depiction of explosions, earth tremors, and even amusement park rides. Theater managers actually warned people seeing movies in *Sensurround* that they would assume no responsibility for emotional or physical reactions of the individual viewer to this new movie theater effect. *Battlestar Galactica* was the last of only four movies to incorporate this effect, the prior ones being *Earthquake* in '74, *Midway* in '76, and *Rollercoaster* in '77 (a post-apocalyptic thriller called *Damnation Alley*, also in '77, used a similar effect known as "SOUND 360"). This format proved very expensive and commercially unjustifiable for many theater owners and didn't last beyond the titles mentioned. Since I had no formal frame of reference or comparison from not having seen the pilot movie on TV, I approached the theatrical version with a fresh and untainted perspective. Thankfully, it played at the local movie theater in town, but it was not equipped with the technological requirements to show it in *Sensurround*. Therefore, I saw it only in its basic format and to this day, I've never experienced the supposedly "feel it" effects of that short-lived motion picture technology.

Initially, the '79 movie version of *Galactica* began just as it did on TV, with the traditional opening score by Stu Phillips, offering an immediate feeling of familiarity. One of the benefits from seeing *Star Wars* a couple of times was that I realized the genre of modern science fiction didn't necessarily require an in-depth knowledge or understanding of the plot details or backstory in order to enjoy what I was watching. This movie's tales of the ancient colonies, the Council of the Twelve, and the numerous references made to Greek mythology weren't easily interpreted by my twelve-year-old mind, or perhaps it was just that I didn't care. The very basic plot elements of good versus evil between the human race and the Cylon warriors were easy enough to understand on the same level that the Rebellion did battle against the evil Galactic Empire. As a kid, what else do you need to know and understand when you're watching an epic space battle on the big screen?

Some of the missing pieces were still coming together regarding the events that took place before the weekly TV series began its run. Now I understood the personal tragedy that took place when Commander Adama and his son Apollo lost younger brother Zak (whom I later realized was played by rock star Rick Springfield) in the opening space battle. I was learning just how Apollo came to meet and hook up with his bride Serina (played by Jane Seymour) and her son Boxey before she was subsequently killed off on only the second episode of the series. Most importantly, though, I realized just why the battlestar Galactica was (seemingly) the only rag-tag spaceship that existed in this galaxy and why they were searching for the planet Earth in the first place.

The true surprise of this movie came at the end when, after just over two hours, the entire story concluded itself, thus practically suggesting that the entire TV series that followed never existed at all. In the movie version, the evil character of Baltar was executed by the Cylons rather than be spared by their mercy, so that no human being whatsoever would remain alive to ever challenge them. The Cylon's base ship was also destroyed, thus suggesting that they'd no longer be a threat to the human race as they continued their journey toward Earth. We who followed the TV series, however, knew differently.

Exiting the theater, I felt better experienced in the history and backstory of *Battlestar Galactica*. Unfortunately, by May '79, the series was cancelled and I had only my weekly Sunday night memories to put the pieces together in one glorious bundle. It was also a great way to begin a year that continued to be filled with more exciting sci-fi screen features. I also learned that Universal pulled the same marketing stunt a couple of months earlier with their pilot movie for NBC's *Buck Rodgers in the 25th Century*. While considerably cheesier than *Galactica*, in my opinion, it was another TV series that I, nonetheless, followed religiously as a kid week after week.

Now

I've not had the opportunity to revisit much of the original *Battlestar Galactica* TV series since I was a kid, other than pieces of it here and there on the Syfy Channel (I tried and failed to get into the 2003 reboot series). In my opinion, many of the episodes look the same to me. I'm not a die-hard sci-fi geek (pardon the term), so I don't take the time and energy to fully dissect and analyze each and every episode and its specific content. That being the case, my only real appreciation for *Galactica* to this day remains in the theatrical motion picture of the television pilot called *Saga of a Star World*. This single, stand-alone film remains a more-than-sufficient requirement to fill my needs for a beloved TV series that (briefly) captured the imagination of kids like myself who loved *Star Wars* and couldn't wait until Sunday night of every week when we could, even for just one hour, reexperience the glory of such sci-fi epic battles and dramas in outer space.

While not a perfect film, the performances of its primary actors Lorne Greene, Richard Hatch, and Dirk Benedict are, at best, wooden to the point where they're suitable for what's still, primarily, a TV movie. There are times when it gets cheesy, particularly the trio of alien female lounge singers who, in my opinion, resemble a knock-off (or maybe homage) to the nightclub trio of female singers in William Friedkin's 1971 film *The French Conncection*. I also find it hard to swallow when the surviving colonists manage to easily restore their happiness and their free spirits following near-annihilation when they're exposed to a Las Vegas-type casino, in which they're well fed and can (seemingly) only *win* money at the gambling tables. The space battle sequences, while looking very much like it's "spiritual father" of '77 (I suppose we can thank producer John Dykstra, who was also the lead special effects artist for *Star Wars*, for that), are exciting to watch (and a young Jane Seymour is always a pleasure to look at too). Fact is, were it not for *Star Wars* and its legacy to not only the history of cinema but also to my own cherished movie memories, the film version of *Battlestar Galactica* would be no more than a cheap and silly knock-off of a far superior piece of work (which it's often considered). As a limited theatrical release, the film was a commercial and critical flop, and perhaps deservedly so. Still, we choose to embrace the films and memories we had as children that continue to inhabit our minds and our hearts today … even if they *suck* by other people's standards.

Alien

Directed by Ridley Scott
(May 25, 1979, U.S. Release Date)

—⊳«◉»⊲—

Then

Ridley Scott's *Alien*, which he called his *"angry version of Star Wars,"*
was a tough sell with my parents. One the one hand, it was sci-fi,
and that genre was usually a safe bet for kids. On the other hand, it
was R-rated, and that was less of a safe bet. Even worse was that my
father was convinced it was a horror movie, and that was damn-near
impossible to sell to either of them. A movie poster tagline that read,
"In space no one can hear you scream," didn't help my case much.
I tried to argue that *Alien* was no worse than a common monster
movie like *Creature from the Black Lagoon* or *The Thing from Another
World* (both of which I'd seen on TV), which they had no problem with. However, the deciding factor in their favor came when my
father read a critic's review in the *New York Times* which stated that
Alien would "scare the peanuts of of your M&Ms." That rather stupid analogy was enough to convince him this was a horror movie he
felt justified in keeping his twelve-year-old son from seeing. During
that summer of '79, *Alien*, like *Jaws* four years prior, existed for me
only through buzz, reputation, advertisement, marketing, and merchandising, and like the great shark movie before it, I was excluded
from a blockbuster phenomenon. Two years later, *Alien* premiered
on HBO in May 1981. Once again, enter my friend Greg B. Like
Halloween before it, the simple task of arranging a weekend sleepover

with my middle school buddy was all it took to finally see this movie uncut and uninterrupted. Despite *Alien* being the great movie it was, I felt severely cheated, nonetheless, by seeing it for the first time on a small television screen.

Unlike *Star Wars*, *Alien* didn't begin with any level of speed, although there was an irresistible creepiness to the opening titles against the silent and dead atmosphere of outer space. Unlike the Imperial Star Destroyer, the cargo spaceship Nostromo crept onto the screen slowly and unassumingly. The movie proceeded at a slow pace as we were introduced to the seven astronauts as they awoke from their long sleep and went on to eat breakfast together. From the moment they discovered the cave on the mysterious planet they'd landed on, I knew things were about to get more exciting. After all, a movie needs time for people to discover the monster before he, she, or it can cause damage and wreak havoc. From what little exposure I had to scary movies so far, I found I was generally tolerable of them; in other words, I didn't get scared too easily. I'd be lying, however, if I didn't tell you my heart jumped when the alien creature violently sprang from its egg and attached itself onto the helmet of astronaut Kane. That brief scare was followed by the jubilant laughter of two young boys, as if what had just happened on the screen was really cool.

What followed soon after could've been considered just as cool by two young (and immature) boys, but a whole lot more disgusting and shocking nonetheless. The infamous "birth" scene of the small alien creature by Kane was, without a doubt, the most horrifying thing I'd seen in the movies so far in my young life. I was shocked, of course, but not too scared because I was intelligent enough to recognize and understand that these were motion picture special effects and nothing more, though blood-curdling as they were. One of my immediate thoughts was that my father had likely been correct about his convictions two years earlier. There was no way he'd ever let me near *Alien* had he known of this violent and bloody scene.

What followed for much of the story was your basic search-and-destroy operation, not only for the crew of the Nostromo and the alien, but for the creature itself and its determination to destroy the remaining humans. Like *Jaws*, there was a strong sense of mystery and ambiguity from not always clearly seeing the killer creature at every turn. You never knew what was lurking around any corner of the spaceship, but you knew that another crew member being killed off was not far away. While we didn't get to see the slayings in great detail, the fear and the darkness of those unseen was always there, and it made the terror all the more real (by that age, I slowly recognized such effective techniques in filmmaking and story telling). Much like Agatha Christie's novel *And Then There Were None* (which I'd read in middle school English class), or even a traditional haunted house thriller, after many of the cast members had been bumped off, there was finally the lone survivor of Ellen Ripley who now had to stand alone to face the killer alien and get off the spaceship before it would be destroyed. I'd seen movies involving a race against time before, but this was the first time I'd seen such a sequence accompanied by a computer voice telling Ripley (and us) just how much time was left to abandon the ship before destruction. This, in my opinion, was true fear; fear in knowing all too well what was going to happen along with the fear of knowing just how much time you had left to save yourself.

The climactic explosion was unlike anything I'd previously seen in sci-fi movies. It wasn't the traditional fireball I was used to, but rather an awesome spectacle of light and energy in the dead of space, and it repeated itself several times before finally disappearing into the oblivion of darkness (again, really cool). But also, I learned something new about movies and that was the ability of the filmmaker to convince its audience that what appeared to be the end of it all was not necessarily so. Greg B. knew what was going to happen because *he'd* been allowed to see *Alien* when it was new. I, on the other hand, was shocked (again) to see the alien was still alive and on board the shuttle with Ripley. She didn't react with immediate bravery and action, but was rather terrified and unsure of what to do at first, even quietly singing to herself. We watched her slowly get into her astronaut's uniform and proceed to shoot the alien with a grappling hook, forcing it out of the shuttle's open airlock door. Even when we thought the alien was *still* not defeated, she acted fast and activated the shuttle's engines and blasted the alien into outer space.

When it was over, despite having loved the movie, I went to sleep that night with a longing to see it again on screen, as it was clearly meant to be experienced. Such a thing would likely never happen because it already had it's theatrical run and was now airing on HBO, and network TV would soon follow. As it turned out, I *did* get to see *Alien* on screen in the fall of 1986 (after the James Cameron sequel *Aliens* had its theatrical run) during a midnight screening at the college campus movie theater. *This* is what experiencing and absorbing Ridley Scott's classic '79 sci-fi epic the correct way finally felt like. Space and the terror it produced was no longer a small-screen television event (though I'm still grateful to Greg B. for providing it to me nonetheless), but rather a giant-screen horror show.

Now

I've owned *Alien* since its first availability on CBS-Fox video in the '80s, right through to today's high definition Blu-Ray. Still, I couldn't resist the opportunity to see it again on screen in the fall of 2003, when it was given a limited theatrical rerelease with restored, never-before-seen footage. The footage was minor and included a fist fight between Ripley and Lambert after she (Ripley) refused to allow the possibly-contaminated crew back onto the Nostromo and also Ripley discovering the body of Dallas in a cocooned, yet still alive, state before mercifully killing him while attempting to escape from the ship. Like so many other *special editions* and *director's cuts* before it, the restored footage did little, if nothing at all, to improve the overall experience of the original film. Even Ridley Scott himself has stated, *"For all intents and purposes, I felt that the original cut of Alien was perfect. I still feel that way"*, and that the original '79 theatrical version *"remains my version of choice."* He's absolutely right.

Looking back on *Alien* now, after three direct sequels (*Aliens* being the only worthy one, in my opinion), two *Alien vs Predator* knock-offs (I didn't see them), and a recent reboot by Ridley Scott himself with *Prometheus* and *Alien: Covenant*, the original film stands out more than ever as a quintessential science fiction thriller. Unlike too many thrillers of today, which makes the point of moving things on screen as quickly as possible, *Alien* holds our attention by taking its time, waiting and pacing itself to create the proper mood of fear based not only on the terror of what we don't know, but also the fear of silence; in this case, the silence aboard the Nostromo and the unknowns that lurk behind every corner and inside every ventilation shaft. The tale of the dreaded extra-terrestrial is a deep, frightening mystery right from the very beginning when the giant ship intercepts the beacon signal from the dark and moody planet, the descent into the cave with the leathery eggs, and the inevitable evolvement of the small, newborn creature into a drooling, murderous monster.

Because the cast is a small one of only seven actors, we can focus on the personal plight of each one of them as they face their own fear of being attacked by the great monster. Unlike the traditional horror of that particular time, namely *Halloween* and *Friday the 13th*, the fear of attack is not limited to the quick kill that motion picture cuts and edits will permit us to see. *Alien* exposes us to the fear that each character is likely to not just be killed off, but to have their body attacked (dare I even say *molested?*) in a most horrible, blood-curdling way by the monster. That's the effect of true fear that not many horror films of that era knew or understood and thus, alienating (pardon the pun) this great film from the typical slasher fare. If it is, as Ridley Scott puts it, his *"angry version of Star Wars,"* then *Alien* is truly *pissed off* and taking no prisoners.

Rocky II

Directed by Sylvester Stallone
(June 15, 1979, U.S. Release Date)

Then

Rocky II may not have been the best movie of the summer of 1979, but it was the one I looked forward to seeing the most when I was twelve years old. I'd seen the original *Rocky* already (once on screen and once on CBS) and was still reeling over the fact that Rocky Balboa had unfairly and unjustly lost his championship bout with Apollo Creed. I and my family wanted restitution quickly, and we couldn't wait for June 15 to arrive so we could finally have it. But we didn't see the movie immediately upon its release. Even back in the late '70s, certain movies had a traveling circuit of their own, not too unlike the famous traveling *"roadshow engagement"* movies of the '60s. The movie opened first in East Hampton, which was further east on Long Island. From there, it opened in Southampton, a bit closer to home but not by much. We could've easily piled into the car and drove many miles to see the new *Rocky* movie, but my parents decided it was easier to wait until the movie made its way to the local theater in Westhampton Beach, which was only a very short drive into town. The waiting inevitably paid off when *Rocky II* finally opened, and my family was there on line, waiting to buy tickets.

The movie began with a format I'd never seen before in storytelling, picking up where the original *Rocky* left off. Actually, it rewound itself a bit to retell the conclusion from the fourteenth round up to the very end. From there, as the opening credits rolled, we watched the ambulance ride through the nighttime streets of Philadelphia where Rocky Balboa and Apollo Creed arrived at the hospital at the same time to verbally confront one another. Apollo was angry (actually, he seemed like a real sore winner) and dismissed Rocky's entire performance of going the distance with him as nothing more than a lucky fluke. He was determined to prove that he was the superior athlete and challenged Rocky to a rematch, which Rocky declined for reasons of immediately deciding to retire.

From there, Rocky and Adrian quietly coasted through life as newlyweds with a new house, a new car, and a new baby on the way. Except Rocky was running out of money and he wasn't experienced to do much else in life (especially do TV commercials requiring him to read cue or "dummy" cards) except be a fighter. He still had a wonderful heart, and it was this heart that prevented him from truly doing his best training to have a solid chance against Apollo for the second championship fight because Adrian didn't support him, fearing he'd go blind if he fought again. When tragedy struck and she fell into a coma while giving premature birth to their son, Rocky chose to spend all of his time at the hospital with her, reading silly poems and a western novel to her in order to remain close and help her to wake up. When she finally woke up, she surprised us all and told Rocky the only thing she wanted him to do now was, "*win!*"

Rocky II took off from that single word, and we watched him train for the big fight with the same inspirational music as before, including what was now the famous running sequence, once again to *"Gonna Fly Now."* The sequence was different this time, as if written for children because like Pied Piper, Rocky led a huge group of children behind him as he ran, including up the museum steps again. The song was also sung by children. Whereas last time Rocky met his challenges for only himself, this time he did it for the love of Adrian and his new baby boy.

The big fight was what we were waiting for. It didn't look too different from the first one, though this time there were moments of slow motion action. For a while, it looked as if Rocky was going to lose again because he got knocked down twice and fell behind in points. By the time the fifteenth round arrived, both fighters had literally beaten each other to a bloody mess. Nobody was going down, and it looked like Apollo Creed would take the prize again. I couldn't believe what happened next. Both men knocked each other down to the floor at the same time. I'd never heard of or seen such a thing in real-life boxing. The winner of the fight would be determined by who got up first. This is my strongest memory of watching *Rocky II* in the movie theater back in '79 because I, my family, and the entire theater were cheering and screaming our heads off for Rocky to get up first (even my usually reserved mother got caught up a little bit in all the joy and excitement, though not as loud). This moment could only be described as my own version of movie heaven because we were cheering for the underdog hero we loved and watching him prevail by standing up first and claiming his right and his honor to be declared champion of the world, and then finally shouting out, *"Yo, Adrian, I did it!"*

Despite the portions of the movie that dragged in its story, my family loved and embraced it for all it had to offer, which was primarily the redemption of a beloved character whom we felt was cheated the first time around (as did the audience, I'm sure). You're probably not surprised when I tell you that we stayed in our theater seats to watch the movie again (yeah, what else is new).

Now

Like it or not, *Rocky II* (even if it's *not* your favorite film in the franchise) *had* to be made. Audiences all over the world (including *this guy*) were simply not going to sit idly by and accept the way things had been left off at the end of the first film. We wanted restitution, dammit, and we sat patiently and waited for the sequel to provide it for us.

I didn't realize this at the time, and maybe it's just me, but somewhere during the course of the first and second film, Rocky's character became just a little *dumber*. Gone, I believe, is the wit and street wisdom of the character we enjoyed listening to in the first film and has now been replaced by an almost mundane simplicity. Even during the tragedy of Adrain's coma, the sadness we're supposed to experience feels limited because Sylvester Stallone (as director also, this time) doesn't take full advantage of this sequence to express his true self with an emotional speech as he'd done so well previously in the first film. It's also unfortunate that Stallone chooses to ruin certain moments of the climactic championship fight by interjecting a very common filmmaking cliché like slow motion action. It doesn't make the fight any better or more thrilling. I give him credit for creating a fresh and original way for this fight to climax, with both opponents knocking each other to oblivion until they've both fallen on the floor and it's up to the one who will have the strength, the stamina, and the spirit to get up first for us to see who'll be the new heavyweight champion of the world. I still get pumped up when I watch that scene.

Moonraker

Directed by Lewis Gilbert
(June 29, 1979, U.S. Release Date)

Then

If *The Spy Who Loved Me* was merely my introduction to the big screen world of James Bond away from the TV set, then *Moonraker* took me over the edge and beyond. By the summer of '79, I was completely pumped up on science fiction from the content of the past two years, so the prospect of Agent 007 blasting off into outer space with spaceships and laser guns was more than I needed to begin the asking (or begging) process with my parents to gain necessary admission into the local movie theater. On top of all that, according to the artwork on the movie poster, Jaws was back (oh yeah, I was *definitely* there!). As a kid, I didn't understand the concepts (if not the rules) of Hollywood marketing and money-making tactics. It didn't occur to me that studio executives at United Artists were making a desperate attempt to cash in on the popularity and financial phenomenon of sci-fi smashes like *Star Wars* and *Close Encounters* (*For Your Eyes Only* was originally supposed to follow *The Spy Who Loved Me*, before *Star Wars* came along and unexpectedly changed things). I was also unaware that at this point in the lucrative Bond franchise, the movie titles were just about all that remained in common with Bond author Ian Flemming's original novels.

I had to wait a couple of weeks before *Moonraker* finally arrived at our neighborhood movie theater. My mother took me and Kevin to see an early show on a weeknight, which meant the theater was emptier than usual. Turns out, she had a mild fondness for James Bond movies, though her tastes and appreciation were stronger for the early Sean Connery pictures of the '60s (most notably, *From Russia With Love*. She loved that one). There was a feeling of pleasant familiarity when *Moonraker* began just as all the others had, with the classic white circle and gun barrel sequence; a feeling that made me think, *It's good to be back here again!* The movie didn't waste much time in its opening action sequence with an awesome explosion of a 747 jet airliner after the Moonraker space shuttle was hijacked in midair. Without so much as a moment to breathe, James Bond was in trouble aboard a small charter plane when he was pushed out of it by Jaws without wearing a parachute. After a bit of high-flying stunts and parachute stealing, Bond was safe (of course) and Jaws went crashing into a circus tent, unharmed (of course), and all of this happened before the opening credits and song.

While I always realized and understood that James Bond movies were strictly meant to be fun and nothing else, I must confess an uneasy and stressful feeling in my stomach during the scene when Bond was strapped (and trapped) in his chair inside the centrifuge chamber. To watch a man sit so helpless as he spun around and around at an unimaginable speed with no way to stop it ... well, let's just say I stopped eating my popcorn until the scene was over and Bond was saved. That uneasy feeling returned twice again when I witnessed the terror of being chased through the woods and killed by man-eating Doberman Pinschers; this time, the victim *not* being saved, as well as the two Italian scientists who were poisoned inside their own secret biological laboratory. Yes, it was safe to say at this point, that as much fun as *Moonraker* was so far, these moments of uneasiness and pensive thought were not an expected part of the James Bond experience ... not for *me* anyway.

My mother, to my surprise, managed to "let her hair down" a bit. She was particularly intrigued by the character of Holly Goodhead (I was still too young to understand the sexually-humorous meaning behind her last name). She admired the character's strength, wit, and resilience that allowed her to keep up and hold her own against a character like James Bond. She loved watching her fight and defend herself against the astronauts under the evil billionaire known as Drax. She also loved the yellow jumpsuit she wore while aboard the Moonraker space shuttle in outer space. Leave it to my mother to always notice and appreciate a female fashion statement, even if it was part of sci-fi fiction.

All of the action, as fun and exciting as it was, was practically immaterial. I wanted the outer space part of the movie, and I wanted it *now*! Once the fleet of space shuttles lifted off and soared high into the reaches of space, I knew I was ready for it. Like *2001: A Space Odyssey* (perhaps even an homage), there were moments of the beauty and simplicity of space flight before they finally docked at the secret city in space and were now positioned for Drax's ultimate evil plan in which he would destroy the entire human race with powerful, poisonous plants inside glass globes before creating his own superior race of human beings to take their place. While I didn't fully understand how this man was going to pull that off, it still sounded like a dreaded plan to me. Like some of the other Bond movies, once James knew of the evil plot, it wasn't too long before he sprang into action with Holly and now even Jaws who'd just turned to the good side because of the the love he felt for his new girlfriend, and the serious action between good and evil began.

The moment that truly paid off for me was the battle in space with laser fire between Drax's people and the United States Marines dressed up in space gear. If the purpose of this Bond movie was to copy *Star Wars*, they'd just achieved that goal with high marks, flying colors, and a great, big gold star. During the battle aboard the space shuttle, Bond shot Drax with a poison-tipped dart and then pushed him into an airlock that ejected him to his death in outer space. In true sci-fi fashion, the great battle eventually climaxed with the destruction of the great city in space that was the heart of the evil plot and the poisonous plants in the glass globes headed toward Earth were finally destroyed by laser fire. Our heroes were safe aboard their own space shuttle, and the brute killer was now on the side of good and considered a friend. He even shocked us all by finally speaking to his new girlfriend over champagne when he said, *"Well, here's to us."*

When *Moonraker* was over, you can probably guess that I begged to stay to watch it again. Alas, though, my mother wasn't as easygoing about that as my father, particularly if she didn't like the movie, and told us it was time to go home. While there were moments she'd enjoyed, she wasn't a fan of sci-fi and never would be. Because this was the first time I'd seen what a space shuttle looked like, the first thing I did was spend some of my allowance money on a movie tie-in space shuttle model kit. The second thing I bought was a few packages of movie photo cards with a sticker and the free stick of hard bubble gum that were considered very popular with kids back in the '70s and '80s. Finally, I also purchased the novelization of the movie which was titled *James Bond and Moonraker* by Christopher Wood, having little or nothing to do with Ian Flemming's original novel. This was actually a hobby of mine as a kid; seeing popular movies and then reading the novelization. I suppose as long as I was reading books without an argument, my parents didn't object to such content.

Reflecting on the Bond movie I'd just seen, I convinced myself that the franchise was very likely over. Not realizing or understanding that Hollywood could drag out a movie franchise for as long as it wanted to, I couldn't conceive of how the movies could possibly continue after this one. Where else could 007 go after having gone through the ultimate voyage of an adventure in outer space? What else lay beyond the far reaches of that unknown? Well, apparently the answer to that question was money, money, and more money. I actually felt a small sense of disappointment when *For Your Eyes Only* was released two years later, as if a sacred position and status of James Bond movie history had been violated (that feeling inevitably didn't last too long).

I didn't see *Moonraker* again until November 22, 1981, when it premiered on the *ABC Sunday Night Movie*. In fact, November 1981 was actually a great month for me in that *Close Encounters of the Third Kind* and *Grease* also premiered on that same channel. These television premieres, as I've descriptively discussed already, were an important part of my childhood rearing in the world of motion pictures, as was the ABC network in my exposure (and *re*exposure) to the great movies of James Bond.

Now

Over the years, it's become necessary for me to acknowledge and understand that not all James Bond films in the fifty-year-plus franchise are necessarily good ones. There are, in fact, many other harder and tougher James Bond afficionados out there who'd unanimously agree that *Moonraker* isn't considered one of the better ones in the franchise. Well, to them I say, "A Bond pox on all of you!" It's my humble opinion that this is not only a great James Bond film, but one of the most underrated and underappreciated ones in the franchise, particularly of the Roger Moore period. It is, in fact, my *second* favorite James Bond film after *Thunderball*. It's unfairly picked on and mocked simply because those who made it, particularly screenwriter Christopher Wood, chose to cash in on the cinematic wonder of *Star Wars* that came along before it.

Moonraker is an easy target for being silly and campy, but take a moment to consider other, more popular James Bond films also guilty of the same "copycat" crime before it. *You Only Live Twice* from 1967 (and also directed by Lewis Gilbert) can easily be accused of choosing to bank on the historical space race of the '60s and actually features space capsules being literally "swallowed" by the ship of the film's enemy. *Live and Let Die* from 1973 can equally be accused of taking full advantage of the "blaxploitation" film genre of the time from movies like *Shaft* and *Super Fly*, even throwing in voodoo art and snakes to boot. *The Man with the Golden Gun* from 1974 can equally be accused of taking full advantage of the popularity of the kung-fu and martial arts genre of the time, thanks to the fame of Bruce Lee. You see my point? Whatever unfair and unjust crimes of filmmaking *Moonraker* can be accused of, had already been grossly committed by James Bond films of the past, in my opinion.

Now that I've made a valiant attempt to defend *Moonraker*, let me tell you why I love it so much. The first is for the very same reason most serious fans of Bond hate it. By '79, sci-fi movies were king and most of us were hooked. Like it or not, the film is a fun and action-packed vehicle of suspense and technical effects during the period of Roger Moore's run that I've always considered to be the most fun of the entire history of actors who have played the iconic role. The performances are solid and a lot less campy than those that followed in later films of the '80s. Moore is as ageless and graceful as the character of 007 he's inhabited many times. Michael Lonsdale is a villain of pure evil who's ultimate purpose of world destruction is actually quite frightening when you consider how he intends to pull it off from outer space through mass genocide by poison gases and then launch a brand-new race of superior physical human beings. If ever there was a Bond villain with a serious "Godlike" complex, Hugo Drax is surely it. Lois Chiles as Bond girl Holly Goodhead (that's the best sexually-explicit Bond girl name I've heard since Pussy Galore in *Goldfinger*) may not be in the same league with Ursula Andrews or even Jane Seymour, but she certainly tops the scale over the likes of other Bond girls like Britt Ekland in *The Man With the Golden Gun* and Denise Richards in *The World is not Enough* (the *worst Bond girl in* the franchise history!). Finally, how can you totally go wrong with Richard Keil back in action as Jaws, who is, in my opinion, the best villain's henchman since Oddjob (also from *Goldfinger*)?

Despite its initial marketing and billing as a sci-fi Bond film, less than a third of the film actually takes place in outer space. Venice, Italy, and Rio De Janeiro are beautifully and exotically photographed for this film's story and purpose. The scene in which Bond drives a hovercraft gondola around St. Mark's Square in Venice may have been widely criticised by film critics at the time (and probably still is), but it's not nearly as cheesy and stupid as the flying car in *Golden Gun* or even the *half* car that drives around the streets of Paris, France, in *A View to a Kill*. Despite its unfair reputation of absurdity over the decades, *Moonraker* was, like it or not, very successful at the box office and scored a lot more positive reviews with critics than you might think. It was a glorious part of the big year that I've come to refer as *"Sci-Fi '79"* that also included *Alien, Star Trek—The Motion Picture,* and Disney's *The Black Hole*. It was an irresistibly entertaining escapist Bond movie back in the day for a twelve-year-old boy sitting in front of the big screen, and it's still just as entertaining in my mind, my heart, and my memories.

Breaking Away

Directed by Peter Yates
(July 13, 1979, U.S. Release Date)

Then

"Eric, I'm taking you to see a *great* movie!"

That's something I *never* heard my mother say to me before. More often than not, she had to be begged to drag her butt out of the house to spend her money and her time sitting in a dark movie theater and eating cheap popcorn. But this really happened with *Breaking Away*. I hadn't heard of the movie, but apparently, she'd not only heard of it, but heard it was a fantastic movie not to be missed. It was playing locally in Westhampton Beach, and she was taking me and Kevin to see it. We weren't asked, we were *told*. Far be it from me *not* to listen to my mother if she really insisted.

I knew nothing about the movie I was about to see. The poster didn't offer much in terms of story content. Four boys sitting together on top of a grass-covered hill hardly indicated a story about bicycle racing, let alone a sports movie of any kind. But as the movie began at an old quarry location, I was intrigued by these four friends who I could tell possessed a good sense of humor. They were funny, and any movie that could make me laugh so early in its story would hold my attention for its duration.

The character of Dave Stoller was particularly amusing in how he drove his parents crazy, especially his impatient father, in his wanting to be a champion Italian bicycle racer and speaking in his own fake Italian accent. Winning seemed to be an easy thing with Dave, as he told his father, *"The victory, she was easy."* When he wasn't pretending to be an Italian, he was just the same as his other friends. Together, the four of them didn't work, nor did they try to find jobs either. They were, as my parents would have put it, "Lazy bums!" When Dave began using his front as an Italian college exchange student to try and win over a beautiful girl on campus, I couldn't help but feel that even though it was entertaining to watch him trick her like this, it wasn't going to be too long before she discovered the truth about him. Her boyfriend Rod, who was a real jerk, wasn't going to make things easy for anybody involved. Still, it was rather fun to watch a good-hearted boy like Dave work his way into the girl Katherine's heart (or "Katerina" as he called her).

The real excitement, despite all the heart and the love, was the sports drama of this movie. The first one-hundred-mile bicycle race with the Italian riders was fun to watch because it became clear that Dave was the champion he'd always set out to be, as he progressively got closer and closer to first place with his Italian racing heroes, whom he was clearly thrilled to be alongside with. My heart literally jumped and skipped a beat when all of his hopes and aspirations came crashing down (literally) when one of the Italian riders cheated in the race and stuck a tire air pump into Dave's bicycle wheel, causing him to fall and be injured. That defeat lead to his depression which, as I'd predicted, lead to his confessing his true self to Katherine. She didn't take it well and even slapped his face.

Thankfully, it wasn't over because I don't think I would've tolerated such a depressing ending. There was still the big championship, Little 500 Bicycle Race, to come. We watched our underdog hero train for the big event and even win over the heart of his intolerant father at the same time. Dave was clearly so much better than the other riders in the final race. While his college boy competitors would periodically switch cyclists every few laps, Dave kept on riding without a break, that is, until he was injured in a crash. This unfortunate incident, however, brought together his other friends who were now forced to get on the bike to make up for lost time and in the process, prove that they could also ride in an effort to maintain good team effort and spirit between them. Of course, the college jerks couldn't help but laugh when Moocher, a rather small teenager, began riding the bike that looked like it was too big for him.

For the climactic moments of the big race, Dave recovered enough to ride the rest of the race himself, with his feet taped to the bike pedals. I sat at the edge of my seat watching the bike riders go around and around the track, not entirely sure if the hero was going to win or not. At the speed in which the riders (and the movie) were going, it really could've been anybody's race. However, by the time of the big finish, Dave overtook Rod on the last lap and won for himself and his friends, who called themselves *"cutters."* I shouted and cheered in glorious joy for the heroic victory I'd had the pleasure of witnessing. My mother, to my pleasure and hers, couldn't resist the urge to express her joy as well. Kevin … well, I think he only smiled. He was never as emotional as I was at the movies.

Breaking Away was one of those rare movies that affected not only my appreciation for sports and drama in stories, but also inspired me to copy its physical efforts. Upon seeing that movie, I swear to you that I started riding my bike more often than I ever had. I even hummed the *Overture from Barber of Seville* in my head while I rode, just like in the first bike racing sequence. Yes, believe it or not, at the age of twelve, I was very familiar with that piece of classical music, thanks to the very popular Bugs Bunny cartoon called *Rabbit of Seville* (hey, sometimes our knowledge of higher culture as children *had* to come from the great rabbit himself!). In high school, I was a member of the bicycle club, though by that time, my desire to join such a group was based more on my own physical efforts and enthusiasms rather than just a mere movie. I found myself quoting Daniel Stern's character of Cyril by saying things like, *"It was somewhere along here that I lost all interest in life."* I didn't say it for long because my parents told me how stupid I sounded by making such negative statements that didn't make sense to my own life. At the time, I suppose they could've just lightened up.

The wait for its TV premiere was not a long one; May 5, 1980, on NBC. That's *less than a year* from its theatrical release date and surely unprecedented in terms of the wait time between theater and television set. My only presumption as to why the movie would come to network TV so quickly was perhaps to serve as a prerequisite and introduce what was to become a short-lived ABC series of the same name that starred ex-Hardy boy Shaun Cassidy in the role of Dave Stoller and ex-Bad News Bear Jackie Earle Haley returning as Moocher. But I suppose even *that* doesn't make much sense since it involved two competing networks (so I'm afraid I have no logical answer).

Now

Breaking Away has become so much more than a fine, dramatic sports film for me. Like *Saturday Night Fever*, I've discovered and understood a deeper meaning of social classes and the effects of social interactions and relationships behind its story and its characters. On its surface, it's clearly a simple film about a young man whose sole purpose in life is to excel in his bicycle riding. However, in a town filled with the everyday working class who are likely never to be educated beyond high school or ever leave their small town of Bloomington, Indiana, Dave Stoller exemplifies himself through his physical skills and repeated victories in his bicycle races. When he's not in his own world on his bike, Dave is as ordinary as the friends he hangs out with. This freedom comes easily as they have all made the conscious decision to avoid getting a job in order to, as Cyril puts it, "*waste the rest of their lives together.*"

Unlike the local teenagers of the town, who are often referred to as "*cutters*" because they come from families of men whose traditional job it was to cut the limestone that would eventually constitute the buildings that went up on the campus, the college kids of Indiana University, who are meant to spend only four years of their lives in Bloomington are rich, spoiled, and known to make no secret of looking down their noses at the local "*cutter*" kids. As a "*cutter*" kid himself, Dave is often not satisfied with his own identity and longs to become something more than just a local kid from the neighborhood with no job prospects and no college education. The spiritual freedom he feels on his bicycle only takes him so far, however, and he longs to be on a more equal level of the privileged college kids in town. To accomplish this, he decides to create an alternate ethnic identity for himself when he meets the beautiful college girl Katherine. Per the film's story, this is a persona he was already testing with his disapproving parents before meeting her, but one he's chosen to commit himself to now once she unexpectedly enters his life. When he's with her, he's no longer the ordinary Dave Stoller, but rather a more colorful Italian exchange student with an alternate colorful Italian name. This sudden switch in identity and character stems from his great love and admiration of Italian bicycle riders, particularly the team Cinzano.

Although Dave hasn't exactly propelled himself to the higher class level of the college kids with this alternate identity, he feels a greater sense of his own self as a fake Italian somebody rather than just a real-life common American working class nobody. His newly-found confidence is just enough to make him feel comfortable sitting in a bowling alley café with Katherine that's normally reserved for only the college kids. During an unexpected brawl involving his best friends, instead of stepping in to help them, he keeps himself well-hidden so as not to expose his secret identity to the woman he's falling in love with. From Katherine's perspective, the man she comes to know as the Italian exchange student, though not being financially well-off or of an upper-class sector, is far more interesting than the typical college jocks with inflated egos she's spent most of her time with up until now.

During the film's first bicycle sequence, Dave takes part alongside the Italian riding team Cinzano that he's come to idolize. From the Italian's perspective, they also sport an attitude that looks down not only on the common working class kids of Bloomington, Indiana, but apparently, also on Americans themselves. During the race, the Italian champions appear to be appalled and flabbergasted that a common American like Dave is not only able to keep up with them, but also has the audacity to speak Italian to them. While Dave's social intentions are to extend his friendship and admiration, the Italian team reacts with anger and malicious intent when they decide to sabotage his bike and subsequently, eliminate him from the race. Dave has not only become the victim of cheats, but has also realized the delusion he held that Italians were supposedly of a higher and more respectable social nature than those he spent his entire life around. During the drive home, his friend Mike even aids his return to reality by telling him, *"I guess you're a cutter again, just like the rest of us."*

This new moment of clarity brings him to the decision to confess to Katherine who and what he really is. His name, his physical appearance, and his very manhood remain the same, but because he's now just an everyday *"cutter"* kid of the local town who lied to her and not the exotic Italian exchange student Katherine thought he was, she reacts angrily and walks out on his life. Despite this blow to Dave's romantic life, he's still able to hold onto the fact that he's gifted in his riding skills and is determined to renew his sense of self-worth. To accomplish this, he takes part in the town's climactic bicycle race with his three best friends at his side. This will not only be a race of human strength and test of will, but shall also bring a new level of competitiveness against a group of college kids also competing in the big race.

This is the film's great moment of triumphant sports victory that audiences are meant to stand up and cheer about, but it's also a race against odds between two social classes of kids who are at the age of trying to figure out who they are, whether it's amidst the environment of the local working class residents or amidst the alternate environment of college wealth and privilege, all within the confinements of the same small town. Of course, the classic cinematic cliché in which the underdog triumphs doesn't disappoint us. Dave Stoller and his best friends win the big race and not only redeem their own self-respect, but apparently the respect of the college riding team as well, as they're seen clapping their hands at the film's end in honor of the victorious *"cutter"* kids.

The film attempts to prove that in at least the world of sports competition, there are no separating classes and those who participate are of equal standing with each other. Realistically, one cannot depart from *Breaking Away* feeling that all social prejudices and disorders in Bloomington, Indiana, will be miraculously healed on a daily basis. But for right now, the love and freedom of riding a simple bicycle appears to give us that small glimmer of hope that things *can* get better between different sorts of people ... or so we can only hope.

The Amityville Horror

Directed by Stuart Rosenberg
(July 27, 1979, U.S. Release Date)

Then

By 1979, I entered my preadolescent phase that included a real fasci-nation toward horror movies. Much of this was due to parents who wouldn't permit me to go anywhere near them. Much like anything else in life, the more you're denied something, the more you seek access to it, and the more you seek access to something as a kid, the more likely you are to sneak around to try and get it (hence, a friend like Greg B.).

There are, in my opinion, two kinds of people who watch *The Amityville Horror*: those who grew up on Long Island and those who didn't. Those who *did* probably know that on the night of November 13, 1974, a young man named Ronald DeFeo Jr. inexplicably shot and killed six members of his family inside their home at 112 Ocean Avenue in the town of Amityville, on the south shore of Long Island. This event wasn't the subject of allegations, nor was it any sort of tall-tale hoax. It was *fact*, and DeFeo is still currently serving his life sentence in prison. It's also forever stigmatized the house, as well as the town of Amityville itself. Those who did *not* may only know these facts because they read the book by Jay Anson or saw the movie. Thirteen months later, in December 1975, George and Kathy Lutz and their three children moved into that same house. Twenty-eight days later, the entire family fled the house, claiming they'd been terrorized by paranormal and supernatural forces that existed inside the house. This would eventually lead to one of the greatest hoaxes ever perpetrated on the American public. For the Lutzs, it meant books, movies, and publicity that made them infamous.

While I was just a child at the time and completely unaware of these events until the movie's release, I was, at the time, living in the town of Melville, located just ten miles and twenty-five minutes from where the *Amityville Horror* events allegedly took place. So when you take into account my desire to expose myself to horror movies accompanied with the fact that I was a Long Island resident during the time of the actual horrors (true or not), the desire to see just what sort of story *The Amityville Horror* had to tell was practically beyond my control. But I wouldn't approach the movie completely uninformed. Shortly after its initial release, I watched an episode of a TV documentary series called *In Search of The Amityville Horror* hosted by Mr. Spock himself, Leonard Nimoy. As a kid, I rarely watched documentaries and didn't yet possess the intelligence to determine whether their contents should be taken as accurate or not. I simply presumed that if it was a documentary narrated by a voice that sounded serious, it *had* to be true ... right?

So, here I was, in Greg B.'s room on the night of Friday December 26, 1980, with what I presumed would be firsthand knowledge of the events of *The Amityville Horror* simply because the guy who played Mr. Spock told me so. I recall my first thought being that it looked as if the movie had been filmed at the actual house in Amityville; the house itself seemingly identical to the real thing. Little did I realize that there were plenty of two-story Dutch Colonial homes all over the place. I also learned years later that this particular one in the movie was converted to look more like the real house and actually located in the town of Toms River, New Jersey.

The movie started with the horrible murders meant to represent the real ones that occurred in November '74. It was impossible for me to know the realities and accuracies of the mass slaying I was watching or even if it really took place in the middle of the night during a violent thunder storm, but it was still a thrilling way to begin a horror movie. The next scene was *One Year Later* and the proper introduction of what was to come next. The Lutz family was a nice family with all the traditional elements of the perfect unit, including three lovely children and a dog named Harry. While I hadn't seen a lot of haunted house movies up until then (just a couple of black and white ones on TV), I knew well enough that things weren't going to start going wrong until the family was settling into their new surroundings. The first incident didn't even happen to the Lutz family directly, but rather to the priest they called in to bless the house. Once inside the sewing room, the door slammed, a swarm of flies in the middle of winter were disturbing him, he started to feel sick and was finally ordered to *"get out!"* by a voice that sounded like the devil himself. I remember smiling and thinking that such a menacing voice was just what a haunted house horror movie needed for proper effect. I think Greg B. smiled too for the same reason.

Much of the movie's actions and implications of supernatural horror came from the simplest things like doors slamming, the front door becoming unhinged during a storm in the night, mysterious musical drumming in the middle of the night, George Lutz's reoccurring insomnia at three fifteen in the morning (the alleged time of deaths one year before), as well as his cold spells and angry moods that took over his personality. The effects of this house also took its toll on people outside the family's world, including the priest, Father Delaney, Kathy Lutz's aunt who was a nun, and George's business partner's wife too. Clearly, the R rating was largely due to bad language, nudity (I can't say I objected to seeing the late Margot Kidder from *Superman* standing partially naked in front of her bedroom mirror) and perhaps the sight of oozing blood from the walls during the movie's climax. It was that very climax that had me at the edge of my seat (or the bedroom floor). After staring at those infamous attic half-moon windows that looked more like evil eyes for nearly an hour and a half, they were finally shattered in a slow-motion shot when a huge tree came crashing through. This was clearly the final straw for the Lutz family, because it was at that moment they decided to run for their lives. Another violent thunderstorm was happening, and it was now that the walls of the house started to bleed. There was an extra degree of intensity in my mind when I watched the entire family having trouble keeping their balance as they made their way down the slimy, red stairs from one floor to another.

I think the real fear crept inside me when they realized they'd forgotten their dog Harry and George decided to risk his life by going back inside the house to get him. When Kathy opened her mouth and shouted, *"N-o-o-o-o-o!"* at her husband, I thought my heart was going to skip a beat. While George was back inside the house looking for Harry, the storm and the horror of the house was all around him, I just hoped and wished he'd get the animal quickly and get his butt back to the family van parked down the street. It wasn't going to happen so easily though. Harry was in the basement outside the dreaded "Red Room," and George fell through the stairs into the horrifying black goo before finally grabbing Harry and escaping the house for the second time. The movie was over, but even before the end credits began to roll, it was the final titles on the screen that really grabbed my attention: *"George and Kathleen Lutz and their family never reclaimed their house or their personal belongings. Today they live in another state."* Did this mean everything I'd just watched was really true? My mind raced as I tried to imagine and even presume who George and Kathleen Lutz really were and what had they really experienced when I was just an eight-year-old boy living in a town only ten miles and twenty-five minutes away from them? Did a haunted house really exist on Long Island? Did people actually live there right now? Were they scared too? How would I react if I was in the car with my family in Amityville and we drove by the actual house? Would I be excited or would I beg my father to turn the car around right now? Most of all, I was asking myself if everything Mr. Spock had told me just one year ago had been nothing but bullshit.

As a teenager, I developed what was … well, not exactly an obsession, but rather an insatiable curiosity behind the truth surrounding the events of *The Amityville Horror*. I don't claim to have permitted myself exposure to the occult or such matters, but I wanted to know just a little more if possible. I read Jay Anson's book in the latter part of 1983, when I convinced my eleventh grade English teacher that it was a viable choice for her assignment of having to read a mystery and write about it (thank you, Mrs. Reece!). Anson's words were very detailed and articulately written, giving the reader the impression that he was documenting incidents and events that had actually taken place in this world. His profile of George and Kathleen Lutz were of reasonable and rational people who had not chosen to flee in fear, a two-story Long Island home with a swimming pool and all of its interior belongings, merely over a simple case of nerves or the jitters. By the time I'd finished the book, my beliefs toward *The Amityville Horror* as a possible true story had grown just a little more. Years later, when I got my driver's license, I swore to my friends that I'd consult the map in the phone book to figure out how to get to Amityville and take a ride to 112 Ocean Avenue to finally see the infamous house for myself. I never did.

Now

We all eventually grow up (*most* of us anyway). I've given up thoughts of ever seeing the real Amityville house. Thankfully, Google Maps provides more than its fair share of photographs of what the house looks like today. Its legal address is now *108* Ocean Avenue, the infamous and dreaded half-moon or "evil eye" attic windows have been replaced with traditional double-hung windows, and about the only interesting thing about the structure itself is that its main entrance at the front façade runs perpendicular to the main road, while the homes surrounding it run parallel. *That's it.* Like it or not, it's just a traditional two-story colonial home, though its history and its cult-like following is likely to stay with it for as long as it remains standing (why it hasn't been torn down and rebuilt, I'll never understand). However, bearing in mind that the purpose of this book is movie memories and not necessarily *house* memories, I still claim the original '79 version of *The Amityville Horror* (remade in 2005) is an entertaining haunted house horror film that effectively uses the ideas of suggestion and psychological human breakdown to deliver creepiness and fear without an excessive use of violence or blood. Because it's a horror film, one must be willing to accept a certain degree of performance that may fall below the par of the full potential one might otherwise expect from talented people like James Brolin and Margot

Kidder. Their performances are as solid as you can expect for actors who must play the role of husband and wife living in fear and whose marriage is deteriorating in the face of a supernatural phenomenon. It's veteran actor Rod Steiger as Father Delaney who honestly carries the performance level of the film, despite a role that's not too large, as a man of religious faith struggling with the reality (the *film's* reality anyway) of what evil truly is and what it can do to good people. It is, however, a film of *fiction* and nothing more. Never forget that.

Despite whatever childish and adolescent curiosities I previously had toward the infamous house in the past, it's more than clear as a thinking and logical adult that the only true event that ever took place at the house on Ocean Avenue was the inexplicable slaughter of a family by a son who was clearly insane. Whatever controversies exist about that house exist only because of that crime that took place on November 13, 1974. But even those controversies and what eventually led up to *The Amityville Horror* hoax (yes, I repeat *hoax*) are fascinating and intriguing nonetheless if you have a taste (even a mild one) for tales of true crime. In 2002, I read a book written by Ric Osuna called *The Night the DeFeos Died: Reinvestigating the Amityville Murders*, which documented not only the murders themselves, but the DeFeo family and all of their dysfunctions as well. Without going into too much detail about the book, it details how DeFeo killed his family with the help of his sister Dawn and two of his friends. It's a well-written account of a true-life crime and what may or may not have led up to it. But even a seriously-written account such as this is open to controversy and discrepancy because apparently Ronald DeFeo has changed his story of what happened that night so many times over the years, it's become virtually impossible to determine what's accurate and what's not.

One issue the book does explain is how the 1974 murders were the origin of what led to George and Kathleen Lutz allegedly purchasing the house with the deliberate intent of not only creating fictional accounts of their experience there, but also deliberately fleeing the house twenty-eight days later in order to create the illusion of what they would try to sell to the public as the truth, when in fact, it was nothing more than a well-crafted and very detailed hoax that the

American people, if not the world, was stupid enough to entertain as truth. Honestly, however the Lutzs may have ended up (George and Kathleen are today deceased), I have to give them their due credit for selling a prize fable to a gullible public and managing to reap the endless rewards that came with it.

The 2013 documentary *My Amityville Horror* features interviews with Daniel Lutz, one of the children who lived in the house at 112 Ocean Avenue during that infamous period in the '70s. Daniel (more or less) defends the original story as told by his mother and stepfather. He also claims that both he and George Lutz were possessed, that George demonstrated abilities of telekinesis and also dabbled in the occult, which may have initiated the demonic events to occur. It's entertaining to watch if you still have any curiosity about *The Amityville Horror*, but come on, give me a break! For Daniel Lutz, whomever he really was then and is today, the only pity I feel for him is as an innocent child once caught up in the middle of all of his parents' bullshit. Still, perhaps he's just a bit smarter than you and I, because like his parents, he managed to (presumably) get paid for his own version of that same bullshit.

And Justice For All

Directed by Norman Jewison
(October 19, 1979, U.S. Release Date)

Then

As I previously mentioned, this was the second feature of a double bill I watched with *The China Syndrome*. It was also the third R-rated movie I saw on screen since *Animal House*. I hadn't known the magic and charisma of such a gifted actor as Al Pacino before. I was still too young to watch the first two *Godfather* movies, *Serpico*, or *Dog Day Afternoon*. I knew from the movie poster that Pacino played a lawyer, but that was the extent of its information. The movie started off ugly. Pacino's character Arthur Kirkland sat in a jail cell next to a man who'd just pissed all over the floor near him. The prison environment was a terrifying setting, filled with convicts, a newly-arrived prisoner dressed as a woman, and policemen who didn't care about what went on inside the jail cells. If nothing else, this scene was a clear message to a young boy to keep himself out of trouble so he'd never end up in such a nasty place. The following scene awakened my familiarity when Arthur was with a man called Judge Flemming. It was Flemming's *voice* that caught my attention because I quickly realized it as the same as Charles Townsend, the authoritative voice from ABC's *Charlie's Angels*. This may sound insignificant, but it was a big moment for me because after more than two years of watching the show, I could finally place a man's face with that mysterious voice I'd heard for so long. Anyway, that was one little mystery in my life finally solved.

I found Arthur Kirkland interesting, if not sympathetic. He was a lawyer, but that was hardly interesting. What intrigued me was his sense of fairness, honesty, and morality in a legal system that didn't appear to share the same values he deemed important. Even *he* was aware of just how useless, if not silly, his ideals were in such a corrupt judicial system. While visiting his grandfather in a nursing home, he asked Arthur if he was an honest lawyer. Arthur's immediate response was that he didn't think being honest had very much to do with the law. Although I knew very little about the law at such a young age, I couldn't help but feel that Arthur had to be wrong somehow. How could one practice a profession of law and justice if one didn't have an honest nature about it? Clearly, I knew very little of how the world really worked.

The scene that caught and held my attention the most prior to the climactic courtroom scene was the late dinner in Arthur's apartment with the woman Gail he became romantically involved with. While eating Chinese food, he told her a story of one of his clients, Jeff McCullaugh, who was stopped for a minor traffic offense one night and mistaken for an assault suspect of the same name. By this time, he'd spent a year and a half in jail due to that false identification. Judge Fleming repeatedly blocked Arthur's efforts to have the case reviewed. Although there was strong new evidence to prove Jeff's innocence, Fleming refused McCullaugh's appeal due to its three-day late submission. Arthur wrapped up the story by concluding that McCullaugh remained in prison because his car taillights didn't work. After taking a moment to catch my breath, I sat there with my mouth open in a moment of disbelief and disgust that such a thing could actually happen in our American legal system. Was this for real or was it just fiction? The thought of its reality sent a minor chill down my back and ended up in my stomach.

I wasn't off the hook that quickly. The discomfort I felt learning of what our precious legal system was capable of continued with another story in which Arthur's legal partner, an unstable man named Jay, arrived drunk at Arthur's apartment late one night and told him that the man he defended for murder and gotten released on a mere technicality, had just murdered two kids. I don't know what disturbed me more; the horrible act itself or the irony of the criminal having been in custody, only to be let back onto the streets to kill again simply because his lawyer was clever enough to make it happen. Such intense adult drama not only taught me a thing or two about the real world, but also left me with a sense of dread over just how bad things could get. On the other hand, the movie wasn't without its lighter side and its outrageous humor. Laughter is contagious, and that was never more true than with the men's bathroom scene when Arthur was not only informed of Judge Flemming's arrest for rape, but also that Flemming wanted Arthur to represent him in the case against him. Oh, how the laughter filled the bathroom and the movie theater! First, with the mild grin across Al Pacino's face as he innocently asked his colleagues, *"Me? Why me?"* and then the explosion of hilarity and insanity as the men were, as Arthur later put it, *"laughing so hard, one of them is choking in the sink."*

Okay, I know what you're really waiting for me to get to is the final courtroom sequence made famous by Al Pacino's shouting at the judge on the stand, *"You're out of order! You're out of order!"* Those were great words, of course, but in all honesty, it's *not* the moment of the scene that truly stands out for me. What really had me holding my breath was the persistent method of Arthur's opening statement in which he slowly built up to what would eventually become his explosion of rage against the very man he was defending. As he spoke, he became more agitated. I couldn't figure out just how his speech would conclude, but I knew it wouldn't be good. It was at the crucial moment when Arthur said to the jury, *"And ladies and gentlemen of the jury, the prosecution is* not *gonna get that man today! No—because* I'm *gonna get him!"* that I knew the shit would hit the fan with all of its might. When all hell exploded in the courtroom and Arthur was led away from the proceedings, despite my joy at such an outrageous victory, I also felt a degree of disappointment in knowing that there wouldn't be an actual trial in this movie. All we were left with was Arthur sitting on the steps of the courthouse and giving us his final stare of confusion and puzzlement. I think by the end, I was also feeling those same feelings.

That afternoon at the movies left me a bit exhausted from my exposure to the worlds of nuclear dangers and our corrupt and imperfect legal system. How does a kid who's spent most of his moviegoing time and energy on sci-fi, monsters, musicals, boxers, and a British secret agent absorb and comprehend the harsh realities of the adult world, even when it's through the eyes of the motion picture? I'd just watched this intense double feature alone, so I didn't have my parents or friends with me to discuss it with or ask questions. For the time being, I was on my own to try and make sense of my thoughts on such subjects. I reminded myself that even hard topics are entertaining in the movies, and that surely helped my thinking. I also repeated a good deal of Al Pacino's climactic dialogue in my head, which brought a smile to my face. At school, there were some friends who'd also seen the movie, and while we didn't get into too much philosophical discussion (when you're a kid in middle school, how much philosophy do you really have?), we enjoyed making each other laugh with our own mimicry of *"You're out of order!"*

When I watched *And Justice For All* again on February 21, 1982, on the *ABC Sunday Night Movie*, I had my father with me this time. By then, I was fourteen years old and just a little wiser in the ways of the world and how it didn't always work the way we wanted. We laughed at the antics of Al Pacino, and I never asked him any questions or tried to offer any intelligent opinions about the movie's contents of reality. Perhaps those confusing and puzzling issues didn't bother me quite so much the second time around. I simply sat there, smiled, and enjoyed reexperiencing the movie I felt privileged to have been a part of on a weekend afternoon back in 1979.

Now

Pacino is my favorite modern actor of all time. I've seen nearly all of his works, and while some may not measure up to the man's true talents (think *Dick Tracy*), he never fails to intrigue me with the intense magnitude of what he brings to his screen characters; from Michael Corleone in all three *Godfather* films, to Sonny Wortzik in *Dog Day Afternoon*, to Tony Montana in *Scarface*, to Lieutenant

Colonel Frank Slade in *Scent of a Woman*, to Lt. Vincent Hanna in *Heat*, to John Milton in *The Devil's Advocate*, the list is endless. No other modern actor manages to hold my attention with such curiosity and interest like he has. When Pacino speaks and Pacino *yells*, I listen. When you consider just a small sample of the great films he's done, it's easy to overlook lighter fare like *And Justice For All*, despite his infamous courtroom line.

The film is best described as a black comedy and courtroom drama that not only conveys the obvious message of just how twisted our legal system really is (and was nearly forty years ago), but also turns the irony and insanity of that same system into situations so outrageous and tragic, you can't help but find them funny. Even when Jay Porter, played by the often eccentric Jeffrey Tambor, finally goes mad due to his exhaustion and disillusionment at our legal system's corruption, he chooses to express his madness by throwing plates down a long corridor. By today's standards of violence, he may have taken a gun and opened fire in a public setting. So when you think about it like that, plates are a rather funny weapon of hate and frustration.

In such a system, Arthur Kirkland appears to be the only shining jewel of a lawyer with any sense of regard for truth and justice. Sadly, he ends up ostracized by the entire Baltimore legal community due to his high ideals. By the end, his partner Jay, despite his nervous and violent breakdown, is permitted to return to the law, while Kirkland ends up disbarred as a result of his moral integrity. This much insanity cannot be completely fictional, can it? Perhaps it's the role of the everyday man, as opposed to the gangster, the cop, or even the devil himself, as only Al Pacino can play him that continues to draw me to *And Justice For All* as one of the best films he's ever made (he's the lawyer I'd want on *my* side were I ever in trouble with the law). I watch the film regularly when I want to experience such an intense man lighten up and give us a look at the world as we know it with all its flaws, its imperfections, and the irresistible drive that compels us to laugh at all of it nonetheless.

Star Trek-The Motion Picture

Directed by Robert Wise
(December 7, 1979, U.S. Release Date)

Then

When NBC's *Star Trek* went off the air after only three seasons in 1969, it resurfaced in reruns and a cult following developed. The success of *Star Wars* and *Close Encounters* demonstrated to the heads of Paramount Pictures that science fiction was pure box office gold. When it was announced that *Star Trek—The Motion Picture* was being made and that virtually the entire television cast would return, the anticipation for those of us already familiar with *Star Trek* was staggering. For myself, one who'd watched only an occasional rerun episode of the show here and there on New York's WPIX Channel 11, and maybe even had a merchandising toy or two lying around in his bedroom, the prospect of the final frontier and boldy going where no man had gone before on the big screen kept me eagerly waiting for many months. Even the marketing tactics in the local newspaper knew just how to grab me and keep me hanging on the edge of my patience by printing a caption like, YOU ARE NOW TWO WEEKS AWAY FROM STARDATE 7912.07 AND THE 23RD CENTURY (I didn't catch this at the time, but 7912.07 switched around, spelled out 12.07.79, the movie's release date).

The Motion Picture was an easy sell with my father. It was science fiction and it was G-rated. However, I didn't get to see it for well over a month or two. By that time, the marketing behind it was in full swing (including a happy meal at McDonalds). My dad finally took me and Kevin to see it during its second run at a local neighborhood theater. I didn't know what to expect at all. If *Star Trek* was trying to compete with *Star Wars* on any level, it would have to be filled with fast-paced action and excitement. As Mr. Spock himself would've said, that seemed *logical*. I couldn't have been more wrong.

As I would've expected from any sci-fi movie, it started out with a lot of visual color and graphics. The crisis of the story began with the mysterious destruction of three Klingon space vessels. Due to specific explanations by its characters, we immediately understood that a massive cloud of energy and power was headed toward Earth and if it reached our planet, it would bring about our destruction. From there, we arrived in the city of San Francisco of the twenty-third century, where everything looked very futuristic and the Golden Gate Bridge still stood as it always had. It was thrilling to see James Kirk again all these years later, even though he was no longer in the traditional *Star Trek* TV uniform any longer and was instead, dressed in a short-sleeved shirt. I suppose the real anticipation in the audience was to see the legendary Enterprise after all these years. I think the movie understood that anticipation because the scene of the travel pod carrying Kirk and Mr. Scott moved rather slow, allowing us in the theater to really take in and absorb the newly-refitted Starship Enterprise as it was being prepared in space dock for launching once again.

"Take us out," Kirk said. This was the moment all *Star Trek* fans had yearned for over the years, and I was no different. It was a thrilling screen moment, and I looked forward to some better sci-fi action as the movie continued (again, I was wrong). The movie moved at a very slow pace, much too slow for a twelve-year-old boy's taste. It *looked* great of course, but I (and I'm sure many others in the theater) were getting impatient for things to pick up. It wasn't happening. Even when crisis hit the crew and ship, including a wormhole, an asteroid, and an energy probe that turned the bald-headed woman into a mechanized robot, things calmed down quickly after some intense crew reactions to the ship's viewing screen and without any casualties or tragedies. Maybe I was judging things too quickly, but I

was starting to feel cheated by those who'd made this movie. Kevin, I don't think really cared too much. My father simply allowed himself to fall asleep in his chair. This wasn't a movie *he* wanted to see, but rather just something to make his son happy.

As the story progressed (*dragged*, is more like it) and things continued to be brighter, more colorful, and beautifully photographed, my hopes of laser gun fire or space battle were slowly shrinking to a likelihood of zero. The Enterprise slowly cruised along its path, and their journey got closer to the end. By now, we were all anticipating the answer to the mysterious question of just who V'Ger really was (if we still cared, that is). I will confess that I was intrigued and fascinated when I learned that V'Ger was a product of Earth's own twentieth century space probe Voyager 6, which was believed to have been lost in space when it disappeared in a black hole. The idea of a space probe developing itself into a living and thinking machine was an interesting concept to consider, even by a kid who didn't fully understand the possibilities of science and space.

The movie's climax of Ilia and Captain Will Decker joining together as a single living entity through the cosmic power of V'Ger was, I'll admit, a little hard to follow. Visually, it looked like it worked and the human race had stopped the threatening cloud from destroying Earth, but I wasn't completely sure how. By that time, just over two hours, I'd reached the point where I decided it was pointless to try and understand every detail behind the story of this movie. I left the theater disappointed, though not regretting having seen it. When I was a kid, *all* sci-fi movies mattered to me, even the ones that turned out to be dull. If nothing else, *The Motion Picture* enabled me to talk about the movie with my friends. Most of us agreed that it was an awesome movie because of how it looked with its special effects. We also agreed that it was a real bore too. Still, we loved all the recent sci-fi hits and we eagerly awaited *The Empire Strikes Back* just five months away. *The Motion Picture* was just another movie that was part of *"Sci-Fi '79,"* and it was worthy of our attention and discussion whether it was actually good or not.

It was just over three years before I saw the movie again, when it premiered on the *ABC Sunday Night Movie* on February 20, 1983 (by that time, I'd seen the first sequel *Star Trek II—The Wrath of Khan* the previous summer). Despite my lackluster reaction to it when I was younger, I watched it again with eagerness because there was additional footage not shown in theaters (this extended cut was also released on video that same year and was the only version available for many decades). While the movie didn't improve too much the second time around, even with the added footage, it was still a fun and worthy throwback to the screen world of the starship Enterprise just the same, even on a small TV set. As I got older and I continued to see *Star Trek* movies on screen and tape them on video when they aired on HBO, I deliberately avoided *The Motion Picture* due to what I considered a low tolerance for boredom.

Now

My appreciation for *Star Trek—The Motion Picture* wouldn't exist today were it not for my deep love of Kubrick's *2001: A Space Odyssey*. Frankly, if this wasn't my favorite film of all time, I don't think I'd ever have given *The Motion Picture* another chance or a fresh and fair perspective. Not to suggest that it's a classic in the world of *Star Trek* films; it's simply that I've managed to develop a more patient, intelligent, and high-concept attitude in how I view it as science fiction cinema.

First and foremost, I consider the genre a *visual* art, not necessarily dependent on speed or action. The *special effects* of *Star Wars* films and such are, in my opinion, a very different experience than the *visual effects* of films like *Close Encounters, Alien, Blade Runner, Dune,* or even George Lucas's slow-paced sci-fi debut film *THX-1138.* To watch *The Motion Picture* now is to do it with the same interest and patience as *2001.* Its visual effects by Douglas Trumbull are astounding, particularly the Enterprise's journey through the massive cloud that clearly echoes the journey of the US Discovery through Jupiter and beyond at *2001's* climax. Both films don't exactly invoke story content and understanding of such content to grab ahold of and keep our attention. We're asked to follow along on a journey of striking visual wonderment and mystery and even, if possible, to ask a question or two about man's place in this vast and dark universe.

For *The Motion Picture*, we have what's best described as the convenience of familiar characters we've previously known and loved on TV. This same point, perhaps, serves to work against us as well, because we're likely to hold those same beloved characters to a higher standard of screen action and excitement. Clearly, those who made the film, including director Robert Wise (his last film, by the way), storyteller Alan Dean Foster, special effects artist Douglas Trumbull, and even scientific consultant Isaac Asimov sought to make a film of thought-provoking knowledge and high-concept scientific possibility, while maintaining a visual feast for the eyes and the senses. I cannot claim they *didn't* succeed in such a bold undertaking. All of this is, of course, my own opinion. Die-hard *Trek* fans or *"Trekkies"* as they're affectionately called, would likely call me crazy and insist the first film of the franchise is still the worst (*my* vote goes to *Star Trek V: The Final Frontier*). Others may see my point entirely. If absolutely nothing else, they might agree the movie poster artwork by illustrator Bob Peak is the finest and the most striking of all films. They may also agree that Jerry Goldsmith provides the most influential soundtrack with its sweeping orchestral fanfares and energetic compositions that truly define the world of science fiction and its deep space journeys.

Kramer vs. Kramer

Directed by Robert Benton
(December 19, 1979, U.S. Release Date)

Then

Kramer vs. Kramer may have been the most ill-timed motion picture of my entire childhood. By the time I saw the movie in early January 1980, my parents had split up for the *second* time in their less-than-perfect marriage. It was unexpected, it was not amicable, and there was a lot of bitterness involved, particularly on the side of my mother. My father was now back in the position of weekend custody visits, and that meant a few extra trips to the movies. It's impossible for me to account for my father's state of mind, if not my own at the age of twelve, in the decision-making process of going to see a new movie about the emotional pains of divorce and its damage to the family when the real thing is taking place in your own life at that time. What's more, how do I account for us staying in the theater to watch such a movie *twice*? Perhaps the old saying of, *"And you thought your family was dysfunctional!"* is an appropriate one here.

Regardless of human motive or rationale behind this movie selection, I was in the theater again with my father and Kevin. I was about to be brought into a very serious world of adult behavior and actions since my double feature experience of *The China Syndrome* and *And Justice For All*. The movie began rather calmly with soft music and a close shot of the face of Meryl Streep as she sat on her little boy Billy's bed looking down at him. As she said goodnight to him, the sadness on her face was immediately easy to read and under-stand. I knew from the information I'd previously learned about the movie that she was leaving her family on this night, and I could only just sit there and wait to see exactly how it was going to happen. Upon breaking the news to her husband, Ted, his immediate reaction was less-than-serious, treating the matter like a joke. I recalled my mother's own attitude toward my father, in which she often accused him of not taking matters in life seriously enough. Honestly, I didn't know whether to smile or frown from such a coincidental scene. Regardless of my reaction, Joanna was out the door and Ted was left alone to be a full-time father to Billy. The next morning was an unco-ordinated mess, as Ted was clueless with what to do with his own son, even finding it difficult to make his breakfast and drop him off with the right teacher at school.

What followed was one of those situations where you feel the contents of the screen having reached out with a large arm and stolen a piece of your own life, as well as those you love. The relationship between Ted and Billy was a constant state of resentment, forgive-ness, and then resentment again, which wasn't too unlike the rela-tionship between my father and his younger son. Kevin was often feisty and challenging with my father. Dear 'ol Dad, while being, at heart, a tough son-of-a-bitch, was often on the defense against his second born, while still trying to maintain the proper level of author-ity and discipline a parent must exercise with their child. This led to resentment between them, which was often resolved easily before it inevitably found a reason to just start up again. Ted and Billy were a reminder of my father and Kevin, not only as they were now, but also perhaps a precursor to what they *would* be under the conditions of a second divorce. While a movie certainly couldn't predict the future of my family, it gave me pause to consider the possibilities.

Sometimes when you're watching a movie for the first time, you can't help but predict what's going to happen next simply by specific camera shots. During the second scene in the neighborhood park, when the camera kept shooting Billy on the jungle gym, I knew with absolute certainly that he'd eventually fall and hurt himself. When it finally happened, I closed my eyes just as poor Billy's face made

214

impact with the ground. I watched my father's face get a more intense when Ted ran like a mad man through the streets of Manhattan with Billy in his arms to get to the nearest hospital. My father later told me of a similar incident with Kevin as a baby, when he fell to the ground and severely cut his lip, leaving my father in the frantic position of driving at top speed to the nearest emergency room. I recall the anger and resentment my mother felt toward the poor man when she came home later and learned what had happened.

As Ted and Billy's relationship became closer, I couldn't help but look over at my father's eyes fixated on the screen. What was he feeling during these moments? Sadness? Regret? Fear? I never asked, though he later told me and Kevin that he would've been just as devoted a dad as Ted Kramer if he ever had to fight for the both of us. I know that he meant it, and I can only imagine such feelings came to his mind and heart as he watched Ted experience the process of hiring an expensive lawyer to help him keep custody of Billy. I recall a feeling of dread when Ted lost his job just before the custody trial was to begin. If ever there was a time when I wanted to shout out, "What are you going to do now?" at the screen, this was surely it. I was relieved when he found another job within twenty-four hours as he promised he would, though I didn't understand the severe loss he was taking in professional status and salary by accepting a job that took him back to the beginning of his career skills. I suppose at my age, I just presumed that any job was still a job. Anyway, perhaps now he had a better chance against his ex-wife in court.

The custody courtroom sequence was, despite my parent's own divorce, a new experience for me in drama and procedure. They didn't go through that process because it was mutually agreed that my mother would retain custody, so I (thankfully) never saw the inside of a family courtroom, nor was I asked uncomfortable questions by a lawyer or a judge. I can only say that I felt for Ted Kramer because from the beginning, he didn't stand much of a chance against his ex-wife who made more money than he did. Her lawyer's attacks on Ted's professional behavior and his apparent inability to hold onto his job looked like the nail in his coffin. I also knew that in many cases of divorce (at least as it was back then in the '70s), the mother almost always gained custody of the child. I saw no reason why the same situation in the movies wouldn't be the same. I was right. Ted lost his court battle and was devastated when he had to tell Billy that they'd be separated and he'd be living with his mother from now on.

Kramer vs. Kramer taught me that life's situations, even the bad ones, are subject to change or even reverse themselves before the entire story is told. The change in Ted and Billy's life followed its due course, right up until the moment when Billy sat in his chair waiting to be picked up by his mother and start his new life. It was the simple call on the apartment building intercom that would alter everything. Good news as it was, it was difficult to understand just why Joanna would change her mind about the entire matter on the very morning she was to take custody. She loved Billy, but she also recognized that he was already home and to interrupt that in any way would be very damaging to him. With a simple hug between her and Ted, I knew it was over but still couldn't deny the feeling of wanting just a little more when the elevator door slowly closed and the end credits began to roll.

By the time I watched the movie again in 1982 when it premiered on the *ABC Sunday Night Movie*, my parents were back together *again* (no joke) for the second time in their marriage for two years already. Any emotional reactions that once existed at the time of the movie's release had dissipated over time. What remained was a wonderful drama of the relationship between father and son and all of the daily quirks that went with it, whether it was fights over chocolate chip ice cream or supermarket decisions on dish washing soap and cereal. This was when I discovered what a great actor Dustin Hoffman was, having seen *The Graduate* and *All the President's Men* on TV. Meryl Streep was still unknown to me. I had no interest in *The French Lieutenant's Woman* or *Sophie's Choice,* and I was still too young to see a movie like *The Deer Hunter*. In short, *Kramer vs. Kramer* slipped into the cracks of time like so many other movies, no longer having much personal meaning for me, at least not until decades later when I became a father.

Now

It's impossible for me not to interpret a film like *Kramer vs. Kramer* without any matured outlook and perspective, now being the father of a twelve-year-old boy. To watch it now is to not only reexamine the relationship I had with my own father as a boy, but to also question what he felt at the time of his second split from my mother and just what sort of man he was at the close of the '70s. He was (and still is) a man of faults as well as assets, but above all else, he was (and still is) a man totally devoted to his two sons. Still, I can't help but wonder if during his experience with this film, might he have been comparing his own status of fatherhood to that of Dustin Hoffman and the emotional challenges his character faced? Did my father consider himself a better or worse man than Ted Kramer? I may never know the answers to such questions unless I ask him (or if, upon reading this book, he divulges such information to me himself). Those questions are easier to answer for myself. I'm not a divorced man and I have only my son. Because he's our only child, I possess a level of love and devotion I consider stronger, if not more intense, than parents who must effectively share and divide their love and devotion between multiple children who are each different in their own way. This self-proclaimed attachment I have toward my child makes the thought of losing him for any reason a much tougher burden with which to bear. Like Ted Kramer, just how would *I* step up and measure up if I were ever in the position of having to raise my son on my own? What sort of emotional battle would I endure if I were put in the position of having to fight for him? Would I be fair and rational or would I become ugly and brutal? These issues and questions are what now make *Kramer vs. Kramer* a film not only possessing the original qualities it's always had, but with an added measure of pain to the mix; the kind of pain only a father can understand and experience when watching a film in which an innocent child is caught in the middle of his mother and father during a difficult and emotionally-trying experience.

As a father, I view Ted Kramer very differently than I did as a kid. Ted is a husband and father solely focused on his own life and career. I suppose many real-life marriages are like that, be it the husband or the wife. It's only when Joanna finally walks out on him without taking their son that he's suddenly forced to deal with Billy not just as a son by name, but a child in need who must rely on his father as not only a supporter but as a trusted friend. Ted's character is one of the gradual changes that's very clear as his relationship with his little boy blossoms into something very special. While the film reflects the era of divorce in the '70's, it also reflects the law's decision that traditionally sides with the mother in these situations and yet still portrays the cultural shift which occurred during that decade when ideas about motherhood and fatherhood were slowly evolving, giving equal weight and importance of story and dialogue to both Ted and Joanna's parental points of view.

Finally, there's a particular scene in *Kramer vs. Kramer* I cannot watch without experiencing a personal, gut-wrenching moment. During Ted and Billy's final French toast breakfast, a scene echoing an earlier breakfast attempt, Ted picks up his son from the kitchen counter, the two embracing each other. Keep silent and you'll hear Billy softly crying to himself. Watch Ted close his eyes and then just attempt to imagine what the man must be feeling at that moment. He's heartbroken over the loss of raising his son, and yet he knows all too well that he must maintain the proper strength and composure for the benefit of his precious little boy. I watch this moment and I feel the pain and emotion, as only a loving and devoted father can, and I'm eternally grateful for my son and all the joy he brings me in a difficult and challenged life.

"I love you, Sam!"

The Black Hole

Directed by Gary Nelson
(December 21, 1979, U.S. Release Date)

Then

Like network television, James Bond and *Star Trek*, Disney wasn't immune from the success of *Star Wars* and their ultimate need to cash in on the new phenomenon of science fiction in the movies. In fact, they were willing to go the extra distance and introduce their very first PG-rated motion picture for the first time in their entire existence. It was yet another sci-fi action space movie about to grace the big screen, and I needed no other excuse to get my father to commit himself to taking me to see it, despite his own personal intolerance for the genre (just one of the many things he was willing to do for his kids, even if he didn't *want* to do them). It was easy to see that *The Black Hole* was the closest thing to a direct *Star Wars* rip-off I'd seen on the big screen thus far (remember that *Battlestar Galactica* was on *TV* first).

First, the movie had the blond kid of Charlie Pizer who, like Luke Skywalker, dreamed himself a hotshot warrior with a blaster. Then it had the older Han Solo-type renegade Captain Dan Holland, the captured female Dr. Kate McCrae (though hardly a princess) in distress and in need of rescue, the little android robot V.I.N.CENT who was, admittedly, a great improvement over R2-D2 with his ability to speak and his educated wisdom. One of the earliest pieces

219

of dialogue between man and robot that quickly jumped out at me went something like this:

"V.I.N.CENT, were you programmed to bug me?"

"No, sir, to educate you."

On the side of evil, there was Dr. Hans Reinhardt, a Grand Moff Tarkin wannabe and finally, the red sinister-looking robot Maximilian, who could have easily given Darth Vader a real run for his money. Yes, it would seem that Disney hadn't missed a beat when trying to cash in an another man's efforts and success.

The movie began with the depths and darkness of outer space and the human beings who occupied it. The black hole itself looked like an awesome sight, and you couldn't help but sense its ultimate destructive power (not too unlike the Death Star, I suppose). Outer space seemed a whole lot more dead and mysterious than the traditional galaxy far, far away. In fact, had I any real memory of watching *2001* on TV back in '77, I might've easily compared it to Kubrick's vision. The Palomino's discovery of the U.S.S. Cygnus as a dark, floating derelict spacecraft raised my curiosity level to high because I knew only too well that it was just a matter of time and patience before that thing lit up like a Christmas tree and startled not only the crew of the Palomino, but perhaps the theater audience as well. I was right, though I think the rest of the audience was likely thinking the same thing I was.

Dr. Hans Reinhardt was a man with evil intentions on his mind, though we weren't entirely sure what they were yet. He was determined to travel into the black hole, and that was clearly a dangerous and potentially deadly stunt, though just how far was he willing to go to achieve his goal? The crew of the Palomino, while needing to stay on to repair their disabled ship, needed to leave as quickly as possible if they were going to avoid being held prisoner. Those hopes were shattered when Dr. Alex Durant (I recognized that actor as the man who played Norman Bates in what little of Hitchcock's *Psycho* I'd managed to catch whenever it was on TV) was brutally murdered by the robot Maxilimilian's spinning blade. At that moment, we were also shocked to learn that the robot crew piloting the Cygnus were actually once human beings now living in a "deathlike" state.

These new revelations finally ignited the real action of *The Black Hole*. Laser gun fire erupted as the heroes of the movie now raced against time to escape their captor. Their own ship was destroyed by the Cygnus, and they'd have to escape using an alternate probe ship. This was challenging, as things everywhere were coming apart as the Cygnus drew closer and closer to the dreaded black hole. The real excitement, both in action and visual effects, came during the meteor storm's impact on the great ship. The gigantic orange fireball that headed straight for the crew as they raced across the suspended bridge was one of the most death-defying, edge-of-your-seat moments I'd ever experienced in a big screen sci-fi thriller and it was absolute destruction at its best.

When the Palomino crew finally reached the probe ship, we learned that they had no choice but to go into the black hole because the ship was going to do it whether they wanted it to or not. I didn't fully comprehend the idea of a ship or machine being pre-programmed to travel somewhere or do anything else for that matter. Regardless, we were hooked and we were going in. As the ship traveled through the unknown void, I remember expecting to see incredible visual and colorful sequences that would blow my mind. Turns out, the trip through the black hole offered no more than the implications of speed and the ship rumbling and tumbling round and round, over and over, as the crew tried to not lose their minds.

What followed afterward was a sequence that I was too young to understand. We were supposed to be inside the black hole now and inside of it was Dr. Reinhardt and Maximilian (I thought they'd both been killed aboard the Cygnus) side by side, floating in the air, until the moment when they became as one. Following that was a freaky landscape setting of fire, robots, angels with white hair, cathedral tunnels, and then a white hole instead of a black one. I leaned over and asked my father, "Dad, what is all this?" His response was a simple one: "I think it's heaven and hell." I knew what both those words meant, though I had no idea how both of them fit into a Disney sci-fi movie. These high concept and even philosophical sequences of *The Black Hole* were confusing to a kid who traditionally expected simple and comprehensible innocence from a studio like Disney. If such thought-provoking issues were now part of the price of their PG-rated movie, then perhaps it was best they go back to their previous level of family entertainment that a kid could understand. These issues might've been wasted on me for years to come had I not purchased the novelization of the movie by Alan Dean Foster after seeing the movie. This helped to fill in some of the holes (no pun intended) that confused me, because unlike the movies and the separate ticket admission required, I had the option to go back and reread parts I didn't understand as many times as required (the book was paid for, and it was mine). It was more than ten years before I saw the movie again on Buena Vista VHS tape. By then, I'd been through various popular sci-fi franchises and had developed a stronger degree of perspective and criticism in which I'd judge *The Black Hole* once again.

Now

Walt Disney Pictures certainly had *balls* back in '79. To join the ranks of the other motion picture studios who were more than eager to commit their own version of copycat sci-fi material was surely expected in the world of movies and money. To practically outright rip off the central characters and relationships of Lucas's previous characters was a far more brazen act than anything *Galactica* was accused of. Perhaps it was Disney he should've sued instead of those who created the popular ABC series (as it turns out, that would've been quite ironic considering it was Disney that he sold the *Star Wars* rights to in 2012 for a cool 4.06 billion dollars).

The Black Hole hasn't aged badly over time, but *differently* than other sci-fi examples. Even if one keeps an open mind and notes the black hole is the true star of the film, it's still nothing more than a cheap matte painting moving in a circular motion. The melodrama is, at times, campy and talky, which is unfortunate for such a talented cast of professionals that include Maximilian Schell, Ernest Borgnine, Anthony Perkins, Robert Forster, and Yvette Mimieux. Perhaps the best performance comes from V.I.N.CENT, voiced by *Planet of the Apes* alumni Roddy McDowall, who gives us what could've otherwise been written off as a forgettable droid, instead of a living entity with wisdom and personality; more than anything Anthony Daniels has offered us in eight *Star Wars* films, thus far.

Though regarded negatively by critics at the time, the cliché of the reclusive mad scientist doesn't fail, in my opinion, as the driving force behind the drama and the action (think of Walter Pigeon in *Forbidden Planet*). Perhaps if you open your mind and memories of classic films, you'll recall Schell's performance in *Judgement at Nuremberg* and notice some of that same intensity in Dr. Hans Reinhardt. The film also effectively incorporates the haunted house concept in its depiction of the forgotten spaceship that was lost from mankind for so many years. When John Barry's pulsating music isn't carrying us through the film's action, there are quieter moments as we follow the Palomino crew through unknown passageways and rooms that define the ship's dark history and its frightening situations. Like the haunted house, there's the introduction of quiet mystery until the moment comes where all hell breaks loose, things come undone, and those inside must fight to escape and survive. One may criticize such a cliché, but it works well enough for me. The standard visual effects of *The Black Hole* are effective for the time. The sequence when the asteroid crashes into the spaceship Cygnus and rolls toward our heroes is still stunning and doesn't fail to entertain (I can't help but wonder if Spielberg and Lucas weren't inspired by this particular scene when they filmed the rolling boulder in *Raiders of the Lost Ark*). John Barry's score is dark and menacing, and that works when considering the whole haunted house effect of the film.

What really holds the film together for me is that now I not only comprehend and interpret the film's complex subtexts, its religious and metaphysical themes, and the climactic visual references to *Dante's Inferno*, as well as heaven and hell in concluding not only the punishment of evil beings as Dr. Reinhardt and Maximilian, but also the salvation of our heroes of the Palomino. At the age of twelve, there was no way I could've (nor any other child my age, I imagine) understood what all of *that* was about. This could only have been Disney's attempt to develop more adult-oriented material into more mainstream motion pictures after decades of cute mice, ducks, and doggies. Whether that actually worked or not is wholly dependent on one's own memory and interpretation. For my own, it was a continuation of the space fantasy genre that so dominated that year, and that was all I needed to have fun at the movies (even if my father hated it).

*****

This is the last film of 1979 I shall discuss in any great detail.

I'll cap off by discussing two films of previous years that I discovered and *tried to* discover on television before the year rounded out.

Monday May 7, 1979, was the day of my twelfth birthday, which meant I was in the annual position of asking for something that I normally wouldn't get. I chose to stay up later on a school night so I could watch the entire movie *Rollercoaster* on *NBC Monday Night at the Movies* (yeah, I know … you're probably thinking I could've gotten away with asking for something more significant, but as a kid, the opportunity to watch movies was enough for me). Despite being billed as a member of the disaster genre, it wasn't so much that as it was a story of *terrorism*, a word I had no real understanding of. A child of twelve might've equated a word such as *sabotage* to have equal meaning. The thought of someone tampering with and causing the destruction of a speeding rollercoaster didn't sit too well with me. Still, what I found most intriguing about the film was the cat-and-mouse interplay between the terrorist demanding extortion money and the safety inspector who was deemed worthy of delivering the suitcase with the money. This airing may have been the first real exposure I had as a kid to the intricate plotting involved when making a modern thriller. Thankfully, I wasn't afraid to go on the rollercoaster after watching that movie on my birthday.

The second *incident*, we'll call it, occurred some months earlier on Friday, February 16, 1979, when I attempted to watch John Schlesinger's film *Marathon Man* on the *CBS Sunday Night Movie*. I'd heard of this movie of three years prior from newspaper movie ads. I wasn't more than fifteen or twenty minutes into the film when both of my parents walked into my room and asked me what I was watching. When I told them what it was, both of them, particularly my mother, flew off the handle and demanded that I turn the TV off right now. When I asked them why, they told me the movie was filled with violence and sadistic, evil torture. As a kid, of course, you want to have your way, and I begged them to allow me to watch the movie, claiming I wasn't bothered by such things on television. That hardly worked because before I knew it, the TV was off and I was ordered to go read a book (or something equally constructive). I finally saw the movie in 1984, when it aired on ABC this time and I was of high school age and my movie viewing (even on TV) wasn't monitored or scrutinized anymore. It's a great film and a very effective thriller. Looking back, however, I'm forced to agree with my parents' cinematic judgment at the time (as much as I hate to admit it); no child of such a young age should be allowed to watch a film like *Marathon Man*, even when it *is* edited for television.

Finally, there's a film that's worth mentioning before concluding this year. In November 1979, Universal Pictures released a Michael Douglas film called *Running*. Though not nearly in the same emotional league as *Kramer vs. Kramer*, it had a strange degree of timing in its theatrical release and how it related to my mother and father. It's the story of a divorced man with high hopes of competing as a marathon runner in the 1976 Olympics. As he struggles with unemployment, his commitment to his running takes him further along the path of achieving his dream and determination. At the time of the film's release, my parents' marriage was slowly eroding into what would inevitably become their second break-up by the end of the year. My father, like Douglas, was obsessed with his daily regiment of running and was even training for a spot in the annual New York City Marathon. My mother would accuse him of putting his running ahead of his devotion to his family. Whether or not this was true was immaterial because he always denied it. Still, the film managed to hit a nerve when he took me and Kevin to see it. While it did little to change his running habits or its impact on his marriage, it was still a wonderful film and I saw it again only one more time when it premiered on the *ABC Sunday Night Movie* in 1982. To this day, it's never been released on American Region 1 VHS video, DVD, or Blu-Ray.

And that, my friends, was the year 1979 for me.

THE YEAR WAS 1980 ...

- Dubbed the *Miracle on Ice*, the United States Olympic Hockey team defeats the Soviet Union team in the Winter Olympics at Lake Placid, New York.
- President of the United States Jimmy Carter declares that the United States shall boycott the summer Olympics in Moscow because of the Soviet war in Afghanistan.
- Mount St. Helens erupts, causing billions in damage and killing fifty-seven people.
- Former California governor Ronald Reagan defeats President Jimmy Carter in the US Presidential Election, just one year after the start of the Iran hostage crisis.
- A record number of television viewers tune into the CBS nighttime soap opera *Dallas* to learn *"Who shot J.R.?"*
- Former member of The Beatles, John Lennon, is shot dead by Mark David Chapman outside of his apartment building in New York City.

... AND THERE WERE MOVIES!

The year 1980 was, without a doubt, the absolute *worst* year of my childhood. It started badly with the second bitter splitting of my parents, and it ended badly with the death of my grandmother (on my father's side). In between those life-changing events was situation after situation that made the life of a twelve-year-old boy (going on thirteen) less than pleasant or bearable. This included a parental reconciliation I never wanted, a Bar-Mitzvah I never wanted, a summer away from our home in Westhampton Beach (my parents choosing to rent it out for the season), and having to study all of my seventh grade French lessons at home during the summer because of my less-than-acceptable final grade. To a kid, these issues are significant enough to cause stress.

In just the first month of the new decade, I had serious issues to face. My mother, Kevin, and I were on vacation in Florida when my father called (on New Year's Eve, no less) to announce that he'd left and moved out (back into Manhattan) while we were away. Upon our return to New York, the family was forced to deal with an entirely new situation. My mother was pissed off, and the two of them went at it while Kevin and I could only sit there and listen to it unfold. Once again, he and I were thrown into the post-marital environment of visiting my father every weekend, though this time there was no girlfriend in the picture. Strange as it may sound though, their second split lasted only a few months before my father begged my mother to let him return home to us. Unlike the first time, however, I wasn't pleased about this move on her part. At the age of thirteen, it was obvious to me that these two people simply *didn't* belong together. Being just a kid though, I didn't feel it was my place to offer such opinions to either of them. So I kept my mouth shut and dealt with the both of them until they split for the third and final time ten years later (thank goodness!).

As oddly as things had occurred over time, January 1980 turned out to be one involving more frequent trips to the movies to occupy the time with my father. While I was forced to deal with another tumultuous event between my parents, I had the comfort of movies like *Star Trek—The Motion Picture* and *The Black Hole* during their extended theatrical runs into the new year to offer me at least two hours of distraction before I had to step outside and face my life again. If ever I needed the true power of escapism through the movies, it was now. It was also a time of numerous theatrical rereleases and double features that included the PG version of *Saturday Night Fever* and *Grease, Rocky* and *Rocky II, Jaws 2, Superman—The Movie,* and the new special edition of *Close Encounters*, as well as TV airings of many films I already loved. Included were encore performances of *King Kong* on NBC in May 1980 (in just one night this time) and *Jaws* on the *ABC Sunday Night Movie* in October of that year, allowing me to experience them for the second time. In fact, with the exception of *Star Wars*, were I to go back in time to reexperience that entire year over again, I would've enjoyed many of my childhood favorites all over again on screen and TV during a time that existed before affordable movie collectibility. Since time travel doesn't exist (unfortunately), the new films of the 1980s would start out for me with horror by the great John Carpenter.

The Fog

Directed by John Carpenter
(February 1, 1980, U.S. Release Date)

Then

From my personal perspective, 1980 will go down in movie history as the year of horror. Not to suggest that this particular year was the birth of the genre (hardly), but it jump-started the new decade thanks to the success of *Halloween*. Knowing nothing about Carpenter except his previous slasher hit, it appeared the man only made horror movies when I first saw the newspaper ad for *The Fog*. This looked like a story involving the fear of the unknown rather than the maniacal terror of the escaped lunatic. Unfortunately for me, the movie wasn't playing anywhere near my neighborhood, so sneaking around town to try to see it was out of the question. Like before, Greg B., who by now had solidified his status as my fellow horror movie buddy, was the ticket to seeing what I wanted, even if I had to wait nearly an entire year to do it (better late than never). On Saturday, April 4, 1981, at 10 p.m., we sat down to continue what had become our sleepover/HBO horror movie tradition as childhood friends.

From the moment the movie opened on a quiet beach at midnight to the background music of soft piano chords, I was hooked because I immediately identified with the idea of the beach as a dark and frightening setting for a ghost story (who could blame me, having spent much of my childhood at the beach already?). The ghost story, as told to a group of children by an old man, wasn't a particularly scary one, as it was merely the tale of a clipper ship crashing onto the rocks off the shore of Antonio Bay exactly one hundred years ago on that very night. Still, I liked the way the movie was setting up the anniversary of the small town as an important story point for what was due to come. I felt a chill of pleasure as I watched the camera pan upward to reveal the nighttime shoreline while the wind howled and the title of the movie was shown on the TV screen. My fascination with the beach as horror continued when I was introduced to the concept of the radio station operated out of an isolated lighthouse overlooking the ocean. I'd never seen or heard of such an idea before, and I appreciated the solitude of the woman running it because it increased the potential danger that would attack her later. In the middle of nowhere, there would be no one to help her when the attack came.

The movie used water as the source of terror, but not in the same way as in the two *Jaws* movies. The water served as the point of origin for the fog, the true enemy. There was an uneasy feeling of isolation being out on the water in the middle of the night on a boat miles away from shore when the three fishermen were killed by the undead ghouls of the fog. Even in morning light, when their boat was eventually discovered by Jamie Lee Curtis's character and her male companion, the mystery of what happened was gripping. *I* knew what had happened because I'd watched it. Those on board were trying in vain to figure out how something very cold and wet stepped aboard and managed to leave everything bone dry. The movie was clearly attempting to step outside the circle of what was considered the traditional ghost story; no house, no rattling chains, and no slamming doors. The entity of evil taking place was in our own outdoor atmosphere, which made it a whole lot harder to escape from it.

Father Malone's reading of his grandfather's hidden diary made the backstory of what was happening a lot easier to comprehend, though I didn't fully understand what a *leper colony* was and how it played into the subject of what happened in that town one hundred years ago (I asked Greg B. to clarify that for me). It was intriguing nonetheless, the idea of the town's entire origin based on the act of murder and the celebration they were about to hold to honor such an unknown, dastardly deed. I think I was getting my first lesson in the art of storytelling irony that night.

When the fog returned and made its way inland, only a small group of people, including Stevie Wayne in the lighthouse, were aware of what was really happening. The evil wasn't something they could outrun, though Stevie used her position as a radio announcer to warn people and even give them direction to find safe shelter. In another example of the movie's irony, the old church where everyone presumed they'd find safety and sanctuary, turned out to be where the climactic showdown between ghosts of the fog and the gold they sought to reclaim from their crashed ship one hundred years ago would take place. The ghosts weren't exactly defeated, but miraculously disappeared once they had what they wanted; their gold melted into the form of a huge crucifix. When it was over, we believed for a moment that all was well and our heroes in the church had survived. That didn't last because there was one more murder to be committed; the beheading of Father Malone, when their sword met his head and the end credits rolled.

Unlike the first two horror movies we'd watched together, Greg B. and I didn't completely agree in our feelings about it. I loved it. I thought it was creepy and mysterious and was particularly taken by the outdoor setting of it all. My horror-viewing companion, however, was disappointed because he felt it wasn't scary enough, nor violent and bloody enough for his tastes, which is what I suppose he truly equated as the quintessential elements of a successful horror movie. His opinion didn't surprise me too much. After all, this was a twelve-year-old kid who had a monthly subscription to *Fangoria* magazine, which at that time had only been in circulation for about a year. I suppose for someone like him, the gorier the better. For my tastes, the elements of frightening suggestion, the mysterious unknown, and that great soundtrack music by John Carpenter are what worked.

The Fog had its TV premiere on the *ABC Sunday Night Movie* on September 12, 1982. By then, I was fifteen years old and had my own small color TV in my room, making it easier for me to watch anything I wanted. The edited-for-television version didn't change the mood of the movie all that much, considering it wasn't violent, bloody, or filled with excessive profanity in the first place. I didn't see it again for well over ten years after that, until I taped an uncut pay-channel airing of it well into my post-college adulthood. Looking back, I can't help but wonder why it took me so long to obtain my own copy, considering how much I enjoyed it as a kid.

Now

The Fog, in my opinion, is not only a very underrated horror film, but has more significance than most people give it credit for. The locale of an isolated coastal town, as well as the lighthouse radio station, is a very original setting for a horror film. The lighthouse not only represents the uneasy feeling of absolute isolation from the world, but also provides the lone DJ Stevie Wayne, played by Adrienne Barbeau, who not only watches over the calm sea to search for the fog, but also serves as the town protector, using her position of communicator to warn the town citizens of the impending evil. John Carpenter effectively uses the beach and the sea as a truly creepy element, despite its initial beauty, during the times of the fog. Tom Atkins as Nick Castle says it best when describing the sea, *"She can get real mean."* Unlike too much of the bloody slasher crap that dominated much of the early '80s, Carpenter's film, in my opinion, maintains a level of style and grace by incorporating the use of atmospheric surroundings and supernatural elements that also helps to capture the essence of a traditional spooky and chilling folktale. Like *Jaws*, the director chooses exactly when to show his entity of evil and when not to, creating the ongoing fear of what's lurking inside what is normally considered a natural weather phenomenon.

The tone of *The Fog* remains dark and complex throughout its tightly-packed running time of just eighty-nine minutes. The one plot point that's always left me feeling a little unsatisfied, however, is the random manner in which the victims are killed by Blake and his ghoulish companion of the *Elizabeth Dane*; practically no rhyme, nor reason to their being chosen. Perhaps I should've read the nov-

elization published just before the film's release. I understand it clar-
ifies the film's implication that the six who must die were, in fact,
descendants of the six original conspirators from one hundred years
ago, rather than random selections (well, *that* makes a big difference
to me). Another effective part of the film is that, much like George
A. Romero's *Night of the Living Dead*, it makes no campy attempt to
fully explain to its viewer why the dead have mysteriously returned
to life. This event happens in a queit, scenic setting like Antonio Bay
simply because it *can* happen and it *is* happening. Carpenter delivers
plausible explanations for the history behind the danger, but concerns himself more with keeping his primary characters out of danger. When it's over, he provides a talented way of leaving his viewer
with an ominous sense of silent terror with just one final scare—the
beheading of Father Malone.

Silly as it may sound, I enjoy watching *The Fog* on April 21 of
every year, echoing the date of Antonio Bay's historical anniversary.
Certainly, it also requires repeated viewing during the annual time of
Halloween, as does much of Carpenter's other early horror material.

Friday the 13th

Directed by Sean S. Cunningham
(May 9, 1980, U.S. Release Date)

Then

By May 1980, I'd reached a degree of independence in which I was finally allowed to take my bicycle into town on my own for several hours to do whatever I chose (within reason, of course). As a result, this newfound freedom allowed me to disappear for two hours to see movies I wouldn't be permitted to see otherwise. At this time, the horror movie was *now*, it was here to stay for a while, and I wanted to be part of it. The newspaper ad for *Friday the 13th* was the most frightening image I'd seen for a horror movie since *Halloween*. The bloody knife, the image of the killer's body, and the dark, threatening woods under the sinister moonlight (I actually own the movie poster) were all I needed to get my enthusiasm going to figure out how I'd get into the the theater to see this. All I needed was my bike and a Saturday afternoon to myself. Oh, yeah, and I *had* to ask Greg B. if he wanted to go too. He did.

Having seen only three modern horror movies so far, I recognized one factor they had in common, and that was they began with an incident or event in the past that determined the present day events of the story. *Friday the 13th* was no different. It began with the brutal murders of two camp counselors at Camp Crystal Lake in the year 1958. Besides the murders themselves, I also noted the chilling, hard-biting soundtrack music that accompanied the killer's attack.

Never had I heard violins sound so horrifying. Following the opening credits (to that same terrifying music), it was the present day and we learned more about the history of Camp Crystal Lake; the murder we'd already seen, the drowning of a boy the year before, mysterious fires, and water that went bad. Despite all this, the camp was about to open up again after more than twenty years and we waited to see just how it would all come apart. At the camp, all was normal as things were prepared for the new summer season. The counselors were young college kids who took every advantage to have fun when they weren't working, including swimming, hiking, cooking dinner, and whenever possible, sex (an exciting thing for a thirteen-year-old boy with raging hormones to see on screen whenever possible).

The unseen killer struck just as a thunderstorm hit the camp, and I remember thinking the most frightening attack, out of what seemed like so many of them, was when Brenda was tricked into going outside at night during the storm because she thought she heard a child crying out for help. When she ended up in front of the archery targets, all of the lights at the range suddenly went on and she was like a trapped animal in headlights. It was easy (and terrifying) to know very well that she was going to get it right then and there. I fully expected to see an arrow or two penetrate her unsuspecting body, but instead, the scene changed and we could only hear her screams in the night. I likely felt cheated in not seeing the actual kill.

As the bodies piled up, there was one girl left, Alice, who stood alone against the mysterious killer. I was surprised to learn the killer was a middle-aged *woman*. From all the physical evidences throughout the movie—the jeans, the boots, the rugged-looking hands—they all pointed to a powerful man. This was when we learned from the woman called Mrs. Voorhees, an *"old friend of the Christys,"* that she was the mother of the young boy who'd drowned at the camp back in '57, an event we'd only heard about in passing from the truck driver at the beginning. She blamed her son's death on the counselors who were having sex at the time of his drowning. She was determined to kill Alice too, though I found it puzzling as to why she'd bother taking the time to reveal herself first instead of just finishing her off without hesitation. I also found it strange that no matter how many times Alice put her down with any weapon available, Mrs. Voorhees kept coming back with plenty of strength to try and finish the job. During their final struggle, I not only got excited, but I practically wanted to stand up and cheer when the camera used slow motion action to show Alice grabbing the machete and cutting off that crazy woman's head. I suppose any half-witted shrink would've argued that this thirteen-year-old boy had an unnatural attraction to murder on the big screen, but rest assured, I turned out okay (kind of).

Friday the 13th was another screen example of learning that a story isn't necessarily over when you think it is. The morning that followed Alice's survival, the entire scene was calm and picturesque as we concentrated on the beautiful morning on the lake and Alice looking at peace with herself inside the canoe on the water. All looked like a "happily ever after" ending, until that peace was shattered when a disgusting, deformed boy jumped out of the lake, grabbed Alice, and took her into the water with him. Whoah! What just happened? This was, as far as I was concerned at the time, horror movie shock and surprise at its best (*before* I saw Hitchcock's *Psycho* in its entirety). But even that wasn't the end. The real end was Alice in a hospital bed, describing what happened to her on the lake with the boy. The police didn't know what she was talking about, claiming they didn't find any boy. It concluded with a simple line that would, as it turned out, provide the setting for many sequels to come: *"Then he's still there."* Greg B. and I were left to wonder how the story had really ended. Did Alice just imagine (or dream) what happened to her or did Jason Voorhees *really* exist?

I can only say that Paramount Pictures managed to answer the latter question with every installment they shoved down our throats during the entire decade that followed. At the time of its release, I'm sure I wanted to see *Part II* because I was left in a state of curiosity and intrigue from the first movie. Somehow it just never happened. As it turned out, the original was the only movie in the extensive franchise I saw on screen at the time of its release. Everything else, with the exception of a midnight screening of *Part 3* when I was in college (I must have been *drunk* to want to see that), I watched on video. Clearly, that was the right decision. It saved a college kid like me a small fortune in ticket and food concession money; money better spent on weekend beer and parties.

Now

Much like *Rocky*, *Halloween*, or any other simple film that inevitably transforms itself into an uncontrollable franchise, one is forced to dissect, reexamine, and even reaffirm one's personal feelings and interpretations of the film that started it all, for better or worse. The *Friday the 13th* films, as released by Paramount in the '80s, was one of the most successful box office franchises in horror movie history. Yet not a single one of them ever received any positive criticism from any credible film critic or journalist. The late Roger Ebert, in his review for the original film, called director Sean S. Cunningham *"one of the most despicable creatures ever to infest the movie business."* In fact, he and his TV partner Gene Siskel spent an entire episode of their show *Sneak Previews* trashing the film, as well as other mindless slasher films of the era, because they were convinced that such films caused audiences to cheer for the killer.

Despite the success of *Halloween*, the bloody horror film wasn't new in 1980. In the '70s, there were many exploitation films of blood and gore playing in grindhouse (think of 42nd street in New York City) and drive-in theaters. Italian director Umberto Lenzi was infamous for such schlock titles as *Eaten Alive* and *Cannibal Ferox* (I've seen none of these types of horror films; not my style). The late Tobe Hooper made a name for himself with his successful 1974 horror show *The Texas Chainsaw Massacre*; a film I've seen only once and never again due to my extremely low tolerance for any sort of horror involving torture. My point is, why pick on *Friday the 13th* for merely continuing something that had already been started by others? It's a slasher film with a very exploitive title; yes, we cannot deny that. But let's go back to the very beginning and examine it for how it is as a stand-alone film. Sean S. Cunningham, while clearly at the behest of his bosses at Paramount, is trying to create the studio's own version of *Halloween*. But to his credit, it's my opinion that he, like Carpenter in *The Fog*, attempts to use atmospheric mystery, in this case the woods, the lake, and the isolated rustic summer camp as characters of fear and danger as the group of unsuspecting and defenseless kids are caught up in a nightmare of terror from which they cannot escape.

The truck driver who gives the innocent (and annoyingly perky) Annie a ride to the camp very casually gives a brief overview of the camp's cursed history, only very casually mentioning *"a boy drowned in '57"* to the point where we could easily ignore or forget it. That very mild setup, of course, proves to be a very important payoff that drives the motive behind the killer and of course the many sequels to come. I also can't deny Cunningham and writer Victor Miller the originality of surprising us with the fact that the killer is a woman; a grieving mother, no less. As you've already read, I was intrigued by this fact even as a kid of thirteen and that hasn't changed. There's also the ambiguity of just *who* Jason Voorhees was before he died (later films suggest he was bullied at camp by other kids) and who he just might be today, at a time before somebody decided to put that stupid hockey mask on him!

At best, the original film is an effective campfire story of the so-called "boogeyman" (sorry ... *woman*) designed to build up the tension and the timely shocks as it moves along through the course of just twenty-four hours. It's a film that manages to set itself apart as its own type in a slasher genre that was still working to establish itself in the first year of the new decade. In the end, I suppose *Friday the 13th* is an easy target for mockery from those who should instead take a moment to see just what sets it apart from not only its inferior sequels, but from many other inferior horror films that dominated the '80s. The film is mysterious, it's scary, it's violent, it's bloody when it has to be, and isn't *that* what a good horror film should be?

The Empire Strikes Back
Directed by Irvin Kershner
(May 21, 1980, U.S. Release Date)

Then

Try to imagine a time *before* social media and entertainment news websites like *TMZ* existed to give us the latest dirt and lowdown on movies and celebrities. There was a time when if it wasn't printed in the newspaper or a magazine or revealed on TV at the behest of the studio, secrets and inside information on a movie were only available through rumor and speculation, and believe me when I tell you that there was just as much of that sort of leaking going on *without* social media. During the immediate success of *Star Wars* in '77, fans already wanted to know more about what was next, and they'd listen to it from any source, even their own mouths. From as early as September 16, 1977, when ABC aired *The Making of Star Wars*, the late Carrie Fisher told us of her understanding that the next movie would take place (partially) on an ice planet. If you were one of the few people who actually watched CBS's *Star Wars Holiday Special* on November 17, 1978 (I missed it), then you may recall (though you would've been unaware of it at the time) an animated Boba Fett, a future character to come.

More than just these bits of information, fans wanted to know what the next movie would be titled. The first presumption was that it would simply be called *Star Wars II*; a logical enough assumption for people who didn't know a thing about the mind of George Lucas.

The next speculation was that it would be based on the 1978 sci-fi novel *Splinter of the Mind's Eye* by Alan Dean Foster, the first original full-length *Star Wars* follow-up novel. These early rumors were finally laid to rest in August 1979 when the rerelease movie poster for the original film announced the *"coming attractions for 'The Empire Strikes Back,' the continuing saga of Star Wars."* Now we knew. We just had to sit back and wait a whole ten months before we'd be back in the theater again to visit that fantastic galaxy far, far away for the second chapter. The release of *The Empire Strikes Back* wasn't just the anticipation of a world I was already head over heels obsessed with, but also the cinematic escape I needed more than ever now during a very stressful summer. So I waited as patiently as I could for my turn at the movies to experience the new *Star Wars* movie.

Released in May 1980, the secrets of *Empire* were impossible to keep from the moment it opened. By Monday morning, following its opening weekend, it seemed as if every kid in my grade had seen the movie already (some of them twice) except *me*. It was impossible not to walk the school corridors without hearing kids talking about it, and with that, came the unavoidable fact that these same kids couldn't keep their damn, little mouths shut! As a result, I learned of the mind-blowing secret that Darth Vader was Luke Skywalker's father months before I'd see it unfold for myself. I also learned that Vader was actually a deformed *human*. Call me ignorant, but for three years, I'd labored under the presumption that he was a *robot*. Learning he was actually a man behind the mask felt like more of a shock than him being Luke's father. Apparently, Luke was going to lose his hand too. By the time the movie was in theaters for only a month, I knew all its secrets, like it or not (definitely *not!*).

Asking my parents to see *Empire* was practically a waste of time. I had nothing to sell them. They knew how important it was for me to see this movie, so it was simply a matter of when, not if. The subject of *when*, however, was more difficult than you'd imagine. The movie repeatedly sold out tickets at every theater we tried. My dad became increasingly impatient trying to get tickets to something he had no personal interest in. He made the effort for his sons, but the effort wouldn't last all summer. It was finally sometime in August when my family was driving in Manhattan, that we passed a single-screen movie theater on 34th Street (now long gone) with the title in bold, blue letters. I practically screamed to my dad, asking if we could give it another try. Reluctantly, he agreed. We parked the car and walked to the ticket booth, my heart practically in my mouth wondering if we'd score or not. We got lucky and had our tickets to *The Empire Strikes Back* in hand (it only took nearly four months!).

Had I bothered to read *Time* magazine at the age of thirteen, I might've seen the May 19, 1980 issue with Darth Vader on the cover. My father subscribed to *Newsweek* instead, so I didn't see it until much later. Had I seen it though, I'd have learned beforehand that Lucas had introduced a new element to his beloved saga in which the second chapter was titled *Episode V*. This was actually one piece of information school kids *hadn't* blabbed about, or perhaps I just neglected to hear it. When I finally took my seat and once again read the title card on black of *"A long time ago in a galaxy far, far away … "*, I fully expected to see a stand-alone title and logo of *The Emprie Strikes Back* crawl across the big screen. Instead, I saw the words *Star Wars*, exactly the way it looked in the first movie, as the opening title on screen. I immediately thought the projectionist had made a terrible mistake and accidentally started the first movie instead. Of course, within a couple of seconds, my mild case of fear and panic was calmed when I read the words *Episode V*, followed by *The Empire Strikes Back*. Okay, that minor issue was cleared up, but I was no less confused as to what was happening here. If this new movie was *Episode V*, then what did that make *Star Wars*? There was no *Episode IV* attached to it when it was first released and subsequently rereleased after that (that technicality, however, was rectified when it was rereleased again in 1981, Mr. Lucas clearly covering his ass).

The story began, and aside from a newly-inserted episode number, the opening crawl and music were just as I remembered it three years ago. This time, however, things started out quietly with the Imperial Star Destroyer flying through space and ejecting a probe toward the ice planet Hoth. Moments later, Luke Skywalker was back on screen, this time covered in heavy winter clothing in what looked like an unbearable world of cold. Slowly, I understood the meaning behind the movie's title. The Rebel Alliance was constantly in danger and evading the force of the galactic Empire. The battle in the snow against the AT-AT walkers was spectacular, but the good guys weren't destined for triumph, their butts getting kicked in the snow. You could even hear one of the rebels shouting, *"Begin retreat!"*, something I'd never heard them say before. The Empire *was* definitely striking back.

Needless to say, the new *Star Wars* movie didn't fail to thrill and excite my senses. I was on the edge of my seat with excitement during the asteroid field chase, particularly noting the hard-driving, pulsating music that John Williams wrote for this scene. I can still picture the huge smile across my face as I watched one of the flaming Tie-Fighters spin out of control after being hit by one of the asteroids. While Han, Leia, Chewie, and See-Threepio hid inside one of the bigger asteroids (later revealed as the inside of a giant space monster), the subject of love was introduced to this space saga as Han and Leia appeared to be falling in love … well, just kissing anyway.

Old characters were always a welcome sight, but new friends could be just as intriguing. My first impression of the puppet Yoda was that he sounded just like Grover from *Sesame Street*, and why wouldn't he? He was performed and voiced by puppeteer Frank Oz, who had, in fact, done some of the muppets on *Sesame Street*, as well as Miss Piggy on *The Muppet Show*. He was a funny, if not silly character at first as he cried, *"Mine, mine, mine!"* like a child when he tried to grab Luke's flashlight. Not too long after, we learned just what a wise and powerful Jedi of the Old Republic he truly was. His wisdom and strength were never more apparent than when he closed his eyes and levitated Luke's X-Wing fighter out of the swamp; something Luke couldn't do himself.

Lando Calrissian was the all-around swashbuckling nice guy of Cloud City and hardly surprising that he was an old friend of Han Solo. He turned out to be anything but nice though, when in an effort to protect himself from Darth Vader and the Empire, he betrayed his old friend by turning him over to Vader and the stormtroopers. I shouted with joy during the long dining table scene because I rejoiced in the fact that only the great Han Solo would have the *balls* to whip out his laser blaster and take a shot at Darth Vader. It did no good though, as Vader simply blocked every shot with his hand. Our heroes were now prisoners of the Empire's mercy. Still, I had no doubt that Han would survive the carbonite. I mean, how could they kill off a major character like him in only the second movie? The climax at Cloud City was, without a doubt, the moment all *Star Wars* fans were waiting for. After a three-year wait, Luke Skywalker and Darth Vader were finally dueling with their lightsabers. Luke did his best to hold his own, but Vader proved to be just too powerful for him. Luke's strength weakened when he (and *we*) learned that Vader was his father. Well, at least that's what Vader *told* him anyway. Was it true? I suppose we wouldn't get the answer to that question right now. Luke, as well as our other heroes, had to escape Cloud City, and the Millenium Falcon had to achieve light speed. Up until the last moment of the climactic space chase, we weren't sure if they'd pull it off or not. They did when Artoo-Detoo repaired the malfunctioning hyperdrive and the Falcon triumphantly escaped the Empire. The entire theater cheered with excitement (except *my* parents, of course).

Chapter 2 of this monumental saga was over for me now. Still, I and others were left with questions. Was Darth Vader really Luke's father? What would happen to Han Solo who was being delivered to Jabba the Hutt by Boba Fett? What was to become of the entire Rebel Alliance as they continued to evade the Empire? We could only wait another three years to find out. In the meantime, my immediate mission was to beg my parents to let me see *Empire* again as soon as possible. That, unfortunately, would take nearly another year when the movie was rereleased on July 31, 1981. The second go-around was more fun than the first because I saw it with a couple of enthusiastic friends instead of two grown-ups who didn't want to be there in the first place. My friends and I also knew what was coming, having already seen it, and that made the experience more fun. One moment I'll never forget was watching the asteroid field sequence a second time, because by that time in '81, we'd all become die-hard fans of the Atari video game *Asteroids*. We laughed as we watched ships in space not only avoid asteroids, but destroy them as well, like a huge video game on screen. Fourteen-year-old, video-game-addicted kids surely get a kickout of that stuff.

It was rereleased again on November 19, 1982, just in time for the anticipation of the third movie in the saga, *Return of the Jedi*. Though I tried, I couldn't get myself to the theater for a third time. The next time I saw the movie again was an interesting set of circumstances. When my family finally got its first VCR in early 1984 (a Quasar pop-up model with a fake, wood grain finish), one of the first videotape recordings I managed to get my hands on was a bootleg copy of *Empire* from a friend. How he got ahold of something like that, I'll never know. It was the first time I'd ever watched anything bootlegged or was even aware such a practice existed. The picture was grainy but watchable. Considering the movie was months away from its official release on CBS-Fox video, I was happy to get what I could. I watched it many times until I finally saved my money to buy an officially-licensed copy in clear, crisp SP videotape mode (those of my generation will recall that these recordings were considered quite top-of-the-line in picture and sound quality, decades before DVD and high definition Blu-Ray discs).

All in all, from the age of thirteen well into my teenage years, *The Empire Strikes Back* was another major "force" that I'm truly grateful for. I thank creator George Lucas from the bottom of my heart for continuing to be such an important and influential part of my childhood (and I thank Irvin too).

Now

It's hard to believe that when *Empire* was released back in May 1980, it received only mixed reviews from film critics. Today, ask any fan or critic and they'll likely tell you it's the best film of the entire saga (though I still prefer the first film), as well as one of the greatest sequels of all time. It's certainly one of the darkest and most thought-provoking installments of the saga. With the exception of Yoda's introduction and childish antics, there's very little camp or fluff. The performances are stronger, more serious, and taken to greater emotional levels, particularly that of Mark Hamill as his character continues to learn of his abilities and ultimate destiny. The middle part of this three-act structure, which has less of the comic book feel of the first film, is still filled with the kind of movie magic, imagery, and technological proficiency that Lucas wants to treat us to.

Taking over the director's chair for this chapter, Irvin Kershner's version of what is still Lucas's creative brainchild, gives the film a more epic dimension and more mature aspect to an already philosophical and mythical premise. His sequel for this universe is darker, harder, and more cynical than the lighter, fairy tale pace of *Star Wars*, which somewhat limits how far and how fast the adventure travels. Events in *Empire* take place all over the galaxy, all the while maintaining the imposing theme that Darth Vader is determined to find Luke Skywalker, though we don't fully understand *why* until that climactic moment during their lightsaber duel. Even while Lucas is deliberately keeping information from us, he also knows exactly when to supply some when necessary. Whether you find this irritating or enthralling is completely up to you.

I'll now pass judgment on the job done to the film for the 1997 *special edition*. Did Lucas really feel he needed to go back and mess with it? I can almost condone his actions for the first film because there were specific deleted scenes that had to be omitted from the final print, including Han Solo's meeting with Jabba the Hutt and the character of Biggs Darklighter and his friendship with Luke Skywalker. For the second film, however, I can only define Lucas's actions as that of a spoiled child who refuses to let go of his favorite toy without a fight. His cuts, edits, and changes for the *special edition* are, in my opinion, not only deplorable decisions, but also an act of *rape* to a product that need never have been violated.

Here are some highlights of the changes that ruined the quality and integrity of the original masterpiece, in my opinion. Let's begin with the wampa of Hoth; the original film left us with an ambiguity of not only what the creature looked like, but its actions when it moved toward Luke in the cave. The new shots show it eating something bloody and screaming in pain when its arm is severed by Luke's lightsaber. There are additional shots that have been revised with

245

CGI, including Cloud City's skyline, both the exterior and interior wall panels of building corridors. Lando Calrissian's public address is revised to show the city's citizens listening to it. But what I consider truly unforgivable is the addition, deletion, and changes to specific pieces of dialogue that were already set in the original film's stone for seventeen years. Included is Luke saying, *"This is it!"* during the battle of Hoth and *"You were lucky to get out of there"* to Artoo-Detoo on Degobah. Worst of all though, is Darth Vader's line of, *"Bring my shuttle"* altered to *"Alert my Star Destroyer to prepare for my arrival."* After this line, a wide-angle CGI shot is added to show Vader boarding his shuttle.

For these reasons, I repeat that I'm glad I keep a working VCR in my life and that I own the two-disc edition of the original trilogy which includes the original films as they were at the time of their release (the Blu-Ray releases do not offer the option of both versions).

The Shining

Directed by Stanley Kubrick
(May 23, 1980, U.S. Release Date)

Then

In January 1980, my grandmother took me and Kevin to a Brooklyn movie theater to see a comedy starring three old Hollywood veterans called *Going in Style* (remade in 2017). The reason I mention this movie, having nothing to do with horror, is because before it began, the trailer for Stanley Kubrick's *The Shining* was shown (its only relation to the main feature being its release by Warner Brothers, too). The trailer was short and to the point; a pair of red elevator doors in the center of a hotel lobby gushing oceans of blood right toward us. As much as I was fascinated at such ambiguous images of horror, I was also scared to death. No actors, no dialogue, no story content— just lots of *blood*. I think my grandmother tried to reach over and cover my eyes, but failed. She certainly covered Kevin's eyes at least. Small children should *not* see such horrifying images on the screen.

At the time of its release, I had no idea who Stanley Kubrick was. I didn't know who novelist Stephen King was either (ironic, considering how much King I've read in my adulthood). I'd heard of the 1976 movie *Carrie* and had watched *Salem's Lot* on CBS back in '79, but made no connection with the book's author. Jack Nicholson was hardly a recognizable name in my small and limited world either. Of *The Shining*, I knew only the trailer I'd seen and what I'd heard in TV commercials for the movie, *"a masterpiece of modern horror"* they called it. What I was able to gather of its story was very simple and to the point; a family alone during the winter in a haunted hotel. Still very much in the process of my horror movie curiosity, I needed no further information on the subject, and neither did Greg B. As luck would have it, *The Shining* came to the local Great Neck Playhouse movie theater and by the first Saturday in June, my faithful horror school buddy and I were in our seats waiting to see whatever was about to hit us.

My first memory was the strange combination of the beautiful Colorado mountains and the sinister-sounding music that opened it. Beautiful or not, we were heading toward something that would mean trouble later. The camera took us straight to the Overlook Hotel, giving us a good look at the front of the building, then proceeding with the story of the Torrance family. Little Danny Torrance was haunted by something (or *someone*) evil named Tony that gave him horrible visions, including the blood-gushing elevators. On the day of the family's arrival at the hotel, during the initial tour, we learned that the friendly hotel cook, Mr. Hallorann, appeared to be gifted (or cursed) with the same strange powers as Danny—powers he called *"shining."* While Mr. Halloran gave a detailed explanation of Danny's abilities, I didn't quite understand every word he was saying, but it was clear that both of them had the ability to see what had happened in the past and what was going to happen in the future. As Mr. Hallorann put it regarding the hotel's history, *"not all of it was good."* The warning he gave Danny to stay out of Room 237 was clear enough even to two thirteen-year-old boys in the theater whose horror movie experiences were still limited.

By the time the family was living in the hotel for a month and the first snowstorm hit, there was (again) that sense of environmental beauty combined with a sense of dread from the accompanying musical soundtrack. We understood that this family was on its own in the middle of nowhere during a crippling snowstorm, and no one or nothing would save them when they faced the horrors to come. They started when Danny disobeyed Mr. Hallorann's warning and went into Room 237. I remember preparing myself for something really horrible to happen to the poor boy right then and there.

Instead, the scene dissolved into a new one. It was only later when Jack awoke from a nightmare that we learned of Danny's experience inside that forbidden room. Apparently, the family wasn't alone in the hotel. According to Wendy, there was a crazy woman inside that room who tried to strangle Danny. When Jack investigated, we witnessed something that may or may not have been real. Again, bearing in mind that this was a tale of a haunted hotel, I presumed the beautiful woman with the great naked body (not for too long) was a ghost or spirit of sorts. Surely, if there was any doubt about the scene in that room, there was absolutely no doubt in my mind during the ballroom bar scene that Jack was talking to a ghostly bartender of the past. It all couldn't have been real, because it immediately disappeared when Wendy entered the ballroom to tell Jack of the crazy woman.

After more than half of the movie had passed, I could tell *The Shining* was not like the typical slasher movies that existed. It wasn't even violent or bloody. It was, instead, able to scare its audience by constantly suggesting what might happen next around any given corner. We also watched Jack Torrance go slowly insane. I recall an intrigued smile on my face during the scene when Wendy discovered that all of Jack's writings consisted of only the repeated sentence, *"All work and no play makes Jack a dull boy,"* and he showed up in her face, proceeding to scream at and threaten her in a completely crazed state of mind. Regardless of exactly what he said as he rambled on, it was entertaining just to listen to an actor like Nicholson (whom I'd never forget after *this* movie) make his presence and his words so well-heard and feared. By the time the story reached its climax, Jack had gone completely insane and was hunting his family with an axe (just as the previous caretaker had done back in 1970, so we were told earlier). It was during the chase scene inside the snow-covered hedge maze that I really noticed the camera work involved (because I almost never paid attention to just *how* a movie was made when I was a kid). The camera made you feel like you were moving along with Danny as he ran for his life from his father, around one corner and another (I learned years later that this is known as a *tracking shot*), as well as Jack's perspective and he chased down his son.

When it was over and it appeared as if every horror of the hotel's past had returned to haunt Wendy, she and Danny finally escaped the hotel with their lives, leaving Jack behind to freeze to death. Things ended quietly with the camera zooming into a series of black and white pictures on one of the hotel walls. In one of the photographs dated July 4, 1921, there was a man who looked just like Jack Torrance, smiling among a crowd of partygoers. What did this final shot mean? Was Jack really alive? Was he once someone else in another life at the same hotel? Was it Jack's grandfather? I was dumbfounded and confused, and so was Greg B. Later, as we sat at the local pizzeria, we tried to come up with a reasonable explanation as to how *The Shining* had ended and what it all really meant. Two pizza slices and two sodas later, we didn't accomplish our goal. Regardless, we gratefully added another awesome horror movie to our growing list of experiences (I think we spent the next week at school repeating the line, *"Here's Johnny!"*).

The Shining premiered on the *ABC Friday Night Movie* on May 6, 1983. I didn't get to watch it because my family was on the road driving to the beach house (by the time we got there, the movie was ending). I didn't see it again until sometime during my senior year of high school. A buddy and I (not Greg B.) rented the video and watched it together. By this time, I'd seen *2001* several times and had also discovered *Dr. Strangelove*. Thought I could now equate the name of Stanley Kubrick to these great pieces of work, it wasn't until the end of *The Shining's* opening credits that I joyously shouted, "Holy shit! This is a Stanley Kubrick film?" My buddy's response (after laughing) was, "You didn't know that?" This is the ignorance I got for waiting five long years before watching the movie again.

Now

The Shining is my favorite horror film of all time by my favorite film director of all time and has been my entire adult life. At thirteen, however, my appreciation for the film existed simply because it was a scary story about a haunted hotel in Colorado and a totally cool spectacle to watch. Those are the cinematic interpretations of a *child*, and they're more than credible for someone that age. Eventually though, you grow up and you (hopefully) learn to watch films and interpret them by not only their story content, but by their hidden meanings and messages as well when applicable. Call me crazy, but I simply cannot resist a motion picture that dares me to use my *brain* and take the time and patience to figure out the complexities of its content. This is why the great films by the great filmmakers often require multiple viewings for the full understanding and appreciation they surely deserve.

Stanley Kubrick's version of Stephen King's novel (a version King considers a poor adaptation) is not simply a horror movie that you watch as you would any other cheap offering. The Overlook Hotel is not merely a mountain resort, but rather an invitation to the dark and evil side of our human personality. There are challenges to the mind and questions that require time, thought, and effort to *try* and answer. There are ambiguities, feelings of open-endedness, and elusiveness that force us to wonder which version of reality we're meant to accept. Is it simply the ghostly disturbances dominating an isolated mountain setting with an evil past *or* are we members of a living nightmare that's possibly manifested through Danny Torrance's powers of *"shining"*? Is it possible that the Torrances are not even *at* the Overlook in the first place, but rather drawn into the abovementioned nightmare through their son's powerful abilities?

Let's begin by examining the Overlook Hotel itself. In many traditional horror films, there's a feeling (if not an *art*) of claustrophobia because the story is set in a limited environment that may be difficult for its characters to escape forces beyond their control. Think of the motel grounds and Victorian house in *Psycho*, the bedroom of Regan MacNeil in *The Exorcist*, the suburban Haddonfield home in *Halloween*, the two-story colonial house in *The Amityville Horror*, and the confined New Jersey camp grounds and woods in *Friday the 13th*; we can't help but feel trapped inside a tight space. The Overlook, however, is a complex space that's so vast, we become frightened of what possibly lurks around the corner of a long, enclosed corridor. Kubrick recognizes this and uses his trademark steady tracking shot to follow Danny riding his big wheel down corridor after corridor, until he finally comes face to face with the supernatural ghostly apparitions of the twin Grady girls, whom we know to be previous victims of their father's homicidal rage. Although we're not sure of what's waiting for us around the bend, we know that Kubrick is setting us up for a good jolt at the end of Danny's ride. This odd combination of grand spaciousness and confinement provides an irresistible uncertainty to just what's real at this hotel and what's not. I suppose it's all as real as the Torrance family is willing to believe and accept as real or not.

The Shining is ultimately a tale of madness and not necessarily of traditional ghosts. Kubrick may even be suggesting the possibility that the ghosts don't exist at all, except in the mind of the Torrances, perhaps victims of the so-called *cabin fever* mentioned by Mr. Ullman at the beginning of the film. Reality becomes an unreliable entity through their eyes and perceptions. Perhaps its only Dick Halloran who's the impartial party in this situation. Like Danny, he has the power of *"shining,"* but he's on the outside looking in, even from as far away as Miami, Florida. His arrival at the Overlook hardly puts together any solid understanding of what's happening, but serves as just a chance participant and concerned human being for the lives of Danny and his parents. His arrival is short, sweet, and cut down violently when he's axed to death by Jack. In the end, the only truly reliable observers to the events of the film are *us*, and we have to decide for ourselves what's real and what's not. These challenges may not necessarily be scary within the film's content, but they create nonetheless a terrifying feeling within ourselves that makes such a horror film work effectively.

During Jack's job interview, Mr. Ullman mentions the previous caretaker of 1970 whose name was *Charles* Grady, who murdered his family with an axe before taking his own life with a shotgun. Later, during the ballroom scene, Jack meets *Delbert* Grady, a butler from the year 1920, in the men's room. Are the two men different people in different lifetimes *or* are they two manifestations of the same inexplicable evil entity of the Overlook, or perhaps even Jack's mind? Delbert Grady tells Jack that he's *"always been the caretaker,"* which somehow suggests that Jack was present at the hotel in 1920, which gives us a clue to his presence in the black and white July 1921 photograph at the end of the film. Or, like Grady, is it possible that Jack is indeed *two* people—one who freezes to death in 1980 and one who lives in 1921? There's also the argument that upon freezing to death, Jack's spirit was *absorbed* into the Overlook itself, transcending him back in time to 1921, where he may or may not have existed before as a member of the hotel's history.

These are tough challenges that are not necessarily easy to answer. *I* don't have the answers. Perhaps in the end, there *is* no right or wrong answer. Like a great painting hanging on a museum wall, it's a simple matter of personal interpretation and just what message and meaning its content offers you. Maybe it's best not to have these questions answered at all. Were they to be answered, *The Shining* may cease to be the extraordinary viewing experience that it is, that it has always been and shall continue to be if everything is so easily delivered in a box with a lovely ribbon on it. I don't ever want that to happen. The thirteen-year-old kid I was once was more than willing to wrap things up nice and neat after just over two hours of film time. The lover of Stanley Kubrick cinema that I am today outright refuses to accept things so neat and tidy.

That's just too damn easy!

The Blues Brothers

Directed by John Landis
(June 20, 1980, U.S. Release Date)

Then

When I first saw the trailer for *The Blues Brothers*, I presumed they were original movie characters. I had no idea they were a fictional act from *Saturday Night Live*, because as a child, I wasn't permitted to stay up late enough (even on a Saturday night) to watch a show that started at 11:30 p.m. (Eastern standard time). I probably thought "The Blues Brothers" was a real band too. Because I'd already convinced my father to take me to see a raunchy R-rated comedy like *Animal House*, *The Blues Brothers* (same director John Landis and same star John Belushi) was no great struggle (conveniently playing in town too). We kept this a secret from my mother because like *Animal House*, it also contained its share of vulgarity.

The movie's opening credits began in a way I'd never seen before. The names of all principal filmmakers, editors, technicians, etc., were listed during the opening sequence when Jake Blues was released from prison. It was only when he was finally outside and facing his brother, Elwood Blues, that the names of both stars John Belushi and Dan Aykroyd, as well as the movie's title, were revealed. The two brothers hugged, and the music began. As they drove together in one of those older-looking police cars, Elwood proclaimed it the new "Blues mobile," despite Jake's dislike for the car. Upon their visit to the nun who raised them as orphan boys, a nun they nicknamed "the

Penguin," I didn't fully understand just why they had to raise $5,000 and what the consequences were if they didn't (what did *I* know of back taxes?). I only understood that it had to be done quick. The other thing that confused me was their near rundown of a group of Illinois Nazis in the sequence that followed. From what I understood as a young boy, the Nazis of Germany had been defeated at the end of World War II. What were they doing in modern-day 1980 at an organized protest? Why weren't they in jail? Why weren't they *dead*?

I knew as soon as they were pulled over for running a red light, the trouble and excitement would begin. If they were arrested, they'd never raise the money in time to save their orphanage from being closed. From the moment they took off, it turned into an action-packed chase movie in the same tradition as a Hal Needham/Burt Reynolds movie. The chase scene in the shopping mall was awesome, especially when accompanied by the jazz and blues instrumental music that gave one the feeling of speed as we watched the cars tear down the strip mall. When they finally escaped the police (for the time being), I remember laughing when Elwood took Jake up to his apartment and I saw just how tiny it was. If that was meant to be comical, it sure worked on me nonetheless. This movie was also using elements of the unbelievable and the fantastic, because when Elwood's apartment building was exploded (by Carrie Fisher, no less) and they crashed to the ground, neither the brothers nor the arresting police were injured in any way. That occurred again when Carrie tried to kill them with a flame thrower while they stood together in a phone booth and came crashing down hard to the ground.

The strongest element of the movie, however, was the musical performances. I even enjoyed the number they did in the gospel church, despite my inexperience and ignorance to relate to gospel music in any way. Even though this wasn't in the same musical league as *Grease* and *Hair*, I still enjoyed it. This wasn't exactly Broadway show tunes either. It had rhythm, blues, and elements of rock and roll too. When the brothers and the band finally made it to the grand ballroom to perform their one-night-only concert, it felt like I was actually at the show from the energy of their screen performance. When the show was over, it was obvious that the light-hearted musical portion of this movie was over. The chase sequences were about to get serious and even destructive because Jake and Elwood were determined not to get caught before delivering the money. From the moment Elwood said, *"It's a hundred and six miles to Chicago, we got a full tank of gas, half a pack of cigarettes, it's dark, and we're wearing sunglasses,"* and Jake replied, *"Hit it,"* I geared up and prepared myself for anything that would happen to these guys.

Everybody was after the notorious Blues Brothers. Not just the police, but the Illinois Nazis and an angry country-western band called the Good Ol' Boys who lost their paying gig due to the brothers' deception in the country bunker scene. The unbelievable and the fantastic continued when the brothers eluded the police with a bunch of very improbable driving maneuvers, including a miraculous, gravity-defying move that eluded the Nazis as well. Not understanding "suspension of disbelief" at my age, I simply accepted the ridiculous as something to laugh at. It was when they arrived at their Chicago destination that their old police car *finally* fell apart after all the insane, reckless, and dangerous driving done throughout the movie. Elwood actually removed his hat, as if paying respect to a dear, departed friend.

Inside the building, they were buying time until they could complete their mission (from God). To watch what looked like the entire city police force, the military, and even helicopters swarming all over the building just to capture *two* men who weren't even armed was simply outrageous, and I loved every minute of it. By the time they did their job and got their receipt, I didn't even realize that the county clerk was Steven Spielberg himself. I'd seen four of his movies already, but I never actually saw what the man looked like (I should've read more magazines other than *Mad* as a kid).

As my father and I walked out of the theater, my first thought was to spend some of my allowance money to buy the movie's record soundtrack. It was impossible to ignore the music from *The Blues Brothers*, despite the fact I generally wasn't a fan of rhythm and blues. However, it was catchy music and I liked the jazz and horn elements of it. I also liked the album's version of "Jailhouse Rock," despite never being a fan of Elvis. Really, more than anything else, it was a way to stay connected to a movie I loved and to try and continue the escape it provided me during a terrible childhood summer (I did the same thing by purchasing the soundtrack for *Empire* as well. I still own them today).

Now

I'm not a fan of films based on *Saturday Night Live* characters. I stopped watching the show following its tenth season in 1985 because I simply wasn't laughing anymore. I suppose I got a temporary kick out of *Wayne's World* when I was in college because its two characters were a couple of rock and roll misfits, and that was the kind of stuff that made a cool movie when you're the type of guy who likes to drink, party, and listen to hard rock music too. But as I matured, such a film became silly and mindless, as compared against stronger material like *Animal House* or some of the selected teen comedies and John Landis films that were popular in the '80s. In fact, since *Wayne's World*, I've seen none of the *SNL*-character-based films, which means *The Blues Brothers* is the only one that's stood the test of time with me and my childhood memories.

Now that I'm of age where I can fully appreciate and even practice the concept of "suspension of disbelief," the over-the-top elements of the fantastic, the unbelievable, and even the outright ridiculous are easy to tolerate when it's up against genuine laughs and stirring musical numbers. Belushi and Aykroyd, close friends that they were, have excellent chemistry with each other as not only brothers, but as musicians who understand each other. There's a moment at the church when Jake declares that their band should reunite and Elwood has his doubts. Seconds later though, Elwood comes around and the two are synced in music and outrageous dance moves. Belushi and Aykroyd's characters are, let's face it, hard-boiled, sloppy men of a lower-class city element, yet are able to achieve dance moves that are irresistible to watch. The two men understand each others rhythms as actors too. Keep your eyes on their facial gestures and the way they slowly look at each other when something out of the ordinary happens to them.

There's an undeniably strong sense of cynicism in this film, despite whatever charm and grace it possesses during the music, the crack-up car chases, and the comedy. Exactly what kind of a world were we living in where an orphanage filled with children would be so calously closed up by its own church and the city? Just how sadistic are people's will to wreak havoc upon an entire city through wreckless auto endangerment, as well as their desire for violent revenge against others? Carrie Fisher as Jake's jilted ex proves (well, at least back then she did) that she could go beyond the likable persona of Princess Leia and become something else entirely (dare I say, over to the *dark side*). Her need for vengeance against the man she once loved is beyond believable as she appears perfectly at home with exploding devices, igniting a blow torch and firing an M16 rifle at her targets. Well, that sort of nastiness lasts for a while anyway. Once her eyes meet with Jake's in the only instance he removes his glasses, she weakens (rather pathetically) and is once again left alone in the mud when Jake takes off on his own agenda.

As a straightforward comedy, *The Blues Brothers* may not necessarily be the funniest thing on film. It's timing may have even been off back in 1980. Belushi and Aykroyd were finished with *SNL,* and their previous screen effort together, *1941*, failed with critics. Perhaps it's because that Belushi died a young man on March 5, 1982, that we cling to and cherish everything he gave before he left us. He was, in my opinion, one of the most energetic and spontaneous men of comedy and mayhem that I've seen on screen and television, not too unlike Robin Williams (who also left us too soon in 2014). When gifted men like them are taken from us too quickly, the laughter they leave behind is more precious to our hearts and our memories. Belushi's style even exceeds Williams's in a way because he was considered such a slob in his mannerism. Maybe that's part of what made us laugh so much. I believe John Landis understood that, and he gave us two of Belushi's best films as a result.

Airplane!

Directed by Jim Abrahams, David, and Jerry Zucker
(July 2, 1980, U.S. Release Date)

———

Then

Another outrageous comedy was just what I needed that summer. My father would have no part of it though. He'd put up with enough stupidity on my behalf with *The Blues Brothers* and didn't want to spend more time and money on that sort of movie. Since it was PG-rated, he told me to just see it with a friend instead. Due to one circumstance or another, I was unable to see *Airplane!* during its initial theatrical run. I managed to see it by myself some months later as a double feature with another comedy called *The Kentucky Fried Movie*. I stayed for all of *Airplane!* and managed to only watch about less than half of the second feature before I had to go home.

At thirteen, I was aware of men like Mel Brooks, though I still hadn't seen any of his movies (yes, I was with my father at the local drive-in back in '74 during *Young Frankenstein*, but I was hardly in a position to pay attention to, nor remember its content). While I was inexperienced at the comic sub-genre called spoof, I *had* seen the first three of four *Airport* disaster movies of the previous decade, so I was familiar enough with that genre to appreciate an attempt to make fun of such material. Still, I wasn't too sure what it meant to *spoof* or *parody* something. Was it an airplane disaster movie with jokes added? Were the passengers in danger going to be funny? From the moment it opened with the airplane's tail end moving through the clouds like a shark fin in water to the music of *Jaws* … well, now I understood what sort of comedy this was, and I loved it. This would have no logic, reason, or sensibility, whatsoever. It was pure and wild laughs from beginning to end. I smiled and prepared myself.

One of the first things I realized watching *Airplane!* was that I had to keep my eyes and ears open at all times. Even while I paid close attention to what turned out to be a silly, personal argument between male and female airport zoning announcers, I could've easily missed something visual that took place in the background. Although I hadn't gone through too many airports in my life, I imagined one expecting strangers to approach you and try to sell you things or ask for a donation. How wonderful it would feel to finally slug one of those annoying creeps. This movie entertained such fantasies. When the main character Ted Striker looked at us in the audience after his girlfriend Elaine dumped him and said, *"What a pisser!"*, I felt I could relate to someone (even myself) wanting to share just how pissed off we were. It was like Woody Allen in *Annie Hall* all over again when he'd look at us and tell us just what he was thinking and feeling. I loved to laugh at stuff like that.

Much of what I determined from *Airplane!* was the idea of life's *"what ifs"* that would (hopefully) never come to pass. *What if* we got stuck sitting next to someone who insisted on sharing his entire life story with us, as Ted repeatedly did with those on the plane who just didn't want to hear it (we'd kill ourselves just like they did!)? *What if* two African American men were so hip, so cool, so *jive*, that their spoken language reflected them as such? *What if* some kindly-looking old woman could actually speak their jive language and communicate what they needed to the stewardess? *What if* it was really possible to remove a single plug from just one electrical outlet (even if you were *"just kidding"*) and darken the entire airport runway? When considering these improbable questions, it was impossible not to laugh out loud at such ideas on screen. I think I finally understood what spoof was all about.

As a kid, I didn't always understand the adult themes behind what I saw, even in comedy. I didn't understand the airplane captain's inappropriate innuendos behind his questions to little Joey such as, *"Do you like movies about gladiators?"* and *"Have you ever been in a Turkish prison?"* (had I been old enough to see *Midnight Express*, then I might've gotten that last one). I didn't understand what Elaine meant when she said to Ted, *"I remember how I used to sit on your face and wriggle."* I didn't understand what the Anita Bryant concert was. I didn't understand why Mrs. Oveur was in bed with a horse. I didn't understand why anybody, in their right mind, would want to sniff glue. Finally, I didn't understand exactly what was happening when Elaine blew air into the small tube of the inflatable automatic pilot between both of his legs (though I'll confess I did have a sneaking suspicion of what it meant). However, not fully understanding the meaning behind adult innuendos doesn't stop a kid from laughing at the humor behind them. It worked with *Animal House* when I was younger, and it worked again now.

Airplane! kept me laughing right up until the very end. Even as the plane experienced its own form of insanity when it came in for a landing, one of the best laughs was the radio DJ's on-air declaration, *"where disco lives forever!"* just before the station signal antenna was destroyed forever, clearly mocking, if not confirming, the end of disco music by 1980. I laughed with a little extra enthusiasm because it reminded me of my own personal decision to stop listening to disco music for fear of being ridiculed by other kids during a time when rock and roll and punk music took over the radio airwaves. When it was over and everyone and everything had "lived happily ever," it was fortunate that I chose to stay for the closing credits because had I left, I would've missed the movie's final gag of the poor man *still* sitting in Ted Striker's taxi cab, continuing to wait for him to return, before looking at his watch and declaring, *"Well, I'll give him another twenty minutes. But that's it."* That was the movie's perfect final laugh. Unfortunately, like other times that summer, the laughter ended eventually and I'd have to return to reality and face the stresses of my home and family.

Now

Since *Airplane!*'s release thirty-eight years ago, the spoof genre has been never-ending; from *The Naked Gun* to *Hot Shots!* to *Scary Movie* to the last (disappointing) efforts that Mel Brooks gave us in the '90s. With so many parodies and so many parody sequels, we're inevitably forced to pause and ask ourselves just how many times we can continuously laugh at the same recycled material over and over again? When does it all just stop being funny because we feel we've seen it before too many damn times? It's also important to note that in addition to Brooks, I've exposed myself to many of the crazy antics in slapstick comedies of such legendary men as the Marx Brothers (thank you, Turner Classic Movies). In other words, the spoof, the parody, and the slapstick comedy is hardly anything new in the history of cinema, so I'm a lot more critical of what I laugh at today.

Airplane! still makes me laugh, but perhaps for different reasons than it did when I was thirteen. Back then, it was practically a requirement for the laughs to be very obvious and in-my-face for them to work. As an adult, I recognize and appreciate the more subtle moments, particulary in the dialogue, where something as simple as a pun can strike the right chrod of humor within us. Even though I've never watched a complete episode of *Leave it to Beaver*, realizing now that the old woman speaking jive is the late Barbara Billingsley, making a cameo appearance completely against her best known all-American purity of June Cleaver, makes the intent behind the joke all the more worthwhile. Understanding now the character of Captain Clarence Oveur is just a sick pedophile doesn't necessarily make his verbal sexual innuendos toward a child funny (that's *never* funny!), but it's still sick and totally insane humor, nonetheless. Knowing now who and what Ethel Merman looks like, it makes her cameo as a mental patient singing one of her own popular songs something to laugh at. Even recognizing now that it's actually Jimmie Walker cleaning the windshield of the airplane before take-off puts a nostalgic smile on my face, because as a kid, I loved him on *Good Times*.

Today, the irresistible humor of *Airplane!* is the little stuff you could easily miss if you turn away too quickly, especially the verbal punning. Just look at how stoic Leslie Neilson looks when he tells Robert Hayes, *"I am serious ... and don't call me Shirley,"* to counteract the true meaning of the intended word *surely*. Then there's the mis-understandings taking place whenever a character asks the innocent question of *"What is it?"* and rather than get the information of the situation that's taking place, they get, instead an explanation of the *thing* in question and that it's really not important right now. Think, *"This woman has to be gotten to a hospital,"* followed by, *"A hospital? What is it?"*, and concluded with, *"It's a big building with patients, but that's not important right now."* It's a repeated gag, yes, but so help me, I never get tired of it. Sometimes even the most professional-looking characters are uttering such nonsense, you can't help but laugh at the lunacy of it. Specifically, I'm describing a very brief scene during the airplane's impending doom when a TV commentator looks bluntly into the camera and declares with merciless conviction, *"Shanna, they bought their tickets, they knew what they were getting into. I say, let 'em crash!"* Perhaps it's not so much *what* he's saying, but rather *how* he's saying it, like a cynical bastard who just doesn't give a crap about anything or anybody. That, in my opinion, *is* funny!

Caddyshack

Directed by Harold Ramis
(July 25, 1980, U.S. Release Date)

***

Then

Between the sci-fi of *Empire*, the horror, and the comedies, the escapism of the movie theater was effectively doing its job. Truth be told, I had no real interest in seeing *Caddyshack*. Perhaps it was because I had no idea what the movie title meant. Perhaps it was because I couldn't relate to golf in any way, even as comedy. Perhaps it was simply because my inexperience with watching *SNL* in the past didn't afford me the knowledge of who Chevy Chase and Bill Murray were. My familiarity with Ted Knight was due only to episodes of *The Mary Tyler Moore Show* I'd watched as a child. Rodney Dangerfield was a complete unknown to me.

When a friend of mine (not Greg B.) asked me if I wanted to go see *Caddyshack* with him and a couple of other boys, I hardly passed down the opportunity. The movie, however, was not playing in town, which meant my friends and I would be driven to a theater in another town by one of their parents. This meant I'd have to have to tell my parents I was seeing something other than *Caddyshack*. While my father was occasionally lenient when it came to R-rated movies, my mother ... well, not so much. It depended on the subject matter, that is *Saturday Night Fever* and dancing. Beyond that, she had a low tolerance level for vulgarity in the presence of her children. In order to be permitted out of the house and into the theater, I was obligated to lie and tell them my friends and I were going to see a PG-rated film released that same month called *Honeysuckle Rose*; a movie with country singer Willie Nelson that to this day I've never had the slightest interest in seeing because I don't like country music. Anyway, they bought it.

Despite the fact that *Caddyshack* opened with a gopher that looked remarkably like a puppet trailing through and destroying a golf course that I suppose was meant to be a funny situation, what immediately caught my attention was the house that the main character, Danny Noonan, lived in. Bedroom after bedroom, behind door after door, there were children upon children, and *more* children after that. Even in the kitchen, there was an extra child eating breakfast who didn't even belong to this family. I concluded that any family that would (and could) have this many children had to be either very rich or very insane. The Noonan's were clearly not rich, as the father immediately scolded Danny for not putting all of his money earned as a country club caddy in the family college fund. As the oldest child of (I don't know how many because I've still never counted) these kids, he was eager to be out on his own, even if it was just the time spent at his meager caddying job.

As a kid watching what was clearly verbal adult humor, I wasn't too knowledgeable to what the characters were talking about half the time. Nonetheless, when you're with your friends watching an R-rated comedy that you all shouldn't have been admitted to in the first place, you feel almost a certain peer pressure to laugh. Just because you don't necessarily get the joke doesn't mean it's not funny. This puzzlement started when Danny and Ty Webb were walking together on the golf course and a conversation started that went like this:

> *"Do you take drugs, Danny?"*
> *"Everyday."*
> *"Good."*

I was a smart-enough kid to understand that taking drugs was wrong and that if someone were to actually say, *"everyday"* and sound proud of it, then there was clearly an intended joke behind it. Still, I remember only sitting there with a mild smile on my face, unable to truly understand the humor behind it. Perhaps I was disappointed because instead of slapstick humor on the golf course, I got dialogue that sounded sincere and serious, even though it clearly wasn't meant to be. The arrival of Al Czervik and Carl Spackler the greens keeper were different stories entirely. These men were just a couple of silly slobs; one rich, one not. Al was disrespectful and foulmouthed. Carl was stupid and determined to destroy a single gopher at any cost. He was also daring enough to actually take a bite out of what was floating in the swimming pool and say, *"It's no big deal." We* knew it was just a wet candy bar, but everyone else thought it was … well, you know. *This* is funny stuff to a kid. Two men smoking what I thought (at the time) was an ordinary cigarette the size of a sausage and drinking wine from a bottle is *not* necessarily funny stuff to a kid who doesn't fully get the joke of drugs and alcohol. There was also the judge, who was an angry, intolerant man who absolutely hated Al and his entire low-class presence at such an upscale place like Bushwood Country Club. In other words, he was a royal snob, and I suppose that made *him* the bad guy and the rich slob and the crazy gopher killer the heroes.

Because my young male hormones were in full gear and virtually unstoppable, the young blonde named Lacey Underall (I didn't get *that* either) was a stunning beauty to gawk at. The moments where she got naked for her bed scene with Danny and showed plenty of skin for her massage scene with Ty Webb was surely worth the price of my ticket, even if I didn't get all of the movie's humor (never let it be said that young boys who like women don't like scenes of female toplessness. They do!).

Both of the golf tournaments were, I suppose, entertaining in their own respect. During the first Caddy Day tournament, I found it funny the way his opponent, the mean Italian guy, and his friends kept trying to distract Danny be repeatedly shouting, *"Noon"* in his face. It didn't work though, because Danny won the tournament anyway. I felt a small sense of victory for that one. The second one was likely intended to create a sense of suspense and tension, as the monetary stakes of the game kept getting higher and higher. By the time it all climaxed, Carl the greens keeper finally decided the only way to get rid of his sworn enemy, Mr. Gopher, was to blow up the entire golf course. Explosion after explosion, the grounds were shaking off their foundation. Still, our eyes stayed focused on Danny's golf ball, which was teetering on the edge of the final hole. It was easily predictable that it would go in and Danny would win the big game. There, I suppose, was the big sports victory that would have us stand up and cheer. We didn't though. We just smiled because it was all supposed to be funny, though I still wasn't sure why half the time. That in mind, when my friends and I left the theater and waited to be picked up, I didn't feel as if I'd been sufficiently distracted enough from my summer problems by what was supposed to have been this great comedy. In short, it's safe to say when I saw *Caddyshack* back in July 1980, even after fabricating a convincing lie to my parents, I didn't care for it too much.

Now

Time can change the way you look at movies you once experienced as a kid, in either a good or bad way. In fact, it's impossible for me to believe there was ever a time in my life that I didn't love *Caddyshack*. Today, when I'm occasionally asked if I play golf, my answer is always the same, "No. But I've seen *Caddyshack* many times." That usually gets a good laugh out of people. I suppose I'm just one of the many people who have come to love this film through a long cult following, because it wasn't well-received upon its release. While I still can't claim that it holds a great deal of slapstick comedy to hold it all together, it is nonetheless happily laced with some of the most endlessly quotable comedy dialogue since *Animal House*. How many times have I and those I know been performing some athletic task and suddenly said to ourselves and everyone around us, *"A Cinderella story, outta nowhere"* or even, *"I'd keep playing. I don't think the heavy stuff is gonna come down for quite a while"*?

The film's entire dialogue process is easier to appreciate as an adult of knowledge and experience. *Now* I understand the irony of Danny Noonan's affirmative response to taking drugs. Rodney Dangerfield is, without a doubt, priceless as a rich slob who doesn't give a damn about anything or anybody except his own private, selfish interests, as well as his leisurely golf games. You *want* a man like Judge Smails to be pissed off throughout the film because it's funny to watch a man like him suffer. While the act of Bill Murray's hellbent intent to kill the gopher may not necessarily be a laugh riot, it's his dialogue with himself throughout the process that's irresistible to listen to (and quote later). We know very well that he never actually caddied for the Dalai Lama in Tibet, but we want to hear the story nonetheless, even if the poor kid with the pitchfork to his throat doesn't. When we've seen the film our fair share of times, we look forward to the moment when Carl concludes his Tibetan story with, *"So I got that goin' for me, which is nice."* I also comprehend the obvious (though still laughable) stupidity behind many of the film's character names that include Lacey Underall, Dr. Beeper, Spaulding Smails, Smoke Porterhouse, and even Mitch Cumstein. Sometimes the joke is so obviously simple and ridiculous, you can't help but laugh anyway.

What makes the dialogue of *Caddyshack* work so well for me is that its four main alumni characters don't necessarily *try* to be funny or *sound* funny when they're speaking. When Ty Webb speaks of the Zen philosophy behind golf and spouts his infinite wisdom behind donuts, donut holes, and danishes, he sincerely means it. When Judge Smails is making that silly speech about his shorts not being too tight in the seat before christening his new boat, he's completely sincere behind it. We laugh because they're silly words comprised into a poem, but Smials believes them to be from the heart. Al Czervik, being the classless guy he is, feels perfectly at home speaking his mind to whomever he feels deserves his frankness. He hates Judge Smails and freely takes a stab at his wife when he tells her, *"You musta been something before electricity,"* or asks her, *"Do you wanna make fourteen dollars the hard way?"* Even the quickest and most subtle of wisecracks, such as Al addressing the bishop Fred Pickering with the words, *"Hey, Rabbi, how are you?"* are hilarious because we appreciate the man's sincere disinterest in not considering other people around him. If the people of *Caddyshack* were sensitive and otherwise socially acceptable human beings, we'd having nothing to laugh at (perhaps this is where NBC's *Seinfeld* got its inspiration).

Looking back at the film now, I can't help but reconsider the negative reaction I had toward it at that young age. Was I *really* that unable to follow along with the adult humor in its dialogue? Was it an impossible film to enjoy even if it wasn't completely loaded with over-the-top insanity? Or maybe, was it simply the fact that I expected, and perhaps *needed*, something a lot stronger to pacify my childhood anxieties at the time? Perhaps it no longer matters because, like it or not, the past is the past and we try to grow as we proceed into the future. But since movies have the power to leave a lasting impression on us, *Caddyshack* serves to remind me of not only who I was and what I liked as a kid, but also how that same film evolved a kid into a man. Maybe I just shouldn't take it all so seriously. After all, it's not Bergman or Fellini. It's just feakin' *Caddyshack*!

As Kenny Loggins sings, *"I'm alright. Don't nobody worry 'bout me."*

Flash Gordon

Directed by Mike Hodges
(December 5, 1980, U.S. Release Date)

Then

The influence of *Star Wars* and the many copycat movies it spawned well into the beginning of the '80s wasn't letting up. I knew the character Flash Gordon went back nearly fifty years, though I'd never seen the original serials on TV, nor had I seen any of the original comic strips from the 1930s. The newspaper ad promised action and excitement. Even the title itself had a lightning bolt going through the center circle of it, so I suppose it *had* to be good. These feelings were confirmed when I finally saw the full movie poster in all its colorful glory. It also had rock music by Queen, a band I'd discovered through their previous rock anthem of '78, *"We Will Rock You/We are the Champions."*

Let me digress for a moment to catch you up on my life by the time December 1980 rolled around. Summer was long past and the routines of the eighth grade were somewhat comforting in settling things down at home and with my parents. I also had a serious boyhood crush on a younger blonde whom I shall call *Robin M.* I mention her because she had some significant bearing on the conditions in which I saw *Flash Gordon*. The movie was due to play at our neighborhood theater. That was a good thing. The word around school was that many kids I knew would attend the Saturday matinee the day following its opening. That too was a good thing. But most important, I learned that Robin M. would be there. *That* was the best thing!

I'll describe the scene to you. It was a Saturday afternoon in December and it seemed as if nearly every kid in Great Neck was gathered at the Playhouse for an afternoon matinee of *Flash Gordon* (it might as well have been the '30s all over again, but without the opening newsreels and cartoon). I was there with Kevin and seated near a couple of my friends. Somewhere, not too far away, Robin M. was there with a couple of her own friends. Did I make a daring move closer toward her? Did I ask her to sit with me so I could take the chance of holding her hand during the movie? Man, I wish I could say *yes*, but I can't. You see, yours truly was, unfortunately, a shy kid and felt awkward around girls, especially the ones I was attracted to. So I did nothing and said nothing. I only took pleasure in the fact that I was seated in the same movie theater not too far away from one of the most beautiful twelve-year-old girls I'd ever seen.

This new movie was (obviously) riding the coattails of *Star Wars, Superman—The Movie,* and *Star Trek—The Motion Picture.* From the opening scene, someone evil was controlling things from another world in order to create chaos and disaster for our planet. The scene was brief before it switched to the opening credits. This is where I really sat up and took notice because the credits were very much like a mini-movie, complete with animated images and a new, awesome song by Queen. The song didn't have much lyrics other than, *"Flash … ahhhh!"*, but it was still a totally cool way to open a new sci-fi movie. We met Flash Gordon, who was a football star for the New York Jets, at a small airport. As he boarded a plane with journalist Dale Arden, the weather surrounding them became very dangerous. During their flight, the plane was hit by a mysterious meteorite and the pilots were lost. Flash, who knew how to fly a plane, took the controls and safely crashed themselves into the greenhouse of Dr. Hans Zarkov, who believed the disasters around them were caused by an unknown source pushing the moon toward Earth. He'd secretly constructed a spacecraft to investigate his suspicions. Before Flash and Dale knew what was happening, they were aboard the spaceship with Dr. Zarkov and on their way to the planet Mongo, which sounded to me like a silly name for a dog ("Here, Mongo! Come here, boy!"). When they landed on the planet, they were captured by the troops of Ming the Merciless (the evil, bald man on the movie poster) and brought before him. Flash was a man of courage because he was soon fighting Ming's troops as if running down the field of a football game, a tactic he knew how to manage. I recall what seemed like every kid in the theater laughing (some cheering) during this silly football game sequence. His bravery didn't last long before he was captured again and sentenced to death. Even *that* didn't last long because he was brought back to life by an incredibly beautiful and exotic Princess Aura, who also happened to be Ming's daughter. So far, *Flash Gordon* was just about the *sexiest* sci-fi movie I'd ever seen.

Alive again, Flash was joined by others, including the group of Hawkmen, who also wanted to defend themselves against the power of the evil Ming, though their alliance wouldn't come too easily. Flash was put through a number of tests, trials, and fights before he was trusted by any of them, including a confrontation in which he and the Prince Barin tried to kill each other with whips on a moving disc that repeatedly had deadly spikes coming out of it at any given time. Once trust was gained, those against Ming had the power of an army. They stood together to forge a plan in which to attack Ming's city. Flash stood out alone in his own rocket ship, heading straight for the city as the battle of flying laser power was all around him. This, by the way, was another one of those great moments in which Queen's music really pumped up the action for this big screen. It looked great and with so much color.

At the climactic moment, Flash's ship crashed through a huge window, and the ship's long and sharp bow ended up right through the back and out the front of Ming's body, just before he was to take Dale Arden by force as his new bride during the wedding ceremony. Before Ming perished, he tried one last time to use his power against Flash with his all-powerful ring, but instead used the power of his own ring against himself until he was completely vaporized. Following a huge victory celebration, Prince Barin and Princess Aura were proclaimed the new rulers of Mongo, and Flash, Dale, and Dr. Zarkov would have to figure out how to get back to Earth. The final moment of the movie had us all wondering what would happen next because we watched Ming's ring being picked up by the hand of an unseen person. Ming's maniacal laugh echoed, followed by the words "The End" accompanied by a big question mark. Was there going to be a *Flash Gordon 2*? As a kid who always wanted more and more, I'm sure I wished for such a sequel to happen.

Outside the theater just a short time later, you'll be happy to know I finally worked up enough courage to walk up to Robin M. and ask her if she liked the movie. She said she did. Unfortunately, that's as far as my sad dose of courage went. I found some excuse to get on my bike and get the hell out of there (Robin, if you're reading this book now, please forgive me for not having grown a bigger *pair* back then). Following that day, *Flash Gordon* all but disappeared from my life. I didn't see it again on screen, I didn't watch it on HBO, and I couldn't tell you when it premiered on network TV without research. The '80s were just getting underway, and sci-fi was about to get darker, more serious, and in many cases, a whole lot better. What possible time did I have to ever consider such a flashy, campy, and colorful state of affairs as *Flash Gordon* ever again?

Now

The year 1980 may very well have been the middle year that divided two great periods of science fiction. Prior to that year, there was the nearly three-year period of content from May 1977 to December 1979 that sought to rip off and bank on *Star Wars*. The years following 1980 brought a darker take on sci-fi with films that included *Escape from New York*, *Blade Runner*, *The Road Warrior*, and John Carpenter's remake of *The Thing*. 1980 was the single year that bridged both these periods with sillier films (*Empire* being the exception) that included Roger Corman's *Battle Beyond the Stars*, *Saturn 3* (with Farrah Fawcett dressed much like a dominatrix, bless her!), and *Galaxina* (with former Playboy playmate and murder victim Dorothy Stratten), as well as *Flash Gordon*. It's the subject of camp, fluff, and silliness that comprises my perceptions of this film as an adult.

The film remained all but dormant in my mind and memory for thirty-two years until I watched Seth MacFarlane's 2012 comedy *Ted*. In the film, the foul-mouthed talking teddy bear Ted and his owner/master John (played by Mark Wahlberg) are serious fans of the 1980 sci-fi movie and often refer to their enthusiasm for it throughout the story (Sam Jones even makes an appearance playing himself to further the ongoing homage). Although *Ted* left no lasting impression on me, it did, on the other hand, renew my interest in rediscovering *Flash Gordon*. Watching it sometime later, my feelings of the film were, at best, lackluster. Still, all was not dead yet. Very recently and for the sole purpose of writing this book and rediscovering lost memories, I watched it again to try and gain some new perspective on it.

Here's what I found out. In all honesty, the film is still a silly mess. That hasn't disappeared over time. But how I interpret and judge the silly mess is, perhaps, a different matter now. There is, first, my experience with many of the principal players of the film, both in front and behind the camera, since I was a kid. When considering the production career of Dino De Laurentiis in American films from the time I was a child, it's impossible to ignore that he was the man behind many films I consider an important part of my upbringing, whether they were box office successes or not. Films like *King Kong, Orca, Conan the Barbarian, Dune*, and *Flash Gordon* are films that have one thing in common: slow theatrical start, big cult following later. Even another film of Dino's that meant a lot to me during my college years, Michael Mann's *Manhunter*, the first film to introduce the world to the character of Hannibal Lecter (played by Brian Cox), falls under that same category. In retrospect, Dino may not have chosen the most profitable projects, but he can still claim legacy, in my opinion, to some very entertaining material.

I also acknowledge the tremendous respect I have for the gifted and prestigious actor Max von Sydow in memorable film roles that include Knight Antonius Block in Bergman's *The Seventh Seal* (the one where he plays chess with death), Father Lankester Merrin in *The Exorcist,* and the cynical Frederick in Woody Allen's *Hannah and Her Sisters*. He's also shown us that he has just as much style and grace when diving into roles of sci-fi and fantasy, including *Flash Gordon, Conan the Barbarian, Dune, Minority Report,* and most recently in *The Force Awakens.* For all of his serious and artistic training as an actor, the man clearly knows how to have a little fun too. By that token, I'm able to respect his role as Ming the Merciless a whole lot more today. I'm also forced to reckon with writer Lorenzo Semple Jr.'s role in this film. He was, after all, the man responsible for the camp in the 1960s TV series *Batman* that I enjoyed watching so much as a kid, as well as *King Kong '76* that meant everything to me as a young boy of nine.

Finally and what I suppose I'd consider most important in my newfound interpretation of *Flash Gordon* is the fact that I've discovered and appreciate many of the original chapter serials of the 1930s as they've become available on DVD. From the beginning, it's obvious that the character was never meant to be taken too seriously. I try to imagine young children in the '30s during the Great Depression who were eager for their fair share of weekly Saturday afternoon fun during a time of great hardship. Buster Crabbe as Flash was the fun and even silly hero they *needed* to forget their troubled lives for just fifteen or twenty minutes each week at their local movie house. By our sci-fi standards of today, or even twenty or thirty years ago, Flash Gordon is not a serious man to be played by a serious actor as Kurt Russell or Harrison Ford. He's a man constantly caught up in a perilous, if not ridiculous, situation in which he must survive and protect others; in other words, the true motion picture screen hero. To have made him a dark figure in 1980 wouldn't have worked. Such figures were still a year or two away with men like Snake Pliskin (*Escape from New York*) and Rick Deckard (*Blade Runner*).

Flash Gordon, for all practical and visual purposes, may well be considered the first (lengthy) rock video by a band like Queen to hit our eyes and ears before MTV made its cable TV debut on August 1, 1981. The music not only drives the action from its opening credit sequence (that still makes me sit up and take notice), but also serves to effectively combine itself with the rich and vividly colorful atmosphere of the film, much like a giant painting that we're drawn into. While clearly acknowledging its influence from *Star Wars,* De

Laurentiis, Semple Jr., and Director Mike Hodges also make it clear that Flash Gordon as a character and a motion picture is derived from decades past when fun, camp, and silliness, even in black and white, was what brought kids to the movies every week. By that respect, I can't ignore that history repeated itself on that Saturday afternoon in December 1980 when we all gathered together to get a small taste of what it was like to experience playful fun at the movies again. As children, we loved it. As grown-ups, we tend to lose at least some of that fun and magic that carries us through our lives. Hopefully, some of us get it back eventually.

In the end, how does *Flash Gordon* identify itself in my eyes and my heart? A guilty pleasure? Surely. A cult favorite? Quite possibly, though I hesitate to use such a corny and repeatedly-used term as that. A childhood memory (complete with a beautiful twelve-year-old blonde) that I'm able to revisit, reexamine, and reinterpret in my adulthood as to its standing in a world of sci-fi films of different themes. Definitely. In a life that's taken seriously day by day, *Flash Gordon*, while not a great film (and really, it never *will* be), is a reminder to me that I should just sit down once in a while and enjoy a little fun, a little color, a little silliness, and a lot of Queen.

Thanks for the memory, Robin M., wherever you are.

*****

This is the last film of 1980 I shall discuss in any great detail.

This particular year was not only a series of opportunities to escape the harsh realities of a time when everything as a kid felt very wrong to me, but it was also a time of revisiting some old favorites, as many of the films I enjoyed in the past made their television debut, including *The Deep, The Spy Who Loved Me, Invasion of the Body Snatchers,* and *Saturday Night Fever.* I also got to see *The Towering Inferno* again for the first time since that night in December '75 when the film premiered on NBC on February 17, 1980, over two consecutive nights with (of course) extra footage never before seen in theaters, to boot. All of this was a welcomed second opportunity at old favorites. But there was also the TV premiere of an earlier motion picture I never got to see on screen as a child, and it was also the one film that changed my perspective of what the horror movie was prior to 1975.

On Tuesday, February 12, 1980, at 8:30 p.m., CBS presented a special movie presentation of *The Exorcist*. This particular week in February just happened to be my winter vacation from middle school, so there was no issue with getting to bed on time on a school night. I remember sitting alone in front of the small color television in my room for two and a half hours, shocked and mesmerized by what I saw. Bearing in mind, of course, that *The Exorcist* had to be heavily edited for television, what I watched was considered only the smallest fraction of what the legendary film's true experience was intended to be, regardless of the network warning of parental discretion advised. Regardless, this horror movie took on a whole new meaning for me. This was the tale of an innocent girl possessed by the devil himself and behaving in unspeakable ways and making things happen at her will. What made the entire story freaky was that nobody in her life, especially her frightened mother, could understand what was happening to her and why. Doctor upon doctor insisted the problem was within her own brain, but we who were watching knew better.

Because this was my first time watching this film, it was impossible for me to know just which scenes were edited or removed entirely. The dubbing of dialogue that couldn't be said on TV was clearer to interpret, on the other hand. Apparently, Ellen Burstyn couldn't even say *Jesus Christ* on TV, and it was replaced with "Judas Priest" instead. I learned years later that it was director William Friedkin himself who supervised and re-shot some scenes for the TV version, particularly replacing the obscene desecration of the Virgin Mary statue with it crying blood instead. Still, to know *The Exorcist* well is to know that one doesn't experience it on television ... ever. It's just not done. To a thirteen-year-old boy, however, who'd never experienced before the concept of demonic possession on film before, the shock value of it all was still very valid even on TV. If nothing else, it planted a seed that hasn't left me ever since. By the time I was in college, I owned my own licensed video copy of the film and was finally seeing all of the content that TV wouldn't dare broadcast (and probably never should). I often enjoyed getting together with friends, particularly at Halloween, to experience the film in all of its uncut and hellish glory.

When the "the version you've never seen" of the film was released on September 22, 2000, I was one of the first ones on line eager to see what sort of changes had been made. With the exception of the digitally-altered infamous *"spider walk"* scene, the newer version is simply comprised of additional footage not included in the original. While the film doesn't suffer the same unacceptable consequences of Lucas's tampering of the original *Star Wars* trilogy, or even Ridley Scott's constant changes to *Blade Runner*, it is, in my opinion, an inferior version to the already perfect film of '73 and a viable example of how sometimes less is indeed more. Still, I'm grateful to CBS, to a timely winter vacation, and to the two and a half hours of bedroom privacy I managed to achieve in order to watch *The Exorcist* for the first time. I'm also grateful that the Blu-Ray edition of the film I own allows me the choice of *both* film versions.

There's one more film that requires mentioning as I round out the first year of the '80s. It was a movie I saw on screen. It was a terrible movie and one I don't deem worthy for the contents of this book. However, it has certain significance to my life, both in childhood and adulthood. During one fine day in the summer of 1980, my mother emphatically declared that I had to get up off of my lazy butt, walk up the street, and introduce myself to the blond boy she'd seen playing out on his front yard so that I'd have the opportunity to make myself a new friend. Really, if that woman was ever trying to portray me as a total loser at the age of thirteen, this was surely it. Regardless, she put her foot down and it seemed I had no choice in the matter. Reluctantly, I walked up the street, knocked on the door of this large Tudor house, and introduced myself to the boy I shall call *Jim R.*, who was one year older than me. I can't honestly remember what we talked about that first time around, but I do know that before the first initial conversation was over, we agreed to meet again to go see a movie in town.

The film we went to see was *Smokey and the Bandit II*. I'd never seen the original from '77 (I think Jim R. *had* seen it), so I was already entering the sequel under a handicap. While it had an excit-ing car chase or two with some spectacular truck stunts, the movie was a undeniable dud, in my opinion. I've never seen the film again since and I suppose it ended up shaping the general negative opinion I've always had toward the films of director Hal Needham (though I admit that *Hooper* and *The Cannonball Run* have an enjoyable moment, or two). Regardless of my opinion and memory of the film itself, it was a day that still brought two boys together for the first time. To this day, Jim R. is one of the oldest, closest, most trusted, and loyal friends I have, and believe me when I tell you that's a very rare thing in life.

So, to Jim R., I say thank you for not judging me too harshly as the pathetic boy down the street whose mother forced him to come to your house to meet you. She ended up doing the right thing indeed.

And that, my friends, was the year 1980 for me.

THE YEAR WAS 1981 ...

- After four hundred and forty-four days of captivity, Iran releases the fifty-two American hostages just minutes after newly-elected president of the Unites States, Ronald Reagan, takes office.
- Ronald Reagan is shot in the chest by John Hinckley Jr. outside a Washington DC hotel. Press Secretary James Brady is also wounded.
- The American space shuttle program begins with the launching of Space Shuttle *Columbia*.
- The first recognized case of AIDS among homosexual men is reported by the Center for Disease Control.
- The wedding of Prince Charles, the Prince of Wales and Lady Diana Spencer is watched by a worldwide television audience.
- MTV, the world's first twenty-four-hour music television video channel, is launched.

... AND THERE WERE MOVIES!

Within the first few months of 1981, things in my life were settled and I was finally able to put the emotional events of the past year behind me. My family reopened the beach house in Westhampton Beach for another season, and we weren't renting it out again this year. Things weren't perfect though. They were still tough for a kid who'd recently turned fourteen and was struggling with his studies in the eighth grade of middle school. It was a time of my childhood when I was still trying to figure out what place I occupied as a boy slowly evolving into manhood. My hormones were raging, and believe me when I tell you that's a tough position to be in when you find it difficult to talk to girls.

Even some of the simple things like my musical tastes were confusing to me. Disco was as dead as a door nail, and I was still a couple of years away from discovering the classic rock that I love today. I was exploring a softer, lighter side of rock and pop music with bands like Daryl Hall & John Oates, Air Supply, REO Speedwagon, and new hit singles by singer-songwriters Kim Carnes and Christopher Cross. Add to the fact that my mother had become obsessed with the new album *"Guilty"* by Barbra Streisand and Barry Gibb and was constantly playing that record, well ... let's just say I was practically turning into a silly, lovesick girl or something.

Spring 1981 seemed a long period of time to endure. School was, well ... *school*, which meant it was nothing to be overly joyous about. I also had to wait until May before we'd return to the beach house. But what really made those first few months of the new year tough for me was that I didn't go to the movies even once (no joke, not even one time). There were movies I wanted to see, but circumstances or lazy parents prevented me from going. Friends were constantly busy, or I had a school test to study for, which meant a lot of extra studying effort on my part. A few movies here and there surely would've helped my outlook a bit.

Perhaps, however, it was just a mental test on my part to see how long I could hold out before summer arrived and a new season of blockbuster movies would arrive, including the return of Superman, James Bond, and a new hero named Indiana Jones. But first, there was someone else, another kind of hero, who caught my eye in the newspaper ads. It was Sylvester Stallone (Rocky Balboa himself). But this time, he looked completely different. He wore glasses, had thicker hair, a beard and mustache, and was carrying a gun. He was a cop now, and he looked like a real badass!

Nighthawks

Directed by Bruce Malmuth
(April 10, 1981, U.S. Release Date)

Then

In the spring of 1980, my family and I were driving across the 59th Street Bridge into Manhattan. As we approached the Roosevelt Island Tramway, we saw huge lights and equipment resembling the kind used on a movie shoot. This was first time I'd ever gotten that close to the world of Hollywood outside the movies themselves. I learned later from the newspaper they were shooting the new Sylvester Stallone movie in New York City and that he'd be playing a cop. Shortly after its release, a friend who'd seen it told me it was one of the best movies of the year. He boasted that Stallone's character was completely different from Rocky. That was enough for me. I begged my (somewhat more lenient) father to take me to see it. Unfortunately, while I could occasionally persuade him to take me to an R-rated *comedy*, a violent crime thriller was out of the question (man, how I wished my parents would just lighten up and allow me to grow up a little and discover things on my own, even if only at the movies).

This being the situation, April 1982 turned out to be quite a month for me. This was when HBO premiered both *Nighthawks* and *Escape from New York*, two thrillers that took me a bit further out of childhood and into the harsh and dirty realities of the modern adult thriller. This was also the first time Greg B. and I got together for an R-rated movie that wasn't horror. On Friday, April 2, 1982, we waited to see what sort of badass cop stuff Stallone would treat us to. The last thing I ever expected to see was the man who'd played Rocky Balboa dressed like a woman, even as an undercover cop. When the wig came off, however, the tough guy came shining through as he taunted the street mugger by saying, *"Come on, badass!"*, and then knocked him out with one punch. We laughed as his character Deke DaSilva dragged the mugger away and continued to read the poor guy his legal rights.

The story then switched to London where we met a charming man who flirted with the pretty girl behind the department store counter. He was hardly a nice guy though, because within seconds of his departure, the inside of the store exploded from a bomb in a backpack he'd left behind on the floor. The following scenes were surprising when I discovered the movie's additional cast. DaSilva's partner was none other than Billie Dee Williams, a.k.a. Lando Calrissian of *The Empire Strikes Back,* and his ex-wife was none other than Lindsay Wagner, a.k.a. *The Bionic Woman* herself (one of my earliest childhood female TV crushes). The terrorist called Wulfgar looked very different by the time he arrived at the New York airport. His face looked younger and his hair was blond. Points in the story told us he'd had facial surgery before escaping from Europe. I'd heard of such surgery before, but I was still in awe of how a human being could change his physical appearance at will without the use of such obvious measures as make-up or costume. This, I suppose, was an effect that made the possibilities of such an evil man even more frightening. How do you catch an international terrorist if you don't know what he looks like and you aren't sure if he's in the city? The English inspector on his trail was sure he *was* in New York, however, and was training the police, including DaSilva and his partner Sergeant Fox, to help find him.

The nightclub scene grabbed me from the moment it started because I concluded that Wulfgar was definitely there. Why else would the scene stay so focused on this one club? It was simply a matter of whether or not DaSilva and Fox would spot him in such a crowded place. I loved the use of "Brown Sugar" by the Rolling

Stones. It wasn't a dance song, but the movie made it look like you *could* easily dance to it. When DaSilva finally stopped moving and stared hard at the man he suspected was Wulfgar, my body froze because I knew it was time for the action to kick in. I was amazed at how DaSilva confirmed his suspicions by using a simple pencil and eraser on a sketch of Wulfgar and then told Fox, *"Because that ... is standing over there!"* The intense stares continued between cop and terrorist for a few seconds until DaSilva finally shouted at the top of his lungs, *"Wulfgar!"* All hell broke loose inside the club with gunfire and mayhem, which is exactly what I expected to happen. What began as a shootout in the nightclub eventually spilled out into the city streets and continued aboard a subway train. When they finally had Wulfgar cornered on the subway platform, he took an old woman hostage and escaped because DaSilva didn't shoot him when he had the chance. His lack of action inevitably ended up with Fox getting slashed with a knife across the cheek. Greg B. and I were practically on the edge of our own excitement when Stallone repeatedly yelled, *"You're fuckin' dead!"* to the now escaped Wulfgar. Yes, from nightclub to subway, this entire sequence was some of the most exciting action (that didn't involve spaceships and laser battles) I'd seen in a movie yet.

I finally understood what I'd previously witnessed on the 59th Street Bridge from the car two years ago. Wulfgar took hostages aboard the Roosevelt Tramway. Although I'd seen my small share of movies filmed in familiar parts of the city, this one hit home for me because I'd once ridden it with my family. This was a hostage situation in which some people would likley die. An innocent woman *did* die, right in front of DaSilva's eyes as he watched from aboard a nearby helicopter. Wulfgar almost got away with his demands to escape with the hostages by bus, but instead, the police attacked him and the bus crashed into the East River where he was presumed drowned. This was another example of screenwriting in which I'd come to understand *presumed* dead doesn't necessarily mean *actually* dead. Wulfgar *did* survive the water and returned to try and kill DaSilva's ex-wife. But the great cop was one step ahead of him and waited for him to strike, dressed in a robe and blond wig to look like his ex-wife from the back (once again, Stallone dressed as a woman), before shooting him dead for good.

Nighthawks was the first cop/crime thriller I ever saw, and I only wish it had been on screen instead of a small color television. I was not only stunned by its harsh reality of the streets of New York City, but also the literal transformation of a man like Stallone from lovable Philadelphia boxer to hard-boiled, street-smart, badass cop ready and willing to blow his enemy away with a gun. I also learned that the street cop, as a general character, didn't necessarily have style, grace, or charm. He wasn't always nice to people and was often hard to get along with. At his heart though, he was a good man and a dedicated cop who was willing to be as nasty and ruthless as he had to be in order to stop the bad guy from hurting the innocent. The movie also had good dialogue that I enjoyed quoting and repeating with friends. Stallone proved to me that he continued to be the great American hero, even if it was outside the boxing ring. By the time I watched *Nighthawks* again when it premiered on the *ABC Sunday Night Movie* in 1983, I'd also seen his 1978 film *F.I.S.T.* on the same network; once again, playing a character putting his neck and life on the line for the better of those around him, even if at times he had to be corrupt in order to serve the greater good.

Now

Nighthawks remains a fast-paced, well-mounted crime thriller focused on the suspense and action of the city streets without overdoing the bloodshed, not too unlike Friedkin's 1971 best picture Oscar winner, *The French Connection* (my favorite cop/crime thriller). The film gives some truly riveting moments of intense confrontation, including the nightclub scene and the final seconds between DaSilva and Wulfgar. But what makes this film standout better, in my opinion, than the typical police action thriller of the '80s and '90s is its higher emphasis on characters playing cops and the moral conflicts they struggle with in their profession. DaSilva and Fox, for all of their street experience, don't understand what they're getting into and misinterpret the mind and actions of the traditional terrorist versus the lowlife street criminal. I use the word *traditional* to define the terrorist of the past who still took hostages and made demands for their release; an era before today's extreme suicide groups like Al-Qaeda and Isis, as well as terrorist attacks in New York City twenty years before the events of September 11, 2001, would occur.

Although DaSilva and Fox are repeatedly instructed by Hartman to learn to *"combat violence with greater violence,"* DaSilva's professional ethics and reservations of judgment work against him when having to stand against the terrorist's actions and he refuses to jeopardize the lives of innocent civilians just for the sake of taking down the bad guy. Wulfgar, played by Rutger Hauer in his film debut, comes nowhere near the profile of the modern terrorist we know in today's world and media. He's stylish, cultured, pleasant, and friendly (when he has to be), and has a genuine agenda of protecting his own life even when he's sadistically threatening the lives of others, not too unlike the classic James Bond villain. DaSilva, on the other hand, is nothing like James Bond. He's hard-edged, foul-mouthed, dresses like a criminal, and is cleary a man of mistakes and human imperfections when it comes to his failed marriage. In fact, I've often thought of him as a mild precursor to the man Arnold Schwarzenegger played in James Cameron's *True Lies*, in which he also played a man of justice pitted against the wills of an international terrorist.

The nightclub sequence still resonates with me, particularly the disco scene during a time when disco was dead and rock and roll and punk had taken over the airwaves. Director Bruce Malmuth attempts to imply that it's easy enough to dance to the classic rock of the Rolling Stones and the keyboards of Keith Emerson (of famed prog rock group Emerson, Lake & Palmer). Well, I totally buy it because when I went through my club-hopping phase in the early '90s, I repeatedly wished the DJ would play "Brown Sugar" so I could dance to it (it never happened). But there's also the crowded situation at the club that intensifies matters. Unlike the gang-related film where those with guns just mindlessly start shooting up the place (think Michael Bay's *Bad Boys* films), *Nighthawks* takes its time through the eyes of the hero as he carefully hunts down and closes in on the man he's hunting. Much like the kid I was when I first saw the film, I sit in anticipation waiting for DaSilva to finally yell out Wulfgar's name in all his fury and then give chase to the inevitable subway climax. Again, like *The French Connection*, the sequence starts off as one form of action before it becomes an entirely different one (in this case, an intense foot chase instead of the cliché car chase that almost kills everyone in its path).

I appreciate and respect the films Stallone made as an actor between 1976 and 1982; essentially *Rocky* and *First Blood*, respectively. Following that year, it's unfortunate the man chose to occupy his film career as a mindless action machine in some very sad and forgettable films, as well as directing *Staying Alive*, the utterly pointless sequel to *Saturday Night Fever*. When I saw *Cobra* in 1986 (and hated, hated, *hated* it!), the first thought that went through my mind was that if Stallone really needed to play a screen cop again, then why didn't he simply choose to make a sequel to *Nighthawks* instead of this mindless garbage? Perhaps it would've even shaped his future cop roles (*Copland* not withstanding). Just watch his 1992 dud *Stop! Or My Mom Will Shoot* and you'll know what I'm talking about.

The Four Seasons

Directed by Alan Alda
(May 22, 1981, U.S. Release Date)

Then

Every once in a while, there were times when my parents were having company over on a Saturday night and wanted to get rid of me and Kevin for just a couple of hours. That's what happened one summer night, and *The Four Seasons* was the only appropriate movie playing in town. Having enjoyed *Annie Hall* and *Breaking Away* when I was younger, I appreciated the so-called *"slice of life"* adult movie. Even more, the prospect of seeing a comedy with Carol Burnett and that funny guy from *M*A*S*H* was interesting too. Although I was unfamiliar with the classical violin piece *The Four Seasons* by Antonio Vivaldi, the title of the movie was easy enough to understand as spring, summer, fall, and winter. The story of a group of friends getting together four times a year for vacations was hardly anything requiring too much thought either.

One of the first things I realized about adult friendships was that they were much closer and more serious than those of children. Children played together, watched movies together, and went out for pizza together. Adults talked to each other, trusted each other, and were more affectionate with each other even in playful situations. From the moment this group of people got together for their first spring trip of the year, I could see just how close they were to each other. However, even as mature and as serious as I presumed adults were *supposed* to be, there was still a time and place for them to act like children when the mood hit them. That was true when Jack stood up in the boat while out on the water with his friends and raised his glass to make a very special toast in their honor to declare, *"this is for all of you...so that we'll never forget this day,"* and then proceeded to jump into the lake. Accepting such a gesture, Jack's friend Nick immediately joined him in the water, and I laughed when the two of them hugged and kissed each other in the water. In fact, I'd also deduced at that moment that friendship between two men who were *not* in love with each other couldn't possibly get any better than that. Before I knew it, everybody inside the boat ended up in the water.

The serious side of adult friendship showed their intense troubles and worries. The closeness between Jack and Nick proved true when Nick told Jack that he planned to divorce his wife Anne because he was unhappy with her. Close as they were, Jack couldn't understand his friend's motives, nor could he offer his immediate support, which disappointed Nick. By the time the next vacation arrived that summer, they all stayed about a rented luxury boat and Nick brought along his hot, young, blonde girlfriend Ginny. Feeling uncomfortable and as though they'd lost Anne in this new situation, the rest of the group treated Ginny as "the other woman." I felt bad for her, or perhaps I only sympathized for this young woman who looked hotter than the rest of the wives. Their attitude continued into the remaining seasons fall and winter, until one night, Ginny finally had enough and told all of Nick's friends off, declaring she'd had enough of their rejection toward her and treating her like a *"blank spot where Annie used to be."* Jack was, by far, the most complicated character as a man who couldn't just relax and go with the flow of things, constantly wanting to get to the bottom of everyone's problems and feelings. He was a sincere man to be sure, but I could totally understand when his other friends just wanted him to shut the hell up.

Not to suggest that *The Four Seasons* wasn't a funny movie, beyond the lake scene. I laughed my ass off when Danny finally had enough of his wife Claudia declaring that she was Italian and then proceeded to stick his head out the window to shout out to the whole world that, *"this woman is Italian!"* I imagined my own father getting

IT'S STRICTLY PERSONAL

so pissed off at my mother that he'd likely do something very similar, if not worse. There was also the moment when Carol Burnett got so mad at her husband that she finally let out that signature scream of hers she'd made so popular on her variety show. When Danny's brand-new Mercedes sank into the frozen lake and he screamed, *"My Mercedes!"* at the top of his lungs, I felt so, so sorry for the poor, fat bastard. Yes, I laughed at all of that. In the world of adults, though thoroughly complicated as they were, they could be very funny people too. I understood that well and I was fortunate to go to the movies one summer night in order to be reminded of it.

Now

In the early '90s, I had an on-again, off-again relationship with a woman (*not* my future wife) I was in love with. We didn't share the same love of films very often, but one title we easily agreed on was *The Four Seasons*. We'd watch it and often talk about our (possible) future together and hoped that we'd also have close friends and take vacations together. Well, let me just say that such idle talk and aspirations didn't quite turn out that way in our real lives (we eventually stopped speaking to each other altogether). Still, I've always thought it would be great to have very special friends in my life to take vacations with. I can easily picture *myself* jumping into the lake for the sole purpose of creating a moment of laughter and insanity among those I love. However, as I've gotten older, I've also gotten more impatient and more intolerant with people and this is *not* a great combination when traveling and spending a great deal of time with other people. In fact, it's very often the people you spend time with the most and whom you love the most that will piss you off beyond belief. With my wife, our life with friends hardly resembles the solidarity of *The Four Seasons*. She has her close friends and I have mine, and with the exception of our wedding day, they've *never* come together.

When studying the film, you'll notice its main structure is focused on the men of the group and the quirky characteristics of men in general, suggesting the women are there only to serve as the "tag along" wives existing only to offer cliché elements of maritial love and support. It seems that even at the start of the 1980s, women's roles in film still had a long way to go. As a collective group of people who care about each other, however, one may regard *The Four Seasons* as a precursor to the popular social films of John Hughes in the '80s or even the friendship vehicle of NBC's *Friends* in the '90s. The film's ongoing point throughout the story though, even after every single one of these people has managed to irritate, confront, abuse, take advantage of, and even betray each other's trust is that in the end, come hell or high water, your close friends are forever and you fight like hell to tolerate and keep them close to you no matter what happens. Perhaps it's perfectly symbolic that the film's final shot is the entire group walking away into the distant beauty of the snow-filled trees off the frozen lake, thus ending the final season of another long year together.

Raiders of the Lost Ark

Directed by Steven Spielberg
(June 12, 1981, U.S. Release Date)

***

Then

For weeks during the spring of '81, I knew *Raiders of the Lost Ark* was coming. Any movie that was the brainchild of the men who gave us *Jaws* and *Star Wars* and also starred Harrison Ford had to be great. In fact, I hadn't seen such a marketing campaign of books, magazines, toys, comic books, etc., since *Star Wars*. Much like that preceding movie, I'd likely have to sit back, wait, and watch everything around me associated with the movie take shape until I'd finally have the chance to see it for myself. That's what I figured anyway. What actually happened turned out to be a completely different story. By the time *Raiders* opened in Westhampton Beach, I regretted seeing *The Four Seasons* at the same neighborhood theater weeks earlier. This issue turned out to be a big fight between myself and my parents about going to the movies. Despite the new Spielberg/Lucas collaboration shaping up to be the biggest blockbuster hit of the summer, they both agreed I'd been to enough movies over the last few weeks (I'd also seen Mel Brooks's disappointing *History of the World—Part I*). Had I known this would be the consequence of going to see two silly comedies back to back, I would've stayed home and kept my mouth shut until it was time for *Raiders*. Instead, I spent several weeks during the movie's duration in town begging and pleading with them to change their minds, but wouldn't give in. It looked like

I was completely screwed for the first time since *Jaws* in '75 (was this some sort of *Spielberg* movie curse happening to me, or what?).

The summer of '81 came and went, and *Raiders* was simply not to be. I tried to compensate by familiarizing myself with the story as much as possible. This meant spending allowance money on the novelization by Campbell Black, the Marvel comic book adaptation, and watching *Great Movie Stunts: Raiders of the Lost Ark* on CBS to get a glimpse at the making of the movie. I also kept the possibility of the movie's rerelease in the back of my mind. I mean, all the great movies of my childhood inevitably had a second run at some point, so why would this one be any different, right? Happily, my long patience finally paid off when the movie *was* rereleased in theaters on July 16, 1982, and it wasn't soon enough. Had it been just a couple of weeks later, I would've been away at summer camp and missed it again. Despite my parents' disinterest in the movie when it was new, the entire family went to see it together at a Long Island theater. By this time, any preconceived ideas I had about it were very minimal. Besides being the colossal hit that it was and even nominated for the Oscar for best picture of 1981, I'd also heard how the spirit of the story was a grand homage to the classic adventure movie serials of the '30s and '40s, which like *Flash Gordon*, I had little knowledge or experience with.

Sitting down in my seat with popcorn in hand, the only thought going through my head was, *It's about time! This was just as bad, if not worse, than waiting to see* Empire! No doubt, the long wait would be worth it. From the moment the movie began in the jungles of South America in the year 1936, the adventures of this famous archaeologist who called himself Indiana Jones grabbed its audience by the throat and wasn't letting go any time soon. I can still hear my father getting a serious case of the *"heebie-jeebies"* when one of Indy's explorers was suddenly covered with giant, hairy spiders. The entire opening sequence was structured much like the two screen James Bond adventures I'd seen already; intense and exciting action before settling down for a moment to map out the overall story due to come. Needless to say, the scene where Indy ran for his life from the giant rolling boulder had me on the edge of my seat and also put a huge smile on my face. I understood now, the homage paid to the movie heroes of another long-gone era, when adventure on a Saturday afternoon truly defined a day at the movies.

Having been raised Jewish, understanding Indy's ultimate quest for the Ark of the Covenant which contained the actual pieces of the Ten Commandments that Moses himself smashed into pieces (I watched Charlton Heston do that on TV every year on ABC) wasn't a challenge. I also knew who the Nazis were in our world history and that they and Adolf Hitler were an evil enemy for a man like Indy to pit himself against. Instead, what I found myself perplexed about was how Indy could go from an action-adventurer to a mild-mannered college professor who wore glasses and looked quite clumsy when he carried too much stuff in his hands. I suppose this could have been an homage to the alternate personalities of Superman and Clark Kent, but it was pretty clear that Indy was *not* Superman. He was brave and daring, but he wasn't invincible. During the big fight at the bar belonging to his ex-girlfriend Mairon Ravenwood, there were moments when his enemies got the better of him. He was, in fact, nearly choked to death until the Nazi commander called Toht ordered his gunman to shoot both Indy and the thug choking him. I found the act of both Indy and his opponent joining forces for even just a moment to save their own lives and shoot back at the gunman, original and exciting. The entire sequence, with the raging fire in the background, was an awesome spectacle to watch. Marion knew just how to handle Indy too, declaring that he would take her along with him from now on in his quest, or as she chose to put it, *"I'm your goddamn partner!"*

By the time Indy and Marion arrived in the city of Cairo, Egypt, to join his friend Sallah, my mother's interest sparked a bit. She was born and raised in Cairo before she came to the United States in 1963 and met my father not too long after. I later learned that what was supposed to be Cairo was actually filmed in Tunisia in North Africa (the same filming location used for the canyon scenes of Tatooine in *Star Wars*). This was where the complex process of archaeology set itself into motion as we watched just how massive the Nazi's digging expedition was in order to find the Ark. In the midst of it all, the action was nonstop. Indy found himself in the middle of a shootout with a group of Egyptian thugs responsible for kidnapping Marion. There were moments of this sequence that were funny, particularly Marion's bravery and spunk, in which she defended herself with a simple frying pan. The humor didn't last long though, because it wasn't too long before Marion appeared to be killed in a truck explosion. However, Indy found her alive later on, bound and gagged, but refused to cut her loose for fear that if he did, the two of them would be discovered before he had the chance to locate and secure the Ark. After an entire night of digging, Indy, Sallah, and a team of diggers finally found the Ark and raised it from its resting place. Indy's arch-enemy, Belloq, however, managed to seize it from him a short time later, reminding Indy that, *"once again, what was briefly yours is now mine."* I actually felt angry at this moment because I couldn't believe our hero was getting screwed again by the same man and would have to get the Ark back again.

This is where the action became relentless with some incredible action footage; from Indy's brutal fight with the large Nazi (who looked more like a wrestler), to the exploding airplane, to the awesome chase sequence with Indy on a horse, and the truck he crawled under in order not to get separated from the Ark. This had to be some of the most eye-popping action I'd ever seen outside of a sci-fi battle movie or a Bond adventure. When it all finally came to a rest, Indy and Marion were together again and traveling with a group of pirates aboard a submarine. The movie slowed down a bit now as the Nazis managed to catch up with the sub and seize the Ark again. I have to say, inasmuch as I was thrilled and excited in keeping up with the story and the action, the constant shifting of the Ark between good guys and bad guys started to test my patience a little.

The story concluded with one of the most original climaxes I'd seen at the movies yet. Once on an island, Belloq intended to test the power of the Ark before turning it over to Hitler. During a Jewish ritual, the Ark was finally opened, and I think my family was surprised to see it contained only sand. I knew better though. This couldn't be the end of it all. Something else was coming. It started with ghostlike images emerging from the Ark and was followed by forms of energy, flames, and bolts of light. I still wasn't sure how this would turn out, but it wasn't going to be good, because in the middle of it all, Indy warned Marion to keep her eyes shut. That was good advice, because when the ghosts finally turned into creatures of death, Indy and Marion were the only ones to survive after all the Nazis were killed, including Toht's face melting and Belloq's head exploding (*whoahh!*). My parents could *not* have liked their boys watching that kind of graphic violence one little bit. They likely covered their own eyes while Kevin and I watched with fascination. After the Ark was magically raised into the air and inside a cloud, presumably returning to God's possession, it all came to a calming quiet. Concluding in Washington DC, the army had the Ark in their hands now and were not taking its power too seriously, choosing to simply store it in a huge warehouse among countless other wood crates. I insisted we stay in our seats to hear John Williams's great ending theme music.

Having waiting over a year, I could finally count myself among the many millions of movie fans who'd experienced *Raiders of the Lost Ark*. The movie seemed the perfect product to come from the two men responsible for two of the biggest blockbusters of the '70s. I was astonished at the creative genius behind such a movie that never failed to keep the story, the thrills, and the action moving at such a steady pace without creating boredom. I also realized just how the Oscars treated such a movie. Despite the fact that *Jaws*, *Star Wars*, and *Raiders* were such perfect motion pictures, the Academy of Motion Picture Arts and Sciences ultimately preferred to give their respective best picture awards to movies about a crazy man in the cuckoo's nest, a neurotic couple living in Manhattan, and runners competing in the 1924 Paris Olympics. Clearly, I was still too young to understand why they did things like that.

Now

The adventures of this unique archaeologist and part time college professor have become synonymous with action and adventure for nearly as long as *Star Wars* has been with not only my own generation of film fans, but with today's as well. It's been a genuine homage to the great Saturday matinee serial cliffhanger heroes of another time (while never directly copying them) that started on a Hawaiian beach in '77 between the two legendary filmmakers. Spielberg confessed he wanted to do a James Bond film, but Lucas convinced him of a better idea. The rest, of course, was motion picture history. It's one of those great films you can't help but reflect on with genuine enthusiasm, and yet can't imagine what you'd say that every other fan around the world hasn't heard before or discussed themselves. It is, in fact, the only film that Sheldon Cooper of *The Big Bang Theory* actually stole from a movie theater when the show was sold out to him and his friends. In other words, if *he* couldn't see it, then no one else would either (you *go*, Sheldon!).

Unlike movie heroes of the past, Indiana Jones is regarded as more of a modern figure in that he's a man, while ultra-brave who's flawed and vulnerable nonetheless. Indy can be hurt and often is. Just watch how fast he goes down when hit with one punch in the jaw during the fight scene with the bald and muscular German soldier. Indy has his fears too, the main one being snakes (who can blame him? I hate them too!). This is simply what makes the hero more human to his audience. His screen adventures that play before our eyes are enthralling and a nonstop, mile-a-minute journey into the unknown of not only ancient religion, but into the heart of evil and the deadly consequences against it. Like our heroes (and our enemies), we long to see the Ark opened to learn its precious secrets. During that climactic and magical sequence, even when it appears there's nothing but sand inside, we know better because we're in the hands of the mighty Spielberg who'd never let us down at such a crucial moments. The Ark possesses the power and the magic to not only protect our heroes, but to violently defeat our enemies of evil. For those of us who choose to believe its religious aspects, I suppose there's also the implying message that you don't want to mess around with God or else you may internally combust in the end (like I said, if you choose to believe in that stuff, be my guest).

Let's now focus some of my attention at key moments of *Raiders* that continue to stand out and hold a dear place in my heart (okay, maybe I'm not that sentimental about it, but these moments are pretty damn cool). There are two moments in the film that stand out as true definitions of Indiana Jones's bravery, in my opinion. The first is in the Egyptian marketplace when he's confronted by the Arab dressed in black who, through his fast moving sword play, can only be presumed as the deadliest and most feared swordsman in the village. Indy, while clearly not afraid of him, simply doesn't have time for this crap and defuses the situation the only way he knows how—by shooting the poor bastard dead. Thirty-six years later, I still laugh my ass off when he fires that shot and the Arab goes down. I can't help but think in my mind, *You're so damn stupid to mess around with Indiana Jones!* The second is the classic desert chase when Indy must regain control of the Ark from inside the truck. At a time when CGI didn't exist and the dependency for movie stuntmen expertise would make or break a great action sequence, I can still cite the truck dragging scene (performed by stuntman Terry Leonard) as still one of the greatest movie stunts I've ever had the pleasure of watching and enjoying over and over again. It's the knowledge of knowing that this isn't CGI taking place here, but a real man making his way under the truck and then dragged side to side along the dirt road (with Ford himself in some of the closer shots). It's simple, it's real, it's raw, it's totally effective, and continues to impress me still far beyond anything a damn computer can do today in a fraction of the time. This is also when John Williams's score rings true for me because the action is so death-defying and the accompanying score just intensifies it all. The scene also simplifies Indy's bravery and hard-edged attitude toward stopping that truck, come hell or high water, in order to keep the Ark from getting to Germany. He may be scared, but we'd never know it because it's simply what he *must* do to get the job done, even if he's just making it up as he goes. It's the highlight that exemplifies how the film can effectively and successfully pile on one incident after another without becoming exhausting or stale.

As the Indiana Jones franchise has grown over the decades, and is likely to continue to grow, my love and affection for *Raiders of the Lost Ark* becomes more faithful. Of the four films made (so far), my response has been an even split, with *The Last Crusade* being the other one I enjoyed. *The Temple of Doom* is, in my opinion, one of the worst films of Spielberg's prestigious career. *The Kingdom of the Crystal Skull* wasn't much of an improvement either. My reasons for disliking it aren't too unlike the reasons of others; weak story line in the form of space aliens (seriously?). Its only improvement over the big dud of '84 is Karen Allen's return to the role of Marion Ravenwood and the priceless bickering between her character and Indy.

Any way that you or I choose to judge the franchise, I take comfort and pleasure in the fact that a film like *Raiders* exists and is forever immortalized in the hearts and minds of its true fans. For that alone, I wholeheartedly say thank you to Steven Spielberg, thank you to George Lucas, and thank you to Harrison Ford for reminding us all of the true meaning behind the fun and adventure of the American motion picture.

Superman II

Directed by Richard Lester
(June 19, 1981, U.S. Release Date)

Then

While I didn't get to see *Raiders* that summer, I did manage to see *Superman II* twice. Since the first movie, the general knowledge among fans was that a sequel was immediately in the works to further the story of the three villains from Krypton and their ultimate battle with the Man of Steel himself. Having lived in a world of movies predominantly ruled by sci-fi and space battles, I put any anticipation for *Superman II* in the back of my head for the time being. I guess you could say I was entertaining a level of patience for its release in that it would simply arrive when the time came. No big deal. I could wait.

After revisiting the trial, conviction, and sentencing of the three Kryptonian criminals to the Phantom Zone (without Jor-El this time), the new Superman movie instead provided a montage of the first movie's best scenes from beginning to end that would lead us up to the new story that began in Paris with terrorism. Though these men who'd seized the Eiffel Tower acted a lot more like the *Three Stooges* than serious terrorists. Regardless, I was old enough to know what a hydrogen bomb was and the massive destruction it would cause, even before Lois Lane confirmed the fact by declaring it could *"blow up all of Paris!"* When she held onto the tower's elevator for dear life as it fell to the bottom at top speed, I got a small knot in the pit of my stomach as if my senses were falling with her; kind of the way you feel as if you're actually riding a rollercoaster if you concentrate hard enough on film footage taken from an actual coaster. Of course, Superman arrived in the nick of time and saved the day by hurtling the bomb into outer space where it would explode and hurt no one. As it turned out, however, the bad side of that move was that the explosion destroyed the Phantom Zone and the three sentenced criminals from Krypton were now free, and it looked as if Superman didn't see any of this happen.

Before flying to Earth, General Zod, Ursa, and Non (who was mute) decided to stop off at the moon first to cause some trouble with the astronauts who just happened to be there. It was on the moon they realized their natural abilities served as extraordinary superpowers the closer they came to the yellow sun. When they arrived in Idaho, they made themselves well-known to the local folks by causing more trouble and destruction. I particularly enjoyed watching Ursa take down a rather hairy and disgusting-looking man in their own little arm wrestling match. That's what he got (and deserved) after telling her, *"Let me know if this tickles,"* just because she was a woman and presumed the weaker sex. Even with damage done to buildings and a series of explosions, the United States military moved in on them to try and stop them, with no success. This was clearly just a small prelude to the harder action that would take place later in the movie.

Meanwhile, Superman ... or rather, Clark Kent and Lois Lane were on a newspaper assignment together in Niagara Falls, posing as a newly-married couple. As they toured the falls, a small boy decided to test his balance on the wrong side of the safety rail. Just before he eventually fell toward the water, I couldn't help but ask myself, *Just how stupid is this kid?* I also recognized the stupidity that immediately followed Superman's rescue of the boy in a line spoken by an old woman watching the action when she said, *"What a nice man!"* (really?). Unfortunately, Superman's heroic feat would have a bad side to it because now Lois suspected just who Clark Kent really was, as he was never around when Superman showed up. She nearly proved her point when she jumped into the water, fully expecting

Superman to save her. It wasn't until later in their hotel room when Clark accidentally fell into the fireplace (was it *really* an accident?) that he revealed himself to Lois when his hand wasn't burned. This was when the movie decided to stop being so light and humorous for a while. Things became serious and dramatic as the two of them realized the truth of Clark's identity and the love they felt for each other. This shift in the movie's mood made sense to me, because even at my young age, I understood that love was a deep emotion that wasn't always funny. After years of Superman keeping his secret from Lois, in comic strips, comic books, cartoons, and an old TV show, the cat was finally out of the bag. With any ordinary movie couple, none of this would've been such a major event. However, this was Superman and Lois Lane, so it meant *something*.

Things stayed focused on just the two of them for a while. When he took her to his home at the Fortress of Solitude, they proclaimed their love for each other over dinner. But the true test of this love was whether or not Superman was willing to give up his superpowers to live as an ordinary mortal man, which according to the spirit of his dead mother, was the only way he could be with Lois. This was a shocking decision to contend with as someone who loved Superman, because we had to watch it happen when he stepped into the molecule chamber that took away his powers forever and turned him into just Clark Kent. Now an ordinary man, he could be hurt as one too. He *was* hurt, in fact, when he and Lois stopped at a local diner and got into a fight with a bully who wouldn't give Clark his seat. Clark was practically fascinated by the sight of his own blood, something he'd never seen before. It was ironic him being an ordinary and powerless man now, because it was at this very moment that he finally learned of General Zod's existence on Earth and that he was now challenging Superman on national TV to come forward and kneel before him. What now? Superman was gone and all the world was left with was the ordinary (and weak) man, Clark Kent. He'd try to get his powers back, but there was no way to know just how he'd do it.

The three Kryptonians, now in a partnership with Lex Luthor, took over the Daily Planet in anticipation that Superman would eventually show up to face them. I wasn't surprised when Superman finally returned with all of his powers intact. This being a movie where the good guy ultimately wins the battle, it seemed clear enough he'd *have* to come back somehow. But how did he pull it off? I knew his rediscovering of the green crystal must've had something to do with it, but the answers weren't clear. I'd have to think about that later because a showdown was taking place between Superman and his enemies in the city of Metropolis with all its citizens watching. The battle was quite a spectacular show, with great visual images of good and bad fighting each other in the air and on the ground. I loved the moment when Superman hurled Non into the giant antenna of the Empire State Building and then watching it fall toward the street; Superman, of course, saving the woman and her baby from being crushed by it. The battle raged on for a while before Superman realized the only way he would defeat these villains was to draw them away from Metropolis. It was a shame though to think the people thought Superman was a coward for flying away when he did. We in the audience knew better.

Kidnapping Lois Lane and taking Lex Luthor along for the ride, the villains followed Superman to the Fortress of Solitude where the fight would continue. For a time, it looked like Superman had his enemies where he wanted them until Ursa and Non grabbed Lois and threatened to kill her. Superman was, for the moment, defeated because he'd never allow Lois to be hurt. The final surprise and climax of the movie came when Superman was forced back into the same molecule chamber in order to be rid of his powers once again. Just when we thought Zod had won, we learned through the hard cracking of Zod's bones in his hand, that Superman had switched the effects of the chamber to take away the villain's powers while he was safely protected inside. The battle was over. Evil was defeated and Superman was, as always, the hero of the hour.

The next morning at the Daily Planet, Clark and Lois still had to resolve the nature of their relationship. They loved each other, and the thought of having to keep Clark's secret and deny her love for him was too painful for her to bare. Clark kissed her, and there was something magical about that kiss because when he finished, she couldn't remember anything that had taken place throughout the movie. It was the *"kiss of forgetfulness"* as we'd call it later. Since it was always a pleasure to watch a bully get beaten up, I loved the movie ending with Clark returning to the diner to teach the one who got the best of him earlier a thing or two with his superpowers restored. Superman was back and we, as well as the entire country, were very glad to have him.

Superman II premiered on the *ABC Sunday Night Movie* in 1984. Like *The Movie*, it also featured extra footage originally not shown in theaters. This time, however, the new scenes weren't nearly as interesting or intriguing as the original movie. Some of this pointless footage included Lex Luthor discovering one of his prison cellmates was a bed wetter and telling Otis to pass it on, as well as a moment where Superman used the heat rays from his eyes to cook a souffle in seconds. Was *this* the best the network could do in order to hold our attention just a little longer? I realized, of course, this footage was originally shot by the director and it wasn't the network's fault, but still, I felt I had to blame *somebody*.

Now

What I knew about *Superman II* back then and what I know about it today are two different matters. As a kid, it was just a sequel released in the United States nearly three years after the original film, the standard wait time. Shortly after the first film, there were rumors and bits of information on TV that the sequel was filmed at the same time as the original and would be released within a year. I dismissed this trivia until '81 came along and it was finally released. It was in 2006, with the DVD release of *Superman II: The Richard Donner Cut* that I learned the secrets and the dirt behind the making of the movie and the difficulties between Donner and producers Alexander and Ilya Salkind, and Donner's subsequent firing from production in March 1979. The specific reasons and details behind Donner replacement with Richard Lester remains a debated issue. One point behind this filmmaking controversy that's always impressed me was the decision among much of the cast and crew to stand behind Donner after he was fired. Creative consultant Tom Mankiewicz, editor Stuart Baird, and actor Gene Hackman declined to return to the film, though Hackman had already completed many of his scenes under Donner's direction. Marlon Brando, who'd also completed scenes with Donner, chose to sue the producers and as a result, all scenes featuring Brando were ultimately cut from Lester's film and replaced with Susannah York playing Superman's mother instead. None of this really mattered though. *Superman II* was a huge success at the box office, as well as with critics and fans, including myself.

As a kid, I felt the sequel outsoared the first film simply due to the fact that it had more action, primarily the fight sequences in Metropolis. I have since changed my position on that opinion due to any cinematic maturity I've managed to maintain as an adult. While *Superman II* remains a fun and effective sequel, I cannot deny that *The Movie* is a more spiritual film. Still, like so many others, I felt compelled to check out *The Richard Donner Cut* to see what all the hubbub was about. While I can appreciate the place the original artist holds with the finished product, I am, at heart, a movie purist and strongly feel that a film should stand as it does without interference or changes later on. Regardless of what may or may not have taken place behind the scenes of production, who was right, who was wrong, who got screwed, and who didn't, *Superman II*, for me, remains the film it was in 1981 under Lester's direction.

Finally, despite thirty-six years having passed since first seeing it as a kid, I still remain unclear about just exactly how Superman got his superpowers back. We know the green crystal had something to do with it, but just *how* remains a mystery to me. Did Clark recreate the Fortress of Solitude with the crystal just as he had in the original film, thus getting his powers back? It's possible, I suppose, but there remain too many holes in that theory which require explanation; explanation I'm likely never to get because I'm not one of those comic book geeks who overthinks these things. It's just a movie ... even if it's a *Superman* movie.

For Your Eyes Only

Directed by John Glen
(June 24, 1981, U.S. Release Date)

Then

Just to recap, after *Moonraker* in '79, I convinced myself there would *never* again be another James Bond adventure, having now gone to outer space. When I saw the newspaper ad of the movie poster, I had two initial reactions. My first was the disbelief that my theory was wrong. My second was the raging hormones of puberty when I saw that woman's incredible ass and legs. My parents never knew it, but I kept that newspaper page hidden in my room for many years during my youth (hey, it was a part of growing up for me). Whether or not I agreed with its release, *For Your Eyes Only* was still a new James Bond movie and I needed no other reason to want to see it.

The opening scene, while exciting to watch, was confusing because I had no idea who the bald man in the wheelchair controlling Bond's helicopter was (I'd not yet seen *You Only Live Twice* in its entirety, so I knew nothing of Ernst Stavro Blofeld, nor his place in Bond's life and history). Regardless, it was a forgettable scene because it had nothing to do with the story that would unfold after the credits. It began much like *The Spy Who Loved Me*, with a ship at sea mysteriously disappearing (sinking, actually) when it accidentally snagged a sea mine, which exploded the ship upon impact). Aboard this ship was something called an ATAC machine that communicated and coordinated with other submarines and was also a threat for nuclear war if it fell into enemy hands. Bond's mission was to retrieve that machine before the Soviet Union could. The race was on.

While investigating who was responsible for murdering a marine biologist and his wife aboard their boat, Bond was captured and escaped not to long after. He met up with the beautiful woman who was the *"Bond girl"* of the movie, Melina Havelock (probably the one with the great legs on the movie poster). They helped each other escape in her car in a scene that was rather silly in how it was shot. From there, they were in Italy and it was some of the most beautiful snow environments and camera shots I'd seen on screen. It was a beautiful resort and I suddenly found myself looking forward to winter, even as I was already enjoying that summer. Like *Spy*, there was an awesome ski chase sequence that eventually took Bond to the top of a jumping ramp; a stunt he attempted to avoid, but by then, the bad guys were behind him with guns pointed out, leaving him no choice. Bond being Bond, of course, managed to survive the entire incident without harm … that is, until he eventually got into trouble again. I have to say though, I thought the attack on his life by a group of hockey players on the ice rink was real stupid. I mean, seriously, were we supposed to believe that a bunch of hockey players are so easily defeated by sliding into the goalie's net?

I recognized signs of traditional scenes that repeatedly took place in Bond movies (*formulas*, as I'd eventually understand them to be). This included an epic shootout and battle between Bond, his allies, and their enemies. This one took place in a huge warehouse and eventually had Bond following the killer known as Locque in a high-speed car chase. I remember gritting my teeth in anticipation when the camera froze for just a second on Roger Moore standing still with gun pointed out, preparing to shoot Locque in the oncoming car. One shot, one bullet, and Locque's car went out of control and hung over a cliff. Moments later, I and other people in the theater that afternoon clapped their hands and cheered when Bond gave the car a single kick and it went tumbling down to the rocks below. As Bond put it afterward in one of his many one-liners, Locque *"had no head for heights."*

When he and Melina went diving to retrieve the ATAC system, their enemy or should I say *"Bond villain,"* was waiting for them at the surface to take it from them. Left to be eaten by sharks, Bond and Melina escaped death (of course) and were on the trail of getting the ATAC system back again. This time, not by sea, but rather a death-defying climb up a great cliff. This sequence toned down the excitement level because there was no soundtrack music to accompany it. The audience got real quiet as we watched Bond and the others climb, wondering what might happen at any given moment. Our job was to keep our eyes closely fixed on every detail, and perhaps even enjoy the beautiful Italian scenery. In the end, as expected, Bond killed the bad guys, saved the day, and got back the ATAC system, which he tossed over the cliff so that neither his country nor the Soviet Union could have it in their possession. As he told the Russian general, *"I don't have it. You don't have it."* Made sense to me and I guess it did to the general, too, because he smiled and laughed the entire matter off. All was well, but I was disappointed at such an anti-climactic ending without a final explosion or something just as dramatic. Clearly, this new Bond movie hadn't been intended to be anything like the two I'd seen on screen before it.

The summer of '81 resonated from *For Your Eyes Only* because my mother bought the single record of Sheena Easton's hit title song and played it on the family stereo all summer. At the time, I didn't like it because it was too much pop for my taste, though my feelings toward it are improved today. My mother never saw the movie until we both watched it on the *ABC Sunday Night Movie* in November 1983. She enjoyed it and found the Bond girl, played by Carole Bouquet, strikingly beautiful. I certainly couldn't argue with her about that. I haven't seen that woman in another movie since. In the end though, I still wasn't sure how I felt about the franchise continuing after *Moonraker*, which was my favorite Bond movie back then. As the years went on though, my feelings changed as I realized the validity of not only continuing with Moore in *Octopussy* and *A View to a Kill*, but with also transitioning the famous character to a new man like Timothy Dalton, whom I believe was a very underrated Bond of the '80s.

Now

The opening sequence of *For Your Eyes Only*, which confused me as a kid, now brings James Bond's personal story full circle. Ernst Stavro Blofeld was last seen at the end of *Diamonds Are Forever* and he'd (presumably) escaped without capture. We saw nothing of him for the past ten years, and United Artists decided to bring that unfinished bit of business back into the fold to tie it all up. For that purpose, we're reminded in the opening shot of the headstone that Bond was once married to Theresa Bond and she was killed by Blofeld at the end of *On Her Majesty's Secret Service*. Clearly, Bond never forgot that impact on his life (you'll recall his sensitivity to the mention of his wife's death by Anya in *Spy*) and it was, perhaps, destiny that he put this part of his past to bed once and for all. While the sequence is exciting to watch, especially since I've always enjoyed helicopter action in movies (think of Roy Scheider in *Blue Thunder*), Blofeld's ultimate demise is silly and comical, and ultimately disappointing because I believe that an infamous Bond villain as he should've perished in a more serious and dramatic fashion. Even though the man in the wheelchair is not officially identified as Blofeld, it's pretty clear to all Bond fans from his bald head and his stroking the white cat, who he really is.

All these years later and my interpretation of the Bond movie franchise changed, I now judge *For Your Eyes Only* with a different perspective. After pretty much *"jumping the shark"* with *Moonraker* in the last installment, there was virtually no choice but to start over and get back to the basics of reality. New director John Glen, new musical composer Bill Conti, new actor in a vague substitute role of "M" (Bernard Lee was dead), and none of the fantastic high-tech gadgetry or weaponry we'd seen twice now under Lewis Gilbert's direction. We also got to see Sheena Easton sing her popular title song during the opening credits, something that hadn't been done before. In short, *For Your Eyes Only* could easily be considered one of the first true James Bond *"reboots."* It's also my opinion that the marketing department for this film knew exactly what it was doing when it pulled audiences into the theaters with the obscure promise of sex by designing a poster featuring that woman's incredibly long, sexy legs and great ass!

The film's entire premise has likely been done more than once, the story being very formulaic; the typical beautiful Bond girl, the threat against the world, the frighteningly evil henchman with a greater physical strength than the average mortal man (think "Oddjob" and "Jaws"), and the resolution in the end that saves the day. In most cases, the formula works well enough to keep you interested. However, *For Your Eyes Only* continues to suffer greatly from a very unexciting and anti-climactic ending when the villain is only quietly defeated with a knife in his back. Even the mountain climbing sequence lacks it full potential due to the absence of the appropriate soundtrack music. I'm sure those behind the film thought they were creating a sense of true tension with that decision, but it just doesn't work for me without the music to give it a stronger sense of drama and even fear.

I've come to classify James Bond films under three rather distinct personal categories. The first being be the "I love this Bond movie!" category for titles like *Dr. No, Goldfinger, Thunderball, Moonraker,* and *Casino Royale.* The second being the "It's not the best, but I still enjoy it" category for titles like *You Only Live Twice, The Man With The Golden Gun,* and *Licence to Kill;* and finally the third being the "This Bond movie really sucks!" category with titles like *Diamonds Are Forever, Die Another Day,* and *Quantum of Solace.* That in mind, after careful consideration, I think I feel justified in putting *For Your Eyes Only* in the second category; a good, solid mixture of action, excitement, humor, and the usual bevy of beautiful women. Not a great movie, but perhaps just enough for the popular franchise to get things started again from the very basics of the classic spy story and inevitably get James Bond to where he is today.

Escape from New York
Directed by John Carpenter
(July 10, 1981, U.S. Release Date)

Then

I don't know *what* I was thinking when I asked my father if I could see *Escape from New York*. Didn't I have good sense to know that as soon as he saw the violent nature of the ad and artwork in the newspaper, he'd deem the movie too unsuitable for his fourteen-year-old son? Still, I thought it was worth a try, despite the movie's R-rating. As predicted, he shot me down faster than I could turn my head and that was the end of that for nearly a year. I'm sure you've already guessed how this turned out; Greg B., HBO, and a weekend sleepover in April 1982.

During the movie's opening narration (by Jamie Lee Curtis), when we learned just how and why the once great island of Manhattan became a maximum security prison for the worst criminals imaginable, Greg B. and I immediately agreed that this horrible future for the city seemed completely probable and conceivable. After all, it was 1982 by the time we saw this movie and Manhattan (as well as the other boroughs of New York City), was still considered a dangerous and deadly crime-ridden filth hole (sometimes I *still* look at them thay way). The impacts and improvements of New York City under future Mayor Rudy Giuliani were still many years away, and there seemed no hope in sight that conditions would ever change under the current mayor at the time, Edward Koch. So why wouldn't they, in the end, finally condemn Manhattan to be a dangerous prison where only the criminally insane would reside? It seemed possible. By that account, the futuristic story behind *Escape from New York* was more frightening than exciting. Even the opening fade-in shot of the movie gave me chills in the way the camera slowly made its way up the fifty-foot containment wall to finally reveal a shot of lower Manhattan in total darkness, which I took to be a very effective visualization of just how dead the island had become in the future (also recalling the infamous blackout in New York City during the summer of 1977).

The hero of the movie, and I suppose that was an interesting thing to call him since he was a criminal and a prisoner, was *Snake Pliskin*. With his tough, unshaven look, his black patch over one eye and his overall don't-mess-with-me attitude, he was just about the coolest guy I'd ever seen in any thriller, sci-fi, or action movie. Even his *name* sounded cool. To amuse ourselves, Greg B. and I repeatedly said the name, "Snake Pliskin ... Snake Pliskin ... Snake Pliskin!" (hey, we were kids, so we still acted silly). Now while I didn't completely understand the full nature of Snake's crime that landed him inside Manhattan, it sounded like it was just a case of robbery. Did he really deserve to be sent into the country's most notorious maximum security prison filled with rapists and murderers just for *that*? He was also an ex-Special Forces man in the military and that made him the best choice to go in and try and rescue the president of the United States (the same man who played Dr. Loomis in *Halloween*), whose plane had just crashed inside the city. If he got the president out in twenty-four hours, he'd be set free. As he told Police Commissioner Bob Hauk, *"Looks like I go in one way or another."*

As I watched and enjoyed *Escape from New York*, my brain repeatedly thought of other things associated with the city of Manhattan. First there was the '77 blackout, and then as Snake was maneuvering his stealth glider and landing it on top of the Twin Towers, I recalled *King Kong* and his final battle atop those same towers. When Snake was on the street, my mind was back to the blackout again. The part of the movie where I concentrated on nothing else was when we met one of the common criminals inside the city; a crazy looking punk with a wild head of blond hair who counted down the seconds that Hauk and his men had to get back into their helicopters and leave the island. There was something very unsettling about the way he counted down at a steady pace, *"Nineteen, eighteen, seventeen, sixteen ..."* Geez, this guy was freaky! If the rest of the criminals inside this place were anything like him, the president was surely going to die (he'd already had his ring finger severed in order to prove to Hauk that they were really holding him prisoner).

Apparently, not everyone inside was crazy. Snake hooked up with a friendly cab driver and even a former military buddy called "Brain" and his girlfriend Maggie (the same woman who played the lighthouse radio DJ in *The Fog*), an angry woman who showed a lot of cleavage for two young high school boys to gawk at. According to "Brain," the big criminal in charge of the entire prison who called himself "The Duke" was planning to use the president as a hostage in order to unify all the of city's gangs in a huge exodus that would take them all across the 69th Street Bridge to their ultimate freedom. "Brain" had developed a map to determine where the explosive mines on the bridge were placed. For a brief moment, Snake managed to locate and free the president, but was captured by "The Duke's" men soon after and forced to fight to the death in a public ring with a nasty-looking wrestler-type prisoner. Meanwhile, "Brain" and Maggie shot their way into where the president was being held and rescued him. "Brian" also killed the freaky-looking punk with the wild hair, and I have to say, even the way his face looked when he died from his stab wound sent shivers up my back (I tell you, *nothing* about this punk looked normal!). Snake killed his opponent and rejoined his partners to try and get the president to safety and freedom.

They were now racing against time across the bridge in "Cabbie's" car and trying to avoid the explosive mines. It didn't work because one of them went off and literally split the cab in two, killing Cabbie. "Brain" was killed by another mine and Maggie was killed when The Duke slammed his car into her. Snake was now the only one left alive to get the president over the fifty-foot wall to safety. The president made it over the wall, but Snake still had to get past The Duke. After briefly fighting each other, Snake was on his way over the wall and almost made it until the winch and rope suddenly stopped. I practically bit my nails to see if The Duke would actually kill Snake before he could make it over the wall. Instead, somebody shot The Duke to death at the last second, and lo and behold, it was the president himself who took a machine gun in hand and killed the man responsible for his imprisonment. Greg B. and I laughed as the president shouted, *"You are the Duke! A-Number One!"* The man may have been leader of the free world, but he was obviously *bad* when he had to be!

It was at the movie's conclusion that I realized just how much I really loved the movies of John Carpenter. The man truly knew how to scare people with his visions and his frightening situations, whether in the present day of the suburbs, seaside villages or the future of one of America's greatest cities. I'd seen three awesome movies of his in a row, and I did it with a good buddy of mine who appreciated the same stories of horror and thrills as I did. The movie was absent from my life for years until I taped a copy of it off of TV when I was in college. This wasn't the way I chose to own such a great movie, but even when I was a student in the '80s, purchasing brand-new movies at the local video store wasn't cheap. Were I to drop what little money I had on movies, such spending was reserved for more important material like *Star Wars* or James Bond movies (that was my thinking back then anyway).

Now

I have occasionally (affectionately and humorously) referred to *Escape from New York* as Fritz Lang's *Metropolis* turned upside down on its ass. Whereas the German black and white silent classic of 1927 depicts the wondrous Utopian glory of the big city (as was Lang's inspiration after visiting New York City for the first time), John Carpenter's film depicts the warped and grimy future of the city at its lowest and most desperate level, where humanity has lost nearly all its meaning and hope. Even our own United States government in the futuristic world of 1997 isn't immune from its lack of humanity, now operating as a dictatorship and responsible for creating the dreaded prison in the first place. As a result, there's a very strong irony taking place when Air Force One is hijacked by a group of self-righteous terrorists standing up against their corrupt government and the president finds himself trapped and fighting for his life inside the very world *he* created; the situation a lot more terrifying than your average futuristic sci-fi thriller. Just look at the blacked-out deserted city streets, the underground-dwelling "crazies," and especially that wild-looking street punk with the crazy laugh who looks like a cross between German actor Klaus Kinski and British rocker Billy Idol, and tell me if don't start to feel the shivers coming on. The entire film feels like one of those low-budget, terrifying movies you might have watched in the middle of the night on 42nd Street decades ago when it was packed with grindhouse movie theaters (and hookers).

As you view this futuristic world, it becomes pretty damn obvious that it was *not* filmed on location in New York City (St. Louis, Missouri, actually). Regardless though, there are enough subtle landmarks of the city to temporarily convince you otherwise; the World Trade Center, the New York Public Library, Central Park, and the 59th Street Bridge (it's referred to as the *69th* in the film for some reason), all of them looking rather post-apocalyptic and menacing in their appearance. There's also one particular scene that still gives me an unsettling feeling. Take a close look at when Air Force One is headed straight toward the lower part of one of the Twin Towers just before it crashes into another building. Carpenter filmed this just over twenty years before the events of September 11, 2001, ever took place. But if ever there was a moment where world history managed to imitate art, it's surely this one. It's a frightening image for those of us who remember that fateful day in our American history all too well.

Carpenter can be credited as a filmmaker who doesn't allow the special effects of his production (even a low budget one as this) deter too far off from the story. But even the effects are just enough to give us the taste of the dystopian atmosphere he's attempting to show us. Many of the visual images are elaborate collections of the city's urban blight, matched against the sounds that make the dark and bleak city so terrifying; from the simple sounds of breaking glass to the more elaborate audio of its crazed elements running their night-time rampage of violence. As an antihero, Snake Pliskin can easily be considered an alter-ego or even a fantasy of Carpenter's. Snake, while a decent man at heart, is nonetheless a man of uncompromising anti-authoritarianism. We can't help but empathize with his feelings and convictions when he blatantly tells Hauk from across the desk, *"I don't give a fuck about your war, or your president!"*, perhaps voicing a sentiment that many of us have felt before and continue to feel today.

While considered a cult classic, I hardly consider *Escape from New York* an action film, nor do I think that's what Carpenter offered us when he made it. Unlike popular action films of the '80s like *Rambo: First Blood—Part II* and *Die Hard*, this film has a much lower level of thrills and excitement, though not low enough to give it a feeling that it's simply shuffling along, in my opinion. While there are moments of action that include Snake's fight in the ring and the climactic chase across the bridge, it's hardly enough to get one's blood and adrenaline pumping, and perhaps that's not even the film's goal in the first place. It's about mood, about setting and a futuristic vision of a city that was already crumbling apart from crime and corruption in 1981. As a kid, I believed this *would* become the future of New York City if things continued to progress the way they were from the filth and scum of the time. As it turned out, by the time 1997 finally *did* arrive, New York City, under Rudy Giuliani's leadership, was not a prison. Instead, it went completely the other way with the demolition of 42nd Street's grindhouse theaters and replaced by Broadway theaters and Disney-style family musicals, as well as the expulsion of all the hookers (too bad about *that*—LOL!).

Heavy Metal

Directed by Gerald Potterton
(August 7, 1981, U.S. Release Date)

Then

During the latter part of the summer of '81, I desperately tried to see *Heavy Metal* when I first saw its full color poster image in the *New York Times* magazine. According to its taglines, the movie promised everything I concluded to be totally cool at the age of fourteen; science fiction, fantasy, battles between good and evil, sexual fantasies of beautiful animated women, and hard rock and roll. It played neither in Great Neck or Westhampton Beach, nor was it in any town nearby that I could get to on my own (the nearest location was a not-so-great neighborhood in Queens). It played at many theaters in Manhattan, but that was impossible for me. I wasn't driving yet, nor was I taking the train into the city on my own yet. I had to wait a year until the movie finally premiered on HBO sometime in 1982, though this time I didn't watch it with Greg B. By my memory, it was a high school get-together in the fall of my sophomore year at the house of a kid I barely knew. It was one of those situations where you're dragged along by the friend of a friend to the house of someone you hardly know. What stands out in my memory of this night was not only getting to watch *Heavy Metal* for the first time with friends, but it was also the first time I drank my first can of *beer* at the age of fifteen.

The memory of Ralph Bakshi's *The Lord of the Rings* and its style of animation was still fresh in my memory, even four years later. It looked like the movie used the same rotoscoping technique of animation in many of its shots. The opening title and the way the words *Heavy Metal* appeared on the screen was an instant attention grabber for all of us boys in the room. I can recall all of us saying, "Cool!" at the same time, and why wouldn't we? It *was* cool! It wouldn't be the only time we'd say that word during the course of the movie, because it was followed by so much more that was also cool, even during the opening credits; from the Corvette released by the space shuttles bay doors, to the car in flight during the first hard rock song, to the astronaut driving the car in space and landing on Earth, to his grisly death by the evil green sphere known as the Loc-Nar. The astronaut's daughter wasn't killed. Instead, she was forced to look deep into the orb so it could show her how it influenced people and societies throughout time, space, and history.

Still fresh off the heels of watching New York City's bleak future in *Escape from New York*, the next scene that followed was also the future city of Manhattan in the year 2031, described by cab driver Harry Canyon as *"the scum center of the world."* Harry reminded me a lot of Snake Pliskin; a dirty, unshaven man who wouldn't take crap from anybody. Even when his cab was robbed by some punk with a gun, he immediately took care of the guy with a disintegrator built into the back of the driver's seat. He appeared to have a good heart though, because he (reluctantly) stopped to help a beautiful girl in trouble with criminals who wanted to get their hands on the Loc-Nar, which her father possessed. They'd killed him and now they were after her. Still, was Harry a nice guy, or did he just want to go to bed with the girl? Turns out it was both. We who were watching couldn't blame him. Animated or not, the girl was hot! It was during the first shot of her animated nudity that I first heard the hit ballad *"Open Arms"* by Journey for the first time (it appeared later on the band's 1981 *Escape* album), and I've been a great fan of the band ever since. After helping her get rid of the Loch-Nar and getting for it by those who tried to kill her, she betrayed him by trying to keep all the money for herself and pointing a gun at Harry while sitting in the back seat of his cab. Remember what I told you about his disintegrator? It was *not* a love story that ended well.

The next story involved a nerdy teenager who found the Loc-Nar, which he mistook for a small green meteorite and simply put it among his bedroom rock collection. During an experiment with electricity, the orb came to life and hurled the boy away from Earth and landed him in another world in another galaxy. By the time he'd landed, he was no longer a skinny kid, but rather a bald, naked muscle man who went by the name of Den. After witnessing a strange ritual in which a naked blonde was to be sacrificed to a mysterious god, he dove into the water which she was thrown into and rescued her. Reaching safety, she introduced herself as Katherine Wells of the planet Earth. My friends and I laughed our asses off when Den's immediate thought upon gazing at her naked body was, *"She had the most beautiful eyes!"* Their sexual encounter together was interrupted, and Den had no choice but to agree to steal the Loc-Nar from the evil queen in order to save Katherine and ended up having sex with the queen too. A second sacrificial ritual would take place, only this time, Katherine was the intended victim. After he rescued her and defeated the queen and her army, Den passed up the opportunity to take the Loc-Nar for himself and secure power over the people of the planet. Instead, he rode off with Katherine into the sunset in what seemed like too happy an ending for a dark movie like *Heavy Metal.*

Such a happy ending was only temporary, because the journey of the Loc-Nar always moved onto something else and something different. In the next story, the orb was the size of a marble, which was discovered by a stupid-looking man with huge ears called Hanover Fiste, who was testifying at a trial on behalf of space captain Lincoln Stern, accused of countless horrible crimes. At first, he stated what a great man Stern was, but as the power of the Loc-Nar showed itself, he was not only blurting out the horrible truth about Stern's evil crimes, but was also physically developing into a bald, muscled giant who was now out to kill Stern. Fiste was raging with fury and destroying the space station as he hunted him down. When the two of them were finally alone and facing each other, it turned out the whole episode was a deception in order to help Stern escape. Fiste transformed back to his old self, was paid off for helping Stern, and then ejected into space by Stern; losing his money and still clinging to the marble-sized orb, even as his flaming hand was severed from his body and travelling through Earth's atmosphere. "Sick" was the word spoken by me and my friends now as we watched the last moment of that scene.

The movie stepped back in time now to World War II and a short story of a B-17 bomber in flight during air combat. While checking on the rest of the crew, one of the pilots discovered nothing but dead bodies and the Loc-Nar following the plane from behind in the night sky. The orb suddenly rammed the plane and had the power to reanimate the dead crew members into zombies. The pilot escaped the horror by parachuting onto a mysterious island where he found a graveyard of airplanes from different periods of history, along with other airmen now turned to zombies, who were now closing in on him. Short as this story was, I was impressed nonetheless of the historical time machine element of how the Loc-Nar influenced a period of our past on our planet.

Earth was now back in the present day for the next story in which our government tried to figure out why ordinary citizens were turning into zombies in what seemed like an offbeat continuation of the World War II zombie tale. While trying to explain the unusual phenomenons taking place, a trusted government doctor gazed at the Loc-Nar inside the locket of the beautiful stenographer sitting across the table from him. At that moment, he went crazy and attacked the poor women right there on the conference table. High above the Pentagon building was a huge spaceship whose front looked like a pair of eyes and a wide smile. The ship burst through the building's roof and took away the doctor and the woman. The ship was controlled by a small robot with big metallic ears who immediately fell in love with the woman. He even convinced her to have robot sex with him. Meanwhile, the two pilots of the spaceship were getting high by snorting a white powder they called *"Plutonian nyborg,"* which clearly resembled real-life cocaine (yes, even at fifteen, I knew what that stuff was and what it looked like, though *not* through personal experience, I assure you). While flying the ship under their intoxication, they crashed the ship inside a huge space station, but still considered it a good landing.

The final story was the most serious and the one most associated with the art and style of fantasy and adventure. The Loc-Nar was now the size of a giant meteor and crashed into a volcano, thus changing a group of human men into sick-looking barbarians who proclaimed, *"Death to all who oppose us!"* and then attacked a peaceful city. The elder scientists, realizing they would be destroyed, made a desperate attempt to summon the last of a race of warriors called the Taarakians, who would fulfill an ancient pact to protect and avenge them. The last of the race was a strong, beautiful blonde named Taarna who arrived to take her rightful place as such a warrior. Along with her sidekick bird, she arrived at the city too late to save its people. She never said a word, but her search for those responsible for the massacre was clear enough. Captured by the barbarians, she was tortured and left for dead. However, with the help of her bird, she escaped capture and fought the barbarian leader to his ultimate death by her hand. To finally defeat the Loc-Nar, she chose to sacrifice her own life by throwing herself into the volcano. In a way though, none of this ever happened because now the movie returned to the little girl whose astronaut father had been killed by the same Loc-Nar she'd been staring into the whole time. Turns out, this little girl was the same one who'd eventually grow up to become the warrior woman Taarna. Realizing that its future was doomed by this girl, the Loc-Nar destroyed itself as she ran for her life before the house exploded. Outside, she met the bird who'd become here sidekick, and the movie concluded itself by offering a chance for hope and peace.

During the closing credits of montage and music, the first thing I recall saying to my friends was that I was running right out to buy the soundtrack album. I played that two record set over and over again. It was fall of '82, and it was a time when MTV was just over a year old and hard rock still dominated the FM radio waves and stereo turntables (before cheesy pop acts like Michael Jackson, Culture Club, and Eurythmics took over). At a time when my music tastes were becoming harder with bands like Journey, Def Leppard, Iron Maiden, and Judas Priest, the rock music of *Heavy Metal*, with awesome tracks by Black Sabbath, Blue Oyster Cult, Cheap Trick, Sammy Hagar, and Grand Funk Railroad, was just the sort of rock music that defined my youth (my adulthood too).

Heavy Metal disappeared from my life for many years after that night, as it wasn't officially released on VHS until 1996, due to legal copyright issues. I did, however, manage to videotape a copy of it prior to that as it had rotated airings on HBO and Cinemax. Prior to that, there was only the occasional midnight screening at the triplex theater not too far from my college dorm room in the late '80s. In many ways though, those nights at the midnight theater were much like that first night back in '82; a young kid (older now) surrounded by friends watching an awesome adult animated movie and still thinking of that reoccurring word in his head, "Cool!"

Now

The adult R-rated animated motion picture is pretty much a dead genre, phasing itself out by the end of the '80s. Today, we have adult-themed animated shows on TV like *Family Guy* and *American Dad.* That in mind, films like *Heavy Metal* and Ralph Bakshi's *American Pop* may be regarded with a great deal of affection and rememberance. Such films should not be taken too seriously. *Heavy Metal* is certainly not a milestone in the art of American cinema. By today's standards of what's considered politically correct, the film may be considered sexist, sleazy, egotistical, sadomasochistic, juvenile, and very dated for its time. But even with today's CGI technology, the mystical and surrealistic animation and graphics are quite eye-popping nonetheless. I know very little about the magazine that inspired it, but I've come to regard the film as a small piece of history in not only its animation, but music as well that continues to take me back to a time when FM radio hard rock still meant something to kids in this country. In fact, there are few films I can easily cite that so effectively blends the art of sight and sound as *Heavy Metal* does.

The landscaping of the film may be considered barren, even as it lends support to characters of fantasy that are superhuman and angry. If we're looking for any sympatic element in this film, it's likely only to be found in the giant bird, which is graphically the most dominant figure in the movie poster's image. The bird is a loyal friend and protector of the heroine Taarna, whom also serves as a young man's (and older one's) kinky fantasy with her black warrior bikini and stunning body (animated though it is). In a film filled with large-breasted women, Taarna proves to be the film's only fully-realized and fully-developed (I'm not speaking physically now) woman, the irony being in that she doesn't ever say a single word.

As the film's epilogue reveals the connection between the astronaut's daughter and Taarna, it lends question to such a possible link. Throughout the story, the Loc-Nar would have us believe that all stories, including Taarna's, have taken place in the *past*. Therefore, how does Taarna come to defeat the Loc-Nar in the future, as we're meant to understand in the end? Such two story segments taking place at the same time are sure to raise confusion in ones sense of logic, if one wishes to take sci-fi and fantasy that seriously. The film's main intent back in the day may have been to simply lure geeky teenage boys with its promise of nudity, kinky fun, and violence (it worked with me and my friends), during a time when a game like *Dungeons & Dragons* was widely popular.

Chariots of Fire
Directed by Hugh Hudson
(October 9, 1981, U.S. Release Date)

⟫⟨◍⟩⟨

Then

As a kid obsessed with sci-fi and superheros, the last kind of movie I would've *ever* shown interest in would've been a lame British movie. It simply wasn't plausible. Those movies were for grown-ups who also liked to watch costume dramas on PBS. During the summer of '81, there was an album in our house that played endlessly on the family stereo. It was the original motion picture soundtrack by Vangelis for *Chariots of Fire*. Despite the fact that this new age music became very familiar in my house, I still concluded the movie's artistic subject matter was far beyond my juvenile interest. But sometimes you get dragged to a movie you don't want to see and probably won't understand too well because your parents want to see it and also because neither of them wish to stress themselves out by negotiating with their kids.

Despite my determined lack of interest, I enjoyed the opening scene of the runners on the beach. I'd already spent the entire summer listening to that popular theme song. Now I could associate a visual image to go with it. Unfortunately, that iconic scene was only a brief one. From there, we were introduced to various students at the all-male University of Cambridge in 1919 England. Though I found it difficult to keep up with exactly who was who and what their backgrounds were, I enjoyed the moments when these men would find any reason to run uplifting, particularly the running of the college courtyard in order to break the University record. The man to do it was Harold Abrahams, the (seemingly) only Jewish man at the university and one who was constantly defending himself against the prejudices of others, including the college staff. He was a man dedicated to his running, but also found time to fall in love with a beautiful, young opera singer named Sybil.

Meanwhile, in Scotland, there was a Christian missionary named Eric Liddel, also a gifted runner. His sister Jennie, also a devout Christian, disapproved of her brother's pursuit of running in the upcoming Olympic games. While Eric planned to return to China to continue his religious work, he needed to fulfill the desires of his running first, even if his sister didn't like it. Though the story didn't make it obvious, I could see things were setting up so that these two young men would eventually compete with each other in Paris. When they first raced and Eric Liddel won, Harold didn't take it well. He acted like a child about it, actually. It was then he met the man who'd become his trainer (played by the same malfunctioning robot in *Alien*) to improve his running technique and beat Eric the next time. This new partnership caused Abraham's college masters to question his amateur standing, as well as his loyalty to the college rather than himself. While Abraham was defensive about this, I understood the religious and class prejudices against a Jew in the story. Perhaps it was because I was Jewish too, though I'd never experienced any anti-Semitism myself (perhaps this was because I was raised in a Jewish town). One moment I remember well was when Eric, after hard work and training, suddenly realized that he couldn't compete in an important Olympic race because it was scheduled on a Sunday, the one day of the week Eric wouldn't run due to his religious beliefs. I wasn't sure whether or not to agree with such an attitude, but I recall thinking just how unfair and unjust the whole thing was. In the end, it was all settled and resolved so that Eric could run, though I didn't fully understand how and why. One minute it was an issue, the next minute it wasn't. I suppose my mother understood, but I didn't bother asking her in a crowded movie theater.

By the time *Chariots of Fire* came to its athletic climax, I felt let down. The final sports competition was only a matter of seconds, and it left me feeling no sense of crowd-cheering victory or triumph. It seems the movie was never meant to excite a young kid like myself as *Rocky, Breaking Away,* or even *The Bad News Bears* had. Perhaps I never should've been in the theater watching this thing in the first place. Perhaps my parents should have left me and Kevin at home while they went off to watch their little British art movie. Clearly, I wasn't ready for, nor was I mature enough for this sort of entertainment. Time, however, changes things, as does *finally* subscribing to HBO. Our first month's subscription was March 1983, and it was also when *Chariots of Fire* premiered. Now I could watch it again, perhaps even more than once, to finally understand what I hadn't quite grasped the first time.

Now

I'm not a kid anymore. I love art films. I love many British films. I love good stories, even if they move at a slow pace. I'm enthralled by *Chariots of Fire,* the Best Picture Oscar winner of 1981, from the moment the film opens with the elderly gentleman Lord Andrew Lindsay speaking these words at a eulogy in 1978:

> *Let us praise famous men and our fathers that begat us. All these men were honoured in their generations and were a glory in their days. We are here today to give thanks for the life of Harold Abrahams. To honour the legend. Now there are just two of us—young Aubrey Montague and myself - who can close our eyes and remember those few young men with hope in our hearts and wings on our heels ...*

And then transitioning into a slow dissolve to the great sequence of young British men filled with pride and promise running together along the shoreline of the windswept beach on an overcast day while the immortal music of Vangelis's instrumental theme song takes us along the journey with them. For a moment, the camera focuses on four of these young men, and we know we're in for an intriguing and moving story surrounding each of them and how their lives shall interact with one another at a higher and more spiritual level. This is what you're likely to think and feel if you open your mind and allow the scene and the music to do the job it was designed to do.

Chariots of Fire is often labelled a sports film, but I find that a difficult pill to swallow. Yes, it's undeniably a film with the athletic competition of the 1924 Olympics as its primary backdrop, but from my perception, this is a story about the internal souls and spirits of young men with strong social values, long before they ever set foot on the running track. Eric Liddell, the devout Scottish Christian who runs for the glory of God and not his own intents, and Harold Abrahams, the English Jew who runs to overcome prejudice; two very different contrast of personal motives. The sports element is actually quick and repetitive, as the track events are inserted almost as fillers to express physical determination of such men, filled with a great sense of honor and meaning. The poetic, slow motion camera shots occurring at the point of victory serve to raise the spirit of the film and maybe even our own personal spirit as we watch men reach their achievements at the end of the finish line. This may sound very cliché, but it's what happens when a film of this sort works so effectively with its audience. These young men racing each other are filled with honor and pride, for not only themselves, but for country, king and God. These emotions are not only definitive for Great Britain at the early part of the twentieth century, but perhaps an example of what there's so little of in modern sports competition today—pride and honor.

Chariots of Fire is best described, in my opinion, in one word and that's *celebration*. The celebration of time and place, of life, of love, of God (if you choose to believe), of the victory of winning, and the life lessons learned from the heartbreak of losing. Harold Abrahams is distraught when he loses his first race against Eric Liddel, to the point of behaving like a spoiled child. However, through the love, encouragement, and even discipline from the woman he loves, he alters his attitude to focus on the positive and the future in which he's determined to beat Eric the next time around, suggesting that without the struggle of his failure, there's no exhilaration in the victory of his success.

For all its historical restoration, old-fashioned feel, flavor, and drama of an independent art film, it was released by Warner Brothers, a major Hollywood studio. I can't help but feel that today, such a studio would never have the *balls* to back a motion picture like this. It is, after all, a strong, character-driven film with very little speed, despite being a sports film. It's a quiet, unassuming British film with young actors who were unknowns at the time, but gave extraordinary performances nonetheless. Today, an intelligent, thought-provoking art film of this quality would likely be released only as an underground independent feature, which just goes to prove what a sad state of affairs the modern Hollywood studio is in. Still, I'm encouraged that this film reminds us to slow down in life. Not just in what we watch, but in how we absorb our own meaning and existence while watching and truly listening to what gifted actors are saying to each other. This is the true essence of *Chariots of Fire*.

Halloween II

Directed by Rick Rosenthal
(October 30, 1981, U.S. Release Date)

Then

Everything about Halloween weekend in October 1981 surrounded the movies *Halloween* and *Halloween II*. On Friday, October 30, 1981, the first movie premiered on NBC with never-before-seen bonus footage added. That same day, the sequel opened at the Great Neck Playhouse. Days earlier, a friend told me that he and others in my grade were going to an afternoon show over the weekend and wanted to know if I'd join them. What made this request interesting was that our group would include a few girls, and I'd be sitting next to one of them in the theater. My friend told me that sitting with a girl at a horror movie was cool because girls that age usually got scared and would grab the hand or arm of the boy sitting next to them. So technically, I was being set up on my first movie *date*. Because of my inexperience with girls at that time, I honestly didn't know how to feel about this. Part of me looked forward to my first so-called "date" with a girl (hopefully, a pretty one), but the other part of me who didn't care so much about the girl was anxious to see the new *Halloween* movie (hey, let's try to remember that I'm still just fourteen and haven't gotten my social priorities straight yet!).

Saturday afternoon arrived, and I sat in the theater with a group of about ten high school freshmen. My "date" was (thankfully) not bad-looking. The movie began like *Rocky II* had, picking up exactly where the first movie ended and rewinding it a bit to catch us up on what happened. Michael Myers had been shot six times by Dr. Sam Loomis and fell to the ground from the second floor balcony of Tommy Wallace's house. Stepping onto the balcony, Dr. Loomis looked down and was shocked to discover that Michael was gone. Six shots, and the killer just got up and walked away. He was on the loose again, and this is where the new movie was beginning. The opening credits began much as the original *Halloween* had with the sinister-looking jack-o'-lantern on the screen. The music was a slightly different version of John Carpenter's original theme. There was also a different director, though Carpenter was still attached as writer and producer. Perhaps there was enough of his involvement to make this sequel just as good.

Unlike the first story, Loomis wasn't a calm person. Convinced that Michael was still on the loose, he was half-crazed with determination to get him and he'd have to do it without the help of the town sheriff who'd just discovered that one of the girls killed that Halloween night was his own daughter, Annie. I thought he might actually *kill* Dr. Loomis when he screamed, *"Damn you! Why did you let him go?"* During that same scene, a young man wearing the same mask as Michael was nearly shot by Loomis, thinking it *was* Michael. We who watched knew it wasn't, but the poor man died anyway when he was hit by a police car and plowed into an exploding van.

Meanwhile, Laurie Strode was taken to the local hospital to treat the stab wound that Michael gave her. Her survival and location had already made the local radio news and Michael just happened to overhear it as he walked along the street. Now *he* was on his way to the hospital to find Laurie and kill her this time. By this time, my "date" took my hand when Michael killed one of the local girls in town and would continue seeking my comfort whenever she felt scared (which was perfectly fine with me!). Arriving at the hospital, Michael cut the phone lines and damaged the parked cars so no one could leave and get help. The story now focused on Michael's presence at the hospital and killing as much of the staff as possible. It seemed to me though that as the murders continued, each one got just a little sicker than the last. One pretty nurse was drowned in a hot tub with the skin of her face completely scalded (that was grue-some!). My "date" grabbed my arm very tight when she saw that. The pretty blonde nurse calling out to Laurie in the corridor was killed when Michael stuck a scalpel into her back and lifted her up off of the floor. While this was a shocking way to die, it wasn't bloody or gross in any way, and I even thought the way the camera focused on it for a moment or two wasn't too unlike the kitchen murder of the young man with the glasses in the first *Halloween*.

In another scene, when Dr. Loomis was driven out of town by one of the local policemen, his assistant revealed a shocking secret. It turns out that when little six-year-old Michael was sent away for killing his older sister, he had a baby sister we knew nothing about. When the baby's parents were killed in an accident, she was adopted by the Strode family. So the baby girl grew up to be Laurie Strode, which meant she was Michael Myers's *sister*. Dr. Loomis was more determined than ever to get Michael now that he knew *why* he'd returned to Haddonfield in the first place. I laughed and said to my "date," "I wonder if Darth Vader is her father too." She laughed too and told me I was funny. Laurie, scared for her life now, escaped the hospital and hid in a parked car. She could barely walk now because she'd been given a shot that weakened her. As she watched Dr. Loomis and the policeman go inside the hospital building, she finally found her voice and screamed for help. She found her legs too because she got up and ran to the building as Michael was now after her again.

Like the first time, she pounded on the door and screamed to be let in before the killer reached her. Dr. Loomis saved her, but when Michael got back into the hospital, he killed the policeman after being shot by him. When Laurie asked, *"Why won't he die?"*, I'm sure many of us watching were wondering the same thing. The final showdown took place inside a surgery room where Michael stabbed Dr. Loomis in the stomach and Laurie managed to get ahold of a gun, shooting Michael in the eyes. Blind, he swung his knife in all directions, trying to stab either of them. Wounded, Dr. Loomis turned on the gas in the room and told Laurie to get out. Declaring, *"It's time, Michael,"* he flicked his pocket lighter and blew up the room with the two of them with it. Now a burning body, Michael stumbled out of the room and finally collapsed onto the floor. The killer was dead and Laurie had, once again, survived the terror of Halloween night in Haddonfield.

You'd probably like to hear that after the movie, I summoned up the courage to ask for my "date's" phone number, we went out on a few high school dates, and she eventually became my girlfriend. Oh, how I *wish* I could tell you that's what happened. The reality was that I was still a shy kid around girls and made no such effort toward her. We thanked each other and said goodbye for the day. My friend who'd set up the whole thing asked me how I did. I told him he was right and she'd held my hand and arm during the scary parts. He laughed and said, "All right, Eric!" (he might just as well have said, "All right, Eric, you're on your way!', echoing a similar line said by *"Fink"* to *"Spaz"* in the 1979 summer camp comedy *Meatballs*). Apparently, he hadn't expected much more to happen between us in a crowded movie theater. He never even asked if I'd asked her out afterward.

I saw *Halloween II* again on TV in 1985 when I was a college freshman. Though I enjoyed it uncut on screen with my "date" by my side, I suppose it left only a minimal impression on me. As I got older, the inevitable franchise it spawned was just another example of how a good thing like the original *Halloween* could spiral into Hollywood overkill. By the time I graduated college in 1992, Michael Myers had come back from the dead and returned in *Halloween 4* and *5*. I saw neither of them because as far as I was concerned, he'd burned to death at the end of the second movie, and I was determined to leave it at that.

Now

The movie poster for *Halloween II* promotes *"More Of The Night He Came Home"* and that's exactly what it is; *more* of the same, though not nearly as good or what I like to affectionately refer to as *SS-NAG* (same shit, not as good). John Carpenter refused to direct the sequel to the same film he'd made already and chose director Rick Rosenthal to follow in his shoes. The sequel attempts to recreate the same thematic elements of the original film, even reusing the opening titles with the sinister jack-o'-lantern and musical themes. In actuality, it's more in tune with the traditional slasher films of the time by using more blood and violence, though it was Rosenthal who claimed that Carpenter stepped in and implemented the extra gore and nudity. I've also never known how to feel about the revelation of Laurie Strode turning out to be Michael Myers's sister. Maybe it's that old childhood joke I made about whether or not Darth Vader was her father, finally catching up with me. Perhaps the old plot twist of a secret personal relationship between two characters presumed to be unrelated to each other is just overused in the movies. Clearly, it's meant to clarify the logical connection between Michael and his victim, but I think there's something to be said for the ambiguity and mysterious circumstances in the original *Halloween* behind an escaped killer's slow and steady rampage against three random babysitters on what's considered the most terrifying night of the year.

I suppose we have to consider that without *Halloween II*, the fate of Michael Myers is left hanging in the air when he gets up and walks away after being shot six times. Still, due to my general distaste for unnecessary sequels, it's my decision to own Carpenter's *Halloween* and nothing else. It can be argued that I've left things unfinished, but that's what adds a real touch of mystery and fear to the entire story in that we're left unsure of what's become of the killer's fate in the end. We know only that a horrible night has taken place and that the film's female protagonist has survived. Maybe that's enough for the *Halloween* saga … enough for *me* anyway.

*****

This is the last film of 1981 I shall discuss in any great detail.

In retrospect, it was a year of classic screen heroes (Superman and James Bond) and new favorites (Indiana Jones and Snake Pliskin). It was also a year where the music of some of the year's most popular films had a strong impact in my family's household. It was dominated by the Vangelis soundtrack to *Chariots of Fire*, but there were also hit singles that I was constantly listening to including "Endless

Love" by Diana Ross and Lionel Richie, "For Your Eyes Only" by Sheena Easton, and "Arthur's Theme (Best That You Can Do)" by Christopher Cross.

During that year, I had the opportunity to catch up with two of the best films of Mel Brooks's career when *Blazing Saddles* premiered on CBS on October 29, 1981, and *Young Frankenstein* premiered on NBC on December 6, 1981. The first film, as funny as it was even on TV, was only a limited viewing for me as it was a school night. Years later, I discovered just how hilarious this western spoof was, with all of its irresistible vulgarity and unapologetic racism. It's the latter film, however, that really left an impact on me. Seven years after accompanying my father at the drive-in, I could finally take in the film for all it was worth. This was a spoof of a monster movie I'd already watched on TV. I sensed the film wasn't too heavily edited for television. There was little to indicate that Gene Wilder and Marty Feldman's words had been altered in any way. The black and white imagery stayed true to the original visual themes of *Frankenstein* in 1931, which it payed homage to and even used some of the original set equipment. Like the drive-in in '74, I watched *Young Frankenstein* with my father, both of us enjoying the laughter that only Brooks could provide us.

The other TV premiere that affected me or dare I say, *impacted* my adolescent upbringing, was Blake Edwards's *"10"* on CBS on November 10, 1981. Over the last year, I'd become very aware of Bo Derek's popularity from this film and saw many pictures of her in magazines (including Playboy). Watching *"10"* now on TV was the first opportunity to see the film that launched her fame, though it was impossible for me to realize just how much I was missing with the edited-for-television version and all its nudity and strong sexual content toned down or deleted entirely. This was a version that only a kid could get away with watching when raised by parents who'd never let him see the uncut R-rated version on screen. Still, even edited, it was a chance for me to get a glimpse of Bo Derek in all her beautiful glory running down the beach in her one-piece bathing suit. One could only sympathize with Dudley Moore's character in becoming obsessed with meeting her and trying to get her into bed.

I mean, if you had to choose between Bo Derek or Julie Andrews, wasn't the choice obvious? Suddenly, her poster on my wall took on a whole new meaning. Now there was a moving image to go with the still one. In short, never underestimate the feelings and reactions of a boy who's just starting to become horny in his life.

And that, my friends, was the year 1981 for me.

THE YEAR WAS 1982 ...

- The Commodore 64 home computer is launched, becoming the all-time best-selling model of its time.
- *Saturday Night Live* comedian and actor John Belushi dies of a drug overdose.
- The Vietnam Veteran's Memorial opens in Washington DC.
- The Falklands War begins when the Islands are invaded by Argentina.
- Actor Vic Morrow is killed in a helicopter stunt accident on the set of *Twilight Zone—The Movie*.
- Michael Jackson releases his second solo album *Thriller*, becoming the biggest selling album of all time.

... AND THERE WERE MOVIES!

This the final year of this book.

The year 1982 is going to be the longest year I write about because by now, I'm an older boy of fifteen and enjoying the opportunity of going to the movies more often with friends, family, and sometimes myself. More movies means more personal memories and experiences to write about. My strongest memory of this year was, by far, the summer. I've often asked myself if the summer of 1982 wasn't quite possibly the *greatest* summer blockbuster season of all time? Perhaps, but what makes such a question or presumption even possible? Previous summers beginning in '75 already gave us many of the spectacular films I've written about. For myself though, and possibly for many others who were there to experience it, the summer of '82 brought blockbuster motion pictures in greater succession than ever before, and many of them had something fresh and new to offer the happy moviegoer (perhaps you agree with me, perhaps you don't).

However, one couldn't approach the summer without winter and spring before it. Sometimes when you're waiting for the *big* season to arrive and you'll finally be out of school for a couple of months, you have to sit back and hope there'll be at least one movie or two that'll offer you sustainable entertainment before the adventures of twenty-third century outer space, a squashy-looking alien visiting Earth, and a familiar Philadelphia boxer's bout with a wrecking machine sporting a Mohawk haircut will finally hit the big screen at your local movie theater. You're not even looking ahead to the fall yet, when you'll be amazed what Oscar-winning gems and other screen surprises are waiting for you.

First, you'll have to start out with a few smaller movies.

Diner

Directed by Barry Levinson
(March 5, 1982, U.S. Release Date)

Then

Diner, the debut movie by director Barry Levinson was something I wouldn't have been interested in at the age of fifteen. Yet every once in a while, I was intrigued by the "slice of life" or "coming of age" movies like *Annie Hall, The Goodbye Girl, Breaking Away, The Four Seasons,* and even the rerelease of *American Graffiti. Diner* was another opportunity to not only experience the simple life on screen, but to also get a glimpse into the past of the 1950s. The time was Baltimore, Maryland, in 1959. A young man entered a dance in progress at a high school. I immediately recognized the song performed was *"Shout"* because I'd heard it by Otis Day and the Knights in *Animal House*. Although I knew it was inappropriate to talk during a movie, there was a question I had to ask my father right away.

> "Dad, is this movie like *American Graffiti?*"
> "I think so. It looks like it."
> "Then I guess you'll love it."

The period and the boys exploring their youth through a series of humorous episodes and time spent talking and relating to their life wasn't too unlike Lucas's '73 masterpiece. These weren't high school graduates, but young men in their twenties trying to figure out exactly what to do with their lives. They were reunited when a friend of theirs came in on the train to attend the wedding of another member of their group. Their favorite late-night hangout place was the local diner, where they feasted on sandwiches, coffee, and french fries drowning in gravy. *Gravy?* That was a new one for me (I never imagined the taste of good 'ol American fries in anything but ketchup). The young man getting married, Eddie, was definitely an odd type. He always took every opportunity to argue with his friends about any topic, whether it was sharing his roast beef sandwich, deciding whether Frank Sinatra was better than Johnny Mathis (my father probably could've decided that one right then and there), or giving his friend a ride home. But what I couldn't understand, for the life of me, was that Eddie was making his fiancée take a football quiz on the Baltimore Colts, for which he was a die-hard fan of. If she failed the quiz, the marriage was off. On the surface, I suppose the idea was funny. Still, I couldn't help but ask myself *why* that idea was funny. Was Eddie really *not* going to marry the girl he was supposed to love if she failed some stupid football quiz? If this was adult humor, I surely had lots more to learn about it.

Another man called *"Shrevie"* was someone I immediately recognized, played by the same goofy actor who was young Cyril in *Breaking Away*. He was a married man with a simple job in a television and appliance store. Although he appeared to love his wife, he wasn't always nice to her. What really made me take notice of him though, was that (not unlike my father) he not only knew the names and lyrics of every popular song of the time, but also knew the flip side of the original 45 single, whether it played on the radio or was part of his extensive record collection. My father smiled and I gave him an affectionate shove to his arm with my elbow, as if directly acknowledging the similarity between both of their quirky musical personalities.

The one who called himself *"Fen"* was the troublemaker of the group (the same kid I'd seen in *Animal House* and *Friday the 13th*). When we first met him, he was breaking windows in the high school basement just for a laugh. Later, he pulled a prank on his buddies by tipping his car over and covering his face with ketchup to look like he'd been hurt in an accident. After that, he was arrested for stripping down to his underwear and beating up statues of the wise men in a church Christmas display. We later learned that he was from a wealthy family and was considered the uneducated "screw-up" among them. He was smart though, because he knew every correct answer while watching a TV game show. He was what my mother referred to as an underachiever (which I think she even managed to quietly whisper during the movie).

The one with the strangest name, *"Boogie"* looked a lot like a criminal with his hairstyle and his clothes. Interestingly, he was the most sensitive and caring one of the bunch. He even worked as a hairdresser in a beauty parlor and also had a gambling problem that got him into a debt of two thousand dollars with a tough loan shark. He was constantly trying to get his friends to take part in bets he offered over silly proposals, including getting his pretty, blonde date to grab his penis during a movie. Although my mother found it completely tasteless, I enjoyed the rather perverted, adolescent humor in the way that he managed to get his penis inside his box of popcorn so his date would grab it without realizing it. He even made a bet that would involve him making a move on *"Shrevie's"* wife, Beth, but at the last minute, his conscience got to him and he told Beth what he'd intended to do with her. She wasn't mad. In fact, she even thanked him for having enough respect for her to call it off. I suppose, even as a boy who knew little about grown-up romantic relationships, I could appreciate such a noble gesture.

The two remaining men had a less important role in the story. Modell was an awkward type who never said exactly what was on his mind, though it was he who gave the wedding speech for the groom at the end of the movie. Billy, the one who returned home for the wedding, was a quiet man who was still in love with his ex-girlfriend and held a longtime grudge against a boy who'd beaten him up years earlier. It was at a bar the night before the wedding that he really came out of his shell when, after expressing his frustration at the slow pace of the band's music, he decided to take matters into his own hands by getting up on stage and playing a smoking tune on the piano that the rest of the band joined in on. Although it was a brief musical moment, I enjoyed the party-like atmosphere it created for the scene.

The movie ended simply with Eddie's wedding and a final shot of these good friends gathered together for a picture at a table. Even as it all came to an end, I couldn't help but notice that this was the first time I'd ever seen a movie that ended with a shot that was exactly the same as the one on the movie poster, as if everything I'd watched on screen was coming full circle. The closing credits had no music, but rather more dialogue, presumably at the diner, between the friends. The one piece of dialogue I took notice of and still appreciate to this day is when Modell, in a conversation about amoebas, says, *"People do not come from swamps. They come from Europe."* I laughed at that and so did my mother (it was indeed a pleasure to listen to my mother laugh at the movies).

Now

I still love the 'ol "slice of life" and "coming of age" film every now and again. I appreciate them more when I discover they're sometimes semi-autobiographical of the person who wrote the story; in this case Barry Levinson and his true life experiences growing up in Baltimore, Maryland. Such films often show the drama, pain, and humor of leaving behind what you once loved and embracing what's to come in the future. The cast includes Steve Guttenberg, Daniel Stern, Kevin Bacon, Mickey Rourke, Paul Reiser, Tim Daly, and Ellen Barkin, who would eventually go on to greater stardom in the '80s and '90s. It's also an interesting look at youth, released at a time shortly before filmmakers like John Hughes, Joel Schumacher, and Cameron Crowe invited us into the world of the *"Brat Pack"* with *Sixteen Candles, The Breakfast Club, St. Elmo's Fire,* and *Say Anything.*

The young men depicted in *Diner* isn't quite like others we've seen on screen before. Although it's still the innocent era of the '50s, they're a little simpler and more subdued than those of *American Graffiti* or even *Happy Days.* High school is over, and with the exception of Billy, none of them have left town for college or any other reason. Some of them, like *"Shreivie,"* have their lives already set in motion within the institution of marriage, good or bad, like it or not. Others like Modell, *"Fen,"* and *"Boogie"* are coasting through life, trying to figure out what to do next. Eddie, on the merge of getting married, struggles to figure out exactly *why* he's doing it. He never once says he loves his fiancé, nor do we ever see her face, even during the wedding ceremony. By his logic, he's been with her so long, that marrying her is simply the right thing to do. The football quiz is either a pathetic excuse to try and get out of the entire commitment (which he almost does when his fiancé fails the quiz by just two points) or a silly attempt to find a viable common bond between himself and his wife-to-be. In the end, only the night before the wedding, Steve is finally satisfied he's doing the right thing by getting married when, in a private conversation with *"Shrevie,"* he's convinced that despite problems with communication and common interests, marriage is still nonetheless *"good."*

Through what is nothing more than an ongoing series of vignettes rather than the traditional narrative, the film explores the relationship among these young men as they near adulthood, though that term in itself can be argued, considering one of them is married already and one is about to be married. Still, the institution of marriage doesn't guarantee any better level of maturity. It's said that Levinson encouraged improvisation among his cast to capture the naturalistic camaraderie among men. The film shows us in many scenes where straightforward dialogue commands the story. One has to presume that the simple idea of putting a bunch of young men together to engage in ongoing conversation at a diner table over sandwiches, coffee, and french fries is likely tougher than one would imagine. Dialogue in any film of social interaction is surely a challenging prospect. For anyone watching *Diner*, there's almost certainly a character or a conversation that will hit home on a personal level. You watch, you listen, and maybe you even find yourself thinking that you know "someone like that" or have "said something like that" yourself. These examples are scripts and characters that have been well-presented if they can "touch" the viewer in this manner.

For myself, there's a part of Daniel Stern's character that I relate to very well. The scene where he very passionately describes his record collection to his wife and how each one of them meaningfully takes him back to a certain part of his life really hits home for me. I still have a large vinyl collection myself. Sure, I own an iPod like every other schmuck out there, but I couldn't (and wouldn't) live without my records. The experience of buying a new record, unwrapping it, delicately placing the needle at the beginning of it, and cranking up the music for all to hear was an experience I don't believe anyone who's a product of modern twenty-first century music technology will ever fully understand or appreciate.

I'll conclude my interpretation of *Diner* by saying that even after all these years, I still don't understand the concept of topping french fries with gravy. I mean, really, who does that?

Evil Under the Sun

Directed by Guy Hamilton
(March 5, 1982, U.S. Release Date)

————))(()((————

Then

As a kid, I always wanted to see an Agatha Christie movie. I caught only pieces of *Murder on the Orient Express* on the *ABC Sunday Night Movie*, missed *Death on the Nile* and *The Mirror Crack'd* entirely, and had read (and loved) *And Then There Were None* as required reading in high school English. Although I was enthusiastic to see *Evil Under the Sun*, it was my mother, in a rare turn, who summoned the entire family to go to the movies to see this one (yes, miracles *did* happen occasionally). She loved British movies and British actors.

The story began with the body of a dead woman on the English moors in the 1930s. As a murder mystery, it wasted no time. However, this woman, nor a diamond briefly mentioned at an insurance company, weren't the real subject of the story. The famous detective of many Agatha Christie's books, Hercule Poiroit, was the main character we should keep our eyes on. I knew nothing of the actor playing the famous sleuth, but from his strong French accent (though his character was supposed to be from Belgium), I never would've imagined that Peter Ustinov was English. I guess he was just that good. At this time, the entire opening sequence of the diamond and the insurance company went completely over my head as far as its true relevance to the story.

Things began for me when the movie shifted to a beautiful Greek island and a fancy vacation resort called Daphne's Place. Guest after guest, the hotel filled up and took shape for what would be the cast of characters in the traditional Agatha Christie whodunit. I remember my mother's eyes lighting up when she first saw the woman who played Arlena Marshall, as if recognizing her immediately. Again, I know I shouldn't have talked during the movie, but I couldn't help but ask my mother a question.

"Do you know her?"

"Yes. She's Diana Rigg. She played a British spy on TV. I love her."

I had no idea who Diana Rigg was. I suppose it didn't matter. Whoever Arlena Mashall was, she was clearly hated by every person at the hotel (except for Poirot himself, who didn't know her). Not the hotel owner Daphne who'd once competed with her as a showgirl. Not Rex who was trying to publish a dirty book about her and would never get her to sign the necessary release. Not Odell and Myra who would lose a lot of money if she refused to star in the stage show they offered her. Not her husband who knew she was cheating on him with the young and handsome Patrick Redfern. Not her stepdaughter Linda who was treated *"so beastly,"* as she put it, by Arlena. Finally, not Christine Redfern, wife of Patrick, who was too weak to stop Arlena from taking her husband from her.

While learning who was who and how everything and everybody related to one another was entertaining, I was impatient because when you're watching a murder mystery, you want to see a dead body as soon as possible. Finally, early one bright and sunny morning, Arlena took a paddleboat by herself to get away from everyone else. Patrick and Myra also decided to take a boat trip for themselves around the island and came across the beach where Arlena was lying. Approaching the body, Patrick realized that she'd been strangled to death. Poiroit took it upon himself to investigate and determine who the murderer was. What followed for much of the movie was a lot of questions, answers, confirmed alibis for each guest, and repeated flashbacks showing exactly what went through Poiroit's mind as he systematically confronted and accused each guest of strangling

Arlena. I liked the use of visual storytelling because it helped me to keep track of all the important information.

At this point, my impatience shifted to wanting the murderer revealed. When the great Hercule Poirot finally assembled all of the suspects together in one room, he accused the last person in the entire group the audience would've ever suspected, the weak and pathetic Christine Redfern. Well, the only thing I could think of at that moment was that an explanation was surely necessary now because there was no way I could possibly understand *this* little woman as the murderer. Poirot determined that Christine had lied to him about a variety of things, including her fear of heights, her pale skin hidden beneath an outrageously colorful mix of clothes, the time of day she left Linda at the sea to play tennis, and a daytime bath none of the guests would admit to taking. By the time Poirot was finsished with his entire speech, as well as the movie's flashbacks that accompanied it, we in the theater were surely convinced he'd nailed the murderer beyond any reasonable doubt. It seemed that Christina had actually *pretended* to be the dead body of Arlena Marshall and then only moments later her husband strangled the real Arlena and replaced his wife's live body with her dead one. The whole premise appeared solid and tight. Trouble was, after listening to everything he'd said and believing every word of it, it turned out he had no real proof or any shred of evidence to back up his accusations against the Redferns. While the husband and wife murdering team of Christine and Patrick appeared to be guilty of their crimes, it looked as if they'd get away with it in the end.

What happened next was startling. We learned that Christine was absolutely *nothing* like the frail and weak woman she'd pretended to be throughout the story. Instead, she was a well-tanned woman dressed in very fancy and expensive white clothes, including a large white hat. My mother's immediate reaction to this revelation was a very enthusiastic declaration of, "Whoah!" She was impressed with the woman's true beauty and fashion *ensemble* as she called it; something that would've been straight out of the many *Vogue* magazines she was often so fond of reading. Just before the Redferns were to leave the resort, Poiroit spoke up again and revealed the proof he needed for their arrest, which was a set of signatures belonging to Partick revealing he'd once been the husband of the dead woman on the moors at the beginning of the movie. It was the valuable (and only briefly mentioned) diamond the Redferns were after. Arlena Marshall had it, they killed her for it, and it was hidden inside Patrick's pipe, which Poirot discovered. The mystery was solved.

Leaving the theater, I was not only glad I'd finally seen my first Agatha Christie movie in its entirety, but glad to have had a movie-going experience I could enthusiastically share with my family, particularly my mother. These movie moments between us didn't occur too often. She loved the movie, as well as the entire British environment surrounding the story and the characters. I suppose when those you've watched a movie with love it as you do, it makes the entire experience all the more rewarding. Sometimes there's nothing quite as awkward than coming away with a positive feeling about what you've seen and finding the rest of those you're with don't feel the same. That's how I felt as a kid anyway. Today, what difference does it really make? Your opinions and your feelings are your own and you shouldn't be ashamed of them, even if it's just the movies.

Now

Evil Under the Sun, directed by the late Guy Hamilton (he did some Bond films including *Goldfinger*), was at the time, the last Agatha Christie film to get a theatrical release until Director Kenneth Branagh's 2017 all-star cast remake of *Murder on the Orient Express*. There's something to be said about the on-location shooting in exotic, worldly locales as well as the glorious cinematography and costume designs that make the entire production such a lavish and exquisite experience for the moviegoer. Unfortunately, many films fans would argue such premises and story lines have no place in our modern world of cinema that is tragically plagued with nothing but unoriginal storytelling and CGI explosions. Today's murder mystery would likely involve more violence, more blood, and an unstable cop rather than a dignified sleuthing detective (kudos to Branagh and 20th Century Fox for growing a pair!).

Like some of the Agatha Christie films preceding this one, particularly *Death on the Nile*, also starring Peter Ustinov as Hercule Poiroit, one can't help but feel left with the feeling of, "Wow, I can't believe how they did it!" or "Why didn't I figure that out for myself?". The fact that we, as witnesses of crime and murder in the film cannot determine the resolution of the classic whodunit, doesn't make us dumb-witted or stupid by any means. In my opinion, it simply means the story has been crafted and executed effectively in order to deceive us throughout the process, therefore making the final revelations and solution to the murder all the more entertaining and startling to our senses. Consider for a moment, the process by which *Evil Under the Sun* sets things up to inevitably lead to the murdered victim of the film. There are numerous scenes and episodes on the morning of the murder that, while perhaps visually mundane and ordinary, are nonetheless important in establishing what we as the audience are meant to believe we're seeing. We're supposed to believe that Christine Redfern is innocently exiting Linda Marshall's room for no other reason than she's looking for Linda to ask her to go sketching with her. We can have absolutely no conception whatsoever that there's a twenty-minute gap in time that's responsible for Christine's ability to take part in the murder of Arlena with her husband. We simply know what the camera and the story are willing to tell us before the truth reveals itself. When all *is* finally revealed by the great detective, we cannot help but feel somewhat dense in our thinking and our logic throughout the process preceding the truth, and yet, it's also an honor to have been a part of it and ultimately let in on the entire substance behind it, delicious as it all is.

There's something to be said for the film's beautiful outdoor photography, with its formal gardens, tranquil turquoise waters, staggering cliffs, and secluded beaches. This is a private, wealthy person's paradise that manages to lose itself in a European world of the 1930s that was at the time consumed with the threat of Adolph Hitler. Characters as these concern themselves more with not only their own precious lives, but also how to destroy the precious lives of others while remaining relatively unobserved by the rest of the outside world (again, that's what makes it all so delicious and decadent). But it's Peter Ustinov that shines in what was, no doubt, his signature role in film. There's an irresistible delight in listening to his impatient, even somewhat hostile demeanor with the guests who are all suspect in his eyes. Still, it's he who provides whatever small doses of memorable comedy the film wishes to show us, including the sight of Poirot taking a morning "swim" which, by his actions, is nothing more than walking back and forth along the shoreline with the water up to his knees, performing short, crawl-like movements with his arms. He also has an outrageous way of distorting the English language as he utters things like, *"Alf an hour"* (that's *half an hour* to you and me) and shouting out *"Abracadabra!"* when performing a silly magic trick with an egg for Linda, who is too stuck up and bratty to even care. To this day, I've never heard the words *"oeuf a la coque"* (that's French for a boiled egg) pronounced quite like the way Mr. Poirot says it.

Deathtrap

Directed by Sidney Lumet
(March 19, 1982, U.S. Release Date)

Then

Ira Levin's thriller *Deathtrap* ran for years on Broadway, and I repeatedly asked my parents if we could get tickets. Back then, they had little interest in live theater and the expense of getting good seats. If I couldn't see it on stage, then it was of some comfort to discover the movie version playing in town. I called my friend Jim R., and while he wasn't particularly interested in seeing it himself, he agreed that we'd go together the Saturday afternoon of its opening weekend. Outside the theater, I stared at the movie poster and its image of the popular Rubik's Cube. It was like staring at the definitive interpretation of what the '80s were all about so far, the decade still only two years old. Labeled a comedy, *Deathtrap* contained humor that came strictly from good dialogue and you had to listen to all of it to truly appreciate the laughs. One of the first moments I laughed at was a scene when Joel Siegel, the film critic for ABC's *Good Morning America*, playing himself on screen, reviewed Sidney Bruhl's new play by declaring these painfully harsh words:

> *Well, Sindey Bruhl's new who-done-it, "Murder Most Fair," opened tonight at The Music Box. But there's no point in you folks going there 'cause I'm*

gonna tell you who-done-it ... Sidney Bruhl done
it! And what's inexcusable is, he done it in public!

Ouch! I don't care what sort of stuff you like to write ... plays, novels, movies ... that's *gotta* hurt! Following that priceless moment, my thoughts turned to Sidney Bruhl's home in the Hamptons (East Hampton, to be exact), a beautiful structure with a giant windmill, which looked as if it was filmed on location in the real town or per- haps a neighboring town. After riding the train all night, Sidney arrived home only to have his wife Myra scream her head off with surprise at the sight of him. Sidney's reaction was to scream back at her, *"Every time I come into this bloody house, you scream!"* I laughed for two reasons. The first being the sharp and brutal way he said *"bloody"* in his British accent and the second being the idea that Myra's screams were an ongoing ritual in their lives (how is that *not* funny?). Michael Caine then went into a long rant about how four of his plays had bombed in a row and that he could no longer cut it as a writer. He suddenly switched gears and was going on about a play called "Deathtrap" he'd received from a former student named Clifford Anderson, an inexperienced amateur who had, according to Sidney, written a masterpiece better than anything he'd written in a long time.

As Sidney plotted a scheme to murder Clifford and claim credit for writing "Deathtrap" himself, this is when I became puzzled. Having never seen the original show, I was confused as to why they repeatedly referred to the play's title of "Deathtrap." I presumed that "Deathtrap" represented the play and its actual content. In other words, I didn't realize that *Deathtrap* was about an unproduced play called "Deathtrap." It was like waiting for the interaction between characters to conclude and the story to move onto a different level of content and action. I was confused and disappointed. Clearly, I didn't understand the intent of *Deathtrap*. Regardless, I hung on and waited to see what would happen next.

The murder of Clifford Anderson was a shocking one. To be strangled by a chain was bad enough, but to be strangled so badly that your neck actually *bleeds* ... well, that was different, if not gross.

Later, when Sidney and Myra were visited by their psychic neighbor Helga Ten Dorp, my confusion continued because I could barely understand much of what she said through her thick accent. Even to a kid who grew up with a European family with thick accents, this seemed unfair (again, I hung on and waited). The shocks of murder and mayhem continued when, just as things were calming down in the Bruhl household, Clifford suddenly burst through the bedroom window, alive and having risen from the grave, and beat Sidney with a wooden log as an act of revenge. Now he was after Myra and before he could get to her, she suddenly dropped dead from a heart attack. For me, this was the moment where (just like an Agatha Christie story), I learned that what you see on screen is not always the truth. Soft footsteps behind Sidney revealed that Clifford was not only alive, but that he and Clifford were in partnership to get rid of Myra (for her money). We'd also learn that Sidney and Clifford were lovers. Back in '82, I suppose that sort of taboo revelation still had an element of surprise.

The truth about these men revealed, the story took a confusing turn for me again because I couldn't figure out *who* was really writing *what* behind *whose* back and what the conclusion would be. I'd learn later that this is what intricate plotting was all about in screenwriting. The relationship between Sidney and Clifford was coming apart as each of them had their own intentions and purpose of what would become of "Deathtrap." Clifford was eager to finish it so he could have a hit play under his belt. Sidney feared the play would expose what he and Clifford did to kill Myra. He also feared being exposed as gay. By the time the movie reached its climax, any and all moments of laughter were long gone and we in the audience waited to see who'd kill who first. Funny or not, it was thrilling, especially during a violent thunderstorm. Despite all the surprises so far, nothing prepared me for the shock of when Clifford appeared behind Sidney in the images of the lightning and it looked like he was about to thrust the axe into his back, only to have the scene change to a Broadway stage with a reenactment of the struggle we'd just seen in the movie. Time had passed and the play had finally made it to the stage. It was a smash hit, and Helga Ten Dorp had stolen the unproduced play and claimed it as her own (smart woman).

Leaving the theater, Jim R. and I talked about the movie. I liked it, despite my confusion during the story and the action. He, on the other hand, wasn't as kind. He just about hated *Deathtrap*, claiming he expected to laugh a lot more than he did. I suppose when you expect to see a comedy, those expectations are shattered if you're not rolling in the aisles with laughter. Well, that's what free opinions among friends are for; certainly nothing a couple of slices of pizza and sodas couldn't fix.

Now

Sidney Lumet's *Deathtrap* is my favorite *dialogue* film of all time. Yes, in the entire history of the cinema, *this* little film unassumingly released in the spring of '82, without fanfare, marketing, or publicity, is the one film I choose as a superior example of what I consider the most irresistible element in film, and that's great dialogue. The key success to this (logically) is a natural flow of words, wit, timing, and chemistry between its participants. Michael Caine and the late Christopher Reeve feed marvelously off each other in both moments of mundane chit-chat and intense interactions in which we're not sure who's going to strike against who first. The art and diabolical schemes of "cat and mouse" are nothing new in film. Just watch any Agatha Christie film or Joseph L. Mankiewicz's 1972 thriller *Sleuth* (also starring Caine with Laurence Olivier) to know what I'm talking about. We wonder who's scheming and double-crossing who and just how far it will go before reaching a murderous climax. Yet, we can't take it too seriously. *Deathtrap* seeks to make solid entertainment of our most traditional human defects that include greed, pride, envy, fraud, and lust. Like Christie, it's all so delicious and diabolical when we know how to have fun with it.

One of the most intriguing moments is the on-screen kiss between Caine and Reeve. By our traditional standards of tolerance (by *most* people anyway), it's nothing. It's a surprise in plot point providing additional motive behind a man murdering his wife, whom he claims he still loved. 1982 may not seem like such a long time ago, yet this single kiss between two men in a thrilling comedy was enough to cause stirs in audience reaction and ticket sales. What did the audience think of watching the man who'd played Superman twice kissing another man? In Jordan Schildcrout's 2014 book *Murder Most Queer*, he describes attending a screening of *Deathtrap* at which a member of the audience shouted at the screen, "No, Superman, don't do it!" at the moment Reeve and Caine kissed. Was that a simple and immature act of homophobia or does one's mind and psyche truly feel threatened when the actor representing the legendary symbol of comic book greatness is about to engage in lip-locking with another man? Why did *Time* magazine report an estimated ten million dollar loss in film ticket sales simply because of a brief kiss between two men?

This was nothing new on screen. Without diving into the history of the celluloid closet, two films (not without controversy) had recently graced the screen with serious homosexual overtones that weren't even close to that of *Deathtrap*. The first was William Friedkin's *Cruising* starring Al Pacino in 1980. The second was Arthur Hiller's *Making Love* with Kate Jackson, released one month before *Deathtrap*. Both films received generally negative reviews from critics and audiences. I've seen neither of them, so I cannot offer additional insight to their impact on modern cinema at the time. My point is that we have our inexplicable quirks about what bothers us in film and what doesn't. We may not be bothered watching the man who played Michael Corleone in two *Godfather* films play an S&M homosexual if we know he's actually an undercover straight cop trying to catch a killer. It may not bother us if Kate Jackson stars in a gay love triangle with the man who played a foul-mouthed hockey player in *Slap Shot* because we'll always affectionately associate her with *Charlie's Angels*. Watching Superman smooch Michael Caine is, I suppose, another matter entirely for some people.

Nothing in *Deathtrap* threatens me. If anything, it solidifies the acting potential Reeve displayed at a time when he was surely fighting any typecasting to the big boy in blue. He and Caine share natural chemistry and are a gem to watch together. I enjoy it to laugh, yes, but I enjoy it more to constantly remind myself that nothing provides me with such exuberant pleasure as listening to and following along with great dialogue (it's a whole lot more fun than watching buildings blow up).

Conan the Barbarian

Directed by John Milius
(May 14, 1982, U.S. Release Date)

Then

Conan the Barbarian played a significant part in my childhood moviegoing. Not so much the actual movie itself, but rather because it was
the last movie I ever saw at the neighborhood Great Neck Playhouse
Theater. It shut its doors forever a short time after screening *Conan*,
though I can't remember for what reason or what their last film was.
Regardless, an era in my life ended and it was a sad one. The town
now had only one movie theater with one screen, which cut my cinematic opportunities there down by half (I can only say that such a
closing really *sucked!*).

I'd never (and have still never) read a Conan comic book in
my life, so I knew nothing of the character. Nor did I know much
about the body builder Arnold Schwarzenegger other than a previous role in a silly 1979 Hal Needham western spoof called *The
Villain* (I've never seen it). Still, to take one look at him and his
bulging muscles was to know that if anyone was perfect to play the
role of Conan, it was surely him. The timing of its release is noteworthy because it continued an ongoing trend of sword, sorcery, and
magic that was the rage of entertainment with previous films like
Dragonslayer, Excalibur, Heavy Metal, and continued later with *The
Beastmaster. Conan* was also the first comic book hero movie released
since *Superman II*. Like Superman and Flash Gordon, the familiarity

of a popular comic book hero transformed into a new movie was enough to stir up the proper enthusiasm and anticipation. I went to see it with a high school friend whom I can no longer remember (not Greg B. or Jim R.). In fact, by this time in our lives, Greg B. and I were starting the slow descent of our friendship into what would eventually become a "falling out." Nobody's fault, no formal goodbyes, or anything that dramatic, but one of those things that can happen between kids as they get older. Today, I doubt he'd even remember who I am.

From the moment the movie began with its powerful soundtrack music and the igniting of a mighty sword, I was hooked and ready for action. We first saw Conan as a young boy listening to the wisdom of his father in his description of the importance of the steel sword in their lives, or as he put it, the *"Riddle of Steel."* That same day, Conan's village was invaded by the evil warriors of Thulsa Doom. After the village was burned down and all its people killed, including his father, his mother was beheaded by Doom himself. I took note of the camera shot on young Conan as his mother's dead hand slowly slipped away from his, leaving him forever orphaned. Captured and taken away with other children, he was now a slave forced to spend his life chained and pushing a giant wheel, even right up until he was a grown man with fierce muscles. He eventually trained to be a fighting gladiator and was the hero of many victorious matches, always taking in the pleasure of the adoring crowd. He was finally freed and set off on his own, where he not only encountered (and made love to) an evil witch, but also discovered a mighty sword in a dead warrior's tomb. The scene with Conan and the witch was about as close to active sex in a traditional, mainstream motion picture I'd seen up to that point.

Conan took on two partners in thievery; the archer Subotai and the beautiful blonde warrior Valeria. Born thieves, they followed a path that eventually led them to the temple of Thulsa Doom, where he stood powerful over hundreds who'd follow his every word and die by his will. There was much action in fighting, slaying, and an awesome-looking python whom Conan defeated quickly with his sword (actually, it was all a bloody mess, but it was cool to watch nonetheless). Fake or not, snakes freak me out, especially the giant ones.

Captured, tortured, and left for dead by Doom, Conan was eventually freed, but almost perished at the hands of spirits summoned by a powerful wizard. Although this was a time before CGI, the images of the spirits trying to take Conan's body from the earth was a wondrous sight to watch. They were images, of course, but I couldn't help but notice some realism to their shapes and forms. They looked angry and determined to win over Valeria's love and devotion to Conan.

Fully healed and revived, Conan was ready to take his final revenge against those who killed his family. After rescuing King Osric's daughter from Doom's temple of worshipers, Valeria was killed by Doom's snake that also served as a puncturing arrow at his command. Even after her death though, Valeria reappeared for a moment as the spirit of a great warrior to fight at Conan's side (as she predicted she would, were she to die) during the final battle with Doom's army of warriors. The battle won, Conan's revenge still wasn't complete until he had the head of Thulsa Doom, which is exactly what he got in the end. Admittedly, I didn't understand why Doom tried to convince Conan that he (Doom) was his father, which made no sense to. By the end of the movie, we learned of Conan's destiny, including his becoming a king by his own hand … but that was another story.

Leaving the Playhouse Theater for the last time in May '82, had I known it would be my last time there, I might've taken some pictures for my everlasting memory (today I can barely find any pictures of it on the web). Following the theater's demise, it became a shop of sorts and then closed again to later become condominium apartments. Years later, those apartments went under for some financial reason. Today, not only is the building itself closed, but practically the entire block sits like an old relic, void of any businesses or activity. Just goes to show what happens to a neighborhood's business and growth when the rent becomes to outrageous to pay.

Now

The world of comic book hero motion pictures today is nothing like I knew it as a boy. From the late '70s to the early '80s, there weren't as many of them on screen and they didn't move with the CGI lightning-fast speed in which they move today. Today, we're assured of catching several new features or continued sequels of every comic book hero known to us every year during every season. The comic book hero movies of the '80s weren't always good ones. In fact, between *Conan* in '82 and Tim Burton's *Batman* in '89, I can't account for a single one of that genre that was either entertaining or successful. Perhaps it's the scarcity of such films, or should I say *good* films, that heightens our appreciation of those few that managed to not only succeed at the box office, but left positive, everlasting memories and impressions. To look back on *Conan* now is to not only look back at the era I've described, but to also reevaluate a film written and directed by John Milius and co-written by Oliver Stone. Surely, a fantasy comic book film written by the man who wrote *Apocalypse Now* (the single best film of 1979, in my opinion) and the man who'd one day write and direct *Platoon* (one of the best Vietnam films ever made) and *Wall Street* deserves a little reconsideration and reevaluation.

When Ang Lee and Christopher Nolan made *Hulk* and *The Dark Knight*, respectively, each of them attempted to deter their films from the traditional twenty-first century comic book action blockbuster already launched with Bryan Singer's *X-Men* and Sam Raimi's *Spider-Man* by painting a more intelligent, if not artistic view of the modern comic book hero. The late Heath Ledger who played the Joker in the second rebooted *Batman* installment even received a Best Supporting Actor Academy Award nomination for his outstanding performance. *Conan the Barbarian*, while successful at the box office, received no such artistic or literary praise from critics or audiences at the time of its release. Whereas the comic book hero films of the early '80s were considered corny and lighthearted, Milius gives us a hero's story filled with ideology and philosophical themes. From the opening frame, we read a quote from German philosopher Friedrich Nietzsche that says, *"That which does not kill us makes us stronger."* The theme of strength, or more specifically, *physical* strength is immediately apparent. The opening theme music of Basil Poledouris, with its pounding drums and blaring French horns, is pulsating and hard-hitting, thus signifying strength, power, energy, and even brutality. The world and time period in which Conan exists is of a fantastic and violent adventure. With violence comes blood and gore, hence the film's R-rating, which was a factor that turned off critics, considering this was supposed to be a comic book film. Still, I don't know how you can effectively tell such a tale without biting the bullet of no-holds-barred viciousness.

Under Milius's direction, *Conan* is mainly a visual experience. Many of the film's sequences contain little-to-no dialogue, which puts the viewer in the position of experiencing the action as a truly moving adventure where characters matter more for what they do rather than what they say. We're told as much about the "Riddle of Steel" as we need to know, enough to know what drives Conan's quest anyway. By the conclusion of the attack on Conan's village at the film's start, it's the gazing and the stares between Thulsa Doom and Conan's mother telling us there's deception taking place even when we think her life might be spared. No such luck. She's beheaded at the blink of any eye before we even have time to think about it. Throughout the subsequent battles that follow, our eyes and senses cannot help but take in the cinematography of the scene in addition to the traditional elements of bloody battle. Even the sight of Conan, recently revived from the brink of death, wielding his sword with the backdrop of the beach and the water behind him is a sight to behold, again signifying the necessary physical strength that feeds his actions and his soul.

Remembering that Milius wrote *Apocalypse Now*, I now draw your attention to the final scene when Conan has his revenge and kills Thulsa Doom. I understand now the metaphoric meaning behind Doom's intent to convince Conan that he's truly his father and the giver of his desire and will to live. After beheading Doom in front of all his faithful religious followers, he throws down his sword, signifying the best has been bested and the reign of terror inflicted on his people is over. Realizing their world is changed forever, Doom's followers lay down their torches and their arms, thus disbanding their cult as Conan slowly descend the great steps to leave this world forever and get King Osric's daughter back to him. The dark mood and setting of the film's entire conclusion is not too unlike Milius's conclusion to *Apocalypse Now* when Captain Willard has finally terminated Colonel Walter E. Kurtz and slowly makes his way out of the village and Kurtz's followers in the Cambodian compound are clearing a path for him, realizing the best has been bested.

As an actor (and I use that word *very* loosely when it comes to him), Arnold Schwarzenegger is a hit-and-miss man with me. For every great film like *Conan,* the first two *Terminator* films and *True Lies,* there's the crap to contend with like *Raw Deal, The Running Man,* and *Total Recall.* As Conan, he barely speaks, allowing his physical actions to do the speaking for him and that's perfectly appropriate for the character. Behind the silence, there's also the true nature of his soul if you just look carefully enough. Conan is a brutal and violent man with no hesitations about killing. Yet we cannot ignore that behind all of that rage is the spirit of love; love for a family lost and love for a woman who understood him best. Even those around him are taught a better sense of love and loyalty. One of the most unforgettable moments in the film for me is when Conan burns Valeria's body following her death. His partner Subotai starts to cry as the ceremony takes place. When asked why he is crying, he simply replies, *"He is Conan. He will not cry. So I cry for him."* Truly poignant and thought-provoking, yes, but also another example of the sense of strength that it ultimately represents for a man like Conan the Barbarian.

Rocky III

Directed by Sylvester Stallone
(May 28, 1982, U.S. Release Date)

***

Then

I had absolutely no idea that a third *Rocky* movie had been made or scheduled for release for the summer of 1982 until I saw the full-page ad in the *New York Times* the Sunday prior to its start date. I was puzzled because I couldn't imagine how this man's story would continue after achieving his ultimate victory of winning the world heavyweight championship at the end of the last movie. My father's opinion was that the story would tell of how Rocky deals with his new success. I didn't know yet if he was right or not, but I did know the Friedmann family wasn't going to miss a new *Rocky* movie (we clearly had a deep love for the big guy).

As returning director, Sylvester Stallone started the third movie just as he had the second one, with the concluding moments of the last fight. After yelling, *"Yo, Adrian, I did it!"*, the scene dissolved into the passing of time following his victory. Something new was added never before in a *Rocky* movie; a great rock and roll song called *"Eye of the Tiger"* by Survivor. Like an MTV rock video, the duration of the entire song showed us how Rocky's life had evolved and progressed since winning the title. He looked cleaner, more refined, and classy. Even Adrian looked different; more made-up, more beautiful, more exotic. Rocky fought various opponents and won every one of those fights. But there was a mean-looking fighter with a Mohawk haircut called Clubber Land that was constantly watching him; an angry man who seemed very jealous of Rocky's success. By the time the song ended, this boxer was screaming, *"I want Balboa!"* and sending out threats to Rocky's trainer, Mickey. All of this occurred on the screen even before the opening credits began.

Rocky's life was not only very civilized, but even silly, which is exactly how I felt about the charity match with the wrestler called Thunderlips (I had no idea who Hulk Hogan was at that time). This was a silly sequence I'm sure was meant to give the audience a good laugh more than anything else, particularly when Thunderlips threw Rocky into the crowd and he yelled, *"Adrian, catch me!"* Later, Rocky was honored by the city of Philadelphia on the very museum steps we watched him run up before, complete with a dedicated bronze statue of him, his arms raised triumphantly in the air. That's when Clubber Lang finally made his presence known and angrily challenged Rocky to a match. He and Mickey wanted no part of it until Clubber made a rude gesture toward Adrian. That sent Rocky over the edge and the two boxers lunged forward at each other. Although against the idea of another fight and urging Rocky to retire, Mickey finally agreed to train him for what would be the final fight of his career. The training was nothing like the first two movies (again, it got silly). He trained with a crowd of people watching him and a disco band performing in the background. He considered it fun, but Mickey found the whole thing ridiculous, even urging Rocky to go back with him to the old gym so they could get the 'ol blood, sweat and tears flowing again. Acting cocky, Rocky wasn't taking his greatest boxing challenge seriously. Meanwhile, Clubber was training like a wild animal out to kill.

On the day of the fight, a brawl almost broke out between Rocky and Clubber backstage. Mickey managed to get in the way of that and was shoved to the wall. This was the moment I'd dreaded because I knew ahead of time that Mickey was going to die of a heart attack (once again, kids can *never* keep secrets!). Rocky tried to call off the fight, but Mickey used his last bit of strength to demand that he *"get out there and do it!"* Rocky got his ass kicked, lost the fight and his heavyweight title. That hardly mattered to him right now. When he returned to Mickey, he had only a few moments with him before he died in front of him. Rocky cried in sorrow, and I actually got choked up for the first time in my life at the sight of a person dying in a movie.

Approached later by his former rival Apollo Creed, he urged Rocky to get back on his feet and challenge Clubber to a rematch to regain his title, his dignity and his *"eye of the tiger."* Apollo would be Rocky's new trainer. He told him that when all of this was over, Rocky would owe him a big favor (what that favor was, we didn't know). The training went nowhere because Rocky was still too demoralized to give it his best effort, which frustrated Apollo. It was Adrian, the woman usually too shy and reserved to speak her mind, that finally straightened Rocky out during a fight on a California beach. I remember my mother being impressed with the dialogue that concluded with:

"How'd you get so tough?"
"I live with a fighter."

His training took off now with the spirit of the first two movies, complete with the ever-popular *"Gonna Fly Now,"* though this time the sequence ended with Rocky and Apollo racing each other on the beach instead of the traditional museum steps. The climactic fight was at Madison Square Garden instead of the Philadelphia Spectrum. It was the most violent and loudest of the three movie fights (though I think the original *Rocky* may have had more blood in it). Still, I wasn't there to judge its staging or choreography. I and many in the theater, including my parents, were pumped up by the action and we cheered with delight and excitement. When it was over and Rocky regained the heavyweight title, we were filled with joy at watching the hero take back what was once his and getting his self-respect, happiness, and *"eye of the tiger"* back. Unlike one and two, however, the story wasn't over in the ring. It was time for us to learn that Apollo's big favor was that he and Rocky finally settle the score between them in a private fight away from people and the media. The final shot of the movie was, in my opinion, a perfect way to end the story and the entire *Rocky* saga (well, I *thought* it was over), with a frozen shot of the two of them hitting each other at the exact same time, giving neither of them the advantage over the other.

My family and I loved *Rocky III*, but we all agreed the first movie was still the best. By July 1983, it was the premiere movie on HBO, and I must've watched it again at least six or seven times. When I went to sleep away camp, they showed it during one of its weekly movie nights. In the span of only several months, I was addicted to the movie and Survivor's popular rock song. For a time in my young life, I'd become a *Rocky III* junkie with nothing but positive and enthusiastic feelings toward the movie (those feelings changed when I grew up).

Now

As a high school freshman, my perception of *Rocky III* was considerably different largely due to the excitement of not only a reformed Rocky Balboa for the '80s, but also a colorful, badass opponent like Mr. T, and the popular rock song. The film was all the rage and practically a fad with kids. However, thirty-five years and four additional *Rocky* films later, I'm forced to take another look and reevaluate my feelings of the third installment. My cinematic tastes and critical abilities have matured in which I recognize a staggering amount of faults taking place here. While I can appreciate Stallone's need and desire to continue Rocky's story after his big victory, the film, while mildly entertaining at times (*few* times), comes off as nothing more than a sensationalized, campy, and even comical version of something else it used to be. Heart and soul are shamelessly replaced by brawl and spectacle. The dramatic performances, with the exception of Mickey's death (still very sad) and the marital squabble on the beach, is ordinary, wooden, and unmotivated. The final championship fight, which we look forward to throughout the film, is cartoonish, with some very unrealistic sledgehammer sound effects accompanying each punch. At the time, even as I thought I enjoyed it, I found it hard to believe that Stallone could take things so far over-the-top. The final moment of Rocky and Apollo's private sparring match as friends is admittedly a poignant one, but it's hardly enough to save a sequel that's gotten worse with age, in my opinion. For what it's worth though, I still love Survivor's "Eye of the Tiger".

I'll briefly give you my feelings toward the remaining films following the third. *Rocky IV* is ... well, how do I put this kindly? Oh hell, I can't! This, in my opinion, is the absolute worst movie ever made in the history of motion pictures. I mean, really, a robot with a nagging female voice given to Paulie for his birthday? A Russian opponent with the mentality and speech pattern of a brick? James Brown's glory of America (was this effort *really* supposed to raise our American spirits during a Cold War that still existed during the Reagan years?)? I still find it impossible to fathom how the 1976 Oscar-winning tale of love, triumph, and spirit could possibly *erode* into something as unintelligent and mindless as this tragic farce.

Rocky V doesn't fare much better, even with John G. Avildsen back at the director's helm, though I enjoyed it when Rocky Jr. finally beat up the school bully. Unfortunately, we don't even get the satisfactory climax of a real boxing match in this one. *Rocky Balboa* was an admirable attempt to get things back to where they belonged with a story of human beings with real feelings, emotions, and drama. But even those positive qualities are only valid in as much as it represents nothing more than a remake of the original '76 film (even the final outcome of the big fight is the same). Still, it was a redemption of sorts because we no longer had to contend with Rocky's final story left in utter shambles as it was at the end of *Rocky V*. *Creed*, is simply a cheap and desperate attempt to keep a dying franchise alive and kicking for no other purpose than Hollywood greed. For me, the story and glory of Rocky Balboa remains a cinematic tale best told during a three-year period in the '70s, when the plight and triumph of the underdog stole our hearts, and even showed us a thing or two we hadn't seen yet in the world of love and drama ... or at the very least, showed a *young boy* who hadn't seen a thing or two in the world of love and drama.

Poltergeist

Directed by Tobe Hooper
(June 4, 1982, U.S. Release Date)

Then

I don't remember what inspired my interest in *Poltergeist* first; the menacing black movie poster of the little girl in front of the TV set or the fact that Steven Spielberg's name was attached to it. I suppose it was the poster more than anything else. When you're a kid, the TV set is practically your best friend. To imagine it a menacing beast that could suck you into a world of evil is intriguing, to say the least. *Poltergeist*, like *Friday the 13th* and *The Shining*, was one of those moments I managed to see it through the privacy of my own Saturday afternoon and my bicycle on a summer day when the weather outside was very nice, so the theater wasn't too crowded. No complaint about that.

The movie began in a very unexpected way. What the United States National Anthem had to do with a supernatural horror story, I didn't know. My confusion was brief. The living room TV was clearly the cause behind what was due to come. Little Carol Anne was fixated in front of it, talking to people or things inside we couldn't see, nor could any of her family. Following the opening credits, the setting was a California town called Cuesta Verde where the Freeling family lived. On a quiet Sunday afternoon, there were thick storm clouds approaching the neighborhood. Little Robbie was afraid of thunderstorms, as well as the big, menacing tree outside his bedroom window. He'd lie in bed staring at the tree with an uneasy look on his face, and I couldn't help but ask myself why he didn't just close his bedroom shades. He was also unsettled by his large clown doll on the chair in front of him. Again, I'm asking myself, *If you're afraid of the clown, why don't you just get rid of it? Why did you buy the thing in the first place?*

Strange events occurred the next day in the family kitchen. Robbie's glass of milk suddenly broke, his spoon mysteriously bent, and the kitchen table chairs stacked themselves on their own when we weren't looking. I remember just how tense I felt when I listened to Diane and Carol Anne whisper about it to each other.

"*TV people?*"

"*Uh-huh.*"

"*Do you see them?*"

"*Uh-uh. Do you?*"

"*Uh-uh.*"

These bizarre events seemed harmless, even playful, at first. Diane was even excited about the whole thing when she showed her husband Steve a sample of it with the kitchen chair that night. By the time they were getting ready for bed during another thunderstorm, it wasn't funny anymore. The unusual ghosts or whatever possessed their house decided to strike. The menacing tree broke through Robbie's window and took the poor boy away in its trunks. While his father rescued him, Carol Anne was sucked away through her open closet door into a strange world outside of our earthly one. The Freelings soon learned that she was no longer in the house with them when they heard her voice coming from the TV.

The family brought in a team of parapsychologists to help them find Carol Anne (did such people really exist in the world?). Their explanations of what they did for a living and what they'd do to help find the girl made it seem probable. They gave detailed descriptions between what they considered a classic haunting and a poltergeist intrusion of the house (I didn't fully understood the difference). Either way, it meant strange things were happening that couldn't be explained. As the scientists and the family understood more about the ghosts dwelling inside the house, Steven also learned from his boss that the neighborhood he lived in was originally built over a cemetery (an unexpected and creepy plot twist). I also wasn't prepared for what took place in the kitchen. The raw steak sliding across the counter was an eerie start, as well as the chicken wing covered with maggots. But to watch that man seemingly peel off his own skin to the point where his skeletal features were apparent, only to be turned back to normal again at the blink of an eye, was brutal while at the same time cool to watch.

The group then brought in a very small woman with a squeaky voice with a history of "cleaning" houses of unknown spirits. She spoke of a terrible presence or the "beast" that was in that other world with Carol Anne, keeping her very close to it. Using Carol Anne's closet as the entrance to that other strange dimension, they also established an exit through the living room ceiling. Diane, being her mother and the only one Carol Anne would come to, bravely passed through the closet entrance with a rope tied around her waist and miraculously rescued her daughter. Once back on the living room floor, the two of them looked like they were covered in red Jell-o. The ordeal was over and the little woman declared, *"This house is clean."* Or was it? The fact that the movie wasn't over yet left us wondering what would happen next. Clean or not, the Freelings were moving away from this place as fast as they could. On their last night in the house, all hell broke loose. The "beast" returned to first possess Robbie's creepy clown doll to attack him. Then the closet door opened again, making it clear it wanted Carol Anne back. *"No more,"* she said in a fearful voice. Meanwhile, Diane was attacked by an unseen force pulling her along the walls and ceiling of her bedroom. By the time she finally got into her kid's bedroom, the closet door had turned into a huge, gaping mouth (looking a lot like foam) eager to swallow up everything in front of it.

After escaping the house, things weren't much better outside. Coffins and rotted corpses erupted out of the ground throughout the entire neighborhood. Fire hydrants exploded and fire shot out of the street. Steven arrived home with his boss and realized that when his company built the neighborhood over the cemetery, they'd only moved the headstones and left the bodies there. All I can say to that is, *"gross"* (or as girls in the '80s used to say in a stupid secret language called "Valleyspeak," *"grody to the max!"*). Like *The Amityville Horror*, the family drove away with their lives. Unlike that movie, however, the house didn't remain for the next tenants to experience. Instead, the entire thing imploded somewhere into the distance, presumably into the unknown portal where Carol Anne had been, as the entire neighborhood watched it happen. It all ended with a small dose of humor, when the Freelings checked into a hotel for the night and immediately rolled the hotel TV set out of their room and out of their sight.

It was a year later that I learned about how Spielberg acted more as director during production than Tobe Hooper. I knew he wrote and produced *Poltergeist*, but it began to look as though he was solely responsible for more of it than originally believed. I hardly cared about any of that though. It was an incredible movie, and it looked like it was shaping up to be the summer of Spielberg with not only this blockbuster, but also a story about a squashy-looking alien visiting Earth that was coming soon to theaters everywhere.

Now

This is the film my generation embraced as one of the true horror greats of the '80s (despite its PG-rating before PG-13 existed), as well as one of the best haunted house films ever made. By its own standards, there's a great deal of originality in its premise because gone is the Gothic stereotype of the isolated, evil haunted house where awful events once took place and continue to live on in the form of white ghosts, freaky skeletons, rattling chains, slamming doors, and whatever other elements of fear may have accompanied men like Vincent Price and Roddy McDowall. From Spielberg's mind, the haunted house is now a simple, comfortable-looking suburban family dwelling on a simple, comfortable-looking street in a simple, comfortable-looking suburban California town, replicated to pay homage to a setting he grew up in when he was a kid. It's a house filled with love, joy, earthly pleasures, and a big, beautiful Golden Retriever named E-Buzz (what's not to love?).

Unlike the Lutz family of *The Amityville Horror*, the Freelings are willing to (temporarily) learn to live with their ghostly guests as they struggle to get their beloved daughter back. Along the way, there are startling spiritual images, horrifying shocks, and bloody hallucinations respectively following the ghastly sight of hungry maggots on that cold chicken wing. Yet, even during all this time of terror, we're never made to experience the Freeling home as physically scary. The house itself still remains a comfortable sight to our eyes and senses. It's only after Carol Anne is finally returned that the house takes revenge and attempts to destroy the family we've come to know and care about. Inasmuch as this is a story about surviving supernatural horror, it's also as much a tale of family love, strength, and bonding.

To know and love *Poltergeist* as much as I do is to also know and love all the infamous events and controversies surrounding the film since its release, including the film's so-called "curse" that claimed the lives of two of its three Freeling child actors and the question of whether or not it was Hooper or Spielberg responsible for the making and artistry of the film. The latter question depends on one's own beliefs and dedication to do the proper Hollywood research. Spielberg himself wrote an open letter to Hooper which was later printed in the *Hollywood Reporter* that read:

> *Regrettably, some of the press has misunderstood the rather unique, creative relationship which you and I shared throughout the making of Poltergeist. I enjoyed your openness in allowing me a wide berth for creative involvement, just as I know you were happy with the freedom you had to direct Poltergeist so wonderfully. Through the screenplay you accepted a vision of this very intense movie from the start, and as the director, you delivered the goods. You performed responsibly and professionally throughout.*

Presuming these words are accurate from a man of honor and integrity like Spielberg, I suppose that's good enough for me to put my faith in Hooper's direction and creativity (he was, after all, the man behind *Salem's Lot* too). All these years later though, I still ask the same compelling questions I asked myself as a kid sitting in the theater; why did Robbie Freeling ever purchase that large clown doll in the first place if it scared him? If the house knows what scares you, then keep scary-looking things out of it. The clown may look innocent enough, but do you really want *this* thing sitting in a chair staring at you while you sleep? As for the menacing-looking tree outside Robbie's window again, if the thing frightens him so much, then why does he repeatedly leave his window shade open night after night (out of sight, out of mind, Robbie!)? Honestly, I feel for the poor kid, but he doesn't seem all that bright to me (though I give him extra points for the great *Star Wars* collection of toys and posters in his room).

Star Trek II: The Wrath of Khan

Directed by Nicholas Meyer
(June 4, 1982, U.S. Release Date)

Then

Like *The Empire Strikes Back* two years earlier, kids *still* didn't know how to keep their damn mouths shut! The word all over high school was, "Spock dies in this movie." Well, thanks a lot, people! Did you *have* to give that one away before I had a chance to see it for myself? The other scoop was that this wasn't so much a sequel to *Star Trek— The Motion Picture*, but rather a direct follow-up to an episode of *Star Trek* called *"Space Seed,"* which I'd never seen before. It looked like I'd enter the new *Star Trek* movie without the benefit of the story that preceded it. That didn't stop me, however, from buying my ticket to what was already marketed as the most spectacular sci-fi movie for the summer of 1982.

Despite having seen *The Motion Picture*, it was apparently not a required prerequisite for the sequel. The story began as a fresh start for the crew of the U.S.S. Enterprise, including a new female Vulcan named Mr. Saavik (a woman called *Mister?*). Within the first few minutes, the ship's entire crew except for Mr. Saavik were destroyed by enemy fire from the Klingons and it looked as if the ship was lost. Then we learned the whole thing was just a simulation or a training exercise for the new cadets of Starfleet Academy. Mr. Saavik was tested and it looked like she'd failed. We were now reintroduced to James T. Kirk (recently promoted from captain to admiral), and he no longer looked like some tennis player in short sleeves, as in the first movie. He was also no longer the energetic, adventurous man we'd all known before. He freely admitted to McCoy on his birthday that he felt old and worn out.

Trouble started with another ship, the U.S.S. Reliant, while searching for a lifeless planet to assist in the development of the Genesis Project. Commander Chekov and Captain Terrel (whom I'd never seen before) beamed down to the planet they believed was the Ceti Alpha VI system to try and remove a piece of matter they thought contained life (*yes*, I actually understood all that when I heard it for the first time). While on the planet's surface, they encountered Khan and his followers. According to the tale (and it's a good thing he told this tale, because I hadn't seen *"Space Seed"* yet), fifteen years ago, Kirk exiled Khan and his people to the Ceti Alpha V system after their failed attempt to take over the Enterprise. After being marooned for six months, Ceti Alpha VI exploded and shifted the orbit to the Ceti Alpha V planet, which is where they all were now, and destroyed the entire environment, leaving it all a sand wasteland. Khan also blamed Kirk for the death of his wife. In order to find out why Chekov and Terrel were really there, he put tiny creatures inside their helmets that entered through the men's ears. Even though this scene wasn't too graphic, it gave me the shivers to think of the extreme pain these things caused entering one's ear canals (this is what suffering from ear infections as a child will do to you later in life). With these things in their ears, the men now revealed to Khan what he wanted to know, even against their will.

Learning of the Genesis Device, Khan escaped, captured the Reliant, and was now on his way to space station Regula 1 to get his hands on the device developed by Kirk's former lover (or wife?) Carol and their grown son, David. The Enterprise was no longer on a training exercise, but rather a mission to investigate Regula 1, which meant Kirk was now back at the helm of the ship as commander. Once they reached Reliant, which was now overtaken by Khan and his people, the Enterprise was attacked and many lives aboard were lost, including this young kid whom I recognized as the boy from *Escape to Witch Mountain* seven years earlier. Looked like he'd grown up a little. He died a bloody mess though. It looked as if *Star Trek* had grown up a little too with some added violence and blood (definitely *nothing* like *The Motion Picture*). The Enterprise struck back, however, and Khan was forced to retreat to repair their damage. Arriving at Regula 1, they discovered that Carol, David, and their crew were hiding deep beneath the planetoid Regula, despite the assumption that it was a lifeless rock in space. Deep inside, the testing of the Genesis Device and its life-creating effects were successful and provided life in a vast world of plants and food.

For a time, we believed that everyone inside Regula was trapped. However, Kirk was smarter than that, and as he put it, *"I don't like to lose."* They beamed up out of the planetoid and were back aboard the Enterprise, ready for action. The ship went into a huge colored cloud called the Mutara Nebula and Khan followed, determined to destroy Kirk once and for all. Inside the Nebula, the shields and targeting systems were useless. It became a manual shooting match instead. Sometimes the Enterprise got hit and sometimes the Reliant got it, so the odds were evenly matched. The Enterprise finally scored the defeating shot to the Reliant which destroyed all of Khan's crew and mortally wounded the man himself. In his last effort to destroy Kirk and the Enterprise, Khan activated the Genesis Device and set it for self-destruction. The Enterprise had to escape the Nebula or it would be destroyed. Even at its top speed, the ship was going nowhere because the warp drive was damaged. Spock went to the engine room to try and repair the warp drive, but had to expose himself to a fatal level of radiation to it. McCoy tried to stop him and Spock performed his Vulcan nerve pinch in order to proceed. He also put his hand to McCoy's head and said the word *"remember."* I had no idea what that was supposed to mean (as it turned out, I wouldn't learn its secret for another two years).

With warp drive restored, the Enterprise escaped just as the Genesis Device and the Reliant exploded, breaking up the gas of the *Nebula*. In the process, the lifeless planetoid transformed into a living, breathing, blue and green planet. The ship was out of danger, but this was the moment everyone in the theater dreaded. Spock was dying of radiation poisoning, and Kirk was the last one to be with him, though they were separated by glass. The two of them shared their final words of friendship before Spock died in front of Kirk's eyes (and ours). Following a funeral, Spock's coffin was shot into space and orbited around the newly-created planet. The final moment was the coffin resting peacefully on the planet's surface. Spock was dead.

As it was common practice for kids at school to talk and give away secrets, even as *Star Trek II* was enjoying its theatrical run, the word already was that Spock would return somehow in the next *Star Trek* movie and it would have something to do with the new Genesis Planet. I suppose given what Genesis was meant to do in its life-giving abilities, that made sense. Even so, I had no understanding of how the dead could conveniently be brought back to life for another movie. Clearly, I still had much to learn about Hollywood's life-regenerating practices for the sole purpose of more movies and more ticket sales.

Now

Forget J.J. Abrams's pointless attempt at rebooting the *Star Trek* franchise that began with his 2009 film. Those of my generation know that *The Wrath of Khan* was the first true *Star Trek* reboot. Although a modest financial success, *The Motion Picture* was met with only lukewarm responses by fans (*Star Trek* creator Gene Rodenberry baring the blunt of the blame for the film's poor performance and initially getting *"kicked upstairs"* by Paramount Pictures and serving only as creative consultant for the new film). We wanted action, speed, and even a little blood. Paramount heard us and gave it to us by reprising Ricardo Montalban's role as Khan Noonien Singh from *"Space Seed"* of the show's first season, originally airing on February 16, 1967. His peformance of pure anger, revenge, and power surely carry the film, though not to take away from equally-engaging performances from William Shatner and the late Leonard Nimoy.

Though I only occasionally and modestly followed *Star Trek* during reruns as a kid, I never considered myself a so-called *"Trekkie,"* so I cannot fully take into account or appreciate the reaction those type of fans had when they learned Spock would die in the new film. Many wrote letters of protest to Paramount at the time, one even paying for a trade press advertisement asking them to revise the film's plot and Nimoy even received a death threat or two. This, in my opinion, is where being a film fan takes a turn for the totally unreasonable (no matter what your feelings, in the end, it's just a movie). While I never take sci-fi and fantasy too seriously or too much to heart, the film does have its recognizable themes of life, death, friendship, sacrifice, regret, and the emotional turmoils of aging. It's impossible not to recognize how much older our beloved *Star Trek* characters were since TV, as well as our own age. The first time I ever heard of or watched an episode of *Star Trek*, I must have been six or seven years old. Now fifteen, I was a high school teenager with feelings of confusion and doubt accompanying that age. Kirk, as it turned out, was not only a man with a romantic past, but a father as well to an estranged son. As a father myself, it can be challenging to determine just how that status makes us feel inside, young or old. Upon realizing his son David's existence, Kirk's immediate emotional reaction is to feel *"old and worn out."* By the film's end, however, even in the shadow of Spock's death, Kirk feels young again in the shadow of the newly-formed Genesis planet. I suppose human emotions, like so many other things in life, are subject to change and reversal.

There are elements to Khan's vengeance that I didn't fully understand as a kid. Some of his dialogue that includes, *"He tasks me. He tasks me, and I shall have him. I'll chase him round the Moons of Nibia and round the Antares Maelstrom and round Perdition's flames before I give him up!"* and *"To the last, I grapple with thee. From Hell's heart, I stab at thee! For hate's sake, I spit my last breath at thee!"*, I had no idea were direct paraphrases from Herman Melville's *Moby Dick*. It's a deliberate homage by director Nicholas Meyer, even making sure that we see a visible copy of *Moby Dick* on the shelf inside Khan's dwelling on Cete Alpha V. Though, to consider a good man like James T. Kirk the sinister white whale is surely a stretch, while considering Khan the more obsessed version of Captain Ahab who continuously pursues his prey against his crew's wishes seems more logical. He also manages to recognize Pavel Chekov upon seeing him on Ceti Alpha V, despite the fact that Chekov was not only an absent crew member in *"Space Seed,"* but also didn't join the cast of characters until the show's second season (it's amazing, the little film flubs we in the audience are meant to try and conveniently overlook when they occur).

For me, a true reboot is what literally saves a franchise from falling on its ass, which is what would've likely happened to *Star Trek* were it not for *The Wrath of Khan*. The interest was renewed and the films continued to thrive, even into the *Next Generation* phase and beyond. The second film incorporates a better pacing than its slow predecessor, though it's pointless to compare such a film with *Star Wars*. The battle sequences are lukewarm and unenthusiastic at best. With this film, or any other *Star Trek* film for that matter, it's the dimension of drama (or even *melo*drama) we're meant to give our higher level of attention to. The dramatic death of Spock grabs us, as we not only (temporarily) say goodbye to a beloved character, but also understand the deeper meaning of friendship and sacrifice between not only Spock and Kirk, but also Spock's feelings of responsibility and devotion to those aboard the Enterprise.

E.T. The Extra-Terrestrial

Directed by Steven Spielberg
(June 11, 1982, U.S. Release Date)

Then

I have no one but myself to blame for not keeping up with the entertainment news of the time in 1982. No internet, no social media, and I hardly knew a show like *Entertainment Tonight* existed. *E.T. The Extra-Terrestrial* took me completely by surprise when I was browsing a magazine and came across a two-page promotional ad for the movie. On the left was a brief summary of the three blockbuster movies Steven Spielberg had given us since '75. On the right was the introduction of his new movie with an image of bright lights shooting down from dark, thick clouds and a tagline that read, "He is afraid. He is totally alone. He is 3 million light years from home." The ad was vague, but its words indicated that Spielberg's new movie was about an alien visitor on Earth. I needed to know nothing else. By this time, I was hooked on the man's movies. If he'd made something about the stupid phone book, I'd have paid to see it.

Like other high profile summer blockbuster movies before it, I needed to exercise patience before seeing it. Not because it was difficult to get to it or that it was inappropriate, but because this summer was the first time I was going away to sleep away camp and wouldn't be anywhere near a movie theater for some time. I didn't see *E.T.* until the end of the summer when I returned home, but even at that late date, it wasn't a problem, as it was still going strong in theaters everywhere. Before camp, the temptation of getting to the movie quickly were everywhere among the vast marketing campaigns. On magazine covers, *E. T.* was all over *People, Rolling Stone, Ebony, Starlog,* and even parodied with Alfred E. Newman on the cover of *Mad.* In supermarkets, *E. T.* was on the box of his own General Mills cereal and he'd practically made Reese's Pieces the hottest candy around overnight. *E. T.* became my top movie priority as soon as I returned home from camp.

By late August, the movie was playing neither in Great Neck or Westhampton Beach. This meant a ride was required, and that meant one or both of my parents (turned to be the entire family). From the movie's opening moment, when we witnessed an alien spaceship resembling a spherical Christmas ornament landing in a forest, my immediate thought was that this, in its own way, played like a moment picking up where *Close Encounters* left off (why not? It's a story by the same man, after all). These aliens, short and squashy-looking things, were here secretly collecting plant samples. When men in vehicles appeared on the scene, the aliens ran for their lives. They all made it back to the ship in time except for one. As he followed, the other aliens did their best to wait for him, but in the end, had to escape immediately. We watched the ship take off and leave their poor, little companion behind. We couldn't see the abandoned alien very clearly, but we could hear him softly moan at his unexpected situation.

As the alien made his way to a particular home in a California suburban neighborhood, I recalled the same sort of neighborhood in *Poltergeist* (again, why not? Same story creator). Inside the house were a group of children that included Elliot, his little sister Gertie, his older brother Michael, and his friends, and Elliot's mother Mary. There was no father. The boys were playing *Dungeons & Dragons.* Feeling left out of the game, Elliot went outside to wait for the pizza delivery man and that's when he heard strange and frightening noises coming from the backyard tool shed. His family didn't believe his claims of something lurking out there, so he waited outside in the middle of the night for its return. Frightened by the alien creature at first, he lured it to his bedroom with Reese's Pieces. Elliot was now hiding an alien in his bedroom, so going to school the next day was out of the question. He faked illness and was left alone with the alien to try and communicate with it. After his brother and sister met it, they chose to keep the creature they called *E.T.* from their mother. As they got to know *E.T.*, they discovered he had magic abilities, including the power to levitate balls of clay and even bring a dead flower back to life.

As the friendship between Elliot and *E.T.* grew, the two of them shared a form of psychic connection in which Elliot could feel whatever *E.T.* felt, including getting drunk from too many beers. This was a funny moment, though I couldn't personally decide whether it was funnier to see a ten-year-old boy or this clueless, little alien acting drunk. At one moment, Elliot went a little crazy and released all of the frogs before they could be dissected in his science classroom. By the time Elliot got home, *E.T.* had learned a little English and even managed to communicate that he wanted to call his home. I finally heard the immortal line, *"E.T. phone home."* When Halloween night arrived, there was a plan among the kids in which Elliot and *E.T.* would go into the forest so *E.T.* could build a phone out of various pieces of machinery and toys he'd collected around the house. The ride to the forest on Elliot's bicycle was truly magical as the power of the alien took them flying over the trees. I was awestruck at the sight of the flying bicycle in front of the background of the giant moon as John Williams's music got louder and more powerful. When *E.T.'s* homemade phone was complete, it appeared to be working, though he'd have to wait until he got an answer. This is where both he and Elliot looked real sick, each feeling the other's illness.

Returning home, Michael decided their mother should know about *E.T.* Her immediate reaction was fear. When she tried to escape the house with her children, government scientists in space suits were waiting for her and proceeded to invade her home. By the time the scene changed, their home was converted into a hospital with wall-to-wall sheets of plastic to keep radiation and other dangers contained within the house. As *E.T.* was slowly dying, his link to Elliot disappeared as Elliot recovered. When *E.T.* finally died, I remember the audience becoming dead quiet. It was then that I looked at the faces of my mother and father. The two of them looked bored out of their minds. I knew neither of them had much patience for sci-fi and fantasy, but geez, didn't they have a *heart*? This adorable, squashy, little creature had just *died* and they appeared to be the only ones in the audience that didn't give a damn (really, how did I end up with these two as a kid?)! They had no emotional reaction either when Elliot was left alone with *E.T.*, expressing his grief (this was the saddest moment I'd seen on screen since Mickey died in front of Rocky's eyes and I got choked up again).

This couldn't be the end. Spielberg wouldn't leave his audience in this sort of state. Something *had* to happen. The sight of a red glow coming from inside *E.T.'s* motionless body, as well as a dead flower coming back to life, told us that *E.T.* was alive and his people were coming for him. With the help of Michael's friends and their bicycles, the race was on to get *E.T.* away from the government scientists/doctors and get him back to the forest to meet his ship. It was an exciting chase, and again, John's music got more exciting with every thrilling moment. While some government men chased the bicycles, others chased the stolen van with *E.T.* in it that Michael managed to drive (without a driver's license). As the kids on the bicycles suddenly faced a roadblock by men with guns, they were magically lifted up into the air by *E.T.'s* magic powers.

Arriving in the forest, *E.T.'s* spaceship was waiting for him. We knew by his glowing red heart that he was happy and healthy again. Gertie, her mother and the government man with the jangling keys attached to his pocket showed up too. This was the moment for a tearful goodbye between *E.T.* and the three children he'd come to love during his stay on Earth. When it was time to say goodbye to Elliot, *E.T.* pointed his glowing finger to Elliot's forehead and said, *"I'll be right here."* I felt my heart jump a bit when he said that, as it was also accompanied by a stronger tone in the music. This was truly a moment in the movies that would live forever in the hearts of those who were young enough and young at heart enough to allow themselves to fall in love with such a heartwarming creature and his adventure on Earth. This was summer blockbuster magic, and it was because we had a man like Steven Spielberg in our lives to give it to us.

Asking my mother how she liked it, her simple response was, "It was cute." Was she just being gracious about the whole experience for my benefit or was that really the limit of her imagination and appreciation for movie magic (what would Spielberg have thought of such a lame response to such an extraordinary movie?)? After playing in theaters all summer, *E.T.* finally "went home" in October '82. It was rereleased in the summer of 1985, and Kevin and I went to see it again (this time, I was eighteen years old and old enough to drive us both). On October 27, 1988, it was released on VHS video, and I immediately plunked down my hard-saved money for my own copy (a copy I *still* have somewhere in my nostalgia archives). In March 2002, it was rereleased again for its twentieth anniversary, and Spielberg (unwisely) chose to do what Lucas did to his original *Star Wars* trilogy by adding extra scenes and computer-generated effects. Despite my negative reaction to such a bold move, my wife and I eagerly went to see it. Changes or not, it was still a pleasure to see the little guy on the big screen again.

Now

I can barely remember a time in the '80s when *E.T. The Extra-Terrestrial* wasn't a beloved member of our popular culture. Take a moment for yourself to not only recall the film, but all that merchandising that included not only some of the stuff I previously mentioned, but also that silly record with Michael Jackson, that really bad Atari home video game, the theme park rides, and of course, the immortal line, *"E.T. phone home."* It was more than just a blockbuster surpassing *Star Wars* as the highest grossing motion picture of all time, but a true pop culture icon of the decade. Despite the fact the alien himself, as designed by Carlo Rambaldi, resembled nothing more than a short, squashy-looking slug, the whole world found him irresistibly cute nonetheless (as did I).

While I don't claim that *E.T.* is my favorite Spielberg film as many people do (that honor *still* belongs to *Close Encounters*), I *can* claim that almost no other family film has ever put such a consistent smile on my face while I'm watching it as this has, and like many fans, that smile turns to sadness during the classic goodbye scene when *E.T.* goes home. However, I'd like to get past the film's "feel good" flavor to explore more serious themes behind its simple story. It's a celebration of childhood, but even childhood has its obstacles. Any Spielberg fan probably knows the separation of Elliot's parents reflects the divorce of the director's own folks when he was a boy. But consider for a moment who *E.T.* represents to Elliot beyond friendship. More than anything else, is *E.T.* not a surrogate father figure to the boy who is growing up fatherless? Gertie is still but a baby and Michael is more the immature goofball than the brotherly mentor Elliot needs. *E.T.*, while abandoned, lost, and confused on our planet, is, in my opinion, the symbol of the smarter, wiser adult that a growing child needs to bond with during a fragile time of questions and curiosity. The father is gone (he's in Mexico with Sally), so *E.T.* seems the worthy replacement. At the same time, *E.T.'s* vulnerability gives Elliot the strength of a grown-up to help him and save his life at the crucial moments when our "evil" government invades our home, our lives and tries to take away our treasured comfort and safety.

E.T. is a true family film in which we see the world through the eyes of children more than anything else. In fact, until the government "bad guys" finally show their faces, Mary is the only adult we actually see in the film (we don't even see the face of Elliot's teacher). Consider also the strong government character actor Peter Coyote portrays. A man with no name, he's dubbed simply as *"Keys"* due to the jangling keys hanging from his pants. The question, I feel, is not so much who is this man, but rather who *was* this man? He tells Elliot, *"He came to me, too. I've been wishing for this since I was ten years old."* Was *E.T.* indeed here before and did he discover *"Keys"* as a young boy too? What sort of childhood memories does *"Keys"* harbor, having met and lost *E.T.*, and then waited for that miracle moment when the beloved alien creature would return to him? If all of this speculation is relevant to our interpretation of the film, is it any wonder why *"Keys"* would grow up to become a government official spending his career seeking out extra-terrestrial life? Makes you wonder, perhaps, if Elliot will inevitably grow up to be the same sort of man as *"Keys"* with the same goal in life. It would make sense.

The little guy and his adventures on Earth not only touched the whole world back in the '80s when I was a teenager, but has continued to touch the hearts of generations since then. Because what's stronger than the memory of seeing *E.T.* on screen for the first time as a kid is the beloved memory I keep when I watch the film with my son and watch his face light up with joy in the belief that there *is* magic that still exists in the world. It's on the screen in front of us and its name is *E.T. The Extra-Terrestrial.*

Blade Runner

Directed by Ridley Scott
(June 25, 1982, U.S. Release Date)

———— ≈«(◉)»≈ ————

Then

In the spring of '82, I shared a freshman class with an Asian American kid. As summer approached, he went on and on about how he looked forward to this new sci-fi movie with Harrison Ford called *Blade Runner*. I knew nothing of it other than the two points just mentioned: sci-fi and Harrison Ford. For a kid still coming off of two *Star Wars* movies and *Raiders of the Lost Ark*, that was enough to peak my interest. However, I was anticipating the new *Star Trek* movie too much to give *Blade Runner* any thought. It would have to wait. When I saw the newspaper ad for it, I was struck by its visual artwork, which looked dark and moody despite its black and white print. I also noticed the movie's R-rating. Not that such a restriction would stop me if I wanted to see the movie badly enough (at fifteen, my parents were relaxing about that and I didn't need to sneak around so much). It was the Saturday night of the movie's opening weekend and my mother dropped me and Kevin off at the theater in Westhampton Beach. She had no interest and that was probably just as well. Nothing kills the buzz of your own movie anticipation more than being accompanied by someone who has no interest in the same enjoyment.

The movie began with an introductory backstory, describing the history and description of an advanced robot called a Replicant, which was a being identical to humans, but with greater strength and equal intelligence to their creators. Considered illegal on Earth, special police detectives called *Blade Runners* were ordered to kill, or *retire* as they called it, any Replicant loose on Earth. The opening scene was striking visual. This was Los Angeles in 2019, and it was represented by nighttime lights, fire, and flying cars. It was a dark and grim world, yet there was unmistakable beauty in all of its visual wonder, while accompanied by an opening musical theme with a mysterious spirituality to it. While new age music meant nothing to me, at best I could say it sounded really cool against the visual shots of the city's future.

An interview took place at the Tyrell Corporation between one of its officials and one of the company's new employees named Leon. It consisted of questions that sounded trivial, particularly that of a desert and a turtle. Within seconds of being asked about his mother, Leon shot and killed the official. Just minutes into the movie and I was confused already. It looked great, but if this was the level of my understanding of the story, then I was in trouble for the next two hours. What made things easier was Harrison Ford as Rick Deckard narrating the movie for us. He was an ex-cop or an ex-*Blade Runner* who was just waiting for a seat at the local outdoor noodle bar while it poured rain outside. Before he could eat, he was detained and flown to his former boss, Captain Bryant. The building they arrived at was the same black skyscraper featured on the movie poster. At Bryant's office, Deckard learned that four Replicants were illegally here on Earth. These models were called Nexus-6, and they were designed to live only four years in order to limit the extent of their own self-developed emotional responses. At this point, we didn't know why the Replicants had come to Earth, but while watching several videos, we learned that the man shot at the beginning of the movie was Holden, a Blade Runner policeman as well who was administering a test called *"Voight-Kampff"* in order to determine if Leon was a Replicant or human, based on his emotional responses to various scenarios (well, thank goodness for small explanations. That explained the desert and the turtle). Other videos introduced us to the rest of the escaped Replicants, including the leader Roy Batty, Zhora (both *Beauty* and the *Beast* as Bryant described her), and Pris. After Bryant threatened him, Deckard agreed to return to his job and hunt down these Replicants.

The events and process of Deckard's search began. First, he visited the Tyrell Corporation to put the *"Voight-Kampff"* test to work. The head of the corporation, Dr. Eldon Tyrell (played by the same man as Lloyd the bartender in *The Shining*), insisted that Deckard first administer the test to Rachael, apparently human. After many questions, including a funny reference to whether or not Rachael was a lesbian, Deckard determined that she was, in fact, a Replicant, though she didn't know herself. She'd been implanted with false memories in order to protect or "cushion" her developing emotions. At this point in the movie, I was fascinated about technology of the future that could create robots resembling, sounding, and acting like human beings (could such a thing ever happen in real life?). I was enthralled by the fictional idea of it.

As Deckard's detective work continued, he used a real cool machine that allowed him to zoom in and out and pick apart an inserted photograph of Leon's hotel room to help find a clue. He eventually determined that buried deep in the photograph was Zhora herself. Trailing her location to a strip club in the city of Chinatown, he approached her pretending to be an awkward city official. Zhora knew he was a fake and hit him hard before trying to strangle him. Interrupted before she could finish the job, she took off running and Deckard raced after her through the city streets. As a chase scene, it didn't move with speed or action, but I was caught up in the dark sights and sounds of the futuristic city it took place in. When Deckard finally caught up with Zhora and fired his gun at her, the entire scene changed. This was an execution, yet it was so perfectly filmed and crafted with slow motion action and music, that it was almost beautiful. Killing Zhora wasn't easy, as she repeatedly got up after each shot that hit her and ran through glass. Deckard's final shot and Zhora's death continued the slow motion pace of the scene, illustrating more than a killing in the streets. I think we were meant to slow down and take a moment to think about what we witnessed and acknowledge our own feelings about, as Deckard put it, *"shooting a woman in the back."*

Harrison Ford was no Han Solo, nor was he Indiana Jones. Rick Deckard was a brave man, but he hurt too. He hated what he did and was sickened by the thought of killing a woman, even a non-human, and it was this sort of killing that drove him to retirement in the first place. After sighting Rachael in the street, he was attacked by Leon. The last words Deckard almost heard in his life were, *"Wake up! Time to die!"* Violent as this moment was, I couldn't help but laugh at such a line. I didn't know whether it was clever or sick, but I found it amusing just the same. It was, in fact, Leon who died instead because Rachael picked up Deckard's dropped gun when we weren't looking and shot Leon through the head. Back at Deckard's apartment, he promised not to hunt her down, even though he knew she was a Replicant, telling her that he owed her one for saving his life. Shortly after their quiet discussion, they were kissing and Vangelis's music turned quiet and romantic with French horns; a perfect sound with the visual beauty of the scene, not just of love and romance, but also streaks of light shining across their faces as they kissed.

Meanwhile, Pris hid inside the apartment of her new friend J.F. Sebastian. Roy Batty eventually showed up, and the two Replicants realized they were running out of time if they would survive on Earth much longer. Sebastian helped Roy gain entrance to Tyrell's penthouse home, and it was here we learned why the Replicants were here, as Roy demanded from Tyrell, *"I want more life, fucker!"* After listening to many reasons why this was impossible, Roy took Tyrell's face in his hands and kissed him. That kiss turned deadly as Roy planted his thumbs deep into Tyrell's eyes and killed him (that *had* to be a horrible way to die!). Although we didn't actually see it happen, it was said later by Bryant on the police radio that Roy had also killed Sebastian.

Deckard was at Sebastian's apartment now. Thinking it empty at first, he was attacked by Pris who used her gymnastic skills and bodily strength to try and kill him. Deckard still had his gun and managed to fire off a couple of shots to kill *her* instead. She died like a desperate, malfunctioning machine rather than a human being (an eerie thing to watch). When Roy showed up, he declared that he'd hunt Deckard down like an animal in a ritualistic-style game he was controlling, even howling like a wolf, at times. The sequence of light, shadows, the sound of hard rain, and the music created a truly captivating moment for my eyes and senses. I'd seen much sci-fi in my childhood, but never anything like this before (it was brilliant filmmaking). Trying to escape Roy's pursuit, Deckard jumped from the roof of Sebastian's building to the next roof over. He didn't make it and was hanging onto a steel beam for his life. Roy made that same jump with ease and took a moment to stare at Deckard and gloat at his predicament. At the moment that Deckard was about to fall to his death, Roy grabbed his arm and pulled him up to safety. Sitting on the roof and facing each other, Roy was dying and spoke of his memories and how they'd be *lost like tears in rain.* After he died, Deckard spoke to us of why he thought Roy saved his life. He spoke of the gift of life and recognizing how much there was to love about it, even if you were a Replicant with only four years in which to live it.

The movie ended with Deckard and Rachael reuniting and taking off for the mountains. Conveniently, we learned that Rachael *"was special"* and wouldn't die in four years. There was an uncertainty to how long the two of them would have together, but it ended on a happy note nonetheless. When the credits started to roll, I remember Kevin standing up from his seat and telling me that it was time to go. I told him I was staying because I was enjoying the music. This closing theme was one of the most intense pieces of music I'd ever heard, and I wasn't going to miss a single note of it. My first priority after seeing *Blade Runner* tonight was to run right out and buy the soundtrack album as soon as possible. That task proved more difficult than anticipated. I waited and waited, but nothing showed up at the local record store (since when did a movie soundtrack's release take so damn long?). It was sometime in the fall of '82, that a record finally hit the shelves, but there was something different about it. It wasn't an original soundtrack release. Instead, according to the album cover, it was an *"Orchestral Adaptation of Music Composed for the Motion Picture by Vangelis"* and *"Performed by The New American Orchestra."*

Not knowing or understanding anything about the business of music or artistic rights at the time, I was confused at the idea of such an album being a copy (or a forgery) of the real thing. I bought it anyway, figuring this was as good as it would get right now. The music *was* quite different from the original Vangelis score I'd heard in the theater. The album was also abridged, containing only eight tracks. But it was all I had, and I simply forced myself to get used to it. Thankfully though, a CD soundtrack of the original motion picture score was released in 1994. Though not perfect, it was a lot closer to the original vision as fans knew it. I still have the '82 record among my vinyl collection, but nothing can ever compare to the real thing. I also purchased Philip K. Dick's *Do Androids Dream of Electric Sheep?*, though the new paperback copy was called *Blade Runner* instead and featured movie artwork on the cover. Try as I might though, I was confused and couldn't get into it, the original story being considerably different from the movie. Years later though, it was required reading for a college English class. I read it with more ease and appreciated the visions and implications about the future before Ridley Scott got his hands on it.

Seeing *Blade Runner* again also proved to be a waiting game. Released in June '82, I figured I'd wait a year before watching it again. June '83 came and went, and nothing. July and August '83 came and went, and still nothing. Just what *was* it about this movie that forced its fans to wait for what would come later? Finally, in September '83, it premiered on HBO. I taped a copy for myself and must've watched it so many times that I inevitably caused damage to the videotape ribbon. I enjoyed it on screen again several times at revival theaters years later in college (one of those times was a double feature with Stanley Kubrick's *A Clockwork Orange.* How's *that* for your perfect dystopian afternoon?). Despite my lack of interest in the movie back in the beginning, I'd since become something of a *Blade Runner* junkie (I even purchased the two-edition Marvel comics version and I still have them somewhere in my archives). I suppose I can thank that Asian American kid in my freshman class who planted the initial seed of interest.

Thanks, kid, whoever you *were*!

Now

Do you know what a *"Blade Runner minority"* is? No, of course you don't. You've never heard it before because it's a term I invented myself. It's how I refer to myself in relation to Ridley Scott's movie for the last thirty-five years. Allow me to explain myself. I was one of the likely few who saw the film upon its original release back in the summer of '82; that makes me a *"Blade Runner minority."* I was one of the likely few who loved the film upon its original release without waiting years for it to become a cult classic; that makes me a *"Blade Runner minority."* Finally, I'm one of the likely (very) few who prefers the original 1982 theatrical version complete with Harrison Ford's voice-over narration and the so-called happy Hollywood ending over the international uncut version, the reworked *"director's cut"* of 1992, and the *re*-reworked *"final cut"* version of 2007; *that*, my friends, makes me a *"Blade Runner minority."* You get the idea?

Only with age and maturity can one truly understand the deeply thematic implications that detract from *Blade Runner's* basic elements of being just a mere futuristic thriller. Its narrative and dramatic levels begin with its rather obvious tribute to the art of film noir from a bygone era. We can almost hear the echoes of classic figures as Humphrey Bogart, Ingrid Bergman, or Lauren Bacall in every frame and every piece of spoken dialogue. Darkness, light, and shadow are just as effective as they were during that period of Hollywood noir, though now in vibrant color. Harrison Ford as Rick Deckard gives us a unique perspective of the morality of the traditional hero, particularly that of his own human nature. Through his eyes and police investigation, we not only see the future for what it is in 2019, but we're also taken to the edge of human distinction. What makes us human? What makes us artificial? Can we even tell the difference anymore? Are we able to control our own emotional responses and actions even when we discover the difference? Can we prevent falling in love against our better professional judgment? These are questions which only the appreciative and understanding viewer can answer for themselves.

The effects of technology is also key to the lives of those in the future. As we watch the film and hopefully never take our eyes off of a single detail, we can't help but notice the tension that exists between the high-tech brightness, glimmer, and gleaming in some sections of Los Angeles and the old, decaying sections that exist elsewhere (note the street location of J.F. Sebastian's apartment building across the street from the exterior of the real-life Million Dollar Theater on Broadway in downtown LA). That technology also expresses a certain degree of control looming over the city, as the all-powerful Tyrell Corporation building stands high and ever-watching above all other structures. Fully realizing what such a powerful corporation is there to do, which is to create life and subsequently use that same power to take it away after just four years, we're forced to realize the consequences for not only the Replicants themselves, but we as human beings for trying to control them in the first place.

Let's recall a piece of dialogue spoken by Jeff Goldblum in *Jurassic Park*, "*Life will not be contained. Life breaks free, it expands to new territories and crashes through barriers, painfully, maybe even dangerously. Life finds a way.*" Such control over our environment has already brought dire consequences over natural life in our future society, as it appears for some unknown reason, real animals are extinct in our world, and if they *do* still exist (such as real snakes), they're unaffordable, as indicated by Zhora in the nightclub scene. Animals, or at least their former existence, play a large part in the *"Voight-Kamff"* test administered to the Replicants. Leon becomes agitated at the thought of a turtle baking in the hot sun, unable to turn itself over. Rachael is asked questions about a wallet made of calf skin, a wasp on her arm, and suddenly becomes silent at the mention of an entrée consisting of boiled dog (seriously? That's gross!). If animals no longer exist in the future, is it any wonder that human beings are relocating their lives to the outerworld colonies in order to possess their own custom-made Replicant which may serve to replace the traditional household pet? Is this sort of control over another living thing (even if it's artificial) just another part of our own humanity?

One of the ongoing points of humanity in *Blade Runner* is that with each new version of the film, the controversial question of whether or not Rick Deckard is a Replicant himself is repeatedly raised. In the 1982 version, through Ford's narration, we understand that like humans, Replicants possibly collect photos in order to instill soothing memories into their psyche. Later, in Deckard's apartment, we see a large array of photographs resting atop his piano, some of them very old and black and white, suggesting not only that the people in them are too old now to have ever been a part of his own life, but to also suggest that he, like Replicants, is collecting photos for his own personal purpose. In the 1992 *"director's cut,"* a newly-added scene of Deckard's unicorn dream (coincidental to Gaff's origami unicorn calling card) suggests he may not only be a Replicant, but also that Gaff may have somehow accessed Deckard's own implanted memories of the unicorn. The answer to this controversy is never decisive, leaving the question open to the perspective and interpretation of the film's fans. By the time the 2007 *"final cut"* version was released, Scott himself came out and confirmed that according to his own vision of the story, Rick Deckard *is* a Replicant (whether we accept his word as truth or not is up to us. I still have my doubts).

A final word concerning these multiple versions of *Blade Runner*. Perhaps it's just me being my usual purist self, but I've always been disappointed in Mr. Scott for "going all George Lucas," as I've come to put it, on this film. Despite its history and controversies, I'm still affectionately attached to the original theatrical version I saw and loved as a fifteen-year-old kid back in '82 (even though I own all versions). But hey, that's me ... the *Blade Runner minority*.

Tron

Directed by Steven Lisberger
(July 9, 1982, U.S. Release Date)

—————◄(◎)►—————

Then

Tron was the first time I went anywhere near a Disney movie since *The Black Hole* back in '79. It was also the second time I'd committed an act of movie-selection stupidity since opting to see *For The Love of Benji* instead of *Star Wars* back in June '77. By July '82, I was away at sleep away camp as a CIT (counselor-in-training). One of the privileges of such a position was that once in a while, we were taken to the movies by members of the senior staff. By my memory, I recall a quad theater somewhere in town near the camp. While I can't recall all four movies playing at the time, I know one of them was *Tron*, and two others were Clint Eastwood's *Firefox* and John Carpenter's remake of *The Thing*. The group consisted of maybe twelve to fifteen boys and girls total and a few counselors chaperoning us. Most of us were evenly split between *Firefox* and *The Thing*, while only a couple of us chose *Tron*. All three choices had awesome visual and special effects to offer, though *Tron* was considered the more childish of the lot simply because it was a Disney movie. Well, if it isn't obvious to you by now, I chose to go with the minority and see *Tron*. While I don't totally regret that decision, because it was a pretty awesome movie, I *do* regret blowing my opportunity to see a gory horror show like *The Thing* with not only the absence of my parents to try and

396

stop me, but also perhaps seeing it with one of the girls sitting next to me in a frightful state (remember *Halloween II?*).

Even before the movie began, I was confused because I'd previously heard of the *Tron* video game already in arcades. So like the egg and the chicken, which came first, *Tron* the movie or *Tron* the video game? Was the game based on the movie or vice versa? Turns out both of them were created together; the movie concept developed first and the game adapted from it. The story proposed the idea of life *inside* the video game and the computer in general, as well as those in the real world who created these games. The opening scene was simple enough when a boy put his quarter into the video game at Flynn's arcade and then took us inside the game to show what was the life-like situation behind the game. This was some of the most incredible animation and live action effects I'd ever seen on screen before; a different class of effects which defined alternate moviemaking effects having little to do with the effects of *Star Wars, Close Encounters,* or *Blade Runner.*

In the part of the story that took place in the real world, Flynn's arcade was owned and operated by Kevin Flynn, played by Jeff Bridges. It took me a moment to recognize him because I'd seen him only twice before in *King Kong* and a 1978 movie he made with Farrah Fawcett-Majors called *Somebody Killed Her Husband* (he had a full beard and mustache as well as long hair in those two). As Flynn, he looked like a younger and almost completely different man. He was like a big kid himself, just as good at the games as his customers were, especially a game called *Space Paranoids.* According to his claims, he was the true inventor of that particularly successful game, as well as a few others, but his ideas were stolen by another man at his company named Ed Dillinger, who was also the big boss. No longer employed there, Flynn spent his free time trying to get into the company's computer system to locate evidence that would prove Dillinger had stolen his video game ideas and passed them off as his own. As Flynn performed his extensive computer tricks, we watched what happened inside the system with Flynn's alternate computerized counterpart (also played by Bridges who looked like a blue and white robotic version of himself). When Flynn hit a snag that crashed the computer, we watched the computer version of himself called Clu crash into a wall and disintegrate into oblivion.

The company called ENCOM was controlled by what was called a Master Control Program (MCP for short). This program talked to its human users and could even control their lives and actions by blackmailing them with information they didn't want leaked to the public, as was the case with Dillinger. One of the things ENCOM was designing was a laser that could take apart an object and then put it back together again. With the help of two friends, Flynn gained access into the building to try and get into the system again, but he was sitting in front of the laser, not knowing what it could do or what was about to happen to him. When the laser struck his back, his body froze and disappeared. He didn't die, but was rather transported into the world of the computer, though once inside, he was still Kevin Flynn the user and not the computerized version of himself. So far, I kept up with the story pretty well, despite my knowing virtually *nothing* about personal computers. This was a movie I expected to draw my attention only for its really cool special effects and images, and nothing to do with story and concept. Looks like I was wrong.

Once inside the computer, Flynn was a prisoner of the MCP who'd not only have to figure a way out, but would also have to play an assortment of combat games in order to survive. Eventually, he encountered computer versions of his two friends from ENCOM, Alan and Lora, or Tron and Yori as they were called inside the computer world. They formed an alliance to not only escape the prion of the MCP and its guards, but to also free and liberate other computer programs held as slaves to the system. As the virtual battles continued, Flynn and Tron got closer to their freedom. In a final battle between Tron and Dillinger's computerized version called Sark, the two tried to destroy each other with flying discs. This was an awesome light show of color and visual effects as they not only hurled the discs at each other, but blocked them with those same discs as well. In the end, Tron disabled Sark and then threw his disc into a gap inside the machine, thus destroying the MCP's rule over its computer slaves. As victory was at hand, all the computer programs communicated with their users in the real world and created a free society inside the computer. This not only sent Flynn back to the real world, but also reconstructed his body with the same laser that had taken it apart. Still seated where he'd been before he disappeared, Flynn now had the printed evidence he'd been searching for to prove Dillinger's guilt. As a result of this, Flynn became the boss of ENCOM and it all was now "happily ever after" in the real world.

When I and the few others who'd chosen *Tron* that night came out of the theater, I remember hearing from some of the other kids, "I can't believe you missed out on *The Thing*! It was sick and so awesome!" I tried (in vain) to defend myself by stating just how cool and awesome the special effects of *Tron* were in the hopes that maybe I'd redeem my less-than-smart selection, but it hardly proved much of a consolation. Still, I couldn't be totally upset with myself for what I did. Like it or not, I enjoyed *Tron* even though I may not have followed every point of the story. The only other consolation I had for my decision that night was those who'd chosen to see *Firefox* all agreed that the movie sucked. Well, that was *something* anyway.

Now

Look how far we've come in the world of video games and computers since 1982. By that perspective, *Tron* may be considered one of the most dated movies to represent another era. It's for that reason above all that makes the film such a treasure today, in my opinion. When we watch *Tron*, we're witnessing several things here; not just the bygone era of the 1980s, which signified the golden age of video games with classics like Space Invaders and Pac-Man, but also the quick rise of the personal computer and machines in our society, both in everyday functions and our popular culture. Months before the film opened, Steve Jobs of Apple Computers made the February 15, 1982, cover of *Time Magazine* as one of "America's Risk Takers." Later, the January 3, 1983 issue of the same magazine declared the personal computer as "Machine of the Year." On February 11, 1983, rock band Styx released their single *"Mr. Roboto"* from their forthcoming album *Kilroy Was Here,* declaring these immortal words:

> *The problem's plain to see*
> *Too much technology*
> *Machines to save our lives*
> *Machines, de-humanize.*

My point is that years before James Cameron depicted the rise of the machines over mankind in *The Terminator, Tron* already suggested a consequential world in which human beings would think less and computers and machines would think more. Because the film was considered a disappointment at the box office, it was easy to overlook such an achievement in story concept and technical moviemaking over the years. By its own right, *Tron* is a milestone in the world of filmmaking due to its use of animation featuring digital patterns of such vehicles as motorcycles, ships, and tanks. The technology to combine computer animation and live action was still experimental in the early '80s, despite the rotoscoping effects in *American Pop* or even the dancing sequence between Gene Kelly and Jerry the mouse in the 1945 movie musical *Anchors Aweigh.* The computer used in *Tron* was limited in how it delivered background detail on film, thus such visual effects were created using a more traditional technique of the time called *"backlit animation,"* incorporating black and white filming for the sequences inside the computer and then later colored with more sophisticated photographic methods to give the action on the screen a greater appearance of technology. As a kid, I never would've understood what any of that stuff meant. Hell, I was still trying to understand just how stop motion animation, blue screens, and matte paintings really worked in films like *Star Wars. Tron* is an example of what it means to create pure fantasy. The computer in our world of the '80s was a simple, mundane tool that rested atop our desks. The film suggests a dramatic, glamorous, and even romantic world inside the great machine, though we can't be expected to take such a suggested world too seriously. We're simply here to witness a dazzling technological show of light, sound, and fluorescent color, perhaps not too unlike watching a planetarium laser light show accompanied by the classic rock music of Pink Floyd or Led-Zeppelin.

Gifted actors like Jeff Bridges and David Warner who provide the equal sides of good and evil are a welcomed plus, even for a plot that's considered weak by some. Nonetheless, it reminds us all of just how much fun and exciting video games were for my generation at a time when they were still enjoying their rise to fame and glory. Those games brought about our spirit of the fun and adventure a few hard-earned quarters out of our weekly allowance money would bring us. Today, don't even attempt to ask me about the modern video games of the world. I don't pretend to understand them and frankly, I don't want to try. In a world where we have games requiring a rating for violence and gore, it's time for me to get off the ride … permanently.

Fast Times at Ridgemont High

Directed by Amy Heckerling
(August 13, 1982, U.S. Release Date)

———◈———

Then

In 1981, one of the many movies I wanted to see was *Porky's*. But my parents wouldn't permit their fourteen-year-old son to go near anything with such vulgarity and filth (despite my secret access to *Animal House*). *Fast Times at Ridgemont High* was compensation at a time when the high school teenage sex comedy of the '80s was on the rise. These kinds of movies were an extra step into a more mature (if not inappropriate) level of screen entertainment where adults got to act like adults, meaning more bad language and more sex. By the time I and my friends saw the movie in its second run, the summer was over and I was into my sophomore year in high school. In its opening credits, I was reminded of many pop culture items representing the early years of the new decade, including tight blue jeans, video games, the popular short-haired look of Pat Benatar, and the Go-Go's's *"We Got the Beat."* The movie itself, much like *American Graffiti*, had no specific story or plot, but rather a series of episodes and events between a selected group of friends designed to represent a real-life look at American high school kids.

On the popular side, there was Brad Hamilton, a senior with a great job, great girlfriend, a classic car to be proud of, and was looking forward to his final year of high school independence before venturing into the real world. Equally popular was Linda Barrett, the senior "hottie" who had no inhibitions about sex and was often smug about the fact that she dated an older man in Chicago instead of the immature selection of boys at Ridgemont High. On the less-than-popular side was Brad's fifteen-year-old sister Stacy who, while very pretty, was still a kid and inexperienced at dating and sex at such a young age (as was *I*). Her best friend Linda gave her as much advice about dealing with her inexperience as possible, including how to give a blowjob with a carrot stick. Stacy seemed desperate to "grow up" sexually. Her first time having sex was with a much older man (believing her to be nineteen) outdoors on a bench at the local softball field dugout. She later developed an attraction to another student named Mark Ratner, who by the standards of high school popularity, was considered a nerd. After their first date, he was lucky enough to be invited into Stacy's bedroom while the rest of her family was away. I wanted to jump up out of my seat and smack him across the head when he suddenly chickened out and decided to go home while he and Stacy were making out on her bed (Mark, you stupid, stupid, stupid jerk! What were you thinking?).

His cowardly attitude cost him his chance with Stacy, because she soon fell for his best friend Mike Damone, who unlike Mark, had a pompous degree of self-confidence. What he didn't have, however, was the ability to have sex with a girl for too long before he came inside her and it was all over (though I enjoyed seeing Stacy naked on the couch). I recall my friend whispering, "What a dork!" Mike was also, according to Linda, *a little prick* for not owning up to his responsibilities and paying for Stacy's abortion after getting her pregnant. This part of the story may have been a message to someone like me about being careful when it came to sex (despite not having *had* it yet!); a moment of pleasure that didn't even last thirty seconds could ultimately result in a big mistake. Mike was also a prick for stealing Stacy away from Mark who really liked her. In the end though, Mark and Mike made up and became friends again. Mark and Stacy also acknowledged that despite their awkward encounter in her bedroom, they still liked each other.

The real star of the movie was, of course, the long-haired surfer dude named Jeff Spicoli. This was a guy who cared about nothing but surfing and getting high. School was pointless, and his teachers were a waste of time. We loved the guy. How could high school boys *not* love a guy who'd have a pizza delivered to his history class simply because he wanted some food while learning about Cuba. The history teacher, Mr. Hand, reminded me of the strict, tight-ass, over-the-hill teachers I had in school who didn't have the time or patience to understand us kids and who we really were. Still, I laughed at Mr. Hand's originality of dealing with Spicoli by not only confiscating his pizza and distributing it among his classmates, but also the daring move of showing up at his home on the night of the final high school dance and forcing him to discuss United States history with him, thus proving what it was like to have one's valuable time wasted. Spicoli was always the one to watch, even when he only stood inside the local mini-mart and declared Brad Hamilton's act of disarming a would-be robber as, *"Awesome! Totally awesome!"*

The story's conclusion was just like *American Graffiti* and *Animal House* in that we learned what became of the main characters (was this some Universal Pictures thing, or what?). The fate of Brad, Stacy, Linda, Mark, and Mike were almost pointless to me and my friends. We wanted to know what happened to the great Jeff Spicoli. We weren't disappointed to learn that he hired Van Halen to play his birthday party with the reward money he got for saving Brooke Shields from drowning (like I said, you *had* to love this guy). It's probably no secret that I and my small group of pubescent, hormonal-raged friends loved *Fast Times* and all its crazy antics. It was everything we wanted to do and wished we *could* do as high school boys, which more often than not, centered around getting laid by high school girls.

The movie was almost forgotten in our minds because there was always another teenage sex comedy that would eventually come along to take its place. It was one year later when it premiered on HBO in September 1983, that it finally resonated with so many of us. Because we were afforded the opportunity to watch the movie over and over again at home, we shared ongoing laughter with each other in repeating some of its most quoted lines. Try to imagine nearly every boy in high school constantly doing their best Jeff Spicoli impression while quoting, *"Hey bud, let's party!"*, *"People on 'ludes should not drive,"* and *"That was my skull! I'm so wasted!"*. It was another reminder of how silly we were as teenagers and how much those silly teenage sex comedies meant to us.

Now

Sometime during the latter part of my high school education, I discovered my love of Led-Zeppelin. This was after seeing *Fast Times at Ridgemont High*. I point this out because it was due to this film that I actually believed the song *"Kashmir"* was on the *Led-Zeppelin IV* album simply because Mike Damone advised Mark Ratner that *"When it comes down to making out, whenever possible, put on side one of Led Zeppelin IV,"* and the scene immediately following featured *"Kashmir"* playing on the car stereo. I eventually learned otherwise, but still, I don't know whether to thank Cameron Crowe (who wrote the screenplay) for introducing me to one of the greatest rock bands in history or *condemn* him for deliberately misleading me regarding what song belonged on what album (I never actually made out with a girl during a Zeppelin song, though I did make out with a girl during the entire second side of Pink Floyd's album *The Dark Side of the Moon*). What I also find interesting about the film since its release is how much I've learned that I didn't know back then. I had no idea who Cameron Crowe was or that he'd gone undercover as a high school student in order to research and write his material. I had no idea that the pretty blonde in the car laughing at Brad Hamilton's fast food pirate hat was Nancy Wilson of Heart who later became Crowe's wife (eventually *ex*-wife). It even took me a few years to realize that the entire Jeff Spicoli surfing sequence was just a dream (I thought maybe he was just *that* good).

I'm reminded of a time before inferior film forgeries like the *American Pie* and *The Hangover* franchise, when high school, college, and young adulthood were a source of antics and fun times with the right amount of tits and ass to entertain (and even *educate*) young, horny men like myself who hadn't lost his virginity yet. Even now, it's nice to return to the wild sexual element of the "coming-of-age" side of adolescence and remember a time when young boys waited in anticipation for the day they'd have sex for the first time. These same boys were also pausing the *Fast Times* videotape at the exact moment Phoebe Cates and Jennifer Jason Leigh took off their tops and treated us to full frontal nudity (yeah, like none of you men reading this now *never* did that when you were my age?). The film may easily be discarded as just another wild teenage romp in a series of films that included *Porky's, Spring Break,* and *Hot Dog—The Movie.* I propose, however, that director Amy Heckerling offers a fresher perspective on such a subject with performances that are far above the norm, particularly by Sean Penn and Jennifer Jason Leigh. I also suggest it's the one film that defines the popular youth culture of America in the '80s, much like *Saturday Night Fever* did for the '70s, *Easy Rider* for the '60s, *Rebel Without a Cause* for the '50s, and eventually what Crowe's *Singles* did for the '90s.

First Blood

Directed by Ted Kotcheff
(October 22, 1982, U.S. Release Date)

Then

From the movie poster and TV spots I'd seen, it looked as if Rocky Balboa had gone ape-shit crazy with a machine gun. When a friend asked me if I wanted to see *First Blood*, I hesitated because I usually preferred to know a little more about a movie besides its artwork and TV commercials before seeing it. Still, my curiosity to see Stallone in something different was impossible to ignore. While still the same brawny character he was in *Rocky III*, he no longer looked like a civilized person. He looked dirty, rough, and damaged by life. I suppose that was the whole point, playing a man who'd fought hard in the Vietnam War. When we first met him, he was a quiet type who visited the home of his former war buddy, only to learn that his friend was dead from the cancer he'd brought back from Vietnam. Sad and angry, Rambo wandered into a small town where he was met by the town's pushy Sheriff Teasle, who considered him an unwanted drifter in a quiet town that wanted no drifters. After dropping Rambo off somewhere and urging him to keep away from his town, Rambo defied his order and started to walk back toward town. Teasle arrested him on the charge of vagrancy (this was the first time I'd ever heard that word and I presumed it described a person with no home or perhaps even a bum). During his arrest, we discovered that Rambo had a huge knife, which he claimed he used for hunting.

At the police station, Rambo was bullied and abused by the chief deputy who despised his existence. The more the abuse continued, the more I thought, *You need to stop this now! You don't want to push this man over the edge!* Upon having a flashback of being tortured in Vietnam, Rambo went wild and escaped, fighting his way through all the police and outside into the street, where he stole a motorcycle to flee into the woods beyond the town. Raging, Teasle was determined to capture Rambo and organized his own search party with guns, dogs, and a helicopter. During the hunt, Rambo proved just how powerful and dangerous he was when he disarmed and overpowered every man that hunted him. We learned that Rambo was a former Green Beret soldier and a war hero. I sensed awe and wonderment from the audience because we not only knew just who John Rambo was, but also had a good idea of the damage and destruction he was capable of. My next thought was, *You people better back off and let him go or he'll kill all of you!* The man may not have spoken much, but his actions clearly did the talking for him.

Rather than heed Rambo's threat of *"Don't push it or I'll give you a war you won't believe!"*, Teasle continued to hunt for him, dead or alive. It was then that Colonel Sam Trautman arrived on the scene to *"rescue you from him,"* as he so bluntly put it. He trained Rambo during the Vietnam War and knew all too well just how unstable he was and the extent of the damage he could cause. He advised allowing him to escape, at least temporarily, but Teasle ignored the warning, believing Rambo was greatly outnumbered by hundreds of state troops. When Trautman warned that with that many men hunting Rambo, he'd need *"a good supply of body bags!"*, my friends and I clapped our hands (we loved that line!). Proving he was just as strong and built for survival as we were led to believe, Rambo survived when a rocket was launched at the cave he was hiding in and destroyed it. For a while, he was presumed dead. He resurfaced though and stole a military truck filled with weapons, which he used to return to the same town he'd escaped from. His reign of destruction really began now. He started by blowing up a gas station, shot out the town's electrical power, and then destroyed a gun shop.

Teasle, now scared for his own life, as well as those in town, positioned himself on the roof of the police station, hoping to get a clear shot at Rambo, but was instead discovered first when Rambo shot him from below a skylight. Still alive after crashing to the floor, Rambo was prepared to kill Teasle when Trautman appeared and warned him not to do it. The police were outside and would kill him if he didn't surrender now. This was the moment we waited for when Stallone would finally break his long silence and tell us about who he was and what he was doing. He broke down in tears as he described the things he experienced in Vietnam, including the death of his best friend, as well as the injustices he endured when returning to the United States. Rambo was not only finished, but he'd also weakened and surrendered to the police, which was something we likely never thought we'd see in this movie. John Rambo, it turns out, was human after all.

Despite also seeing Stallone in *F.I.S.T.* and *Nighthawks*, it was Rocky Balboa I never failed to associate him with, especially after three movies. *First Blood* and John Rambo, in a way, shattered my childhood image forever and even expanded my perception of just who Stallone could be on screen. It was a new and startling experience I didn't regret, despite my initial hesitation at seeing the movie. As time went on during its theatrical run, I not only read about reactions from audiences and critics, but there was a lot of chatter about the movie at school. Chatter that usually concluded with, "You *have* to see *First Blood!* Stallone is awesome in it!"

He definitely was.

Now

I consider *First Blood* Stallone's last great film of his lengthy career as a true actor (though I give him points for *Copland*). Based on David Morrell's original novel, it serves as the introduction to John J. Rambo before he (unfortunately) became a major pop-culture slab of meat in the sequels that followed. Beyond the familiar action, blood, and guts, the first film in the *Rambo* franchise offers Stallone the opportunity to act and perform without saying too much. Sounds easy on paper, I'm sure, but it represents a challenge because his inner silence not only expresses the man he is while trying to evade capture by the local police idiots, but also the man he was as a soldier of the United States Army Special Forces in Vietnam.

When we first meet him, we're given every indication that he's an unstable psychopath, and perhaps that's not altogether untrue. Because there are two sides to this story, the mistreatment and abuse he undergoes after his (unjust) arrest is very clear. These are local law enforcement morons of a hick town who push Rambo to his limit simply because they don't want his type, a drifter, in their small, quiet, and boring town, and it's possible they deserve everything that Rambo dishes out to them for having violated his human rights. However, if you look closely at the action, you'll see that Rambo never actually *kills* anybody by his own hand. The abusive deputy who falls to his death from a helicopter is only because Rambo throws a rock at it in his own defense. All other police officers in the hunt are merely injured and maimed at the hands of their hunter. Does this mean that Rambo is a sympathetic, kind-hearted human being, even before his tearful collapse at the end of the film, or does it simply imply that even during the hunt, he's remembering to use his *brain* in which he intentionally terminates his aggressive actions before he can commit murder against civilians?

As Will Teasle, Brian Dennehy's performance is especially effective because you know he's an unfair and pushy little prick while still giving the viewer a sense of sympathy for his determination to not only protect his little town from Rambo's rage and onslaught, but to protect his own life as well. Stallone's silence builds up to that rather gripping speech expressing his pain and anguish of not only his past in a very unpopular war, but also his struggle to survive in the world he came back to afterward. At a time in the '80s before the struggles and consequences of the Vietnam War came to the public light in films like *Platoon, Hamburger Hill,* and *Full Metal Jacket,* John Rambo may have been the first cinematic example of that decade in which the Vietnam veteran was meant to be regarded with sympathy, understanding, and respect. He's suffered the tortures of the damned and seeks to take action against somebody, *anybody* who can serve as a justifiable means of vengeance. The film makes its best effort to portray Rambo as a misunderstood and tormented victim of war rather than an evil sadist, while still possessing the outstanding and admirable resources and skills of pure survival (by that reference, I'm reminded of Charles Bronson's character Paul Kersey and his vengeful New York City rampage in *Death Wish*).

Watching *First Blood* today prompts me to ask a question or two of myself. The first is obvious, and that's, why doesn't Rambo just walk away from trouble? He says he's headed for Portland, Oregon, and Teasle, for whatever prejudice motives he's harboring, drives him in the right direction. Nobody likes to be pushed around, of course, but Rambo could've still walked away and avoided the entire mess that followed (I suppose we'd have no movie if he'd done that). The second is far more complex, and that is, were Hollywood to remake and reboot the story of John Rambo, who would he be in today's world? In my opinion, that's an easy question to answer. He'd be a modern war veteran returning from Afghanistan or Iraq with post-traumatic stress disorder. He'd also be an African American man. The trouble would likely start when he's unfairly and unjustly pulled over in his vehicle by some racist Mark Fuhrman-type police officer. Rambo's violent retaliation against such a man would surely echo the modern racial conflicts between the American police force and the African American community. Such a story line could cite unrest among those who watch it, but it's not my function here to take sides on social or political matters. I'm here merely to express such opinions and speculations with regard to *film*.

Creepshow

Directed by George A. Romero
(November 12, 1982, U.S. Release Date)

Then

Despite the fact that *Creepshow* opened in theaters *after* Halloween in 1982, this horror movie was the talk of all the kids (well, the *boys* anyway) in high school. One look at the movie poster and you'd know why. It promised *"The Most Fun You'll Ever Have BEING SCARED!"*, with a skeletal creature buying his movie ticket. By this time in my life, I was well aware of Stephen King's popularity, having already read his early novels *Carrie* and *Salem's Lot* (I read many more in the years to come). The late George A. Romero, I associated only with his two most popular movies, *Night of the Living Dead* and *Dawn of the Dead*, both of which I'd not yet seen. Still, the two of them joining forces had to mean something pretty special was on the way. The movie was playing in town and finding someone to go see it with was not difficult. As usual, going to see a horror movie, even at an older age, still meant the same white lie to my parents in order to get out of the house.

I'd heard of an old comic book called *Tales From the Crypt*. Beyond that, I knew nothing of the horror comic books that were once popular in the '50s. This movie was supposed to be a homage to such comic books. In fact, it started out with an argument between a young boy and his father over such a comic book. The boy Billy (I didn't know this at the time, but he was Stephen King's real-life son) was being punished for reading a trashy horror comic book called *Creepshow*. The fight ended with the confiscation of Billy's comic book and it was thrown outside in a trash can. Outside Billy's window was a ghostly figure known as *"The Creep"* who, once animated, would be our guide to the horror tales about to begin.

The first story was called *Father's Day*. As a family of descendants gathered for their annual dinner on that very day, we learned of how a mean and wealthy old man was killed by his own unstable daughter Bedelia (whom he hated) when he pushed her too far with his emotional abuse and demands for his Father's Day cake. Bedilia, arriving later than the rest of the family, stopped at her father's grave site first to not only visit, but to tell her father off as well. Without warning, his decaying corpse emerged as a hideous creature from the burial plot to seek revenge not only on his daughter, but the rest of the family, whom he considered nothing but a bunch of scheming, greedy crooks who just wanted to get their dirty hands on his money. After killing a few of them, he finally got what he wanted— his Father's Day cake, topped with a severed head (totally gross, but still so much fun to watch!). This was when I discovered just how much like a comic book this movie really was. When the first story ended, the picture freeze-framed into an animated image, like a real comic book, before flipping its pages to what would be the movie's next tale. *Pretty clever and original,* I thought.

The second story was called *The Lonesome Death of Jordy Verrill* and starred Stephen King himself as an idiot yokel farmer who discovered a meteorite crashing on his farmland. Touching the hot meteorite burned Jordy's finger and left an unusual blister on it. He splashed the meteorite with water, causing it to crack open and leak a mysterious green and glowing liquid. This liquid, whatever it was, was slowly transforming not only the entire farm, but Jordy himself, into a plantlike organism that was covering his body. Thinking that a hot bath might help, he was suddenly warned by the ghost of his dead father not to take the bath. He ignored it, and the next morning, he looked like a giant weed. In his last desperate act as a thinking man, Jordy blew his own head off with his shotgun. Outside his house, we learned that the entire town had fallen victim to the spreading plant from outer space. The radio report of expected heavy rain was only going to make all of this much worse.

The third story was called *Something to Tide You Over*. I immediately recognized the old man who played the doctor aboard the plane in *Airplane!* as Vickers, an eccentric man who discovered his wife Becky was cheating on him with a much younger man named Harry Wentworth. He had a plan to do away with both of them by luring them separately to different parts of the beach, at which time he'd force them to bury themselves up to their necks in the sand below the line of high tide. He told Harry that he could survive this ordeal if he managed to hold his breath long enough for the sand beneath him to loosen and allow him to break free. To make the event more fun for him, Vickers set up a closed-circuit TV camera and VCR on the beach in front of Harry so he could enjoy it all from his own TV at home. This was truly a sick and twisted man, but still, this being a horror movie promising fun, it was certainly delivered. Like the first story, the undead returned to seek vengeance, this time as a pair of waterlogged ghouls covered with seaweed. The final shot of the movie showed Vickers as a victim of his own crime, now buried in the sand up to his neck and shouting at the top of his lungs, *"I can hold my breath for a long time!"*

The fourth story was called *The Crate* and took place at a local college where a janitor accidentally discovered an old, dusty crate with the date 1834 printed on it, hidden under the stairs while he was chasing a dropped quarter. Rather than open it himself, he summoned a professor named Dexter to tell him of his find. The two of them went through the process of moving the heavy crate to one of the science laboratories and opening it with crowbars. Inside the crate was one of the most hideous and monstrous-looking creatures I'd ever seen in a movie. It was an Abominable Snowman with long, disgusting, razor-sharp teeth who, despite its small size, could easily kill and devour an entire human body in just seconds (this was the most violent and bloody tale of the movie so far). Escaping the scene, Dexter was hysterical and sought help from a student, but it wasn't long before the poor kid was a victim of the same monster, as he suffered deep, bloody wounds on his throat from the monster's sharp claws. Still hysterical, Dexter went to his friend and fellow professor Henry. Henry was a quiet man who suffered the emotional abuse of his wife Wilma. While Dexter stayed at Henry's home, Henry decided to not only investigate the matter, but to use this opportunity to finally get rid of Wilma, whom he not only hated but had frequently fantasized about killing (we even got to see one of his fantasies when he shot her in front of party guests). Luring Wilma to the stairwell, he got what he wanted when the monster mauled her to death. Henry secured the crate and dumped it in the lake, but we were meant to believe the monster had escaped and was still alive beneath the water.

The fifth and final story was called *They're Creeping Up on You*. This one wasn't particularly violent or bloody, but in its own way, was the most difficult tale to watch, especially if cockroaches gave you the creeps (pun *totally* intended), and they *did* for me. Mr. Pratt, a cruel and ruthless businessman who lived alone in his New York City penthouse apartment, was very paranoid and cautious against germs in his home. On this night, the city was hit by lightning storm that resulted in a blackout. Mr. Pratt's home was also slowly invaded by an army of cockroaches. At first, Pratt was able to keep up with them and destroy them one by one, but this wouldn't last all night. As the cockroaches continued to multiply, Pratt realized there was nowhere to escape, except a to safe room in his apartment. That didn't work either because he was swarmed by cockroaches until he suffered a fatal heart attack. In the final scene, after the electricity was restored throughout the city, Pratt's dead body opened, as thousands of disgusting cockroaches burst from his mouth and body, totally engulfing the safe room. Some poor woman in the theater screamed her head off when those roaches burst from the man's mouth and body. My friends and I found her reaction funny, despite my own rattled nerves at the sight of so many cockroaches.

The movie concluded as it had began, returning to the scene of Billy and his father the next morning after their fight. His father complained of neck pain, which became worse when we realized that it was his own son causing him that pain through the use of a voodoo doll he'd sent away for from the *Creepshow* comic book before being trashed. When it was over and my friends and I were outside the theater preparing to head for the local pizzeria, we asked each other which tale was our favorite. Between the bunch of us, I was the only one who chose *The Crate*. Despite our conflicting opinions, we agreed that *Creepshow* delivered the fun it promised, with all its chills, thrills, and nastiness. I suddenly felt jealous of another kid I knew at school who'd purchased that awesome movie poster for himself upon its release. I wondered what my parents' reaction might've been if *I'd* hung such a poster on my bedroom wall? My mother probably would've (unfairly) tossed it in the trash as well.

Now

Horror film or not, I still consider *Creepshow* pure light-hearted fun. It's just fun-filled with *terror*, that is all. While seeking to scare us out of our socks, it also tells us in its own way to sit back and enjoy what it offers. There's very little that's grim or moody about it. On the contrary, it's colorful and even funny, never forgetting that its inspiration comes from very tacky comic books of the '50s, including *Tales From the Crypt, House of Mystery,* and *The Witching Hour* (all of which I've never read myself). Gifted actors such as Viveca Lindfors, Ed Harris, Leslie Neilson, Fritz Weaver, and Hal Holbrook are in *Creepshow* to have fun and be silly when the moments call for it. Regardless of whatever terrifying predicament they find themselves in, we can hardly take it as seriously as we might, say, a gifted actor as Jack Nicholson in *The Shining*. It may not exactly conform to all the textbook qualifications a horror film purist may take to heart, but I believe that's the very point the film tries to make. Instead of the classic elements that may scare us, such as the devil, the knife-wielding fiend that won't die, or the murderous alien creature from another world, we're entertained with five grisly tales, or even vignettes, having nothing to do with each other other than a discarded comic book designed to bring shock value with a smile rather than the tradition blood-curdling fears. On the other hand, who can possibly watch the monster in *The Crate* or the cockroaches in *They're Creeping Up on You* without feeling the chills along their spine and in their stomach?

These are mixed feelings of horror and humor, scary and satire, that the collaboration of King and Romero seek to instill in us because they enjoy it so much themselves (and it works).

Speaking of *The Crate*, let's revisit that tale and I'll explain why it's still my favorite one of the five. Like *Jaws* and *Alien*, we're dealing with the mystery of the unseen monster. The dusty crawlspace under the stairs is a creepy place, and we cringe at the idea that something unknown and evil has been living under there for so long without our knowledge. The fear of not knowing what we're going to find inside the crate haunts us, especially when the process of getting the damn thing open takes an inhumanly long time. We long to see what's inside, and yet we're terrified. Like the great white shark and the alien, when the monster finally appears, it's a merciless murdering creature with no conscience, no understanding, and no reason. It simply eats, devours, and then returns to the safe environment from which it sprung. It's fun and humorous when a mean bitch like Wilma, played by Adrienne Barbeau, gets her just dues when she's torn apart by the beast, but it's a completely terrifying and altogether different feeling and experience when we watch that poor janitor get slowly pulled and mangled by the same beast, whose attack ends in a river of blood pouring down the front of the crate.

Perhaps the best and only real way to approach a film like *Creepshow* is to treat it as the simple horrific bedtime story that it is, with the animated skeletal ghoul as our beloved host. Turn off the lights, have some fun while you're watching it, and hope it doesn't all *get you* in the end.

Gandhi

Directed by Richard Attenborough
(December 8, 1982, U.S. Release Date)

———⟫⟪⟨⟫⟪———

Then

I never liked school. From my elementary years right up to the moment I graduated college, school was something I had little enthusiasm for. It was, year after year, something I simply had to work myself through in order to progress through life. Even today, when I try to help my son with his math homework, I humorously tell him, "Hey, I graduated. It's not my job to know this stuff anymore." In high school (aside from math), social studies was the class I detested the most because I considered it nothing but dates, facts, and events I couldn't keep up with (or perhaps I just didn't care). However, it was because of my tenth grade social studies and history class that I saw Richard Attenborough's *Gandhi*.

On a day like any other in high school, there was a press kit mini-movie poster of *Gandhi* sitting on the teacher's desk. At the top, it said, "*A WORLD EVENT.*" That was different. I'd seen movies considered blockbuster events on screen, but never one advertised as something big enough to involve the whole world. Then I read carefully the various taglines on the poster describing this great man of history, whom I knew little about, as someone who'd not only defied the entire British Empire, but had also brought freedom to three hundred fifty million people. This was intriguing. At the bottom of the poster, it only said, "*COMING SOON.*" Exactly how soon? My interest was peaking, but was this a movie that would open in Great Neck or would it be one of those big movies that played only in Manhattan for a long time, in which case, it would be months before I got to see it? My prediction was wrong. Our teacher announced that in the days to come, all of his tenth grade classes would take a field trip together to see *Gandhi* at the Zeigfeld Theater in Manhattan. This meant we'd have the entire day off from school just to go to the movies. This would also be the first time I'd return to the Zeigfeld Theater since seeing *Close Encounters* there at the age of ten. That grand theater with its giant screen in itself was something to look forward to. This would also be a private screening for the students only.

Gandhi, the story of one man's life, began with a screen statement from the filmmaker himself in which he explained the difficulty in telling such a complex life story in one motion picture.

> *No man's life can be encompassed in one telling. There is no way to give each year its allotted weight, to include each event, each person who helped to shape a lifetime. What can be done is to be faithful in spirit to the record and to try to find one's way to the heart of the man.*

I'd never seen a movie begin like this, and I took note of such a statement attempting to justify its intent even before the story began. It wasn't an apology, but rather an understanding between those who created and those who would experience what was created (at least that's how *I* interpreted it). Before we'd understand who Gandhi was in life, we were introduced to him by watching how he was assassinated in January 1948. Shot in the chest by one of his own people, Gandhi's only chilling words before he died was, *"Oh, God!"* The movie then cut to his massive funeral, attended by what looked like every citizen of India, including other world leaders as well. Although I wasn't familiar with the art of epic moviemaking, I was amazed at how such a procession could be organized for the purpose of a motion picture.

It then flashbacked to Gandhi's young life as an attorney in South Africa and an incident of racial prejudice he experienced aboard a train when trying to sit first-class rather than the third-class section he was told he belonged in (despite having a first-class ticket). Rather than give in to intimidation, he used common sense and logic to humiliate those trying to push him around when he told them, *"I think we can deduce that there is at least one colored attorney in South Africa."* My friends and I reacted with mild laughter, expressing admiration for such a man who wouldn't hide his feelings toward unjust actions, though he was thrown off the train regardless. This was the inciting incident of Gandhi's life that pushed him forward to his inevitable destiny as a leader. Upon learning more of the unjust laws against all Indians in South Africa, Gandhi proposed a nonviolent campaign of protest. These protests were met with violence, arrests, and very unwelcomed attention against South Africa from the rest of the world. As a result, its government finally gave in and released all Indian prisoners, thus realizing and recognizing *some* of the rights for Indian citizens. Victory won, Gandhi headed home to India. He was a national hero, though he wanted no such glory. He was urged by Indian officials to join them in their fight for India's independence against the rule of the British Empire. His campaign of nonviolence protests and speeches continued, bringing millions of Indians together nationwide. As progress was made, I was drawn into this man's story I'd never known before today. Looking around, I saw the faces of my classmates and could tell that they too were enthralled at the life of this simple man.

One of the most tragic setbacks of Gandhi's movement was a bloody massacre that occurred when British and Indian soldiers were ordered to fire upon defenseless civilians gathered together in peaceful protest. Any feelings of pride and awe we felt up until then were shattered when we watched hundreds of innocent men, women, and children mercilessly shot to death. Even those who tried to escape by climbing a stonewall were inevitably fired upon and killed. This horrific sequence ended with a little baby girl crying at the side of her dead mother and later with Gandhi himself looking over the aftermath of the massacre in shock and shame. The audience was dead quiet when a fifteen-minute intermission was announced (as this was my first screen epic, it was also the first time I was allowed the convenience of an intermission). Outside, students were somber, but permitted themselves the brief conversation of what we thought so far. There wasn't a single negative opinion from anyone. This was as close to a perfect biographical motion picture I'd ever seen, and it was only half over.

The massacre didn't deter Gandhi's efforts or that of the Indian people, and Great Britain was facing increasing public pressure to change their rule over India. In a scene I'll never forget, Gandhi himself was seated with important British politicians and one of them asked him, point blank, *"You don't think we're just going to walk out of India!"*, to which Gandhi promptly responded, *"Yes. In the end, you will walk out. Because one hundred thousand English men simply cannot control three hundred and fifty million Indians, if those Indians refuse to cooperate."* This was one a moment of such great dialogue, it prompted my friends and I to say, "Oh, shit!" as a true sign of unanimous support. In the end, after one final protest ending in a bloody conclusion, India was finally declared a free nation from the rule of the British Empire. By this time, I would've predicted the movie's end, seeing as the ultimate victory had been won. However, India now faced the problem of their nationwide religious division between Muslims and Hindus. While Gandhi encouraged all Indians to live together in peace as one nation, violent civil war broke out all over the country. Gandhi went on hunger strikes to protest the violence and killings and wouldn't end them until the fighting stopped. In his name and his honor, the fighting *did* finally stop. Even as it appeared peace and understanding would prevail, the story brought itself full circle to the point where Gandhi was assassinated. As his body burned and his ashes were scattered at sea, we were left with these words from Gandhi's voice-over:

> *When I despair, I remember that all through history the way of truth and love has always won. There have been tyrants, and murderers, and for a time they can seem invincible, but in the end they always fall. Think of it. Always.*

As I read the closing credits listing its primary players, there was one thing I was certain of and that was I'd never forget the man who'd played Gandhi, Ben Kingsley, ever again. Such an extraordinary performance. I also asked the question of whether those final words were spoken by the actor or perhaps by Mohandas Gandhi himself in a vintage recording from the past. No one I knew had the answer, not even my teacher. No matter. I loved *Gandhi*. The details of my experience at the grand Manhattan Zeigfeld Theater and my emotional reactions during the movie say it all.

Now

Over the years, it's been hard to digest any of Sir Kingsley's films which I consider nothing better than the common Friday night multiplex selection; films like *Species, Iron Man 3,* and *Ender's Game*. In my opinion, these are an extraordinary waste of the man's talent. I watch Mr. Kingsley in such films and I find it hard to believe it's the same man who played Monhandas K. Gandhi and won the Academy Award for Best Actor of 1982. I'm consoled, however, by alternate performances in films like *Schindler's List, Sexy Beast,* and *House of Sand and Fog*. For *Gandhi*, Kingsley can only be praised. With only a single virtue preaching non-violence, the man's presence on screen is a spiritual one. Whether we agree with his philosophy or not, we cannot help but be enthralled by his courage, conviction, and persistent stubborn attitude.

Kingsley's intelligent and moral spirit behind this character of great importance is so dead on, that one should take a moment to remember he's portraying a real man who lived and died in history and not personally taking on the burden of freedom fighter for himself as a mere actor on film. We, as an audience, are challenged when we watch the film because of the historical consequences, good and bad, that came from a person of such profound political and revolutionary discipline. Gandhi's philosophies may be debatable, but its results, according to film and history, are indisputable. *Gandhi* represents a personally significant turning point in my moviegoing experience. Besides it being my first epic screen motion picture, it was a major step in my maturity level that defined my perception of what great cinema truly was. It was at this time I realized that, perhaps, I was no longer a child in the world of film. Unlike milder adult drama I'd seen in the past, this was serious material in its telling of a major historical figure and the first true grown-up art film for a fifteen-year-old boy like me. The year was drawing to an end by showing me a piece of world history and a single man that made such a significant difference in freedom and world peace.

There are two points about *Gandhi* I'd like to mention because I think about them whenever I watch the film. The first is a specific sequence when Gandhi sets off on his march to the Indian Ocean where he'll make salt as a campaign against the British government. There is a particular moment when a young Indian boy is climbing a tree to get a better glimpse of the great man passing through. The camera takes a second to get a close-up of his face. *Who is this boy?* Throughout the entire film, why does the director take the opportunity to show us *his* face among others? It may seem very trivial moment to you and the next guy, but I can't help get the feeling that it's *this* boy who will eventually grow up to be Nathuram Godse, the man who will assassinate Gandhi on January 30, 1948. The film gives no such indication of this point whatsoever, but it's a theory I like to entertain nonetheless. The second point is a characteristic trait of Gandhi's the film touches upon here and there and that's his laughter. While Gandhi's life is filled with struggle and sorrow, every once in a while, he has an irresistible tendency to enjoy a good joke and express joyous laughter. It's a minor point, but it has the ability to put a smile on your own face because you realize your own joy in the joy of another man facing insurmountable tyranny and injustice.

Speaking from a personal view of Gandhi's philosophies, I can only say that while they're truly admirable, they're not those I agree with. Turning the other cheek and loving thy enemy doesn't conform with my own beliefs and feelings. If I had to lend my agreements to a historical figure's beliefs and opinions, I'd likely go with those of Malcom X, who considered it unintelligent not to strike back at those who'd seek harm against you. In the film, Gandhi says, *"An eye for an eye only ends up making the whole world blind.*" Perhaps he was right. But we're only human, and human nature (like it or not) has a very ugly side, and that ugly side often says hurt those who hurt you. Can't say I completely disagree with that. Can *you*?

48 Hrs.

Directed by Walter Hill
(December 8, 1982, U.S. Release Date)

———«(◉)»———

Then

This was Eddie Murphy's first movie, so I was hot to see it. At that time, his outrageous performances on *Saturday Night Live* were legendary. The circumstances in which I saw it were interesting. It was a weekend trip to the movies with my family, though we didn't go to see *48 Hrs.* We had, in fact, gone to see *Gandhi*. I'd already seen this very long epic and after nearly an hour of it, I decided I'd had enough. Upon entering the theater earlier, I noticed the start times for *48 Hrs.* and I kept an eye on my watch the entire time. When the moment finally came, I whispered to my father next to me,

"Dad, since I've seen this movie already, I'm gonna go see *48 Hrs.* in another theater."
"How long is it?"
"It'll definitely be over before *this* movie is."
"Okay."

It was that quick and simple. It was also the first time I'd ever *"movie-hopped"* from one theater to another without paying for another ticket admission (I did a *lot* of that during the '90s). This was also the first crime/cop thriller I saw on screen (some may cite *Blade Runner* as the first, but I consider that more sci-fi noir than crime

425

thriller). Finally, it was my first exposure to the "buddy cop" movie, which eventually led to others in the '80s like *Running Scared, Lethal Weapon,* and *Stakeout.* In the beginning, my immediate reaction was to the character Albert Ganz and the plan he and his American Indian friend used to escape the prison gang as a very clever one, as I never imagined the Indian had slipped him a gun during their staged fight in front of the guards and prisoners. When they started shooting, it was obvious these two men were afraid of no one and would kill anyone who got in their way, even cops.

These two convicts were now loose in San Francisco, and they had another plan. They were on the hunt for a large sum of money hidden somewhere in the city by a former partner of a robbery they'd committed in the past. To find it, they grabbed another member of their gang, Luther and his girlfriend, Rosalie. They would hold her prisoner until Luther located the money and delivered it to them, and he only had a couple of days to do this in order to save her. This is when we met the hero cop of the movie, Jack Cates, played by Nick Nolte, whom I remembered well from *The Deep* back in '77. That was only five years ago, yet the man looked much older and his voice was also very scratchy. Was this how Nolte really sounded now or was it just part of his performance as an angry city cop? On this day, he joined two fellow detectives at a hotel where they believed Ganz, his Indian partner called Billy Bear, and Rosalie were hiding. What should have been an ordinary search-and-question task turned into a violent and deadly shootout when Ganz killed the two detectives, one of them with Jack's gun. Jack survived, but was left with the guilt and anger over watching two of his fellow cops die.

Determined to find Ganz and Billy Bear, Jack's plan was to get a member of the former gang, Reggie Hammond, out of jail for forty-eight hours in order to help him find the two killers. Reggie was no ordinary convict. He was a loud and boisterous man who enjoyed a good laugh (what else would we have expected from a guy like Eddie Murphy?). When we first saw him, he was sitting in a big, comfy chair in his jail cell wearing dark glasses and singing real loud to a song I'd never heard before called *"Roxanne."* Since I didn't discover The Police until months later with their *Synchronicity* album, that means I heard *Eddie Murphy* sing *"Roxanne"* before I ever heard Sting sing it (how sad is that?). Still, it was a funny way to be introduced to his character. His new partnership with Jack wouldn't be a friendly one, as Jack laid down the law only minutes after meeting, declaring, *"We ain't brothers, we ain't partners and we ain't friends!"* and *"If Ganz gets away, you're gonna be sorry you ever met me!"*. I hadn't heard too much "cop talk" in the movies so far, but Jack's little speech to Reggie was some of the toughest dialogue I'd ever heard. I smiled as I considered the idea that Jack was someone you didn't want to mess around with, and wasn't *that* the true substance of the tough movie cop who wanted justice served?

During their investigation, they entered a country redneck bar called Torchy's, where Billy Bear had once worked as a bartender. On a bet, Reggie pretended to be a police detective using Jack's badge. Inside, he was about as bad as he could be in his interrogation of the racist patrons who very likely wanted to tear him apart for stepping into their place. This scene was some of Eddie's funniest material as he continuously pushed these county boys around, pretending to be someone he wasn't. In the end, returning to his normal voice, the whole theater shared a good laugh when he said, *"Y'all be cool! Right on!"* It was Eddie simply being *Eddie*, and we loved it. Shortly after the bar scene and a brutal fight between Jack and Reggie, we learned that Reggie, Ganz, and Billy Bear were all after half a million dollars they'd stolen from a dealer during a sale—the kind of money nobody reported stolen. This is where confusion hit me for the first time. Because I was still only fifteen at the time, I had no idea that *"hitting a dealer during a sale"* had anything to do with drugs. I thought (I swear, this is true) that Reggie described a *retail establishment* they'd robbed during a sale. I suppose that makes me sound ignorant, but perhaps if Reggie had just said "drug dealer" instead of just "dealer," I would've comprehended it a lot better (just sayin'). The money was hidden in the trunk of Reggie's car, parked in a garage for the last three years. They simply had to wait for Luther to show up and exchange it for Rosalie's return.

Jack and Reggie followed Luther carrying the money to a subway station, but their tail went wrong, and Luther, Ganz, and Billy

Bear got away. They escaped again when they were chased while driving a stolen bus. It seemed no matter what these two boys tried to do together, they repeatedly failed to get Ganz. It was finally a chance visit to Chinatown where they found both Ganz and Billy Bear hiding out with their girlfriends. After a brief confrontation in which Reggie was shaking with fear in front of his old partner in crime, he shot Billy Bear to death. Ganz escaped the apartment building and eventually grabbed Reggie as a hostage. Once again, Nick Nolte didn't fail to impress me as the ultimate figure of the tough city cop. He appeared out of the steam in the back alley and told Ganz, *"You're not gonna make it!"* I just *loved* the tough lines that came out of this man, and tough lines were met with tough action. Jack didn't hesitate for a moment to the point where he shot Ganz to death and then returned Reggie, the two of them now respected friends, back to the prison.

As I'd promised, *Gandhi* was still in progress when I returned to that theater. Turns out this long epic was my best friend that day when I wanted to see something that wasn't necessarily appropriate for an underage kid. Despite the popularity of *48 Hrs.*, there was only one other kid in my high school classes who'd seen it too. He was just an acquaintance, but he was the only one I could share my memories of the movie with, and the only one I could repeat many of the wise-ass Eddie Murphy lines with. In fact, looking back on it, having to sit and listen to two boys constantly say, *"Y'all be cool!"* is probably an obnoxious experience (to all those at school who had to listen to us sound like a couple of Eddie Murphy-wannabe-idiots, I apologize).

Now

In any "buddy cop" film or any story where you have two main characters pitted with or against each other, the key word is *chemistry*. Without it, the film is over before it starts. As the two leads in *48 Hrs.*, the chemistry between Nolte and Murphy works well because they're such opposites who generally despise one another and are constantly trading insults with each other. I'm not just talking about the relationship between cop and convict, but also a clash of person-alities as well. Jack Cates is a no-nonsense, mean-talking guy who has little time or patience for humor or even to look at the lighter side of life. Even after a night of sex with his beautiful girlfriend, played by Annette O'Toole, his immediate impulse to start the day is to pour alcohol in his coffee and pick a fight with her, saying, *"I make you feel good, you make me feel good—now what the hell more do you want from a guy?"* His damaged 1964 sky blue Cadillac DeVille convertible suggests a man who simply doesn't give a damn about his appearance in life. Before we know what Jack's purpose will be in this film, we know he's a man who's seen and apprehended his share of city scum-bags to the point where his cynicism almost makes sense to us. Why else would a man consider a candy bar from a police station vending machine a suitable dinner?

This is also where Murphy's presence makes sense. Reggie Hammond, though a convicted thief, is still a good man with a good heart. Even as he serves time in prison, he happily embraces his life with a wise-ass sense of humor without taking things too seriously. To this day, I've never quite heard anybody enjoy a song by The Police on screen quite the same way he does. To spend forty-eight hours with Reggie Hammond, if not less, means inevitably light-ening up in a job and city filled with so much filth. It's this obser-vation of filth that's one of the first elements of the film to notice. San Francisco, "the city by the bay," that has often looked so pictur-esque and beautiful with its famous landmarks like the Golden Gate Bridge in other films like Hitchcock's *Vertigo* or even *Star Trek IV: The Voyage Home*, represents a visual stink-hole atmosphere more in tune with Los Angeles and New York City at that time. As a city in a seedy crime film with two psychotic cop killers on the loose, it echoes the first *Dirty Harry* film before considering anything even closely related to beauty.

Reggie Hammond may, in fact, be the only thing that comes close to beauty, as he's constantly determined to maintain his sharp appearance despite his criminal background. As Jack bluntly puts it, *"Class isn't something you buy, man. Look at you, you've got a five hundred dollar suit on and you're still a low-life."*, to which Reggie simply replies with overconfidence and without apology, *"Yeah, but I look good!"* It's his overconfidence, in fact, that supports the film. We know the man can carry himself in just about any situation, but we can't help but be amazed when he actually talks his way out of Torchy's with its confederate flags hanging on the wall without getting his ass kicked, or worse. His verbal attack on the bar's patrons is a merciless, racist onslaught toward a bunch of, as he puts it, *"backward-ass country fucks!"* Seeing as he's the minority guest in a world that doesn't want him, we cheer him on for turning the tables against people who contemplate racial thoughts and motivations toward him. It's the overconfidence at work, sure, but in the case of this particular bar, it's survival too, and survival has never been this funny.

Tootsie

Directed by Sydney Pollack
(December 17, 1982, U.S. Release Date)

———«(())»———

Then

In March 1982, I got into a big fight with my mother because I told her I was seeing the movie *Victor/Victoria* with a friend. She absolutely refused to allow me to see "a movie like that," as she put it. "Like what?" I replied. She proceeded to describe how the movie was about degenerate people who dressed up in drag costumes. "Mom, it's a musical!" I said, to which she concluded the fight by declaring, "I don't care!" It took me a while to understand her (unreasonable) feelings, but it appeared my mother suffered from some form of homophobia. Nonetheless, I was faced with the embarrassing task of telling my friend I couldn't go to the movie. When he asked why, I made up a silly excuse because frankly, I just couldn't wrap my head around the real reason. I mean, it was just a movie; it's not like I was going to a porn theater in Manhattan. This memory is relevant to me because by the end of that same year, when my family prepared to see the new comedy *Tootsie*, I started a conversation with my mother that went something like this:

"Mom, do you remember last spring when you wouldn't let me see *Victor/Victoria*?"
"Yes. What about it?"

"That was a movie about a woman who dressed like a man. How come we're going to see a movie about a man who dresses like a woman?"

"This movie is different."

"Why?"

"Because it's *funny*!"

Was she serious? What the hell did that mean? Whatever logical conviction she thought made sense to *her*, made absolutely no sense to me. There was a hypocrisy taking place here that I didn't understand. Unfortunately, when you're a kid who's practically been told to shut up by his mother, you simply do it without argument because you just want to go to the movies with your family in peace.

Despite my love for the movies, I never once had any aspirations to be an actor. My conviction was confirmed once *Tootsie* began. Listening to Michael Dorsey, played by Dustin Hoffman (whom I remembered well from *Kramer Vs. Kramer*) I believed actors spent their lives looking for work and not getting any. Instead, they ended up as waiters in restaurants. Despite these difficulties, Michael was determined to make it as an actor and encouraged his friends to have the same discipline and commitment. As a perfectionist, however, Michael was impossible to work with. Even his well-known agent George Fields (played by the director himself Sidney Pollack) couldn't help him. During an argument in George's office, he and Michael shouted each other about the time Michael played a tomato for a commercial and refused to sit down. As they went back and forth about the tomato, the theater was in stitches. This was the funniest and most stupid argument I'd ever heard in a movie, and I loved it! To finally get a good-paying job, Michael went to extremes and auditioned for a female part on a soap opera *dressed as a woman*. Instead of Michael Dorsey, he went by the name of *Dorothy Michaels*. It worked because he got the part by performing the role as a tough, no-nonsense feminist who wouldn't take crap from men. He fooled them all and he even fooled his agent for a time when he met him at the Russian Tea Room. The moment when George was shocked to see how Michael had transformed himself was hilarious not just because of the surprise element, but also because of the look on poor George's face when he realized just how far Michael had gone to get a job. This was a rare moment where I appreciated just how far one's facial expression could take a scene in a movie. Sometimes words weren't necessary to get the point across.

As Dorothy became a TV soap opera sensation, Michael was living two lives and was intrigued by just how far he could take his new female personality. In a scene inside the bedroom of his best friend Sandy, he stood in front of her mirror staring at himself. The audience (especially my father) cracked up when he altered his facial expression and said, *"Why, yes!"* at himself in a feminine voice. That wasn't enough though. He got undressed while Sandy was in the shower so he could try on one of her dresses. She caught him in his underwear, and the only way he could get out of the situation was to tell her that he wanted her, even if he really didn't, because after all, they were just friends.

"Sandy, I want you," he said as he walked toward her in his underwear.

"You want me*?"* she asked in disbelief pointing to own body, lacking any self-esteem.

This wasn't much dialogue, but it said wonders about the two characters, their history as friends, and the drastic step they were about to take. The unexpected sex between them began an act of deception by Michael toward Sandy. At the same time, Michael was falling in love with his beautiful co-star Julie, played by Jessica Lange (who still held my fixation from *King Kong*), who only knew him as Dorothy and who was also dating the show's director, Ron. By all accounts, he was a sexist and a total jerk because of the way he disrespected the women in his life. There was a scene at a party in which I learned a great deal about the flaws of human nature. Michael was there (as Michael) with George, and Julie was there too. In a previous scene, at Julie's apartment, she confessed to Dorothy that it would be a relief if just once a guy would come up to her and skip the usual pick-up lines and role playing and just come right out and say, *"I find you very interesting and I'd really like to make love to you."* Having that knowledge, Michael said that very line to Julie at the party. It backfired when, instead of being relieved and flattered, she threw her drink in his face. My mother laughed in hysterics at that move. It seemed that people, regardless of what they may *say* to other people, didn't necessarily want what they said to actually *happen*, and if it did, they wouldn't necessarily react the way they thought they would. In other words, I'd just gotten my first life lesson of "be careful what you wish for—you may get it."

As Dorothy, life got very complicated. On top of everything else, *she* was being pursued by two men: Julie's father and an older cast member on the show. Did men *really* find Dorothy attractive? Sorry, but I just couldn't see it. As a straight man, Michael fought off such advances. Julie's father even proposed marriage and gave her/him a ring. All of this was too much to handle. If Michael didn't think of something fast, he'd spend the rest of his life as Dorothy Michaels. The opportunity to get out of this gig presented itself when the show was in the unexpected situation of having to perform a party scene *live* instead of being taped. Before any of us in the audience knew what was happening, Dorothy was off on an uncontrollable verbal rant, improvising a strange backstory as she went along, almost to the point of a stuttering panic. Finally, at the crucial moment, with the audience watching live (including Sandy and Julie's father), Dorothy wiped off her makeup, took off her wig, and revealed herself to be Michael Dorsey. The jig was up, the mask was off, and Michael was free, but not before he received a good punch in the stomach from Julie.

The aftermath was what I expected it to be, with Michael making amends with those he hurt, including Julie and her father too. She confessed to missing Dorothy, and Michael tried to make it better by telling her, *"I was a better man with you as a woman than I ever was with a woman as a man."* She didn't understand, but I did, and I thought that was a great line. We knew she forgave him when she asked him to lend her a yellow dress. My family and I not only loved *Tootsie*, but it was one of the most fun times we'd had at the movies in a long time. Laughter being contagious, it was always a pleasure to see my mother let herself go for two hours and give in to the feeling and freedom of allowing herself the joy to laugh at wild situations and stupidity. My own laughter at such a movie took on extra meaning because I was able to share it with someone who didn't laugh too much at the movies. However, I *still* never got a reasonable explanation to why *Tootsie* was acceptable and *Victor/Victoria* wasn't.

In a way, this movie represented strange timing for me because I'd recently gotten caught up in the popular ABC soap opera *General Hospital.* It started in 1981 when nearly every kid in my high school freshman class was going on about the wedding of Luke and Laura as the biggest event on TV. Plagued by curiosity, I couldn't resist seeing what all the hubbub was about. Well, after one hour of drama and intrigue, I had to see what would happen in the next episode … and the next … and the next (I surrendered *nine years* of my life to that show until 1990, when I finally decided the writing became too stupid to bother with anymore). Watching the actions and drama of the soap opera in *Tootsie* gave me a somewhat interesting insight as to what possibly went on behind the camera of a real-life soap opera … minus the man in drag, of course.

Now

Tootsie remains one of the funniest films I've ever seen (the "tomato" argument still cracks me up every time). It's noteworthy that in his long career, this was the only real comedy Sydney Pollack ever directed (sorry, but *The Electric Horseman* just wasn't funny). Besides paying homage to the Billy Wilder classic *Some Like it Hot*, as well as other slapstick comedies of the 1940s, the film perfectly combines the outrageous farce of the modern TV soap opera and New York City show business with relevant social points about sexism. At the beginning of the film, we're unclear on Michael's position on women, having no romantic interest in his life. As his life progresses as Dorothy Michaels, however, he develops a better understanding of women as he lives through his own hell in their shoes. Aside from the defense he's forced to maintain against men who want him physically, he preaches his own public sermon regarding a woman's need for respect and to be treated fairly and equally among men. At the very least, they should be referred to by their name and not some cheap pet name like honey, baby, or Tootsie.

As the traditional situation comedy, this is far from traditional (forget even the best set of circumstances you've seen on *I Love Lucy* or *Three's Company*). The film doesn't go off half-cocked by trying to shove cheap laughs in our face. Those responsible for writing it use as much common sense as possible. Michael isn't going all out in drag just to deceive people or pretend to be something he's not for his own personal gratification. This is a man that's been mostly unemployed for twenty years, and enough is finally enough. When the chance presents itself to work steadily for a good paycheck, Michael does what he has to do, even if it means screwing his best friend Sandy out of a possible audition he could've helped her get. Whatever moral intentions and obligations that follow his acting success are primarily fueled by his love for Julie, and the fact that *one* of the reasons he can't have her (besides the *obvious*) is because she's lowered her own standards to be the girlfriend of her chauvinist pig director. To have to watch a woman he cares about go through this brings out his own need to try and improve the lives of other woman, both on TV as a character actress and in real life with Julie.

Dorothy is *not* attractive, and Micheal knows this. She is, however, very well-groomed and very confident in herself, and it's this alone that likely makes her a turn-on to certain men who admire these qualities and even find them sexy. Despite being a kind woman with a big heart, she also knows how to defend herself very well against those who go too far with her (even men on the street who try to take her taxi away from her), the reason being because as a man who was, perhaps, also a chauvinist before he put on the dress, is finally learning how it feels at the other end.

The film is perfectly cast. I can't think of any combination of actors in which the chemistry doesn't work well. From Dustin Hoffman and Bill Murray as roommates, to Dustin and Jessica as girlfriends, to Dustin and Sydney Pollack biting each other's head off. Pollack is particularly funny as Michael's nervous and impatient agent trying to cope with his clients insane antics. I can only feel for the poor man immediately wanting a double vodka when he sees just how far Michael went to get ahead in show business. The tomato argument is played out so flawlessly, I'd find It hard to believe if the two men didn't get it right in just the first take. The two of them make you believe that an otherwise intelligent man would throw away a good job opportunity simply because he cannot comprehend the logic behind a tomato that's required to sit down.

Tootsie was, in its own special way, a poignant film of laughter that reminded us of the pleasure of life's silliness, even while maintaining its common sense, its intelligence, and its social messages.

*****

This is the last film of 1982 I shall discuss in any great detail, and subsequently, the end of the last year of this book.

At this time, I invite you to turn back to the beginning of the book to 1975 to see where we began and just how far we've come together to the point of conclusion. What started out as safe and innocent G-rated material in the form of two children with witchcraft powers and a bumbling French detective to the eyes of a small child slowly progressed into the more mature and adult-oriented material of a world freedom fighter and a man in a dress to the eyes of a growing teenager. The year 1982 was, without a doubt, filled with more moviegoing experiences than I'd had as a child. It wasn't just limited to what I saw inside the dark movie theaters, but also what I watched on pay movie channels one year later. The great films of '82 were rounded off with titles like *The Road Warrior*, *The Thing*, *The World According to Garp*, *An Officer and a Gentleman*, and *The Verdict*. Let's also not forget one of the most awesome video rentals I ever experienced of a film from '82, which was Alan Parker's *Pink Floyd The Wall*. Watching this tale of madness just one time began a long chain reaction that inevitably lead to Pink Floyd not only being my favorite rock band in my youth, but my favorite rock band of all time today as well (I'm getting my son hooked on their music too).

And that, my friends, was the year 1982 for me.

Before We Say Goodbye

The time has come to ask the big question: *Why stop now?* Why do I choose to terminate the tale of my motion picture upbringing at the conclusion of 1982? What exactly happened the following year to prompt me to take an alternate turn in how I perceived and experienced the movies? Did I suddenly grow into a *man*? Not really. While I did turn sixteen in May 1983, I hardly considered myself a man yet, despite whatever Jewish traditions of my Bar-Mitzvah dictated when I was thirteen years old. There was still very much a kid in me, though the way I viewed and perceived movies was due to change. Was it because movies were no longer great after '82? Hardly. In fact, I can't imagine my youth being what it was without the great blockbusters of the '80s like *Ghostbusters, Back to the Future, Top Gun, Die Hard,* and *Batman.*

However, there was *one* particular film that started to turn things around for me, and not necessarily for the better. You'll probably be astonished to learn that film was *Return of the Jedi*, relcased in May 1983. What does that mean? What did the third chapter in the original *Star Wars* trilogy have to do with what movies meant to my life? Allow me to explain. Like every other fan of the galaxy far, far away, I spent months waiting in anticipation for the saga to conclude the cliffhanger we were left with at the end of *Empire.* When *Jedi* finally opened on Wednesday May 25, 1983, it played at the recently renovated triplex theater in Great Neck. My father, having already experienced the pain-in-the-ass impatience of his two sons for the first two films, decided they should see the new movie right away so as not to spend the entire summer bothering him about it. Kevin and I went to see it that Friday afternoon after school, just two days after it opened. The theater was packed to the brim with kids, and I prepared myself for another spectacular movie in a saga that began six years ago.

What happened over the course of the next two hours astonished me. While there were notable scenes of real intense action and space battles (the battle of Endor looking pretty awesome), something just wasn't right about this movie. To begin with, there were too many redundant points from the first two episodes; beginning with the lack of originality of the *second* Death Star, to the constant recycled musical themes of John Williams, to yet *another* lightsaber duel between Luke Skywalker and Darth Vader. The acting and the dialogue were terrible. The Ewoks were silly creatures that made *Sesame Street* look mature. See-Threepio's entire personality had turned very feminine and Darth Vader became a complete wimp, constantly sucking up to and kissing the Emperor's butt.

What I honestly believe happened to me that day in that movie theater was that I learned for the first time in my life that the familiarity of what was previously such a miraculous element of action and fantasy the first two times did *not* necessarily guarantee a good movie by the third go-around. The new *Star Wars* movie was flawed and flawed badly, in my opinion, and I discovered I possessed a higher and more mature level of criticism toward what I watched on screen. Great films and franchises of the past like *Star Wars, Superman, Psycho, Jaws,* and even *Saturday Night Fever* didn't necessarily mean their follow-ups of the '80s would continue to be great, because as I'd soon learn that fateful summer, *Superman III, Jaws 3-D, Psycho II,* and *Staying Alive* were just awful movies.

The tide had finally turned. Movies would now be approached more carefully, more critically, and with an altered frame of mind. Not everything I watched would be so good at the time I watched it, as was often the case when I was younger. My thoughts, feelings, and perceptions of movies were very likely going to be right on target the first time, with little room for reconsideration or reevaluation. I *still* loved movies, but they were changing for me now, and I'd have to change with them.

But that, perhaps, is another story.

CPSIA information can be obtained
at www.ICGtesting.com
Printed in the USA
BVHW030212230119
538439BV00001B/5/P